THE
GLOBAL
EXPANSION
OF
JUDICIAL
POWER

Major support for the publication of this work has been generously provided by the Italian National Research Council (CNR) and the Foundation SER.IN.AR of Forlí.

THE
GLOBAL
EXPANSION
OF
JUDICIAL
POWER

Edited by

C. Neal Tate
and
Torbjörn Vallinder

NEW YORK UNIVERSITY PRESS
New York and London

NEW YORK UNIVERSITY PRESS
New York and London

Library of Congress Cataloging-in-Publication Data
The global expansion of judicial power / edited by C. Neal Tate and
   Torbjörn Vallinder.
       p.   cm.
   Some papers were originally presented at the theme meeting
"Judicialization of Politics", hosted by the Centro studi
sull'ordinamento giudiziario, Bologna, University of Bologna, Forlí,
Italy, June 1992.
   Includes bibliographical references and index.
   ISBN 0-8147-8209-4 (alk. paper)
   1. Judicial power.   2. Judicial review of administrative acts.
3. Judicial process.   I. Tate, C. Neal (Chester Neal), 1943-
II. Vallinder, Torbjörn.
K3367.G58   1995
347'.012 — dc20
[342.712]   95-11510
                   CIP

New York University Press Books are printed on acid-free paper,
and their binding materials are chosen for strength and durability.

Manufactured in the United States of America

10   9   8   7   6   5   4   3   2   1

To Chester and Pearl Tate
for the values
and to Carol and Erin
for the inspiration.

To Ulla and Per Anders,
companions
before, in, and after Forlí.

Acknowledgments

Most of the chapters included in this volume were originally presented as papers to the theme meeting "The Judicialization of Politics" of the Research Committee on Comparative Judicial Studies of the International Political Science Association. This meeting was graciously hosted by the *Centro Studi sull'Ordinamento Giudiziario* of Bologna at the University of Bologna's campus in Forlí, Italy, in June 1992. The dedicated work of the staff of the *Centro*, especially its founding director, Giuseppe Di Federico, and the principal meeting organizers, Carlo Guarnieri and Patrizia Pederzoli, made the Forlí meeting not just productive, but positively enjoyable for all who attended. The editors and contributors thank these fine colleagues—and all the others who contributed to making the meeting so successful. It is an understatement to say that without them neither the meeting nor this book would have been possible.

Major funding support for the Forlí meeting, as well as for the publication of this work, was generously provided by the Italian National Research Council (CNR) and the Foundation SER.IN.AR of Forlí. Additional support was provided by the Institute of Public and International Affairs of the University of North Texas.

Subsequent to the Forlí meeting, several of the chapters in this work appeared in somewhat to substantially different forms in a symposium issue of the *International Political Science Review* edited by Torbjörn Vallinder (vol. 15, no. 2, April 1994). The relevant chapters include those by Martin Edelman, Christine Landfried, Barry Holmström, Peter H. Russell, Martin Shapiro, Maurice Sunkin, C. Neal Tate (chapter 24), Jan ten Kate and Peter van Koppen, and Vallinder (chapter 1). The chapter by Jacqueline Lucienne Lafon appears in a different form and in French in the same issue. In addition, the chapter by Nico Steytler appeared in somewhat different form in the *South African Journal on Human Rights* (November 1993), portions of the chapter by Alec Stone appeared in *Comparative Political Studies* (26, no. 4, January 1994, pp. 443-69), and portions of the chapter by W. A. Bogart appear in his *Courts and Country: The Limits of Litigation and the Social and Political Life of Canada* (Toronto: Oxford University Press, 1994).

Contents

THE
GLOBAL
EXPANSION
OF
JUDICIAL
POWER

1.

The Global Expansion of Judicial Power: The Judicialization of Politics

C. NEAL TATE AND TORBJÖRN VALLINDER

THE EXPANSION OF JUDICIAL POWER

Bob Bullock, the lieutenant governor of Texas, plaintively appealed to a television newscast audience in May 1993: "We really need help. I'm not a proud man. I'll accept suggestions from anybody, because we *really* need help!" What was the cause of Bullock's distress? As presiding officer of the Texas Senate, he was reacting to the overwhelming rejection by the state's voters of a so-called Robin Hood constitutional amendment state leaders had devised to equalize funding of the state's school districts. The amendment was the latest effort of the legislative and executive branches of the Texas government to solve a school funding crisis that had plagued them for four years. The rejection of the amendment meant that the legislature now faced the task of coming up with yet another solution to the funding dilemma—within one month, if they wished to avoid a promised cutoff of state funding and possible shutdown of the state's public schools. Whence came the dilemma and the deadline? From a state district judge who was implementing a decision of the Texas Supreme Court that had declared the system of funding public education to be in conflict with the requirements of the state's own constitution.

It has not been very common in Texas for state judges to cast the leaders of elected governmental institutions onto the horns of such a policy dilemma. The same cannot be said for federal judges. Indeed, a single federal district judge, William Wayne Justice, is famous/notorious for his decisions requiring Texas to reshape its policies regarding public education, mental health, juvenile justice, prisons, and other areas (see Kemerer 1991). The experience of Texas is far from unique. Virtually every American state has been, in recent years, under a variety of mandates from its own courts or those of the national government to revise its policies governing the provision and funding of basic state services of one kind or another.

If we shift our attention from Texas and the other individual states to the United States, such vigorous policy-making by judges is even less surprising. For better or worse, students of American government and politics are used to the phenomenon: cussing and discussing, analyzing and advocating, and commending and condemning it have long been the favorite political and intellectual activities of many.

Shifting our attention once more, from the United States to the world, those who are blasé about the ubiquity of judicial dictates of public policy in the United States might be surprised to learn that the phenomenon of judges making public policies that previously had been made or that, in the opinion of most, ought to be made by legislative and executive officials appears to be on the increase. In fact there are several factors that support this development, this move toward what all would recognize as the American pattern: the expansion of judicial power.

Several of these factors are international in their scope. Perhaps the most stunning of these has been the breakdown of totalitarian communism in Eastern Europe and the disappearance of the Soviet Union, leaving the United States, the home of the judicialization of politics, as the one and only superpower.

Closely connected is the trend to democratization in Latin America, Asia, and Africa. Being for democracy does not necessarily require one to support the expansion of judicial power, as we shall see. But given the circumstances under which many new democracies are being constructed, the inclusion of a strong judicial wing seems almost inevitable to some governmental architects.

Another international factor of a less spectacular, but nevertheless probably important, character is the mounting influence of American jurisprudence and political science. The interest in, perhaps obsession with, courts and legal procedures among scholars at U.S. universities has certainly made an impression on their colleagues from different parts of the world. For example, at the beginning of this century almost no Swedish legal scholar or political scientist had been to the United States. Today such visits are routine matters for young Swedish political scientists and certainly are more common than in the past even for Swedish legal scholars. In the U.S. these academics learn what their old-fashioned textbooks did not tell them: that courts are related to politics, and vice versa. Then they return home and tell their teachers.

In Europe, the European Convention and Court of Human Rights in Strasbourg have been of great importance in spreading the gospel of judicialization, not only through the rulings of the court, but also through the debates initiated through the working of the system. Even the Swedes have slowly come to realize that they are not world champions of human rights and that strengthening the domestic courts may be an appropriate move toward achieving that goal.

Of course domestic developments have been important in many different countries. In the U.S. harsh criticism of elected politicians has always been a major industry—witness the works of Mark Twain, among many others. In more recent decades, such events as the Watergate affair have enhanced the prospects for investors in that industry. One must remember that in that affair, the third branch of government came out less badly than the second one, not to mention the first.

A similar pattern can be found in many other democratic countries: distrust of ministers and MPs is now more marked than distrust of judges. All three branches may be regarded as corrupt, but some are more corrupt than others.

Turning to developments within individual nations, one finds much evidence for the global expansion of judicial power. For example, next door to the U.S. exemplar, the Supreme Court has become, at least since the adoption of the Charter of Rights in 1982, a major influence on the policies of provincial and cultural autonomy that persistently threaten to break up the Canadian Confederation. Across the Atlantic, judges in the United Kingdom are increasingly involved in reviewing the discretionary acts of the administrators of a wide variety of government programs, contrary to their tradition.

On the Continent, the activities of Italy's "peculiar judiciary" (see chapter 13 by Giuseppe Di Federico) have been, for better or worse, largely responsible for publicizing and prosecuting patterns of large-scale corruption that have thrown the whole country into a political turmoil that is shattering, perhaps permanently, the basic structure of Italian politics and government. Although the American judiciary came out of the Watergate scandal with a better reputation than the other institutions, that reputation would nevertheless pale in comparison to the outright popularity and celebrity status developed in recent years by some of the Italian magistracy.

Somewhat to the north, French and German legislators and executives now routinely alter desired policies in response to or in anticipation of the pronouncements of constitutional courts, and, as we have already noted, member states of the European Community are beginning to alter domestic policies as a result of rulings of the Court of the European Community. In such unlikely locations as Sweden and the Netherlands the prospect of elected governments changing policies in response to the dictates of their courts seems certain to increase as a result of decisions made at the European level and also because of local developments. In tiny Malta changes in governments have led in recent years to periods of intense conflict between majoritarian and judicial institutions.

In Russia the legislative-executive confrontation over the constitutional distribution of authority and Boris Yeltsin's economic policies regularly wended its way in and out of the Constitutional Court—before Yeltsin suspended that court in the wake of his 1993 conflict with and victory over the "hardline" parliament dominated by his political opponents. In Israel the politicians have learned to live with policy limits imposed by a judiciary that has, for all practical purposes, invented a binding constitution where none exists. In India the Supreme Court has established extraordinary procedures to encourage "public interest litigation" designed to protect and enhance the economic and political interests of disadvantaged classes and groups (see Barr 1992). In the Philippines, as well as in Latin America and in Africa, courts are or will be important participants in ongoing efforts to establish constitutional rules and policies that will protect newly established or still fragile reestablished democracies from the threats of military intervention, ethnic conflict, and revolution. Even as this is written, Namibians are being governed and South Africans are contemplating elections and majority government under the rules of new constitutions that grant a prominent and inevitably controversial role to courts: protecting the rights of minorities against the majority—in this case, the rights of the white minority that for generations used its power to deny any substantial rights to the nonwhite majority.

THE JUDICIALIZATION OF POLITICS

The phenomenon we have just described represents the most dramatic instance of the global expansion of judicial power, which, for brevity, we shall frequently refer to as "the judicialization of politics." Another, less dramatic instance of the expansion of judicial power, or judicialization, is the domination of nonjudicial negotiating or decision-making arenas by quasi-judicial (legalistic) procedures. This instance also appears to be on the rise. Again for better or worse, the judicialization of politics may be or may become one of the most significant trends in late-twentieth and early-twenty-first-century government. It deserves careful description, analysis, and evaluation.

We seek, in this book, to make a substantial contribution to the understanding of the judicialization of politics. Drawing on the expertise of political scientists, law scholars, and other students of courts and judges around the world, we provide careful definitions of the term and its intellectual origins, descriptions of its occurrence—or lack of occurrence—in specific nations, analyses of the circumstances and conditions that appear to promote—or to retard—judicialization, and, not least, evaluations of the phenomenon from a variety of intellectual and ideological perspectives.

Some students of the topic appear to approve of the judicialization of politics. Asha Gupta (1992) seems to say that the needs of the poor in India are so great and also so unlikely to be fulfilled by majoritarian institutions alone that courts and judges *must* be actively involved in politics. Justice Carmel A. Agius and Nancy A. Grosselfinger (in chapter 21) approve the active defense of rights inconsistently provided by Maltese judges. Salvador Lozada (1992) probes the perils inherent in what he feels to be a necessary judicialization of politics in the reemerging Latin American democracies.

But analysts of the judicialization of politics are not necessarily fans. Many politicians and scholars have long been suspicious of a process that substitutes the policy judgment of usually unelected representatives of the socioeconomic and political elite for that of majoritarian political institutions. Agius and Grosselfinger's discussion of the Maltese case provides graphic evidence of the hostility of the supporters of that nation's principal leftist party to "interference" by judges in policy matters, if one accepts sacking the courts when they decide against the interests of the left as evidence of hostility. The expansion of the policy role of Canadian courts since the adoption of the Charter of Rights in 1982 has been viewed with concern not just from the left (see Mandel 1989, as an example), but also from the right and center, as the chapters by W.A. Bogart and Peter H. Russell and the work of Patenaude (1992) document.   The chapters by Brian Galligan and David R. Slater, Christine Landfried, and Michael Mandel and the work of Edward A. Fitzgerald (1992) illustrate that such suspicion exists among observers representing a variety of ideological orientations.

THE BOOK

This work has five parts, of unequal size. Part 1 introduces the book's theme, defining the "judicialization" concept that underlies our exploration of the global expansion of judicial power and exploring the likely institutional and behavioral conditions under which such expansion is likely to occur.   In two chapters, Torbjörn Vallinder defines the judicialization concept and traces its intellectual roots, and C. Neal Tate explores the institutional and behavioral conditions that promote the judicialization of politics.

Part 2 explores judicialization in the major English-speaking democracies that share the common-law tradition.   It begins with a base-laying chapter by Martin Shapiro summarizing the experience of the putative home of judicialization, the United States.   Shapiro concludes that the long-term expansion of judicial power in the United States may have leveled off at the national level, even though the expansion of judge-like or legalistic procedures to new decision-making arenas continues apace.

Part 2 proceeds with an analysis by Maurice Sunkin of the expansion of judicial power in the United Kingdom, the common-law country that by most standards would appear to be least hospitable to judicialization. Sunkin finds considerable expansion of judicial power via judicial review of the acts of administrative agencies, but little judicialization that has directly affected the policy-making prerogatives of Parliament. He also finds that even the judicialization that has occurred has not necessarily served to provide citizens a useful check on the administrative decision-making.

The remainder of part 2 surveys judicialization in Australia and Canada, two nations in which judicialization appears to be an increasingly relevant, if not always approved, aspect of national politics. For Australia, Brian Galligan and David R. Slater investigate how the judiciary intruded into what many would have regarded as the most sacred precincts of cabinet government, before finally retreating. John Power explores the increasing role of the judiciary in immigration policy and processing, showing how judicialization has progressively removed them from the control of majoritarian institutions and the administrators who report to them. For Canada, W.A. Bogart explores the extent to which judicialization can be expected to support progressive social policies, reaching skeptical conclusions after a careful analysis of the arguments surrounding the issue. Perhaps reacting to those who have seen the Supreme Court as likely to engage in a wholesale usurpation of majoritarian policy-making, Peter H. Russell analyzes what he feels are likely to be self-imposed constraints on the further judicialization of Canadian politics.

Part 3 considers the expansion of judicial power in the European democracies that share, to a greater or lesser degree, the Romano-Germanic legal tradition. History and tradition would deny the appropriateness of judicialization in these polities. Nevertheless, current evidence suggests that it has entrenched itself firmly in Italy, France, and Germany, and that it is becoming more common in the even less likely settings of Sweden, the Netherlands, and the Maltese microstate.

Part 3 begins with several cross-national analyses that lay foundations for subsequent country-based investigations. Anna Mestitz and Patrizia Pederzoli review the training and selection of Italian, French, and German judges, showing how these processes relate to strengthening or weakening judicial decision-making and how the distinctive Italian practices support an irresponsible expansion of the power of possibly ill-trained and less-than-competent legal personnel in that nation. Francesca Zannotti supports the analysis of Mestitz and Pederzoli and the subsequent chapter by Carlo Guarnieri by exploring how salary provisions affect the patterns of judicial independence in the United States and Italy. Alec Stone's examination of the expansion of the power of the constitutional courts of France and Germany demonstrates the striking similarities, as well as the differences, in the ways those institutions have reshaped majoritarian politics in their nations.

Subsequent portions of part 3 scrutinize the expansion of judicial power in individual political systems. The case of Italy is the subject of extended analysis because it offers perhaps the most striking current illustration of the consequences that have emerged from judicialization in the Romano-Germanic tradition countries. Giuseppe Di Federico introduces the "peculiar" magistratorial institutions of his country that have led to one part of this striking judicialization. Carlo Guarnieri then demonstrates how rules designed to guarantee the independence of Italian judges also provide a basis for the extraordinary judicialization of politics. Michael Mandel, a well-known critic of the expansion of judicial power in Canadian politics, compares the Italian case with what has happened in Canada and argues that, despite relatively favorable conditions for promoting more equalitarian social policies, the Italian judiciary has also essentially judicialized politics in favor of conservative interests.

Turning to France and Germany, we find that by focusing on the principal regular and administrative judicial hierarchies rather than on the work of the *Conseil Constitutionnel*, Jacqueline Lucienne Lafon paints a rather different portrait of the extent and prospects for the expansion of judicial power in France than does Alec Stone. Even so, Lafon's purpose is to show how judicialization has still emerged within the stringent constraints of the classical perspective on French law. The expansion of judicial power in German politics is analyzed critically by Christine Landfried because of its apparent impact on the effectiveness of parliamentary and executive institutions. Unlike some critics, however, Landfried argues that there will be occasions on which courts make what is, from her perspective, a positive contribution to policy and to the effectiveness or representativeness of majoritarian institutions. Thus she concludes with an attempt to specify the circumstances under which judicialization is appropriate. Finally, H. G. Peter Wallach reviews the prospects for judicialization from the perspective of the problems resulting from reunification. Wallach argues that, while the possibility of the expansion of judicial power as a result of reunification was great in the abstract, the architects of reunification took steps to reduce the chance that it would occur in fact.

For the smaller democracies, Barry Holmström describes a clear but perhaps surprising history of the progress of judicialization in Sweden. His account reveals that Sweden has experienced contrary judicialization patterns: the adoption of judicial procedures in nonjudicial settings has actually declined, while the intrusion of the judiciary into policy areas frequently dominated by majoritarian institutions continues to rise. Jan ten Kate and Peter J. van Koppen describe the development of a limited judicialization through a form of judicial review in the Netherlands and speculate about its probable growth under the impact of European Community norms and requirements. Justice Carmel A. Agius and Nancy A. Grosselfinger recount the tempestuous course of judicialization in Malta, finding it to be deeply intertwined with the interests and objectives of the personnel who staff both the judiciary and the majoritarian institutions. Finally, Martin Edelman's chapter reviews the extraordinary case of Israel, where substantial judicialization has occurred without judicial review or even a written constitution to be reviewed!

Part 4 focuses on the prospects for judicialization in some of the world's most volatile polities, the post-Communist nations and a pair of "troubled" and "rebuilding" democracies in Asia and Africa. The difficulty of assessing political trends in the post-Communist states clearly shows in Cheryl A. Thomas's and William Kitchin's analyses of judicialization in Russia. Time pressures and the continuing turmoil of Russian judicial-executive relations forced each author to cut off her/his story before its finish. But this is less of a problem than it might seem because no one knows the finish to their stories, and no one is likely to know for some time. The sea change in Russian judicialization that has occurred since Thomas and Kitchin drafted their chapters only prefigures what one may expect in the future. How judicial policy influence has expanded or may expand in the troubled democracy of the Philippines is the focus of C. Neal Tate's inquiry. Tate depicts the Philippines as a case in which the effort to reestablish democracy appears to place great emphasis on the role of a powerful judiciary, one that has the authority to review at its discretion the actions of almost any government agency on almost topic. Whether this emphasis on the expansion of judicial power will strengthen or weaken majoritarian democracy and whether it will protect Philippine citizens against abuses of their rights like those that occurred under the former regime of Ferdinand Marcos remain a part of the unknown finish to Tate's story. Finally, the role of judicialization in the new democracy of Namibia is discussed by Nico Steytler. Steytler finds that an expansion of judicial power was essential to achieving an agreement on which Namibian democracy could be built. At the same time, however, it may pose a serious threat to the success of that democracy because of the entrenched protection it provides for the interests of the white minority.

A concluding chapter by the coeditors reconsiders the arguments and analyses of parts 1–4 in an effort to generalize concerning the importance and future of the judicialization of politics.

REFERENCES

Note: "Paper presented at the Forlí Conference" is shorthand for the following complete citation: Paper presented to the Interim Meeting of the Research Committee on Comparative Judicial Studies, International Political Science Association, *Centro Studi e Richerche Sull'Ordinamento Giudiziario*, University of Bologna, Forlí, Italy, June 14–17, 1992.

Baar, Carl. 1992. "Social Action Litigation in India: The Operation and Limits of the World's Most Active Judiciary." In *Comparative Judicial Review and Public Policy*, ed. Donald W. Jackson and C. Neal Tate. Westport, Conn.: Greenwood Press, 77–88.

Fitzgerald, Edward A. 1992. "New South Wales v. Commonwealth: The Australian Tidelands Controversy." Paper presented at the Forlí Conference.

Gupta, Asha. 1992. "Judicialization of Politics: Ram Janambhoomi Babri-Masjid Controversy in India." Paper presented at the Forlí Conference.

Kemerer, Frank R. 1991. *William Wayne Justice: A Judicial Biography*. Austin: University of Texas Press.

Lozada, Salvador. 1992.   "The Successful Appeal from Bullets to Ballots: The Herculean Hardships of Judicializing Politics in Latin America." Paper presented at the Forlí Conference.

Mandel, Michael 1989. *The Charter and the Legalization of Politics in Canada*. Toronto: Wall and Thompson.

Patenaude, Pierre. 1992. "La Judiciarization des droit linguistiques en Canada et la politisation du pouvoir judiciaire." Paper presented at the Forlí Conference.

PART I

CONCEPTS AND CONDITIONS

2.

When the Courts Go Marching In

Torbjörn Vallinder

Meaning

When we speak of the global expansion of judicial power, we refer to the infusion of judicial decision-making and of courtlike procedures into political arenas where they did not previously reside. To put it briefly, we refer to the "judicialization" of politics.

To judicialize, according to the best of sources, is "to treat judicially, to arrive at a judgement or decision upon." In this connection judicially should mean either (1) in "the way of legal judgement, or in the office or capacity of judge; in, by, or in relation to, the administration of justice; by legal process; by sentence of a court or justice," or (2) after "the manner of a judge; with judicial knowledge and skill" (OED, 297).

Thus the judicialization of politics should normally mean either (1) the expansion of the province of the courts or the judges at the expense of the politicians and/or the administrators, that is, the transfer of decision-making rights from the legislature, the cabinet, or the civil service to the courts or, at least, (2) the spread of judicial decision-making methods outside the judicial province proper. In summing up we might say that judicialization essentially involves turning something into a form of judicial process.

In democracies, primarily in their popularly elected assemblies, decision-making is based on the majority principle and a free, public debate among equals. What about the courts?

According to standard works on legal procedure, the organization and working methods of the courts regularly include
- a special staff (judges), normally with legal training,
- the resolution of conflicts between two parties in a regular and authoritative way, according to
- preordained rules, thereby
- ascertaining the facts of the case and weighing the arguments of the conflicting parties, with
- prospective effects on similar cases in the future.

The differences between the judicial and the political ways of conflict resolution may be further illuminated through the more detailed comparison between a court and a legislature in table 2.1.

Table 2.1: A Comparison of a Court and a Legislature		
Characteristics	**Court**	**Legislature**
Actors	two parties and a third participant (the judge)	several parties
Working methods	open hearings weighing of arguments	bargaining, often behind closed doors compromise, logrolling
Basic decision-making rules	decision made by impartial judge	the majority principle
Output	settling of individual cases (but cf. precedents, especially judicial review)	general rules (laws, budgets) policy-making
Implications	ascertaining of the facts (what has happened) and the relevant rule (what should be applied) "the only correct solution"	allocation of values (often economic) "the politically possible solution"

These two decision-making models can perhaps be looked upon as ideal types. However, the borderline between them is by no means crystal clear. In the judicial field there are instances of discussion between the parties and the judge behind closed doors, that is, plea bargaining, widespread in the United States and practiced also in the United Kingdom and other European countries. It is also quite obvious that in practice the courts make law through precedents. That activity is especially important in judicial review of legislative enactments.

It is nevertheless quite clear that the two models embody two different principles and two corresponding roles, both of which are indispensable in a democracy. Quoting Herbert Wechsler, we should put "emphasis upon the role of reason and of principle in the judicial, as distinguished from the legislative or executive, appraisal of conflicting values" (Wechsler 1959-1960, 16). In this connection it is the task of the courts to shelter the fundamental rights of citizens, what we, following Isaiah Berlin, call "negative" freedom. The legislature, on the other hand, has to take care of the rights and obligations of the (legislative) majority. The judicialization of politics may roughly be said to signify upgrading the first principle at the expense of the second.

FORMS

Using the definition above of judicialization of politics, it is possible to distinguish several forms of it. Quite obviously, one major form is ~~DeFiN of Judicial Review~~ judicial review of executive and legislative actions. In a way, this form would amount to placing the third branch of government above the first and second ones. However, the basis of judicial review of legislative action is, of course, the codified constitution of the country. Since that document has been enacted by the legislature, or, as in the United States, by a constitutional convention, this form of judicial review should really imply keeping the legislature within its proper limits as stated in the constitution and thus protecting it from wrongful use of its powers. Somewhat in the same vein, judicial review of executive action may often be said to entail enforcing the decisions of the legislative majority by applying the ultra vires principle to the action in question.

The scope and efficiency of judicial review can be enhanced through the enactment or the expansion of a bill of rights. Here Canada provides a recent example (Russell 1990, esp. 120ff.; also see Jackson and Tate 1992).

Judicial review may be termed judicialization from without. There are also different forms of judicialization from within, that is, the introduction or expansion of judicial staff or judicial working methods in the administrative sector.

Here one example can be found in the development within the administrative tribunals in Britain. Partly following the recommendations of the Franks Committee of 1957, "a large measure of judicialization has occurred, in part through the stimulus provided by the Council on Tribunals. Some changes, such as the duty to give reasons on request, were incorporated in the Tribunals and Inquiries Act 1958, while others, for example, the opening-up of hearings to the public, have come about either through delegated legislation or administrative action" (Harlow-Rawlings 1984, 97).

That means more adjudication, less administration. A similar example is provided by the American Administrative Procedure Act of 1946 and the fact that U.S. agencies have "administrative judges" who hold hearings on many decisions, often of no great adjudicatory character (cf. Bell 1987).

Somewhat different examples of judicialization from within can be found in Sweden. Owing to traditions going back to the Code of Laws of the Kingdom of Sweden, enacted in 1734, the similarities in working methods between the civil servants, several of them with law degrees, and the judges are clear and important. It is thus quite logical that the English separation between the civil service and the judiciary has never existed in Sweden (cf. Strömholm 1981, passim).

Even more striking is another Swedish tradition, with roots going back to the second part of the nineteenth century. In their earlier middle life, many Swedish judges, on leave from the courts of appeal, work for some years in the ministries as drafters of governmental bills or in ministerial commissions as secretaries. Then they go back to the courts at various levels.

This tradition may also be seen as a way of judicialization of executive work. However, Swedish critics of the system maintain that it is rather an example of an executive indoctrination of middle-aged judges before their return to the courtrooms.

BACKGROUND

Several of the earliest champions of democracy did not envisage a conflict between the two principles under discussion here. That very American Englishman Thomas Paine was a typical example. In his book *Rights of Man*, published in 1791–1792, he stated (in italics) in the chapter "Of Constitutions" that *"representative government is freedom"* (Paine 1976, 223). In his mind the only threat to the rights of the citizens came from the hereditary monarchy and the hereditary nobility, that is, people of no ability (128) and their henchmen, including corrupt judges. Consequently, positively if briefly, he referred to Charles James Fox's Libel Act of 1792, which expanded the power of the English jury (222 fn.).

However, somewhat earlier the American Founding Fathers of 1787 had taken a more skeptical view toward strict majority rule and were consequently much more interested in the constitutional role of the courts. In *The Federalist Papers* (no. 78) Alexander Hamilton stated that the judiciary is beyond comparison the weakest of the three departments of power and that "the general liberty of the people can never be endangered from that quarter." Hamilton continued:

The complete independence of the courts of justice is peculiarly essential in a limited Constitution. By a limited Constitution I understand one which contains certain specified exceptions to the legislative authority: such, for instance, as that it shall pass no bills of attainder, no *ex post facto* laws, and the like. Limitations of this kind can be preserved in practice no other way than through the medium of the courts of justice, whose duty it must be to declare all acts contrary to the manifest tenor of the Constitution void. Without this, all the reservations of particular rights or privileges would amount to nothing. (Madison et al. 1987, 438)

Thus, Hamilton clearly and enthusiastically endorsed the judiciary and judicial review.

The subsequent American development in the area should be well known. In 1803 the first instance of judicial review occurred, the famous *Marbury v. Madison* case. During the latter part of the nineteenth century, the Supreme Court established judicial review as a basic feature of the American governmental system (see, e.g., Abraham 1985).

During the nineteenth century several liberals, most notably Benjamin Constant, Alexis de Tocqueville and John Stuart Mill, took as skeptical a view as Hamilton did of strict majoritarianism and assemblies elected by universal and equal suffrage.

Constant, scared by his experiences during the French Revolution from 1789 onward, designed a constitutional system that should provide the necessary checks to popularly backed despotism. He stressed the importance of independent judges and praised the jury system (Constant 1988, 295 ff.; Holmes 1984, esp. 4).

Tocqueville and Mill worked, in the main, along the same lines. In his classical book *Democracy in America* (about 1840) Tocqueville extensively discussed the roles and importance of the American courts, judges, and juries. Three typical sentences run like this:

> [T]he Americans have given their courts immense political power; but by obliging them to attack the laws by judicial means, they have greatly lessened the dangers of that power. . . .
>
> I wonder if this way in which American courts behave is not both the best way of preserving public order and the best way of favoring liberty. . . .
>
> Restricted within its limits, the power granted to American courts to pronounce on the constitutionality of laws is yet one of the most powerful barriers ever created against the tyranny of political assemblies. (Tocqueville 1969, 102 ff.)

Like Tocqueville in his later works, Mill was very much upset by the revolution in France in 1848 and the subsequent return of the popularly backed Napoleonic despotism. In his books *On Liberty* (1859) and *Considerations on Representative Government* (1861), indispensable reading for all democrats ever since, Mill reviewed possible checks to the tyranny of the majority, including the tyranny of public opinion. However, he had been brought up in the British traditions of parliamentary supremacy and of utilitarianism, and he accepted in principle Jeremy Bentham's critical attitude toward lawyers. Thus, Mill had not much and, indeed, nothing favorable to say about judges, not to mention judicial review (cf. Mill 1989, 68 fn. 1).

Going on to our own century, we may take Lord Bryce's well-known standard work *Modern Democracies* as a starting point. It was published in 1921, when the world was supposed to have been made safe for democracy. It comprises two volumes with about thirteen hundred pages in all. The section on the United States, needless to say, contains a comprehensive treatment of "The judiciary and civil order" (Bryce 1921, vol. 2, 89–120). In other sections there are also some remarks on the courts in a few countries, for example, Switzerland.   Bryce further included a general chapter on "The judiciary," but this chapter is very short and contains nothing about the constitutional role of the courts (Bryce, vol. 2, 421-427).   There is also a chapter on "Liberty" which is very short and does not mention the courts or the judges (vol. 1, 57-67).

Proceeding rapidly to the period after the Second World War, we may safely say that the role of the courts and the judges has clearly and considerably expanded. A certain amount of judicialization of politics has occurred in many democratic countries. The precise causes behind these developments differ from country to country. However, it is certainly possible to point to some general determinants.

One important factor was the rise in the 1930s of the totalitarian regimes in Europe and their horrible outrage against the rights of the citizens, especially during the war.   After the war, against that background, democrats everywhere had to ask themselves some crucial questions: How could all this happen? How can we prevent a recurrence of it? In other words: How can we protect the rights of the citizens in the future?

These questions were especially burning in Germany, for obvious reasons. At the end of the 1920s Germany was still a highly developed country, economically, politically, and culturally, certainly a *Kulturstaat*. There were totalitarian parties, Nazis and Communists, but they were not looked upon as major political actors.

During the first three years of the 1930s the political situation in Germany changed totally. In the general election in July 1932 the Nazis and the Communists together received more than 50 percent of the seats in the Reichstag. This majority, of course, was not a working one. Nevertheless, it was an antidemocratic majority emanating from a democratic election, something unheard of so far.

In January 1933, formally in good constitutional order, Adolf Hitler was appointed chancellor and formed a coalition government. The Reichstag was dissolved and a general election, neither fully democratic nor totally rigged, was held in March, giving the government an absolute majority. After the election, using the notorious emergency article (no.

48) in the constitution, the Reichstag was purged of Communists, thus securing an absolute majority for the Nazi party. Then the dictatorship was established through a decision of the Reichstag, only the Social Democratic Party voting against (see, e.g., Bracher 1983).

To say that Hitler came to power in a democratic way is thus at most a half-truth. However, even half-truths may be frightening and require countermeasures. The Federal Republic of Germany took them in 1949: a new constitution, the Grundgesetz, was enacted included an extensive bill of rights, a constitutional court and judicial review.

Another background factor can be found in the economic sector of political life. During the later war years the leaders of political parties in different countries were planning for economic reconstruction and development in the approaching peacetime. In the socialist camp central planning, including an extensive social security system and some measures of nationalization, was considered instrumental in achieving those goals. According to the tenets of the Labour Parties in, say, Britain and Sweden, the suggested policies would promote not only economic equality but also political liberty.

In the liberal and conservative camps dissenting opinions were put forward. To liberals of the classical persuasion central planning was certainly not a way to freedom and security but *The Road to Serfdom* (Hayek 1944). They pointed out that such a planning had been put into practice in the Soviet Union and, to some extent, in Nazi Germany, with disastrous results.

Representatives of the Labour Parties retorted that, in their view, *Freedom under Planning* (Wootton 1945) was not only indispensable but also quite attainable. However, by and large, at least some British laborites conceded that there was something valid in the liberal criticism, that there existed a real problem (Crossman 1956) which could be labeled *Socialism and the New Despotism*.

In his pamphlet, R. H. S. Crossman, a well-known member of the political science profession, discussed the relations between the law and personal freedom:

> To restore parliamentary control of the Executive, however, is not sufficient for our Socialist purpose of liberating the community from the abuse of arbitrary power. The next step will be to reform the Judiciary, so that it can regain its traditional function of defending individual rights against encroachment. That function

has been steadily narrowed for the last hundred years, as small-scale capitalism has been transformed into oligopoly and the flimsy structure of the Victorian State has developed into the Leviathan which now dominates our lives.

Thus, Crossman insisted that the Labour Party should "go on to discuss the reforms of the law and the reorganization of the Judiciary which will be required to defend the individual against the oligopolists and oligarchs who threaten his freedom" (Crossman 1956, 19ff.).

In Scandinavia, maybe especially in Sweden, the general distrust of courts and lawyers among socialists and social reformers was more intense than in Britain. However, even in Sweden the Labour Party has in recent years accepted a certain amount of judicialization of politics. In 1979 judicial review of legislative action was explicitly written into the new constitution of 1974 (Heckscher 1984, 130ff.; Stjernquist 1992, esp. 136ff.). In 1988 as a consequence of rulings by the European Court of Justice in Strasbourg, which had convicted Sweden, a very restricted measure of judicial review of executive action was introduced. However, this second reform, in contradistinction to the first, was not enacted through a constitutional amendment but through a provisional act (Warnling-Nerep 1991).

Another background factor can be found in the recent developments in political theory and legal theory. In the middle of the 18th century the classical theories of natural law and natural rights were demolished by David Hume. That destruction took place at the philosophical level and did not, at the political level, prevent the American and French revolutionaries from using those theories as an ideological platform.

However, up to the middle of the twentieth century, natural law theories were on the decline, at least in the non-Catholic world. In countries such as Britain, the United States and Scandinavia several departments of philosophy, jurisprudence, and political science were dominated by a more or less Benthamite, utilitarian philosophy, emulating Hume and thus strongly critical of natural law. Also, several party leaders, educated in those university departments, were influenced by utilitarian principles.

After the war we have seen a change on this score also. We have experienced a remarkable revival of natural law theories or, maybe better, deontological theories, in several academic quarters. Once more philosophers, political scientists, and legal scholars have taken down from their shelves the works of, say, Locke, Rousseau, and Kant, not for their historical contributions but for their topical interest:

> One could say, to paraphrase Benjamin Constant, that the liberty of today is not that of other times, and the same can be said of justice and all other values. But the utopian desire which natural law doctrines express is an irrepressible facet of human nature, and thus natural law theories will be continually revived, especially in moments of acute crisis." (Cappelletti 1971, vii)

In the same vein Judith N. Shklar has written that natural law ideology is in "a permanent state of revival" (Shklar 1986, 68).

However, that development has not stopped at the revival of classical theories. Inspired by the older thinkers, several modern philosophers have developed rights-based theories of their own, for example, *A Theory of Justice*, (Rawls 1971). *Taking Rights Seriously* (Dworkin 1978) has become a much more common practice than during the heyday of positivist philosophy. Against this background, *Judicial Review in the Contemporary World* can be described as "a fascinating synthesis of two seemingly contradictory schools of thought" (Cappelletti 1971, vii).

When talking about background factors we should not, finally, forget the comparative and international aspects.

After the Second World War the United States emerged as the democratic superpower. To many democratic countries, old and new, the American political system, with great power and prestige for the judiciary and for judicial review, became an ideal to be emulated (cf., e.g., Russell 1990).

In the 1930s many liberals, in the United States as well as in Europe, had been very critical of the performance of the U.S. Supreme Court. Using its power of judicial review the Court had declared unconstitutional some important proposals of President Franklin D. Roosevelt, thereby almost destroying his program for fighting the economic depression.

However, after the war, especially in the Warren Court period (1953–1969), the justices followed a more liberal line, making several rulings favorable to underprivileged groups, such as the blacks (Abraham 1988, 393 ff.). This development strongly enhanced the reputation of the Court and of judicial review, inside and outside the United States.

There is also a specifically European tradition of judicial review. It is not, and could not be, wholly independent of the American one. It is nevertheless a tradition in its own right.

The most important roots of this European tradition are to be found in Austria. "*Au commencement était Kelsen!*" (Favoreu 1986a, 42) (In the beginning was Kelsen!). Hans Kelsen became a law professor, of a liberal persuasion, in 1911 at the University of Vienna. After the First World War he was entrusted with the task of drafting a constitution for the new Austrian republic.

This Austrian constitution of 1920 included rules for judicial review. However, and in contradistinction to the American system, the review was not to be handled by the ordinary courts but by a constitutional court, especially designed for the task by Kelsen.

In several of his works in jurisprudence Kelsen defended judicial review and expanded upon the Austrian model of it. During the interwar years that model was extensively discussed among European legal scholars and was also, to some extent, emulated outside Austria (e.g. Kelsen 1923, 214 ff., Kelsen 1925, 254 ff., Kelsen 1929, 52ff., Favoreu 1986b, 4ff.).

Kelsen left Vienna in 1929, moving first to Cologne and then to Geneva. In 1943 he was appointed professor of political science at Berkeley. However, after the fall of the Nazi empire in 1945 and the reintroduction of democracy on the Continent outside the Soviet bloc, his Austrian model of judicial review once more became influential in several European countries (Cappelletti 1986, 302, Favoreu 1986b, 4ff.).

Not only the developments in model countries like the United States and Austria but also the efforts of different international organizations in defense of human rights have influenced the judicialization process in some states. The United Nations Charter of 1945, as should be well known, begins by expressing homage to human rights, as does the Organization's Universal Declaration on the matter of 1948. The UN also established several conventions to the same purpose (cf., e.g., Russell 1990).

However, more important is the European Convention for the Protection of Human Rights. Primarily through the European Court, it has been provided with fairly strong legal teeth, which have made their mark also in countries where the rule of law was supposed to be firmly established, e.g., Britain and Sweden. The parliaments of those countries have been forced to amend legislation pertaining to the rights of the citizens, yielding to judicialization from abroad.

PROSPECTS

Adjudication and political decision-making may be looked upon as the two ends of a scale. At the one end is what a French scholar several years ago called *Le gouvernement des juges* (Lambert 1921), that is in English *Government by Judiciary* (Berger 1977). At the other end we might place, say, total majoritarianism. In this perspective the judicialization of politics that we have seen in recent decades means a movement toward the first end of the scale.

What about the future? The prospects clearly differ from country to country, depending on the constitutional traditions and the political situation. However, it seems hardly likely that the ongoing process of judicialization will be reversed or even brought to a stop. It has already, to some extent, spread in Eastern Europe. Hungary, for instance, has enacted a bill of rights and established a constitutional court. Similar developments can be found in former dictatorships outside the Western world. In the end a new equilibrium will perhaps be established in many countries between the rights of the citizens and the rights and obligations of the (legislative) majority.

Note: Most valuable advice has been provided by Professor John S. Bell, Faculty of Law, University of Leeds, Dr. Geoffrey Marshall, The Queen's College, Oxford, and Professor Hans F. Petersson, Department of Political Science, University of Lund.

REFERENCES

Abraham, H. J. 1985. *Justices and Presidents: A Political History of Appointments to the Supreme Court.* 2nd ed. Oxford: Oxford University Press.
———. 1988. *Freedom and the Court: Civil Rights and Liberties in the United States.* 5th ed. Oxford: Oxford University Press.
Bell, J. 1987. "The Judge as Bureaucrat." In *Oxford Essays in Jurisprudence*, ed. J. Eklaar and J. Bell, 33–56.

Berger. R. 1977. *Government by Judiciary: The Transformation of the Fourteenth Amendment*. Cambridge: Harvard University Press.

Bracher, K. D. 1983. *Die deutsche Diktatur: Enstehung, Struktur, Folgen des Nationalisozialimus*. Frankfurt am Main: Ullstein.

Bryce, J. 1921. *Modern Democracies*. Vols. 1–2. London: Macmillan.

Cappelletti, M. 1971. *Judicial Review in the Contemporary World*. New York: Bobbs-Merrill.

———. 1986. "General Report." In *Le contrôle jurisdictionnelle des lois*, ed. L. Favoreu and J. A. Jolowics, 301–314.

Constant, B. 1988. *Political Writings*, ed. Bianca-Maria Fontana. Cambridge: Cambridge University Press.

Crossman, R. H. S. 1956. *Socialism and the New Despotism*. London: Fabian Society.

Dworkin, R. 1978. *Taking Rights Seriously*. London: Duckworth.

Eklaar, J. and J. Bell, eds. 1987. *Oxford Essays in Jurisprudence*. 3rd series. Oxford: Clarendon Press.

Favoreu, L. 1986a. "Europe occidentale." In *Le contrôle jurisdictionnelle des lois*, ed. L. Favoreu and J. A. Jolowics, 17–68.

———. 1986b. *Les cours constitutionelles*. Paris: Presses Universitaires de France.

Favoreu, L., and J. A. Jolowics, eds. 1986. *Le contrôle jurisdictionnelle des lois*. Paris: Economica.

Harlow, C., and R. Rawlings. 1984. *Law and Administration*. London: Weidenfeld and Nicolson.

Hayek, F. A. 1944. *The Road to Serfdom*. London: Routledge.

Heckscher, G. 1984. *The Welfare State and Beyond: Success and Problems in Scandinavia*. Minneapolis: University of Minnesota Press.

Holmes, S. 1984. *Benjamin Constant and the Making of Modern Liberalism*. New Haven: Yale University Press.

Jackson, D. W., and C. N. Tate, eds. 1992. *Comparative Judicial Review and Public Policy*. Westport, Conn.: Greenwood Press.

Kelsen, Hans. 1923. *Österrichislles Staatrecht: Ein Grundriss entwicklungsgeschichtlich dargestelt*. Tübingen: J. C. B. Mohr.

———. 1925. *Allgemeine Staatslehre*. Berlin: Springer.

———. 1929. "La garantie jurisdictionnelle de la Constitution. (La Justice constitutionnelle)." *Annuaire de l'Institut international de Droit Public*, 52–143.

Lambert, E. 1921. *Le gouvernement des juges el la lutte contre la legislation sociale aux Etats-Unis: L'experience américaine du contrôle judiciaire des constitutionnalité de la lois.* Paris: Giard.

Madison, J. et al. 1987. *The Federalist Papers*, ed. Isaac Kramnick. Harmondsworth, Middlesex: Penguin.

Mill, J. S. 1989. *On Liberty*, ed. Stefan Collini. Cambridge: Cambridge University Press.

Oxford English Dictionary. 1989. 2nd ed. Prepared by J. A. Simpson and E. S. C. Weiner, Vol. 8. Oxford: Clarendon Press.

Paine, T. 1976. *Rights of Man*, ed. Henry Collins. Harmondsworth, Middlesex: Penguin.

Rawls, J. 1971. *A Theory of Justice.* Oxford: Oxford University Press.

Russell, P. H. 1990. "The Diffusion of Judicial Review: The Commonwealth, the United States, and the Canadian Case." *Policy Studies Journal* 19:116–26.

Shklar, J. N. 1986. *Legalism: Law, Morals, and Political Trials* Cambridge: Harvard University Press.

Stjernquist, N. 1992. "Judicial Review and the Rule of Law: Comparing the United States and Sweden." In *Comparative Judicial Review and Public Policy*, ed. D. W. Jackson and C. N. Tate, 129–141.

Strömholm, S., ed. 1981. *An Introduction to Swedish Law.* Stockholm: Norstedts.

de Tocqueville, A. 1969. *Democracy in America*, ed. J. P. Mayer. Garden City, NY: Doubleday.

Warnling-Nerep, W. 1991. "Rättsprövning av förvaltningsbeslut," *Förvaltningsrättslig Tidskrift* 54:129–165.

Wechsler, H. 1959–1960. "Toward Neutral Principles of Constitutional Law," *Harvard Law Review* 73:1–35.

Wootton, B. 1945. *Freedom under Planning.* London: Allen and Unwin.

3.

Why the Expansion of Judicial Power?

C. NEAL TATE

The thesis of this book is that there is an expansion of judicial power afoot in the world's political systems. For convenience we also refer to this expansion as "judicialization." The authors of the various chapters find judicialization present or developing in a wide variety of places. Though not all are treated here, Canada, France, Germany, India, Israel, Italy, Malta, the Philippines, Sweden, the United States, Latin America, the former USSR, and the European Community (at least) all appear to be settings in which the expansion of judicial power/judicialization of politics is relevant, even controversial.

Accurate description and perceptive analysis of the judicialization of politics depend on having a better understanding of the meaning and development of the process. This chapter enhances that understanding by suggesting the political conditions that appear to promote the judicialization of politics and logically analyzing how those conditions interact with the values of those who are the prime actors in the process, the judges, to determine whether or not the judicialization of politics is likely to occur in a particular setting.

JUDICIALIZATION: DEFINITIONS

For clarity and consistency, I follow Vallinder's conceptual survey of the judicialization of politics (chap. 2 of this volume), which suggests two core meanings for the term:

1. the process by which courts and judges come to make or increasingly to dominate the making of public policies that had previously been made (or, it is widely believed, ought to be made) by other governmental agencies, especially legislatures and executives, and
2. the process by which nonjudicial negotiating and decision-making forums come to be dominated by quasi-judicial (legalistic) rules and procedures.

From the point of view of traditional views of the legal process, which ought not to be taken seriously by any scholar seeking to understand the global expansion of judicial power, the former involves "nonpolitical" judges in the exercise of "political" discretion, that is, in acting like politicians. The latter meaning, in turn, implies that discretionary, frequently "political," decision makers act like rules-bound, "apolitical" judges. I shall argue that both forms of the judicialization of politics emerge under some common conditions. But there appears to be no theoretical or practical reason to expect the two forms to develop together. Holmström's analysis of the Swedish case concludes, in fact, that the first form has developed in that country precisely as the second form has declined.

CONDITIONS FACILITATING THE EXPANSION OF JUDICIAL POWER

Democracy

Much discussion of the judicialization of politics considers it a threat to such essential features of democracy as majority rule and popular responsibility (see Linz 1978; Valenzuela 1978). Despite this, it seems very unlikely that one will encounter the judicialization of politics outside democratic polities. It is hard to imagine a dictator, regardless of his or her uniform or ideological stripe, (1) inviting or allowing even nominally independent judges to increase their participation in the making of major public policies, or (2) tolerating decision-making processes that place adherence to legalistic procedural rules and rights above the rapid achievement of desired substantive outcomes. The presence of democratic government thus appears to be a necessary, though certainly not a sufficient, condition for the judicialization of politics.

Separation of Powers

Given democracy, what conditions appear to further the prospects for the judicialization of politics? A constitutional condition that is frequently cited is the presence of a "Montesquieuean" or separation-of-powers structure for government (see the discussion in chapter 2 by Vallinder and chapter 19 by Holmström). It certainly seems plausible that decision makers in a constitutionally independent and coequal branch would be in a good position to assert themselves in policy-making against or in competition with the legislative and executive branches.

On the other hand, one should remember that in separation-of-powers systems the formal duty assigned to judges is always to interpret, and not to make, the laws. Leaving aside the difficulty of distinguishing interpreting from making the laws, a difficulty that is well recognized by practicing judges and attorneys as well as by sociolegal scholars, coequal status and personal and institutional autonomy for judges hardly *require* them to substitute their own policy judgment for that of others, or even to put their own policy judgments into place when others have failed "adequately" to address a policy issue. A separation-of-powers system may thus facilitate a judicialization of politics that occurs for other reasons, but it does not appear to be a necessary, much less a sufficient, condition for judicialization.

Politics of Rights

A much more relevant condition for the judicialization of politics may be the presence of a "politics of rights," as several analysts note (see chapter 2 by Vallinder, 19 by Holmström, 9 by Russell, and 22 by Edelman). Such a politics is perhaps more likely to develop if can be founded in a constitutional bill of rights, although the experience of Israel demonstrates that, again, the structural condition represented by a formal, constitutional bill of rights is facilitative but not necessary (see Edelman's chapter).

Regardless of whether there is a formal bill of rights, an acceptance of the principle that individuals or minorities have rights that can be enforced against the will of putative majorities seems very likely to increase the policy significance of those—the judges—whose institutional location usually makes it easier for them to make rules that favor minorities over majorities. When legitimacy is accorded to a politics of rights, it spills over to the procedures associated with the work of the courts, who become key players in this politics. With their new legitimacy, these procedures then become archetypes available for use in the many nonjudicial forums into which the politics of rights penetrates.

Interest Group Use of the Courts

It would be misleading to leave the impression that the judicialization of politics develops somehow in isolation from the central social and economic interests that structure system politics. In fact the development and expansion of even a politics of rights may often more properly be seen as the achievement of interest groups who find majoritarian decision-making processes not to their advantage (see Holmström's chapter) than as the product of the devotion of political actors to some elevated vision of human rights. As groups increasingly discover the potential utility of the courts in the achievement of their objectives, they may be able to expand the understanding of "rights" to include interests that may appear to some to be only remotely connected to any constitutional foundation in a formal bill of rights. The politics of rights may become distinguishable from the politics of interests only in its relatively more legalistic discourse.

Opposition Use of the Court

Stone's research on constitutional review reveals an equally impressive linkage between national system politics and judicialization. In France the primary constitutional "court," the Constitutional Council, has increasingly been the instrument of the judicialization of politics (1) as the parliamentary opposition has used it effectively to oppose major government initiatives that it could not defeat through ordinary majoritarian processes, and (2) as the government has prospectively modified legislation to avoid negative scrutiny by the council. One of Stone's major points is that as it exercises constitutional review, a constitutional court might be more accurately regarded as a third branch of the legislature than as a regular court. Since the French Constitutional Council exercises no judicial functions other than abstract constitutional review, Stone's argument is especially applicable in its case. But it seems likely that the experience of many other nations will document that political oppositions frequently judicialize politics by attempting to use the courts to harass and obstruct governments, regardless of whether those courts have the especially useful tool of abstract review.

Ineffective Majoritarian Institutions

There are no doubt many conditions affecting the desire and ability of political oppositions and interest groups to drag or entice judiciaries into disputes that many argue should be left to majoritarian decision-making processes. As noted, one condition is the presence of a politics of rights. If the opposition can redefine a "legislative" dispute as one that involves a "right," it can shift it from a forum in which the majority's right to rule is accepted, into one in which minorities are acknowledged to have rights that can be asserted against majorities by nonmajoritarian institutions like courts.

A second condition may be the weakness of political parties and governing coalitions (see the chapters by Holmström and Edelman). When executives are unable to govern through disciplined parties with effective legislative majorities, they will find it difficult to develop effective policies with the political and public support that can sustain them through opposition challenges directed to the judiciary.

Perceptions of the Policy-Making Institutions

Functioning as both consequence and possible cause of this inability of majoritarian institutions to make effective public policy are mass public and elite attitudes toward the executive, legislature, and judiciary. When the public and the leaders of interest groups and major economic and social institutions view the majoritarian institutions as immobilized, self-serving, or even corrupt, it is hardly surprising that they would accord the policy-making of judiciaries, who have reputations for expertise and rectitude, as much or more legitimacy as that of executives and legislatures. This tendency should only be accelerated when judicial institutions are accorded *more* respect or legitimacy than other government institutions (see the chapters by Edelman on Israel and Tate on the Philippines; Caldeira and Gibson 1992).

(Willful) Delegation by Majoritarian Institutions

Occasionally, the judicialization of politics occurs when majoritarian institutions decide that there are certain issues that they do not wish to be burdened with deciding. Though the leadership of the majoritarian institutions might well deny it, it often appears to an outsider that this delegation is willful. Why do such delegations occur? At times the reason appears to be that the political costs of dealing seriously with the issue are too great to risk, that the issue is a no-win proposition for elected decision makers. For example, many (certainly not all) American state legislatures have appeared to be more than willing to leave abortion policy in the hands of the courts because of their assessment of the political costs of taking any action on the issue. Similarly, in Texas and several other American states prison and education reform and funding have become major policy concerns of the courts because legislatures and executives did not wish to face the excruciating choices involved in raising taxes or reallocating existing funding to benefit an unpopular group, prisoners, or an otherwise easily-ignored group, poor communities. It has also appeared to me that the judicialization of Canadian politics that has occurred in the last decade results in large part from an at least semiwillful decision on the part of the national and provincial leaders of that nation to remove certain very difficult issues of provincial and linguistic autonomy (see Patenaude 1992) from the normal purview of legislative politics. The notwithstanding clause, which Russell now finds to be a dead letter, except in Quebec, was the elected politicians' safeguard against the courts taking their policy role in these issue areas too seriously—their guarantee that they could "take back" the policy issues that they were delegating to the courts.

Delegating policies to the judiciary usually occurs in the context of a politics of rights—the policies being delegated are otherwise too clearly within the normal discretion of majoritarian institutions to allow them to become the subject of judicial decision-making. In addition, the delegations may also represent the ineffectiveness of majoritarian institutions. However, one might also argue that failure to delegate these issues to the courts would only guarantee ineffectiveness of legislative or executive policy-making, since the issues would hamstring the majoritarian bodies and make it difficult for them to make any other kind of policy effectively.

JUDICIALIZATION AND THE ATTITUDES OF POLICY MAKERS

The presence of democracy, a separation of powers system, a politics of rights, a system of interest groups and a political opposition cognizant of judicial means for attaining their interests, weak parties or fragile government coalitions in majoritarian institutions leading to policy deadlock, inadequate public support, at least relative to judiciaries, and the delegation to courts of decision-making authority in certain policy areas all contribute to the judicialization of politics. It seems highly unlikely that judicialization could proceed very far in the absence of these conditions. But I cannot conclude this discussion of the conditions facilitating the judicialization of politics without noting that even in the presence of all of them, significant judicialization is still not a given.

Even under a very favorable constellation of facilitating conditions, the actual development of the judicialization of politics requires that judges have the appropriate personal attitudes and policy preferences or values, especially relative to the values of other decision makers. Under otherwise favorable conditions, *judicialization develops only because judges decide that they should (1) participate in policy-making that could be left to the wise or foolish discretion of other institutions, and, at least on occasion, (2) substitute policy solutions they derive for those derived by other institutions.* To clarify, I must note that I accept the aphorism "not to decide is to decide." In choosing not to participate or not to substitute their own policy prescriptions for those of others, judges affirm existing policies, including the policy of "no policy," just as surely as if they had imposed those existing policies of their own volition. In this sense, they cannot escape their policy-making role. But "the judicialization of politics" implies a more positive policy role than that involved in a judicial "nondecision" (see Bachrach and Baratz 1962).

What are the judicial attitudes or values essential to the development of any significant judicialization of politics? The massive literature of judicial politics suggests two: judicial activism/restraint and judicial public policy preferences, normally arrayed on one or more left-right dimensions. The two sets of attitudes are not mutually exclusive; indeed they are theoretically independent. Any judicial system could in principle be populated by leftist-activists, leftist-restraintists, rightist-activists, and rightist-restraintists.[1]   As an empirical matter, I am convinced that the evidence supports a hierarchy of these two types of values, with judicial policy preferences more likely to determine judicial activism than vice versa.   But what is important for present purposes is that, given a sufficient cumulation of the conditions discussed above, judicial policy preferences and activism orientations will interact with the policy orientations of majoritarian institutions to produce judicialization under some specific circumstances, but not under others.   The accounts of Russell, Stone, Di Federico, and Agius and Grosselfinger, among others, provide clear evidence that it is the choices judges make to be more or less active in imposing their own policy solutions that determine just how far judicialization will go under favorable sets of facilitating conditions.

Table 3.1 presents the likely judicialization results one can expect, given specific combinations of facilitating circumstances, majoritarian institution orientations, and judicial attitudes or values.   It appears to suggest that the judicialization of politics should be a relatively rare phenomenon.   It presumably will not occur at all when facilitative conditions are unfavorable because the constitutional structural supports that make it feasible are absent and majoritarian institutions are effective and well respected, or perhaps both.   Yet because of the importance of the orientations of majoritarian institutions and the values and attitudes of judges, it can be expected to occur in only two of eight possible combinations of circumstances even when conditions are favorable.

Logically, restraintist judges should be expected to resist judicializing politics regardless of their personal policy values, or how those values relate to the values dominant in majoritarian institutions, even when conditions for judicialization are favorable.   Activist judges, by definition, may be expected to take every opportunity to use their decision-making to expand the policy values they hold dear.   But when those values are *consistent* with the values dominating majoritarian institutions, there will be much less incentive for activist judges to seek to judicialize a political process that is already producing such good policy results, even though the conditions are favorable for doing so.

Table 3.1 thus implies that only rightist-activist judges in an environment dominated by leftist majoritarian institutions and leftist-activist judges in an environment dominated by rightist majoritarian institutions should be expected to promote the judicialization of politics vigorously. Given the logic underlying table 3.1, why is there—as available evidence

Table 3.1: Conditions Promoting the Judicialization of Politics							
Facilitative Conditions **Favorable**							
Majority Institutions Values							
Leftist				Rightist			
Judicial Policy Value				Judicial Policy Values			
Leftist		Rightist		Leftist		Rightist	
Judicial Activism		Judicial Activism		Judicial Activism		Judicial Activism	
Acti-vism	Re-straint	Acti-vism	Re-straint	Acti-vism	Re-straint	Acti-vism	Re-straint
No Judicial-ization	No Judicial-ization	Judicial-ization	No Judicial-ization	Judicial-ization	No Judicial-ization	No Judicial-ization	No Judicial-ization
Facilitative Conditions **Unfavorable**							
Majority Institutions Values							
Leftist				Rightist			
Judicial Policy Value				Judicial Policy Values			
Leftist		Rightist		Leftist		Rightist	
Judicial Activism		Judicial Activism		Judicial Activism		Judicial Activism	
Acti-vism	Re-straint	Acti-vism	Re-straint	Acti-vism	Re-straint	Acti-vism	Re-straint
No Judicial-ization	No Judicial-ization	No Judicial-ization	No Judicial-ization	No Judicial-ization	No Judicial-ization	No Judicial-ization	No Judicial-ization

suggests—the correct perception that the judicialization of politics is a growing phenomenon worldwide? The answer is that the categories of table 3.1 do not occur with equal frequency in the real world. There appears to be considerable evidence—presented in many of the chapters of this book, for example—that the conditions promoting the judicialization of politics are on the increase in many nations. In addition I have contended that the balance of the empirical research documents that judicial activism is for most judges an instrumental value, one that is chosen when it will help them maximize their basic policy values and avoided when it will not. If this is true, then there must be relatively few judges who, under favorable conditions, choose to exercise judicial restraint when their own policy preferences could be advanced by promoting judicialization against a regime with contrary policy values.

Also, one should remember that table 3.1 is undoubtedly an oversimplification, in part because the policy values represented in the political process at large and in the minds of judges are multiple: there is not a single left-right dimension on which all policies can be easily placed and against which the policy orientations of majoritarian institutions can be assessed. It is likely, therefore, that activist judges even in political systems dominated by majoritarian institutions whose general policy orientations agree with their own will find some issues on which they assess the performance of majoritarian institutions to be inadequate. On those policy matters they may seek to judicialize, even while they restrain their activist tendencies on other issues.

In the real world, (1) the frequency in the top half of Figure 3.1 must be increasing, relative to that in the bottom half, and (2) the frequencies in the cells where judicialization is predicted to occur must be disproportionately large compared to the frequencies in the "restraintist" cells immediately to their right. The result is an increasing globalization of judicial power, the judicialization of politics.

NOTE

1. I use dichotomous classifications for simplicity. In fact, both judicial activism and judicial policy preferences are best operationalized as continua. For a more complete understanding of the relationship between judicial attitudes and the judicialization of politics it might be necessary at least to provide for a "moderate" category.

REFERENCES

Note: "Paper presented at the Forlí Conference" is shorthand for the following complete citation: Paper presented to the Interim Meeting of the Research Committee on Comparative Judicial Studies, International Political Science Association, *Centro Studi e Richerche Sull'Ordinamento Giudiziario*, University of Bologna, Forlí, Italy, 14-17 June, 1992.

Bachrach, Peter, and Morton S. Baratz. 1962. "Two Faces of Power." *American Political Science Review* 56:947-52.

Caldeira, Gregory, and James L. Gibson. 1992. "Legitimacy, Judicial Power, and Emerging Transnational Legal Institutions: The Court of Justice in the European Community." Paper presented at the Forlí Conference.

Linz, Juan J. 1978. "Crisis, Breakdown, and Reequilibration." In *The Breakdown of Democratic Regimes*, ed. Juan J. Linz and Alfred Stepan, Baltimore: Johns Hopkins University Press, 3-124. Also published separately as *The Breakdown of Democratic Regimes*, Baltimore: Johns Hopkins University Press, 1978.

Patenaude, Pierre. 1992. "*La Judiciarization des droit linguistiques en Canada et la politisation du pouvoir judiciaire.*" Paper presented at the Forlí Conference.

Roelofs, Joan. 1992. "Judicial Activism as Social Engineering in the U.S.A." Paper presented at the Forlí Conference.

Valenzuela, Arturo. 1978. "Chile." In *The Breakdown of Democratic Regimes*, ed. Juan J. Linz and Alfred Stepan, Baltimore: Johns Hopkins University Press.

PART II

WESTERN COMMON-LAW DEMOCRACIES

The United States and the United Kingdom

4.

The United States

MARTIN SHAPIRO

AMERICAN LEGAL CULTURE

If any nation is the peculiar home of the expansion of judicial power, it
is the United States. The phenomenon is so massive and multifaceted
that it is probably the result of multiple, interactive causes. The
American revolution, with its natural law–social contract ideology was
particularly legalistic. Lawyers had played a major part in the preceding
English revolutions. The colonies themselves were organized under
royal charters that were viewed as legally binding contracts. The
revolution was not expressed as an assault on the existing system of law
and courts but as an assertion of the legal and constitutional rights of
Englishmen against an overbearing Parliament.

Subsequently American politics have been notably Constitution
centered. The American two-party system emerged in the fight over
adoption of the Constitution, with one party as its champion and the
other its opponent. Because the Constitution established three separate
and equal branches, two elected and one not, it was natural that the party
experiencing electoral losses would attempt to preserve an enclave of
power in the judiciary. The Federalists did so with the appointment of
John Marshall at the time of the Jeffersonians' sweep of Congress and
the Presidency in 1800. In a federal constitutional system, the Court
almost inevitably became the referee of many of the most controversial
political issues that would arise, that is, issues about the boundaries

between the state and national governments. Subsequent to the initial assertion of judicial power in *Marbury v. Madison* (1 Cranch 137 [1803]), most of the great Marshall Court decisions were about federalism. The Court served as one of the principal instruments in building a strong central government.

It has been early and widely noted that lawyers play a disproportionate role in American politics (Eulau and Sprague 1964). This phenomenon is in part probably both a cause and an effect of the highly constitutionalized politics of the U.S. In part, too, it is probably the result of deeper socioeconomic causes such as the absence of a hereditary aristocracy, the prevalence of small, market-oriented agricultural land holdings, and rapid economic development through competitive corporate capitalism. For most of America's history, entry into the legal profession was particularly easy, and legal and political activity enjoyed a kind of natural synergy. The great number of self-employed and under-employed lawyers offered skills obviously relevant to legislation and public administration and had the time to engage in democratic grass-roots politicking, while the political activity itself was a means of enhancing their private law practices.

The distinctive American mode of selecting judges from this broadly recruited, highly politicized and overwhelmingly private- practice bar may be the crucial cause of judicialization. Judges in many countries theoretically are granted as great a power of judicial supervision over government as those in the United States, at least in certain spheres. For instance, the administrative law competence of United States, British, and French judges really looks about the same on paper. The markedly higher propensity of American judges to interject themselves in major administrative decision-making must be more a function of the nature of the judges than of the nature of the law.

Continental judges are recruited right after their initial legal education and spend their lives in a government service that itself is closely aligned with the rest of government service and neatly segregated from private practice. The British judiciary is recruited from a relatively closed and elite subclass of lawyers who are relatively isolated from direct involvement in business enterprise and take their briefs indifferently from both government and its opponents. The American judiciary is recruited very largely from among middle-aged, successful private practitioners who have been deeply and directly involved in private enterprise, typically have little or no experience in government, and typically have built some substantial portion of their success on representing interests heavily regulated by government. The American judge typically comes to the bench after a life of deep and direct involvement in the private sector and of representing private clients against government rather than vice versa. American judges thus bring to the bench a wealth of knowledge of the everyday affairs of the private sector that their continental counterparts certainly do not have and their English counterparts have far less. And they bring the perspectives of the governed rather than that of the governors. Thus they have both the knowledge needed and the inclination to intervene in affairs of state to a far greater degree than do European judges.

THE GROWTH OF JUDICIAL REVIEW

Undoubtedly the constitutional judicial review powers of the Supreme Court, with the usual chicken-and-egg caveat, constitute the central engine of the expansion of judicial power in America. We have already noted that the Supreme Court almost inevitably played a major role in the issues of federalism that dominated American politics before the Civil War. Because of federalism the moral issue of slavery tended to be transposed heavily into legal arenas. Citizens in Northern states could not use direct electoral politics to reach slavery in Southern states, and so slavery necessarily became a constitutional question.

The Populist and Progressive era in the decades just before and after the turn of the century set the stage for contemporary judicialization. These movements, which dominated a number of state legislatures and occasionally Congress, called for a stronger, more technically expert, more regulatory government that could deal more adequately with the growing corporations and problems of industrialization and urbanization. These movements were reinforced by labor-union and other concern for better working conditions and general amelioration of the lives of the poor. The result was a spate of regulatory laws, most notably railroad regulation and antitrust laws, and new labor and welfare laws, most notably wages-and-hours and industrial-safety laws.

The United States Supreme Court responded to constitutional challenges to these laws quite frequently between the 1880s and the 1930s, striking down some and upholding others, but generally asserting its ultimate authority to strike down economic legislation that violated sound economic principles or trenched upon the proper state-national boundaries of federalism. The Court frequently portrayed itself as the protector of individual rights—in this instance property rights—against the occasional aberrations of democratically controlled legislatures. It was in this period that Americans came to assume that every major piece of legislation would somehow or other reach state and/or federal supreme courts for constitutional testing, and that all of this legislation involved rights (McCloskey 1960).

The great upheavals of the New Deal are usually portrayed so as to emphasize the disjunction between the old and the new Court and the contrast between property rights on the one hand and civil rights and liberties on the other. In terms of judicialization, continuities are more significant than contrasts. The judicial power and legitimacy that the Court had built up as the protector of property rights was not destroyed by the New Deal. That power was preserved and transferred from "property rights" to "civil rights and liberties," that is, from the constitutionally expressed interests of Republicans to the constitutionally expressed interests of Democrats. The Court did not stop declaring laws unconstitutional. It only changed its targets (Shapiro 1986).

The judicial review powers of the Court have never gone uncontested. Marshall's assertions were opposed by the Jeffersonian-Jacksonian Democrats. The abolitionists attacked the Supreme Court's proslavery decisions. The elaborate doctrines of judicial self-restraint based on the conflict between review and democracy were first spelled out by academic spokesmen for the Populists and Progressives when the Court threatened the new regulatory and welfare laws of the 1880s and 1890s. Exactly the same arguments were taken up by New Deal commentators in the early 1930s. When the New Dealers captured the Court in 1937, some New Dealers persisted in judicial self-restraint themes. They died out in liberal circles with the liberal successes of the Warren Court. By the 1960s the same arguments were being arrayed by conservatives against the Warren Court. In the slightly different language of "strict construction," they appear again in Republican attempts to curb the Court in the 1980s.

BROWN V. BOARD OF EDUCATION

In spite of these countercurrents, the expansion of judicial power in the United States, and perhaps even worldwide, is essentially associated today with the great movement toward judicial protection of human rights initiated, or at least most dramatically signaled, by the great desegregation decision *Brown v. Board of Education* (374 US 483) in 1954. That event provided a paradigm of mythic proportions. An interest group employs a concerted campaign of individual-rights litigation to persuade a court to undertake a major change in public policy that legislatures and executives have refused it. The judicial process is developed as an alternative to the more explicitly political processes of partisan electoral politics and interest-group lobbying. A nonelected, "independent" and "neutral" court steps in to correct a "failure" or "pathology" of the democratic process. The substitution of judicial policy-making for legislative-executive policy-making is legitimated in part by the invocation of minority rights against majority will and in part by the argument that in certain rare instances democracy is not self-correcting without judicial intervention. Finally, *Brown* represents the intervention of a national court to achieve uniform national norms. These norms are supported, albeit perhaps at low intensity levels, by a national majority. They have, however, been thwarted by local norms, often with high intensity, by local majorities, or by local elites (Kluger 1977).

Brown becomes a model for a long series of major policy changes initiated by the Warren and Burger Courts at the behest of groups conducting conscious litigation campaigns. Through case-by-case lawmaking the Warren Court introduced a nationally uniform and reformed set of police procedures for dealing with the accused, a new national law of obscenity, profound reform of the system of electing state and federal legislators, and a new libel law more protective of criticism of public officials. The Burger Court continued this judicialization by attempting, with somewhat less success, the enactment of national standards for prison conditions and death-penalty and abortion laws while consolidating most of the Warren Court "advances" and cutting back on a few of them (see, e.g., Fisher 1990).

SUPREME COURTS AND POLITICS

This judicialization generated both political struggle and political awareness. The legitimacy of the U.S. Supreme Court had suffered a major crisis in the 1930s but had survived in part by tapping long-built-up reserves of public support and in part by a timely shift in policy and personnel. In the 1950s the Court generated a powerful opposing coalition of Southern Democrats and Northern Republicans as it coupled desegregation decisions with decisions seemingly providing constitutional protections to Communist "subversives." The Court broke up this coalition by continuing its desegregation policies while retreating from its protection of leftists. After the crisis had subsided the Court returned to partially rebuild protections for unpopular speakers. More and more interest groups were instructed by events to lobby courts as well as legislatures and bureaucracies. The general public learned that one of the significant aspects of their votes for President was presidential choice of Supreme Court justices. Most notably in relation to the growth of crime and crime control as a public issue and the Warren Court's multiplication of protections for those accused of crime, the Court has become a normal partisan issue in presidential elections. There has been growing public attention to and controversy over the advice and consent of the Senate to Supreme Court appointments. The great national controversy over the justices' abortion decisions have brought the Court to center stage politically and subjected it to the single-issue politics and "divided government" (one major party controlling Congress, the other the presidency) that are central features of contemporary American politics.

Finally, the deep American ambivalence about racial policy also continues to bring the Court to the center of political life. Affirmative action is a major party issue of Congressional-Presidential politics. Judicially ordered busing and other coercive pupil assignment schemes are less a national political issue than they were a few years ago, but they remain very potent in local politics.

Moreover, as the Burger and Rehnquist Courts have proven less welcoming of rights initiatives than their predecessor, rights groups have shifted their litigation to the state supreme courts—many of which are or were until very recently controlled by liberals. State supreme courts, invoking state constitutions, may extend constitutional protections further than does the United States Supreme Court. In a number of states radical changes in the funding of schools and the provision of housing for the poor and minorities and less major movements on rights of accused and freedom of speech have occurred through state court action when the federal courts have refused to act. A number of supreme courts in states whose constitutions and/or laws authorize the death penalty have fought long-term delaying actions against it, verging on judicial lawlessness. In many American states judges are subject to popular election or at least diselection. In at least one, California, the voters have turned state supreme court justices out of office over death-penalty and other crime issues.

INSTITUTIONAL REMEDIES

So far in dealing with constitutional judicial review, the law-declaring aspects of judicialization have been central. Courts, however, have also become more and more active in public affairs as law implementers, typically of constitutional law itself created by courts. The desegregation decisions of the Supreme Court called for the dismantling of local dual school systems "with all deliberate speed." In practice that meant separate lawsuits for hundreds of school districts filed in dozens of federal district courts scattered all over the South and later over the whole country (Peltason 1961). Where violation of the equal-protection clause was found, the district courts, in a further "remedy" stage of negotiation and/or litigation with and by the parties, constructed often elaborate, detailed, time-staged, long-term plans for desegregation. These plans often covered every aspect of school administration from teacher assignment to curriculum and spending for equipment. They included such devices as voluntary and/or compelled busing, "magnet" (specially upgraded) schools, altered school attendance boundaries, school closings, and new construction. The remedial court order typically remains in place indefinitely until desegregation is achieved. The parties, typically the local school board and a local chapter of the National Association for the Advancement of Colored People or other Black or Hispanic group or groups, may keep coming back to court with requests for modification of the order as circumstances change. Many such initial orders have been followed by so much white flight from the district that there are fewer and fewer white students to integrate. American school districts pass through frequent budget crises. So all sorts of circumstances change often, suddenly, and radically. The judicial ordering of these plans and changes in them falls under the "equitable remedies" power of federal courts and so is almost unlimited by statute or even Supreme Court doctrine. It lies almost entirely at the discretion of federal district court judges who are appointed for life. Thus a sort of judicial constitutional dictator has been in charge, often for years at a time, of fundamentally reshaping a basic local public institution. Here again, school desegregation served as an instructional model for other political actions. Judicial "institutional remedies" have also been widely employed in employment discrimination suits either brought under the equal-protection clause itself or under civil-rights statutes. Such orders often involve the courts in continuous supervision of the hiring, promotion, assignment, testing, and evaluation practices of large public organizations such as police forces and fire departments. Occasionally they have even included court orders directing chief executives and legislatures to provide additional budget. Many courts that have issued such orders feel compelled to appoint "special masters" to administer them because the judge has neither the time, expertise, nor staff resources to participate in the detailed, continuous administration they require. Under the cruel-and-unusual-punishment clause, courts have similarly involved themselves in prison administration sometimes to the point of determining the water temperature of showers and the weekly rate of intake and release of prisoners. Cases involving racial discrimination in public housing also generate these kinds of institutional remedies (Cooper 1988).

Such institutional remedies represent a very deep involvement of the courts in politics along a number of dimensions. Judges become active and continuous administrative decision makers in major public affairs. They become enmeshed in the internal politics of large organizations where, like any other "top" executive, they must invent all sorts of carrots and sticks to overcome resistance and inertia among organizational subordinates. Without being electorally responsible, they make decisions with major budgetary and therefore tax consequences for local and state governments. And if they are to achieve the goals they themselves have defined, they must shape their policies not only in the light of the predicted behavior of the particular parties to the lawsuit but the behavior of large political institutions and masses of citizens. There is a lively debate over whether institutional remedies have been effective in achieving the large social reforms at which they have been directed. There is little doubt, however, that they have plunged the judges issuing them deeply into public affairs.

ADMINISTRATIVE JUDICIAL REVIEW

In dealing with the expansion of American judicial power, it is natural to concentrate, as we have so far, on constitutional judicial review and thus on the U.S. Supreme Court and on the federal district courts carrying out Supreme Court constitutional mandates. There is, however, quite a different realm in which judicial power has accelerated dramatically in the United States—that of judicial supervision of administrative action. Most of this supervision occurs as a matter of administrative rather than constitutional law. The governing law is the Administrative Procedures Act and the host of procedural and review provisions in hundreds of federal statutes.

In the 1950s federal courts almost invariably deferred to the "expertise" of federal administrative agencies. By the 1980s nearly every significant decision of a federal regulatory agency was litigated in the federal courts. And, while their batting averages varied over time, federal agencies had come to expend enormous efforts to defend themselves against adverse court review. As a result of judicial intervention, the whole behavior of federal agencies in making rules and regulations has fundamentally changed. And the policy-making process in Washington has changed from the iron triangle of Congressional committee, interest groups, and administrative agency to the iron rectangle of those three plus the courts. American regulatory politics today is justly characterized as living in a culture of "adversarial legalism" (Kagan 1991)

The vehicle for these changes has been a large body of new, judge-made administrative law generated by the Court of Appeals for the District of Columbia and the other federal courts of appeal, with only occasional intervention by the U.S. Supreme Court, but with substantial, sporadic assistance by Congress.

In the modern regulatory, welfare, administrative state, administrative agencies wield enormous power especially in the enactment of the myriad rules and regulations needed to supplement and implement statutes. In theory this administrative lawmaking is held democratically accountable through legislative oversight and the election of the chief executive, be it cabinet or President, who controls its administrative subordinates. A second mode of accountability is the law itself, or rather mechanisms to insure that the agencies obey the laws enacted by the legislature. A third mode is transparency, or a set of devices for insuring that the citizenry may know how and why agencies reached the decisions they did. And finally, there is the general, substantive norm that the agencies must act reasonably rather than arbitrarily, capriciously, or abusively. In United States statutes authorizing supplementary rule making by agencies, judicial review is almost always authorized to provide these supraelec-

toral controls. It is also provided by a general Administrative Procedures Act (APA).

In the 1940s and 1950s federal judges routinely assumed that the
agencies had established the facts necessary to support their rules and
deferred to agency interpretations of the statutes that their rules were
designed to implement. The language of the APA called for only the
most rudimentary procedures for rule making, did not require any
substantial record of rule-making proceedings, and provided the most
lenient standard of judicial review. Most factual and legal issues were
left to the agencies, which could easily satisfy the few and pro forma
procedural requirements. Any rule that they adopted that was not clearly
insane passed judicial review muster. By the 1980s, with no changes in
the language of the APA at all, although with much new language in the
regulatory statutes of the 1960s and 1970s, courts demanded extremely
elaborate agency procedures, including an exhaustive record to demonstrate that the agency had invited participation by all interested groups,
had responded to every point raised by those groups, had given good
reasons for every choice it made, had considered every possible issue,
and had arrived at the best possible rule. Judges declared that they
would take a hard look at everything the agencies did, that they, not the
agencies, were the final authority on statutory meaning and that they
were in "partnership" with the agencies in rule making. Nearly every
significant agency-made rule was challenged in court. And given the
number the judges struck down, there was no doubt who the senior
partner was. Agencies spent more and more time and resources during
the rule-making process in insuring that rules once enacted would survive
the inevitable litigation.

The result was an enormous increase in the transparency of government action and in public participation and an enormous increase in the
care that agencies took to get both the science and the law straight on
which their rules depended. Because Congress had enacted a sweeping
new, health, safety, and environmental regulatory regime that required
thousands of new rules, these great changes in rule-making processes
were especially significant. Yet judicial review not only improved the
transparency, responsiveness, rationality, and law abidingness of agency
rule making; it also came to demand a rule-making process that was
extremely slow, cumbersome, and uncertain. It took years to write a
rule and then often years more after the first and perhaps even the second
and third version failed to survive review. The system often simply

failed to provide the timely flow of rules needed by the new sweeping regulatory regime. Although part of this failure undoubtedly stemmed from antiregulatory Republican forces that often controlled the White House even as Congress pushed new regulation, there was a widespread belief that hyperactive and super-perfectionist judicial review was also a major culprit.

The Supreme Court weighed in occasionally with opinions warning the courts of appeal not to simply substitute their policy judgments for those of the agencies and not to demand impossibly perfect procedures. On the whole, however, the Supreme Court accepted the new administrative law jurisprudence. Various means of avoiding the confrontational and litigation-oriented style of rule making have been proposed and occasionally pursued, such as environmental mediation. There are also attempts to substitute market and other incentive methods for detailed command-and-control regulations. Such methods do not eliminate the need for rule making but may work with fewer and a less continuous stream of rules. Moreover, as reviewing courts have demanded more and more of agencies, the agencies have learned to armor themselves in thicker and thicker and more and more technically complex rule making records that more and more survive litigation. Thus, to a certain degree, superactivist judicial review is self-limiting over time. Eventually judges receive records so large, running to thousands of pages, and so packed with technical data obviously beyond their capacity to comprehend that they must return to deference to administrative judgment.

During the crucial periods of the 1960s, 1970s, and 1980s, when major new legislation required massive new bodies of rules and when the agencies had not yet perfected their armor, the courts certainly became major participants in health, safety, and environmental policy and politics in the United States as well as fundamentally reshaping both the teams and the rules of the regulatory game. Judicial policy-making may now be decreasing, in part because of agency self-protection and in part because of voluntary judicial withdrawal. The new rule-making regime, very transparent, highly participatory, laden with extraordinarily complete fact finding and policy analyses, highly adversarial, highly litigation-oriented, and consequently extremely cumbersome and slow and excessively confrontational, is quite firmly in place. It is unlikely to change much, short of a new revolution in Washington politics. This new regime is in part a product of the new Congressional regulatory statutes. They were replete with "technology forcing" and "agency forcing" provisions, highly aspirational goals stated as legal rights and special procedural provisions. All of these measures encouraged very vigorous enforcement, very vigorous interest-group pressures on the agencies for more enforcement, and very vigorous resistance on the part of the regulated. In part the new regime is a product of public sentiment that wants the government to fix everything while hating big government, thus generating regulatory and counterregulatory waves at the same time and conflict between Democratic statutes and Republican presidents. In large part, however, the current rule-making regime is a product of direct, self-initiated, and extremely self-confident judicial intervention in the regulatory process (Shapiro 1988).

THE LITIGATION EXPLOSION

The activist constitutional judicial review initiated by the Warren Court and the radical shift from the passivity of the 1950s to the activism of the 1970s of the courts of appeal in the exercise of administrative judicial review are easily documented in streams of leading cases. Far less easily documented is the so-called litigation explosion in the United States. Beginning in the 1950s juries came to make startlingly high money awards in some tort cases, particularly in wrongful-death actions. Tort doctrine also shifted from emphasis on fault to "deep pockets," the notion that whoever had the largest resources to compensate for injury should pay without regard to how much at fault they had been. Traditionally in the United States tort litigation has been done on a contingency fee basis. The plaintiff's lawyer is not paid a fee but receives a large share of any award. Thus high awards encouraged lawyers to advise their clients to litigate, and litigating lawyers had special incentives to achieve high awards. The growth in the number of automobiles and of liability insurance, the tendency of juries to be generous with insurance company money, the high cost of litigation, the crowding of the courts, the tendency of insurance companies and other defendants to settle cases before trial to avoid the costs of trial and the risk of high jury awards, the capacity of tort lawyers to advertise their services on television as a result of Supreme Court opinions overturning traditional bar-association bans on lawyer advertising, all contribute to high levels of tort litigation (Sugarman 1989).

In fact it is extremely difficult to assess the comparative propensity of people in various societies or at various times to litigate, although there is a lot of folklore on the subject (Galanter 1983). The American "tort explosion" may be no more than the normal growth of litigation and the normal growth of cash awards to be anticipated in a society whose enormous postwar economic growth greatly escalated the number of accidents, the prevalence of insurance, the costs of medical care, and the value of the lifetime earnings that were the basis for calculating the size of awards. The jury system, which is almost unique to the United States in civil actions, may account for the special prominence of tort law in America.

Extremely crowded American court dockets, even when the number of judges was markedly increased, were not entirely due to tort filings. The number and size of large law firms that serve corporate clients has shot up. Contract and other business disputes are very numerous. Are American corporations more legalistic, litigation prone and lawyer led in their relations to one another than those of other industrialized, capitalist states? Again the answer is not clear. The American corporate structure has been much less cartelized than that of Europe, more vigorously competitive, and has operated over a much wider geographic range, necessitating relations with thousands of local suppliers, agents, distributors, and buyers, compared to the hundreds dealt with by European national corporations in pre-Community days. Rapid economic growth and the mergers and acquisition fervor of the 1970s and 1980s necessarily generated an enormous amount of new legal business. Much of that business was not litigation but "deal making," negotiating, business advising, contract writing, property transfer, and financial development. Growth in legal business is not necessarily growth in judicial power. Although shaped by the possibility that litigation might someday occur, very little of the corporate business of large law firms ever involves a judge.

Moreover, a part of the cause of the growth in number and size of large, corporate-serving firms has been the growth of government regulation of corporations rather than any particular propensity to litigate. Mergers and acquisition and stock and bond issuance to finance corporate growth meant major corporate involvement with existing antitrust and securities regulation. New worker-health-and-safety and environmental regulation generated enormous new legal problems for business. Even deregulation, by disturbing and requiring the reordering of existing business relations, generated new legal business.

Neither the crowding of court calendars nor the growth of large law firms necessarily indicates that Americans have become peculiarly prone to seek judicial intervention in their affairs. Both may simply be commensurate with the growth in the corporate capitalist, regulated economy of the United States. Nor does even the enormous growth in legal billing and litigation necessarily indicate growing judicialization. Most of the billing does not involve litigation, and most of the litigation involves only routine matters of settled law in which, even collectively, the judges are making little or no new policy.

CASE-BY-CASE DECISIONS

Indeed, looking at American law in the most general way, there has been a marked decrease in judicial power in the twentieth century. For during this period the legal system taken as a whole has shifted from being essentially one of common-law to one of statutory law and regulation. Statutes and regulations, to be sure, generate a lot of cases, and judges do a lot of supplementary lawmaking in those cases. But most of the primary law of the U.S. today is no longer common-law made by judges but law declared by legislatures and executive-branch agencies.

Whenever we move from particular high courts making particular major policy changes in leading cases to large numbers of trial courts that, without conscious collaboration, cause shifts in public policy by the collective impact of numerous routine decisions scattered over time and place, the argument for judicialization is attenuated. Whether such collective judicial policy statements are causes or effects becomes increasingly difficult to determine. And instead of being able to show that the particular policy preferences of some particular judge or small number of judges led to policy change, we are reduced to arguing that some highly generalized class, professional, or institution-based ideology shared by all or most of the judges resulted in some policy change that itself must be discovered by subtle analysis of the shared drift of many cases. The movement from fault to deep pockets may be such a major change in public policy achieved over time by uncoordinated, shared judicial policy preferences. There may be a half dozen others. Standing alone, however, without the far more tangible constitutional and administrative judicial review interventions against legislatures and administrative agencies by the Supreme Court and the courts of appeal, and the dramatic "institutional remedies" imposed by federal district courts, all this general proliferation of lawyers and litigation would not have led to much alarm about the expansion of judicial power.

For ultimately the concern about judicialization is a concern about whether we have turned to litigation as a substitute for or a supplement to "normal politics." Such a phenomenon is seen as quite distinct from the kind of common-law, case-law drumbeat in which changes in life lead to changes in the claims made in litigation, and changes in those claims lead to gradual changes in legal doctrine and thus in public policy. In that arena litigation is seen as essentially a conflict-resolution device with some incidental policy-making fallout. That fallout may indeed constitute relatively significant judicial lawmaking, but not the conscious intervention of judges into what otherwise would be left to "politicians." Litigation campaigns or the lobbying of courts by interest groups bent on winning in court what they cannot win in the political process and major policy-making and institutional change consciously instituted by appellate court judges in leading, "test" cases, is the stuff of judicialization.

LITIGATION AS PLURALIST POLITICS

The American political science literature quite early recognized that the pluralist political theory of interest groups gaining access to government decision makers in order to attain policy goals applied to courts as well as to the rest of government. Litigation as lobbying is a long-established theme. Yet as late as 1964 the following statement was viewed with dismay and hostility by most American academic lawyers.

> The Supreme Court is an agency of American government. So are the Interstate Commerce Commission and the House Rules Committee. The taxpayer who descends on Washington to have his tax status altered may turn to the Internal Revenue Service, the House Ways and Means Committee, the Supreme Court, or his own congressman. The businessman who is worried about government regulation of his enterprise may deal with the Department of Commerce, the Supreme Court, one of a half-dozen regulatory agencies, the Justice Department, and the President himself. The labor union seeking freedom from government curbs on the strike weapon begins with the Supreme Court, the Secretary of Labor, the Justice Department, Senator Humphrey, or a Congressional investigating committee. The Chamber of Com-

merce president who wants a new yacht basin for his community may visit a Senate committee or the Corps of Engineers—but probably not the Supreme Court. Washington is a place where specific agencies or individuals can do specific things for specific people. For some people, the Bureau of the Budget is more helpful and thus more important than the Secretary of the Treasury. For others, the Senate Foreign Relations Committee is more helpful than the Supreme Court. (Shapiro 1964, 1-2)

Such a statement would hardly cause a ripple today.

Taking the NAACP's long litigation campaign against segregation as a model, a number of sets of litigators have mounted campaigns designed to persuade the Supreme Court to employ its constitutional judicial review powers to achieve major policy changes refused by other segments of government. Often such campaigns were not actually mounted by cohesive interest groups employing lawyers, but rather by loose affiliations of lawyers seeking to transpose into constitutional rights interests that had not actually organized. The lawyers created the clients as often as the clients created the lawyers. The long litigation campaigns to get Supreme Court-made law protecting accused persons, improving prison conditions, and banning the death penalty involved such shadow clients. The abortion-right campaign, on the other hand, began with organized birth-control interest groups and later was largely supported by feminist organizations. Legislative districting litigation was usually sponsored by whichever of the two major political parties was disadvantaged by the state electoral arrangements being challenged. Yet the role of organized interest groups in pushing the expansion of judicial power through constitutional judicial review should not be overstated. Many of the Court's major constitutional interventions were initiated by individual clients and/or individual lawyers.

Judicialization by interest group is at its peak in administrative judicial review. There a mutually supporting interaction exists between interest groups and courts. The courts have intervened decisively to require the agencies to afford exhaustive access to the regulation-making process for any group that wants to participate. The courts have also opened their own doors wide to interest-group litigation against the agencies. The interest groups have litigated nearly every important administrative rule announced and thus push the judges toward more and more intervention in agency policy-making. The impression is often left that it is largely "public interest" groups, such as environmental organizations, that have benefited from this mutual support arrangement. But business interests have also been major players. And the government agencies themselves sometimes use litigation as a vehicle to acquire amendments to their governing laws by judicial statutory interpretation that they cannot get out of Congress by requesting formal amendment.

All the players in the game of judicializing administrative regulation are likely to move freely among Congressional, executive, and judicial branches, constantly active in all three and content to enjoy success wherever they can find it. Judicialization does not substitute judicial policy-making for legislative or administrative policy-making or even provide judges with the last word in the policy process. It simply adds judges as another category in the broad and multifaceted array of policy-makers.

Some interest groups, notably those concerned with civil rights, play the constitutional game in the same way. They pursue test-case constitutional decisions, new Congressional civil rights legislation, Presidential initiatives, and administrative regulations all at the same time, as do their opponents. Civil-rights legislation may push statutory antidiscrimination or affirmative action rights further than the Supreme Court will push them as constitutional rights. Court interpretations of those statutes may cut back statutory rights, and Congress may push them onward again by amending the statutes. There is a certain tendency, however, for constitutional court victories to turn interest groups away from other realms of politics and encourage excessive reliance on judicial allies. As pro-abortion forces won major Supreme Court victories barring state legislatures from limiting abortions, those forces tended to ignore the state legislatures. Their savior was the Supreme Court. Antiabortion forces, finding the Court unfriendly, concentrated on the state legislatures and won many victories there, which then began to bolster their access to the Supreme Court itself.

JUSTIFICATIONS OF EXPANDED JUDICIAL POWER

One way to look at judicialization in the U.S., then, is as a sort of logical and pragmatic extension of American pluralist, interest-group, single-issue politics from legislatures and executives on to courts. Courts are, after all, one of the three independent and equal branches of American government. Why shouldn't they be as pluralist as the other two? Growing out of the felt need to legitimate judicial review in a democratic state, another perspective is that courts intervene if and only if the electoral process experiences some massive failure in its normally self-correcting mechanisms. If racism among majority whites keeps blacks from voting or forming the coalitions with whites that would bring some political victories, then the electoral mechanism cannot fix itself. It cannot achieve fairness to blacks in the electoral process. Then the Supreme court is justified in engaging in judicial intervention to increase black political capacities enough that black interests can be represented in the normal electoral and representative political process. Legislators who owe their seats to malapportioned or gerrymandered electoral districts cannot be expected to vote themselves out of office by voting for new fair electoral districting. So courts may legitimately intervene to redraw district boundaries. Or it may be argued that certain widely held values or interests, such as that in freedom of speech, are too diffuse to be reflected in voting and so are never adequately represented in elected legislatures. Courts should protect those values. This correcting-the-failures-of-democracy rationale is the narrowest democratic justification for a rather narrow judicialization (Ely 1980; Shapiro 1966).

The broadest justification for the broadest expansion of judicial power is the assertion that the Constitution or the universal human-rights tradition contains a set of certain and knowable rights and that judicial review is supposed to defend those rights from infringement by the majority. The judge is portrayed not as exercising policy discretion but simply as enforcing preexisting legal rights (Dworkin 1977). This position is reoffered and rebutted in every generation and moves from the mouths of political conservatives to those of political liberals and back again depending upon whose legislative will the Court is thwarting at any given moment.

Another justification rests on the special institutional capacity of courts. Granting that Congress and the President also are responsible for enforcing the Constitution, the Court is more capable of focusing on long-term constitutional values than are legislatures and executives pressed to meet immediate problems with immediate solutions (Perry 1982). Moreover, the litigation process is one in which equal attention is paid to both parties, no matter what the disparities in their political resources, and special respect is paid to systematic and responsive argument. Thus the litigation process provides a quality of policy deliberation unavailable elsewhere in government (Fiss 1979). Finally, the judges are neither technical specialists nor program operators. So they bring a generalist or lay perspective to a policy-making process otherwise badly distorted by the narrowed perspectives of the various specialists who are the real authors of most legislation and regulation (Shapiro 1968). Thus the courts are actually in a better position to recognize the real public interest among the various special interests masquerading as the public interest than are legislatures or executives (Sunstein 1990). Indeed in contemporary government it is the judge's mind that most closely mirrors that of the demos, as the rest of government is more and more fragmented into the various specializations needed to cope with an increasingly complex environment.

Ultimately this justification comes down to the proposition that judges should wield political authority because lawyers, or at least lawyers once they mount the bench, think more clearly and are more dedicated to the commonweal than the rest of us. This argument is probably more persuasive within the community of scholars who write about law and courts than in the more general community.

Perhaps the best argument for judicialization is grounded in the virtues of redundancy. It is not really true that governing power can be divided among three great branches, one of which legislates and legislates only, one of which administers and administers only and one of which judges and judges only. Segments of government can only check and balance one another if they share the same power rather than wielding different ones. In all governments that divide powers, each branch legislates, administers and judges. Thus the presidential veto power in the U.S. is clearly a legislative power, as is the Supreme Court's constitutional veto. And the court's "interpretation" of statutes or "findings" of law are inevitably and unavoidably a species of law-making just as are the same activities when conducted by administrators. Ultimately, all legislative judgments must be made the same way. Whether made by legislators, administrators or judges, they always constitute a set of prudential guesses made under conditions of great uncertainty. The judge deciding whether a statute is constitutional or a rule is lawful necessarily replays the same analysis of facts, values, policy alternatives, and predicted outcomes that was earlier undertaken by the statute and rule writers (Shapiro 1968). If the legislative analysis has been done already, why should judges do it again? Perhaps because three heads are better than two. High levels of redundancy are a standard and sensible design response for systems that must handle high-risk, high-uncertainty, high-value situations (Landau 1969). Judges may not be better than other governors, but they are slightly different. Allowing them some of the power to govern gives us more governors of more sorts and more reiterations of crucial policy calculations. The case for some measured level of judicialization ultimately may rest on nothing more. How much or how little judicialization is best will depend upon a cost-benefit analysis of whatever level of redundancy is proposed. Americans appear to prefer high levels of redundancy.

THE UNCERTAINTIES OF JUDICIALIZATION

This picture is somewhat confused by two tendencies in contemporary American culture. The first is a widespread, highly vocal although superficial disaffection from political institutions. Precisely because the courts have somewhat succeeded in preserving the myth of their apolitical, neutral independence, there is some tendency to grant them additional governing power precisely because they appear not to be part of government. Of course the more they govern, the less apolitical and neutral they appear, and the more independence comes to be seen as irresponsibility. The United States Supreme Court has suffered a loss in perceived legitimacy as have the other segments of United States government, but it and courts in general still retain some margin of perceived legitimacy over other governors precisely because they are seen as places of law and of rights rather than mere political places.

Moreover, the American electorate is showing decreased partisan loyalty to particular political parties and a curious mixture of voting heavily in favor of incumbents while despising incumbency. The voters often divide governing authority between legislatures of one party and political executives of the other. They are attracted by candidates who run against the "ins," even if they are "ins" themselves. Here again, judges enjoy a certain advantage because they, unlike the other governors, are supposed to stay in, and they are not supposed to be strongly party oriented.

So Americans are relatively less disaffected from their courts than from their legislatures and executives at the moment. But these relative disaffections do not serve as a firm basis for nor do they promise a particularly high level of judicialization. The phenomenon is largely self-limiting. As courts are moved by these disaffection disparities to govern more, the gap in disaffection soon closes against them precisely because it depended on their seeming to govern less.

It is sometimes claimed that the central phenomenon of the increase in judicial power in the United States is that Americans have abandoned the ballot box for the courtroom. It is certainly true that what they cannot win at the ballot box they will try to win in the courtroom. But they don't care where they win or where they win first. Litigation is viewed as an alternative, supplement, and response to legislative and administrative politics, but not as a substitute for them. Everyone moves from arena to arena as circumstances change. The current disaffection with normal partisan, electoral politics may or may not signal a coming major change in the American party system, but it surely does not signal any general tendency to abandon legislative and executive politics. No particular area of policy has been or promises to be the exclusive domain of courts.

Finally, there is a natural tendency to confuse legalization, judicialization in Vallinder's second sense, with the expansion of judicial power into other political arenas, judicialization in his first sense. There are tendencies to transform certain previously private and/or informal relationships into more formal, rule-bound ones. These tendencies are fueled by, if not caused by, litigation and often are seen as ways of protecting oneself against litigation. Medical practice has been substantially altered by a large paraphernalia of "informed consent" and "defensive medicine" devices. It is now being seriously urged that the cure for "sexual harassment" and "date rape" is wooing by contract, in which each romantic advance is preceded by a formal offer and acceptance. ("Do you consent to a kiss?" "Yes I do." "How about another?") This tendency to convert more human relationships into formal, rule-bounded announcements of rights, duties and arms-length transactions may lead to more litigation about matters that previously could not be litigated. It may entangle judges more in day-to-day human affairs. But it is only tangentially related to the expansion of judicial power through the transfer to courts of political authority to make policy decisions. The new law on sexual harassment, for instance, may be made far more by statute and administrative regulation than case-by-case. Some of this legalization may be judicial imperialism in which courts force formal rules and procedures on people. Much of it, however, occurs because people seek, often by ill-understood analogy, to improve aspects of life by making them more rule bound and rights asserting. To the extent that such movements lead to more litigation and to the extent that public policy is constructed case by case in masses of routine court decisions, some accretion of judicial policy-making authority occurs. Legalization, however, is as likely to magnify the political power of other parts of government as that of the courts.

CONCLUSION

Judicialization waxes and wanes in the United States. Startling increases in judicial policy-making began in the 1950s in constitutional judicial review and in the 1960s in administrative law review. Increases in personal-injury and corporate litigation also occurred at roughly the same time, so that it began to appear as if judges were intervening in every area of public and private life. The role of the courts and the qualities of individual judges became major campaign issues as did many of the courts' specific interventions in such areas as civil rights, rights of accused, abortion, and obscenity. Administrative agencies enhanced their legal staffs and expended great time and effort to render their decisions litigation proof. Few significant government actions in the domestic sphere escaped some judicial contribution. By the late 1980s the Supreme Court had slowed its pace of innovation, cut back somewhat on some of the rights announced earlier, and issued some warnings to the courts of appeal to be less intrusive in administrative policy-making. Some attempt was also being made to cut back on sweeping, intrusive institutional remedies. State supreme courts had, however, become somewhat more active. In part because the agencies were doing a better job of protecting themselves, and in part because there were more Republicans on the bench, the courts of appeal were intervening somewhat less in agency rule making. And much of the growth in legalization entailed rather piecemeal low-level judicial governance where policy choice was less a matter of conscious policy decision by a few judges than the collective impact of accumulated decisions. Legalization may continue to grow in the United States but conscious, active judicial policy-making on major political issues seems to have plateaued or to be slightly on the wane.

REFERENCES

Cooper, Phillip. 1988. *Hard Judicial Choices*. New York: Oxford University Press.

Dworkin, Ronald. 1977. *Taking Rights Seriously*. London: Duckworth.

Ely, John. 1980. *Democracy and Distrust*. Cambridge: Harvard University Press.

Eulau, Heinz, and John Sprague. 1964. *Lawyers in Politics*. Indianapolis: Bobbs-Merrill.

Fisher, Louis. 1990. *American Constitutional Law*. New York: McGraw-Hill.

Fiss, Owen. 1979. "Foreword: The Forms of Justice." *Harvard Law Review* 93:1-87.

Galanter, Marc. 1983. "Reading the Landscape of Disputes." In *Litigation in America*. Los Angeles: University of California, Los Angeles, Law School.

Kagan, Robert. 1991. "Adversarial Legalism and American Government." *Journal of Public Policy Analysis and Management* 10:396-406.

Kluger, Richard. 1977. *Simple Justice*. New York: Vintage.

Landau, Martin. 1969. "Redundancy, Rationality, and the Problem of Duplication and Overlap." *Public Administration Review* 29:346-58.

McCloskey, Robert. 1960. *The American Supreme Court*. Cambridge: Harvard University Press.

Peltason, Jack. 1961. *Fifty-Eight Lonely Men*. New York: Harcourt, Brace.

Perry, Michael. 1982. *The Constitution, the Courts, and Human Rights*. New Haven: Yale University Press.

Shapiro, Martin. 1964. *Law and Politics in the Supreme Court*. New York: Free Press.

———. 1966. *Freedom of Speech: The Supreme Court and Judicial Review*. Englewood Cliffs, NJ: Prentice-Hall.

———. 1968. *The Supreme Court and Administrative Agencies*. New York: Free Press.

———. 1986. "The Supreme Court's Return to Economic Regulation." *Studies in American Political Development*. 1:91-142.

———. 1988. *Who Guards the Guardians?*. Athens: University of Georgia Press.

Sugarman, Stephen. 1989. *Doing Away with Personal Injury Law*. New York: Quorum Books.

Sunstein, Cass. 1990. *After the Rights Revolution*. Cambridge, Mass: Harvard University Press.

5.

The United Kingdom

MAURICE SUNKIN

The United Kingdom has an essentially political constitution (Griffith 1979). It is, of course, unwritten and contains no statement of fundamental rights. This, together with the absence of judicial review of primary legislation, means that courts and law have traditionally played a marginal role in political life. Such a constitution does not lend itself to an expansion of judicial power, but a judicialization of politics has occurred and is likely to become a more important feature of the system as the impact of European Community law grows.

Vallinder defines judicialization of politics as normally meaning either the expansion of the province of the courts at the expense of politicians and/or administrators or the spread of judicial decision-making methods outside the judicial province proper. There is clearly much room for debate as to what constitutes judicialization, and those seeking it might find it in the most unexpected places. The second aspect of Vallinder's definition appears broad enough to include administrative use of rules and principles that have been developed by the courts as well as the use of adjudicative techniques (see further: Jowell 1973). The work of the Social Fund commissioner and her inspectorate in reviewing decisions of Social Fund officers using principles analogous to the principles of judicial review would on this basis be an example of judicialization even though their working methods are not adjudicative in nature (Drabble and Lynes 1989).

The definition might also be pushed to include two other important developments. One is the increasing use of law to define, contain, and control local government that has "juridified" central/local relations and to "judicialize" local government administration (Loughlin 1986; Leach and Stoker 1988). The other is the increased emphasis placed upon law and legal procedures in central government administration that has occurred as a result of the growth in use of judicial review over the past 15 years or so (Sunkin and Le Sueur 1991).

An expansion of judicial power implies greater judicial involvement, more open and more rational decision-making, and generally a system in which decision-makers are more accountable to the law. But judicialization is not a coherent trend necessarily aimed at (or leading to) greater public participation, more legal accountability, or an upgrading of fundamental rights at the expense of legislative majorities. On the contrary, judicialization may occur because government seeks to centralize its control, reduce its accountability to the courts or curtail citizen's rights. From this perspective it is ironic that judicialization may be an aspect of "delegalization." Delegalization has a variety of meanings, but in essence it is concerned with a movement away from formal constitutional systems of accountability in favor of more informal, less accessible, and less accountable methods of decision-making (Lewis 1985). Delegalization may be achieved by judicialization when, for example, judicial techniques are introduced within administration schemes in order to minimize judicial review and to keep decision-making out of the judicial province. Again, the Social Fund inspectorate and the managerial strategies aimed at reducing government's vulnerability to challenge are examples of this.

In order to emphasize the diverse nature of judicialization I intend, very briefly, to examine some of the most significant recent developments from two perspectives: court-inspired judicialization and politically inspired judicialization.

COURT-INSPIRED JUDICIALIZATION OF POLITICS

Today it is perhaps common-place to observe that . . . there has been a dramatic and indeed a radical change in the scope of judicial review.

—Lord Roskill

increasing anxiety at the highest levels of government as to whether judicial review is inhibiting the implementation of governmental decisions and policy to an extent which is becoming intolerable.

—Lord Justice Woolf (Woolf 1990b, 17)

The past decade or so has witnessed a dramatic growth in the use of the courts to challenge decisions of local and central government (Sunkin 1987, 1991). This has been accompanied by a general liberalization in the standing requirements, an extension of the scope of judicial review, and improvements in the grounds upon which challenges may be mounted. The result is that Courts are now regularly drawn into areas of government that would have been regarded as beyond judicial competence even 20 or 30 years ago. There are many examples of judicial involvement in local[1] and central government politics. They include decisions adversely affecting educational policy[2], television licensing[3], airline regulation,[4] local government finance[5], and social welfare.[6] In this section I will look briefly at three contexts in which the extension of judicial review has been particularly prominent: prison discipline, City regulation, and review of prerogative powers.

Prisons

A senior administrator likened the traditional culture of the prison service to that of an army unit, consuming its own smoke and ensuring that nobody looks in.[7] Prior to the late 1970s this view was respected and encouraged by the judges, who refused to interfere with prison disciplinary procedures.[8]

The situation started to change when the Court of Appeal, in *ex parte St. Germain*,[9] asserted jurisdiction to review disciplinary decisions of the Prison Board of Visitors. The decision apparently came as something of a shock to administrators, who thought that the roof had fallen in on them. *St. Germain* was followed by a series of decisions holding that prisoners retain their civil rights while in prison;[10] that Boards of Visitors have a duty to consider allowing legal representation;[11] and that Governors' disciplinary adjudications and certain managerial decisions are also reviewable.[12] These English cases were reinforced by decisions under the European Convention on Human Rights.[13]

At each stage of this history the Home Office vigorously opposed judicial intervention, fearing that "opening of the door to judicial review . . . would make it impossible to resist an invasion by . . . 'the tentacles of the law'"[14]   and that such an invasion would undermine the governor's authority and "seriously aggravate the already difficult task of maintaining order and discipline in prisons."[15]   The judges, however, were not impressed.   "No one," said Lord Bridge, "can predict the consequences" of judicial intervention with any certainty.   Judicial intervention might have some adverse effects, but "(n)othing . . . is so likely to generate unrest among ordinary prisoners as a sense that they have been treated unfairly and have no effective means of redress."[16] In his view, freer access to the courts would probably make it easier, rather than harder, to run prisons.

As it happens an invasion of the tentacles of the law has not occurred. Far from increasing, the number of prisoner applications for judicial review substantially declined during the late 1980s (Sunkin 1991). Whatever the reasons for this, the decline in prisoner litigation does not reflect a general improvement in conditions in British prisons or an improvement in morale among prisoners or within the prison service in general.   Recent years have seen some of the most violent disturbances ever to have taken place in our prisons.   The riots at Strangeways Prison during April 1990 are probably the best known.   The report of the inquiry, headed by Lord Justice Woolf,[17] into the events at Strangeways emphasized the need to improve the quality of justice for prisoners and is likely to lead to greater judicialization of disciplinary and complaint procedures within prisons (Woolf 1990a).

City Regulation

In *R v. Panel on Take-overs and Mergers, ex parte Datafin Plc.*,[18] the Court of Appeal held that decisions of the City Panel on Take-overs and Mergers could be judicially reviewed.   The case indicated judicial willingness to intervene in the work of a body that had been established by the City of London as part of its internal mechanisms for self-regulation.   The Court of Appeal justified intervention on the ground that although the panel did not derive its powers from a public source, such as statute or the royal prerogative, its functions are of public importance and it therefore operates in the public domain.   *Datafin* showed the courts prepared to impose principles of public law upon bodies operating at the fringes of government but not politically accountable.   The imposition of accountability to the courts will become increasingly significant as government policy 'hives-off' a wider range of governmental functions to departmental agencies and the private sector (see, further, Birkinshaw, et. al. 1990). As in the rather different context of prisons, judicial attitudes reflect wider European trends that are leading to greater legal regulation of City life (Jowell 1991).

The Royal Prerogative

From the perspective of constitutional law, perhaps the most significant extensions of judicial review are made possible by the decision of the House of Lords in *Council for Civil Service Unions v. Government Central Communication Headquarters*.[19] Acting under prerogative powers the prime minister, as head of the Civil Service, ordered workers at the Government Central Communication Headquarters (GCHQ) to relinquish their trade union memberships. The Unions challenged this action on the grounds, *inter alia*, that the prime minister's refusal to consult with them prior to reaching her decision was contrary to natural justice. For the prime minister it was argued, *inter alia*, 1) that prerogative powers could not be judicially reviewed; 2) that there was no obligation to consult; and, 3) even if there were, in this case the decision not to consult was taken in the interests of national security and was therefore unreviewable.

It was held that the mere fact that the prime Minister had acted under prerogative powers did not mean that her decision could not be reviewed. What matters is not the source from which the power derives but the nature of the decision being made. Provided decisions are justiciable, the courts will be prepared to intervene. Here, the court accepted that there had been unfairness but was not prepared to quash the action because of the government's claim that it had acted in the interests of national security. The decision means that the Executive can no longer claim immunity from legal challenge simply by relying on the ancient prerogatives of the Crown. Its importance, however, was diminished by the willingness of the judges to accept the national security justification, even though it was supported by slight and even contradictory evidence (Griffith 1991, 155).

According to Vallinder, judicialization of politics occurs when the province of the courts expands at the expense of politicians. The deference shown by the judges in *GCHQ* to the executive's national security defense suggests that extensions in the potential scope of judicial review are not necessarily at the expense of the government.

In the United Kingdom politicians always have the last word, and the judges know this. If judges "fly too high, Parliament may clip their wings. They entirely lack the impregnable constitutional status of their American counterparts" (Wade 1988, 30). Statutory reversal of decisions unfavorable to government and exclusion of judicial review is a common feature of political life and seems to have assumed a new prominence since 1979 (Graham and Prosser 1979, 11; McAuslan and McEldowney 1985, 28-31; Prosser 1983, chap. 5).

Judicial wings may also be clipped more subtly, as we shall see when I discuss politically motivated judicialization. Suffice it to say that judges are well aware that there are dangers in the "over invasive use of judicial review" (Woolf 1990b, 19) and that the prevailing judicial mood is rather more cautious than it might appear. Extensions of jurisdiction tend to be tentative and are often proclaimed in cases in which the courts decline to intervene.[20]   Moreover, there is a tendency to erect new barriers to intervention as the old ones are being dismantled. In recent years concepts such as justiciability have come to the fore[21] and the courts have refused to intervene in areas they regard as being politically sensitive[22] or where they believe that their intervention will create undue administrative inconvenience.[23]   All the evidence shows the judges jealous to maximize their discretion over the scope of judicial review, but it should not be assumed that this necessarily implies a more invasive use of their jurisdiction.

POLITICALLY INSPIRED JUDICIALIZATION

Judicialized procedures, such as tribunals and inquiries, are used to inform decision-making and resolve conflict in a vast array of contexts. It is commonly said that tribunals were established because courts were unable to provide the cheap, accessible and informal justice demanded by social welfare programs (Street 1975, 2). So perceived, this form of judicialization fits well with the theory that judicialized procedures further the relative status of individual rights. But this benign view of the rationale of tribunals is disputed. It is said to neglect political motivations behind judicialization, such as the desire to legitimate controversial policies and depoliticize conflict (Harlow and Rawlings 1984, 67-78; Bridges 1975; Prosser 1977, 42-44).[24]   Recent use of forms of judicialization—although not necessarily of adjudication—by politicians and administrators in the context of central government administration, central/local government relations, and the Social Fund illustrate some of the political uses of judicialization.

Judicialization of Central Government Administration

By the early 1980s it had become obvious that central government was vulnerable to legal challenge (Kerry 1983, 1986). The underlying reason for this vulnerability lay in the cultural ethos of the civil service that had traditionally placed a low priority on law and the need for officials to be legally aware (Drewry 1986). Prompted by their political masters, senior managers responded by encouraging more careful draftsmanship and introducing a program of training aimed at improving legal awareness (Sunkin and Le Sueur 1991; Bradley 1987). From the outset the main thrust of the strategy was defensive and, as one eminent judge has remarked, it has led to the introduction of procedures "which appear to be designed to remove particular decisions from the area of judicial review" (Woolf 1990b, 17). The emphasis is upon improving the defendability of decisions and, while this may improve aspects of decision-making, the new culture (so we are told) encourages officials to go through a charade of formality in decision-making in order to protect their authority from legal challenge.[25]

My purpose in focusing upon the negative aspects of the managerial strategy is to show that judicialization can be used in ways that are perceived to reduce accountability, and that may have an uncertain positive effect on the overall quality of decision-making.

Local Government

Local government litigation was one of the areas in which government appeared particularly vulnerable. What made this all the more worrying for Government was that the litigation was an immediate by-product of its own policy.

Increased central control of local government was a main plank of Thatcherite policy throughout the 1980s. This has been achieved by "the aggressive use of the law" (Leach and Stoker 1988, 98), which has led to a collapse of the traditionally flexible structure within which local and central government could bargain and negotiate. In its place was imposed a juridified relationship that forced conflict into the courts (Loughlin 1986, 193; Grant 1986, Bridges et. al. 1987).

As well as enabling central government to define the obligations of local authorities, judicialization helped shift politically contentious issues, such as education, transport, and housing (issues on which the Tory central government was politically vulnerable) into the judicial sphere, thereby diminishing the political power of authorities, particularly those in Labour strongholds.

The Social Fund

The Social Fund was introduced amid considerable political controversy by the Social Security Act of 1986 (see Drabble and Lynes 1989). The fund is designed to help those already dependent on state support to cope with financial crisis and emergencies. Payments, in the form of grants or loans, are made on a discretionary basis by local Social Fund officers. Payments are made in accordance with need, but local officers must always keep within their budgetary allocation even if this means that needs cannot be met. When the scheme was originally presented to Parliament, there was no provision for appeals against decisions of Social Fund officers. The ministerial view was that appeals would undermine the strictly budgetary nature of the scheme because appellate bodies would not be constrained by the budget. The absence of appeals, however, attracted widespread criticism and became the focus for hostile opposition in Parliament, which eventually forced a concession out of the government. While still refusing to allow an appeal, the government agreed to introduce a system for reviewing decisions of Social Fund officers on procedural grounds akin to the principles of judicial review. The purpose of the review is to ensure that decisions have been properly made in accordance with the appropriate law, but not to second guess the decision itself. Thus the discretion of the Social Fund officers within their budget is retained while providing a degree of redress.

The reviews are carried out by Social Fund Inspectors who are responsible to the Social Fund commissioner. Although their work is akin to that done by high court judges when considering applications for judicial review, the inspectors are not legally qualified and tend to be drawn from within the Department of Social Security. The scheme is an example of judicialization being adopted by a reluctant government in order to buy political support for, and to add legitimacy to, a controversial and unpopular scheme. Here the judicialization is combined with discretion in a way that accepts the desirability of catering to procedural rights, even if substantive rights cannot be protected.

CONCLUSION

Judicialization, as it has been defined here, takes many forms, occurs for many reasons, and is present at many different levels of the system. It is a technique that does not necessarily increase levels of participation, accountability, or legal rationality. Moreover, judicialization at one level of government or in one context of administration may well be at the expense of judicialization and accountability at other, more public and more important levels of government.

I have made passing references to the influence of European Community Law and the European Convention on Human Rights. These, and particularly the former, are exerting fundamental pressures on the constitution of the United Kingdom and upon its legal culture. In-so-far as there are coherent pressures to judicialize, they come primarily from Europe. They will doubtless increase, and it is almost certain that our courts will be drawn further into political and economic life. Already concepts as fundamental as the supremacy of Parliament are being refashioned as the courts find themselves obliged to adjudicate upon the compatibility of primary legislation with community law. Who knows how long it will be before we have some form of written constitution, or at least a modern Bill of Rights?

NOTES

1. The best-known local government decision is that quashing the Greater London Council's decision to reduce fares on London Transport in accordance with its election manifesto: *London Borough of Bromley* v. *G.L.C.* (1983) 1 A.C. 768. See also *Wheeler* v. *Leicester City Council* (1985) A.C. 1054, in which a decision to withdraw the license of a local rugby club because the club had refused to prevent four of its members from participating in a tour of South Africa was quashed.

2. *Secretary of State for Education and Science* v. *Tameside MBC* (1977) A.C. 1014.

3. *Congreve* v. *Home Office* (1976) 1 All E.R. 697.

4. *Laker Airways* v. *Department of Trade* (1977) 2 All E.R. 182.

5. *R* v. *Secretary of State for the Environment* (1982) 2 W.L.R. 693.

6. *R v. Secretary of State for Social Services, ex parte Cotton & Waite, The Times*, December 14, 1985.

7. Interview with author, July 1988.

8. *Fraser v. Mudge* (1975) 2 All E.R. 79.

9. *R v. Hull Prison Board of Visitors, Ex parte St. Germain* (1979) All E.R. 701.

10. *Raymond v. Honey* (1982) 1 All E.R. 756.

11. *R v. Secretary of State ex parte Tarrant* (1984) 1 All E.R. 799.

12. *Leech v. Parkhurst Prison Deputy Governor* (1988) 1 All E.R. 485; *Hague v. Parkhurst Prison Deputy Governor* (1991) 3 All E.R. 733.

13. For example, *Golder v. U.K.* series A No. 18; 1 EHRR 524; *Silver v. U.K.* series A No. 61; 5 EHRR 347; *Campbell & Fell v. U.K.*, 5 EHRR 207; series A No. 80; 7 EHRR 165.

14. Per Lord Bridge in *Leech v. Parkhurst Prison Deputy Governor*; see note 12 above, 499 referring to Home Office submissions.

15. Per Lord Bridge in *Leech v. Parkhurst Prison Deputy Governor*, 500.

16. Per Lord Bridge in *Leech v. Parkhurst Prison Deputy Governor*, 501.

17. The use of judges to carry out inquires of this type is itself an example of judicialization; see further Griffith (1991, chap. 2).

18. (1987) QB 815.

19. *Council for Civil Service Unions v. Government Central Communication Headquarters (1984)* 3 A1 E.R. 935, at A.C 374, at 953.

20. *Ex parte Datafin* and *GCHQ* are themselves examples of this reticence.

21. See *GCHQ*. Lord Diplock said, of national security, "It is par excellence a non-justiciable question." See note 19 at 952; also, *F v. Secretary of State for the Home Department, Ex parte Cheblak* (1991) 2 All E.R. 319.

22. For example: *Nottinghamshire CC v. Secretary of State for the Environment* (1986) AC 240; *Hammersmith LBC v. Secretary of State for the Environment* (1990) 3 All E.R. 589; *Brind v. Secretary of State for the Home Department* (1991) 1 All E.R. 720.

23. For example: *Puhlhoffer v. Hillingdon LBC* (1986) 1 All E.R. 467; *R v. Secretary of State for Social Services, Ex parte the Association of Metropolitan Authorities* (1986) 1 W.L.R. 1.

24. Judicialization is said to depoliticize controversy by: providing an appearance of neutrality; emphasizing procedural fairness and directing attention away from substantive injustice; creating the impression that conflict can be resolved on an individual basis by formal and rational means; and focusing on individual cases and deflecting attention away from the underlying ideology of policies.

25. Michael Warr, Address to the Administrative Law Bar Association October 26, 1987, quoted by Lord Justice Woolf (Woolf 1990b, 18).

REFERENCES

Birkinshaw, P., I. Harden, and N. Lewis. 1990. *Government by Moonlight*. London: Unwin Hyman.

Bradley, A. 1987. "The Judge Over Your Shoulder," *Public Law*, 250.

Bridges, L. 1975. "Legality and Immigration Control", *British Journal of Law and Society* 2:221.

Bridges, L., et. al. 1987. *Legality and Local Politics*. Aldershot: Avebury.

Drabble, R., and T. Lynes. 1989. "Decision-Making in Social Security: The Social Fund—Discretion or Control," *Public Law*, 297.

Drewry, G. 1986. "Public Lawyers and Public Administrators: Prospects for an Alliance," *Public Administration* 64:173.

Graham, C., and T. Prosser, eds. 1979. *Waiving the Rules: The Constitution under Thatcherism*. Milton Keynes: Open University Press.

Grant, M. 1986. "The Role of the Courts in Central-Local Relations." In *New Research in Central-Local Relations*, ed. M. Goldsmith. Aldershot: Gower.

Griffith, J. A. G. 1979. "The Political Constitution," *Modern Law Review*, 42:1.

———. 1991. *The Politics of the Judiciary*. 4th. ed. London: Fontana Press.

Harlow, C., and R. Rawlings. 1984. *Law and Administration*, London: Weidenfeld and Nicolson.

Jowell, J. 1973. "The Legal Control of Administrative Discretion," *Public Law*, 178.

———. 1991. "The Takeover Panel: Autonomy, Flexibility, and Legality," *Public Law*, 149.

Kerry, Sir Michael. 1983. "Administrative Law and the Administrator." *Management in Government*, 3:170.

———. 1986. "Administrative Law—The Practical Effects of Developments over the Past 25 Years on Administration in Central Government," *Public Administration* 64:163.

Leach, S., and G. Stoker. 1988. "The Transformation of Central-Local Government Relationships." In C. Graham and T. Prosser, eds., *Waiving the Rules: The Constitution Under Thatcherism*, Milton Keynes: Open University Press.

Lewis, N.   1985. "De-Legalization in Britain in the 1980s."   In P. McAuslan and J. McEldowney, eds., *Law, Legitimacy and the Constitution*. London, Sweet and Maxwell.

Loughlin, M.   1986. *Local Government in the Modern State*. London: Sweet and Maxwell.

McAuslan, P., and J. McEldowney, eds.   1985. *Law, Legitimacy and the Constitution*. London: Sweet and Maxwell.

Prosser, T.   1977. "Poverty, Ideology, and Legality: Supplementary Benefit Appeal Tribunals and the Predecessors." *British Journal of Law and Society*, 4:39.

―――.   1983. *Test Cases for the Poor*. London, Child Poverty Action Group.

Street, H.   1975. *Justice in the Welfare State*. London, Stevens.

Sunkin, M.   1987.   "What is Happening to Applications for Judicial Review?" *Modern Law Review*, 50:432.

―――.   1991. "The Judicial Review Caseload: 1987-1989." *Public Law*, 490.

Sunkin, M., and A. Le Sueur.   1991. "Can Government Control Judicial Review?" *Current Legal Problems*, 44:161.

Wade, H.W.R.   1988. *Administrative Law*. 6th. ed.   Oxford, Oxford University Press.

Woolf, Lord Justice 1990a.   *Prison Disturbances 1990*.   Cm 1456. London: HMSO [Her Majesty's Stationery Office].

―――.   1990b. *Protection of the Public—A New Challenge*. London: Stevens.

Australia

6.

Judicial Intrusion into the Australian Cabinet

BRIAN GALLIGAN AND DAVID R. SLATER

In the past fifteen years the Australian judiciary has breached the executive citadel of cabinet secrecy and privilege by making itself the arbiter of what documents are to be produced for court proceedings. The High Court, in *Sankey v. Whitlam* (1978), ruled that no class of documents, not even cabinet papers, are immune from compulsory disclosure at the court's discretion. Moreover, the court held that it was the responsibility of the judiciary rather than the executive to determine the balance of public interest in deciding which documents were to be produced. Applying this decision in a liberal way in *Commonwealth v. Northern Land Council* (1991), the Federal Court upheld a decision ordering the delivery and inspection by counsel of 126 cabinet notebooks. This decision entailed judicially sanctioned intrusion into the very interstices of cabinet decision-making because these cabinet notebooks are the most complete record of the cabinet's proceedings and provide the raw documentary basis for drafting official minutes recording executive decisions. Previously, the courts had accepted that cabinet papers were in a special class immune from compulsory disclosure in judicial proceedings, and justified such residual Crown privilege on the ground of maintaining cabinet secrecy and collective responsibility. The High Court subsequently reversed the Federal Court in the *Northern Land Council* case (1993) and gave greater weight to the public interest in maintaining confidentiality of cabinet records, but it nevertheless reaffirmed the principle that it is for the judiciary rather than the executive to determine.

This assertion of judicial review over the most sensitive aspects of executive decision-making is clearly a major advance in the judicialization of Australian politics. Indeed, it represents a crucial qualification to claims of executive dominance or "elective dictatorship" said to characterize Australia's system of parliamentary responsible government and disciplined party politics.

Australia has a strong tradition of judicial review of constitutional issues by a powerful and independent High Court that is well entrenched in its federal constitution (Galligan 1987, 1991; Solomon 1992). In the last couple of decades, this strong form of political "judicialization from without" (see chap. 2 of this volume) has been complemented by a range of measures for judicial review of administrative action. The New Administrative Law was a response to widespread dissatisfaction with traditional parliamentary review and ministerial responsibility for protecting individual rights in an era of big government, and reflected confidence in alternative judicial tribunals and procedures (Administrative Law Seminar 1989; Administrative Law Forum 1991). It entailed partly an extension of judicial procedures through such bodies as the Administrative Appeals Tribunal and partly an extension of judicial review by means of the Federal Court. Australia also has a well-developed national system of industrial arbitration based upon the judicialization of industrial relations—bringing working conditions and the setting of wage rates within "a new province for law and order," according to Justice Higgins, who was one of its early champions and a prominent High court judge.

The extension of judicial oversight to the production of cabinet documents for court proceedings, which is the subject of this chapter, is a rather specific, but nonetheless significant, instance of the judicialization of Australian politics. Like the more extensive New Administrative Law, it runs counter to the widespread perception, particularly among the judiciary, of the increasing power of the executive. As with the enhanced administrative law, this is something of a counterbalance to executive dominance and is broadly sustained by public confidence in the judiciary.

This chapter explores the historical development of the courts' role in determining the accessibility of departmental and cabinet documents to prospective litigants and the respective roles that the executive and the courts play in this task. The chapter examines the various claims that support the executive's demands for absolute immunity and the way the courts have surmounted these. To appreciate the significance of the judiciary's extension of its purview to cabinet records, we begin with a detailed sketch of how Australian cabinet government works and why secrecy has been justified.

CABINET PRINCIPLES AND CONVENTIONS

The early development of the English cabinet process remains obscure, primarily because of the secrecy that surrounded its operation. The cabinet's origins stem from seventeenth-century England, where an inner circle of privy councilors, known as the Cabinet Council, acted as advisers to the monarch. Even when the cabinet supplanted the monarch as the real executive in British government, it remained highly secretive, as Bagehot emphasized in his classic exposition:

> The most curious point about the Cabinet is that so very little is known about it. The meetings are not only secret in theory, but secret in reality. By the present practice, no official minute in ordinary cases is kept of them. Even a private note is discouraged and disliked. The House of Commons, even in its most inquisitive and turbulent moments, would scarcely permit a note of a Cabinet meeting to be read. . . . The committee which unites the law-making power to the law-executing power—which, by virtue of that combination, is, while it lasts and holds together, the most powerful body in the State—is a committee wholly secret. (Bagehot 1867, 68)

As if continuing this tradition of formal secrecy, the Australian constitution makes no mention of the cabinet whatsoever in its chapter 2 on the executive. Section 61 vests the executive power of the Commonwealth in the queen, exercisable by the governor general as her representative. Section 62 of the constitution established a federal executive council to advise the governor-general in the government of the Commonwealth, thereby grafting into the constitution the principle of responsible government. Quick and Garran (1901) argue that the practical result of sections 61 and 62 is that executive power is placed in the hands of the Cabinet and that the real head of the executive is the chairman of the cabinet, the prime minister. In 1987 the constitutional commission concluded that the reason for the absence of an express recognition of the cabinet within the constitution was:

> because the cabinet is essentially an informal body, it is unsuited to a formal statement in a Constitution. Practices as to its composition and operation can and do change from one government to the next. It is even possible that some system other than the present one of cabinet might evolve. Again, much of this desirable flexibility could be lost if the cabinet were written into the Constitution. (Constitutional Commission 1988, 15)

As the cabinet system developed, so did a number of conventions that underpinned its operation. The key ones were the principle of collective responsibility and the convention of cabinet secrecy, which were used to justify demands for absolute immunity from production of any records of its proceedings. It is difficult to deny the constitutional significance of the conventions that regulate the behavior of the cabinet because it is the center of executive decision-making. "Its proximate relationship to the *de jure* powers of the Executive Council under section 61" according to one judicial view, "enhances that significance" (Mason in *FAI Insurances v. Winneke* 1982, 364; also Murphy at 373-74).

Collective Responsibility

The convention of collective responsibility emerged as a convention of cabinet government in the nineteenth century. The trend toward solidarity developed as an incident of the British two-party political system (Mackintosh 1968, 520-21). In their early exposition of the Australian constitution, Quick and Garran give a strong statement of the convention in the following terms:

> The principle of the corporate unity and solidarity of the Cabinet requires that the Cabinet should have one harmonious policy, both in administration and in legislation; that the advice tendered by the Cabinet to the Crown should be unanimous and consistent; that the Cabinet should stand or fall together. The Cabinet as a whole is responsible for the advice and conduct of each of its members. If any member of the Cabinet seriously dissents from the opinion and

policy approved by the majority of his colleagues it is his duty as a man of honor to resign. (Quick and Garran 1901, 705)

Mackintosh argues that those who worked together to guide national affairs ought either to be in sufficient agreement to give genuine efficacy to collective decisions at the formulative stage or should resign. The doctrine, he argues, lies in the field of convention, being strictly no more than a generally accepted political practice with a record of successful application or precedent. And, by definition, political conventions are not rules of law (Mackintosh 1968, 520-21; Munro 1975, 231-34; Crisp 1978, 352). Current Australian doctrine, including the governing Labor Party's practice of binding caucus solidarity, is set out in the *Cabinet Handbook* which lays down the procedures for handling and presentation of cabinet business:

> The convention of the collective responsibility of Ministers for Government is central to the Cabinet system of government. Cabinet minutes reflect collective conclusions and are binding on Cabinet Ministers as Government policy both outside the Party and within. All Ministers are expected to give their support in public debate to decisions of the Government; non-cabinet Ministers, however, are not prevented from debating in Caucus decisions in areas apart from their portfolios. Caucus decisions are binding on all Ministers. . . . Administrative procedures have been adopted to support the convention of collective responsibility. With limited exception (e.g., national security and budget matters), all Ministers receive copies of all Cabinet documents, including Submissions, Memorandums, Notices of Meeting, Business Lists and Programs, so that they may be aware of the business coming to Cabinet. (*Cabinet Handbook* 1991, 5)

The importance of collective responsibility cannot be underestimated from either a practical or a political perspective. In the complexity of modern bureaucracy, collective ability is important because many issues and programs arising on the political response agenda cross ministerial portfolio boundaries. In such an environment, unilateral decision-making would tend to be fragmentary, whereas collective consideration ensures cohesion and collegiality.   Furthermore, collective responsibility promotes party unity and purpose, which are important for political cohesion and electoral survival. Thus it is not surprising that all Australian prime ministers have embraced and zealously guarded the principle of collective responsibility.

That is not to deny that the convention of collective responsibility is not at times the subject of political expediency in Britain as well as in Australia. In *Attorney-General v. Jonathan Cape Ltd* (1976), the court found "overwhelming evidence that the doctrine of joint responsibility is generally understood and practiced and equally strong evidence that it is on occasion ignored" (770). According to one leading Australian practitioner, however, there is a danger in taking the principle of collective responsibility too far—especially if every issue that is seen to require the attention of more than one minister is automatically regarded as a matter for the cabinet. Michael Codd, cabinet secretary for most of the 1980s during the Hawke Labor government, argues that the risks become apparent if the position taken by Quick and Garran, that "the Cabinet as a whole is responsible for the advice and conduct of each of its members," is taken too literally (Codd 1990, 3).

Cabinet Confidentiality

Associated with the convention of collective responsibility and also underpinning the operation of the cabinet is the principle of confidentiality. The *Cabinet Handbook* articulated the principle as follows:

> Collective responsibility is supported by the strict confidentiality attaching to Cabinet documents and to discussions in the Cabinet Room. Ministry, Cabinet and Cabinet committees are forums in which Ministers, while working towards a collective position, are able to discuss proposals and a variety of options and views with complete freedom. The openness and frankness of discussion in the Cabinet Room are protected by the strict observance of this confidentiality. (Cabinet Handbook 1991, 6)

In the *Northern Land Council* case (1991), the Federal Court noted that the relationship of cabinet decision-making to the tendering of advice to the monarch or to the governor general in council may support a rationale for secrecy. In addition, the court linked the basis of secrecy to the political imperatives for collective responsibility. From a political and practical perspective, the court argued that it is difficult for ministers to make an effective defense in public of decisions with which it is known that they have disagreed during the course of discussions in the cabinet. Confidentiality is important to ensure that collective responsibility is not undermined by identifying in public the voting patterns of individual ministers within the cabinet room. To this end the *Cabinet Handbook* states: "Having regard to the obligations imposed on Ministers by the conventions of collective responsibility and Cabinet confidentiality, officers should not seek from Ministers or Cabinet officers information about the views of individual Ministers or about aspects of discussion in the Cabinet Room" (*Cabinet Handbook* 1991, 6).

One Australian judge, Chief Justice Blackburn, (in *Whitlam v. Australian Consolidated Press Ltd* 1985, 414), penned an eloquent tribute to the virtues and venerable tradition of cabinet secrecy: "Cabinet secrecy is an essential part of the structure of government which centuries of political experience have created. To impair it without a very strong reason would be vandalism; even wanton rejection of the fruits of civilization." Rhetoric aside, the need for cabinet secrecy is best assessed in the context of its modern structure and operation, which have become highly complex, structured, and bureaucratized.

Cabinet Structure and Operation

The procedures by which the Australian cabinet system operates are laid down by the *Cabinet Handbook*. The *Handbook* is revised as necessary in the light of experience and changes to procedures that may be authorized from time to time. Subject to the Ministers of State Act of 1952, the organization and structure of a government's cabinet is unrestricted. When the Hawke Labour government came to office in 1983, it adopted the more conventional practice of having cabinet ministers and an outer ministry, although this was a notable departure from the Labor tradition followed by the earlier Whitlam government in 1972-75. After the 1987 election, this two-tiered cabinet structure was reinforced by creating a number of megadepartments, such as education, employment, and training, with senior cabinet ministers and junior ministers under them *(Canberra Bulletin Of Public Administration* 1988). Former Labour prime minister Mr. Robert Hawke described the relationship of this structure to cabinet operations in the following terms: "Portfolio ministers will represent the interests of the portfolio in Cabinet, but other ministers will be entitled to bring forward submissions related to their allocated areas of responsibility, and to be present when Cabinet discusses those submissions" (Hawke 1987).

Cabinet Meetings and Attendance

Throughout the year, the cabinet meets generally on Mondays when the Parliament is in session and Tuesdays when it is not. As chairman of the cabinet, the prime minister determines the times and business for all meetings. Generally, cabinet and committee meetings avoid meeting when the Parliament is in session. Ministerial attendance takes priority over all other committees apart from unavoidable parliamentary commitments such as when a Minister is involved in the passage of a vital piece of legislation or dealing with a question in the House requiring his personal attention. Leave to be absent is generally sought in writing from the prime minister, and a minister may seek agreement with one of his colleagues to represent the absent minister for portfolio specific items on the cabinet's agenda. Apart from ministers, the secretary to the cabinet or the deputy secretary attends all cabinet and committee meetings and is usually accompanied by two other cabinet officers, who may be rotated depending upon the duration of proceedings. The officers are present to record the outcome of cabinet discussions and to generally assist with the smooth running of the meetings. When private discussions take place, the officers withdraw from the meeting. The officers are permitted to take notes for the purpose of writing up minutes, which, for security reasons, may be recorded only in special cabinet notebooks. These notes are not a verbatim transcript of cabinet room discussions but aides to the formulation of minutes that, when initialed by the prime minister, formally endorsed by executive council, signed by the governor general, and promulgated in appropriate ways, are the substance of executive decision-making.

Officers other than those associated with the cabinet do not attend cabinet or committee meetings unless they have been specifically requested by a minister and approved by the prime minister or deputy committee chairman after consulting about the matter with colleagues. Such officials are present at such meetings only in order to aid their minister, and through this conduit to provide advice to the meeting if requested. They do not participate in discussion but are expected to explain factual or technical material when requested. Notes of cabinet deliberations are not to be kept by officials and there must be no disclosure outside the cabinet room of the contents or nature of those discussions. The conventions of collective responsibility and cabinet confidentiality extend to public servants, who are barred from seeking from ministers or cabinet officers information about the views of individual ministers or details of discussion in the cabinet room.

Cabinet Decision-making

The Cabinet is "the supreme organ of the decision-making processes of the Government" (Hawke 1988, 5). Business coming before the cabinet arrives in one of the following forms: (a) formal submissions and memorandums, (b) committee minutes for endorsement by cabinet, (c) appointments proposed by ministers, and (d) matters without submission. The latter covers only matters of exceptional urgency that require cabinet discussion immediately but are not so complex as to require cabinet submission.   To enable ministers adequate opportunity to consider proposals and to arrange the programs for cabinet business, submissions and memorandums are not normally listed until at least 10 clear calendar days have elapsed after the documents have been lodged with the cabinet office. The cabinet office may reject a submission when strong criticism from other departments has not been addressed or significant issues have not been canvassed, especially when the document was requested by the cabinet.

The nature of business discussed in the cabinet rooms is diverse in its formality, complexity, and economic and political importance. The bulk of matters bought before the cabinet are in the form of proposals initiated by other ministers. In order to maintain the volume of matters coming before the cabinet, ministers are encouraged to consider settling a matter by correspondence, especially when it is perceived that all ministers will be in agreement. If this is the case, then the initiating minister would write to the prime minister, advising of the outcomes of the consultations and seeking his approval for the course of action he proposes. Apart from considering submissions, the cabinet is also responsible for the endorsement of committee minutes.

The endorsement of committee minutes by the cabinet is then normally a formal process that generally does not involve reopening the discussion. If there are aspects of a committee minute that a minister wants to raise, when the minute is put forward for endorsement the minister must in writing beforehand inform the prime minister or the secretary to the cabinet. If the request is made by a minister who is not a member of the cabinet, he is co-opted as a matter of course to attend the cabinet meeting for that item. In endorsing a committee minute, changes of substance are not normally made unless the minister responsible for the original proposal is present. If such a matter is at issue, the cabinet may refer the matter back to the committee to be considered further. The same procedure is adopted when the cabinet requests additional submissions or memorandums or a corrigendum to a document before it, and such matters may be returned to the relevant committee for consideration before being considered before the cabinet again.

Once decisions are made, all cabinet documents except those for official records are destroyed and registers kept. The cabinet office retains a full set of all cabinet documents which are eventually released according to the Archives Act of 1983, generally after the standard thirty years. In some instances special access to documents can be granted within the thirty-year period to ex-prime ministers and ex-ministers in order to refresh their memory of events for biographical purposes. This is a minor exception, however, and special provisions of the Freedom of Information Act of 1982 in effect exempt such documents from public access. Special procedures apply to security documents which are returned to the office of security and intelligence coordination after meetings. The doctrine of confidentiality also ensures that cabinet documents are confidential to the government that created them, with access to succeeding governments only being granted when approval of the appropriate political party has been given.

The Cabinet Office

Within the cabinet structure, an important role is also played by the cabinet office. It is responsible for servicing cabinet and committee meetings, tendering advice to the prime minister concerning the programming of cabinet business, the preparation, distribution and custody of cabinet documents, which remain the property of the Commonwealth and not of individual ministers, and are held on behalf of the government in the custody of the secretary to cabinet and issued to ministers and departments. The most important of these documents are, programs, notices of meeting, business lists, submissions, memorandums and minutes. These documents are held separately from other working documents involved in the government's administration. Generally, access to such documents is on a need-to-know basis. Cabinet documents are given a level of protection at least equivalent to that given to a document that bears the national security classification "confidential."

The cabinet office is responsible for the delivery of cabinet documents to the office of each minister who has nominated up to three members of his staff to receive and handle these documents. These must be signed for on receipt, and the signer is responsible for their safe handling and delivery. Generally, such documents cannot be reproduced except by the cabinet office on request. An access record is kept of all persons who have had access to each cabinet document. The cabinet office is not responsible for the circulation of copies of the final document to officers of other departments and authorities consulted regarding a proposal. This responsibility lies with the department lodging a submission or memorandum. Whether an individual minister wishes to be briefed by his or her department after receiving a submission or memorandum remains at the discretion of that minister.

The handbook also sets out guidelines for the preparation of cabinet documents, detailing the presentation and format to be adopted when presenting submissions, memorandums, the handling of business without submission, and appointments. In general, the aim of a cabinet submission is to obtain cabinet's agreement on a course of action. Submissions should be presented in straightforward language, examining the issues logically and concisely, enabling ministers to focus upon the issues that have to be considered and decided. Generally, memorandums contain additional information or the development of options, prepared by departmental officers in response to requests by the cabinet but do not contain recommendations.

The cabinet has clearly come a long way since Bagehot described it as "a committee wholly secret" about which little was known and certainly no official minute of its affairs kept. With the growth in volume and complexity of government business, the cabinet has not escaped the increased bureaucratization that has been characteristic of government generally. The cabinet is no longer synonymous with an informal meeting of ministers that decides issues of state in complete secrecy but has become a highly structured and formalized process of collective decision making replete with an associated system of subcommittees, published procedures for the preparation of submissions and conduct of its affairs, an office to service its requirements, attendance and detailed note-taking by officials, and preservation of its records. Despite all these developments, however, collective responsibility and confidentiality have remained hallmarks of this system of executive government with cabinet documents, until quite recently, being considered sacrosanct.

In an era of enhanced judicialization of executive action, which has also spawned Australia's New Administrative Law, it is not surprising that the courts have also extended their oversight to executive decision-making and cabinet records. The rest of this chapter examines the erosion of absolute protection that cabinet documents once enjoyed, culminating in the recent High Court decision that swung back to acknowledging a high public interest in respecting confidentiality of cabinet documents but nevertheless reaffirmed the right of courts to decide the issue.

CABINET'S EXEMPTION AS JUDICIAL RESTRAINT

In colonial Australia as in mother England, the courts eschewed review not only of the cabinet but more broadly of departments of state. Such exclusion of the affairs of state from judicial scrutiny was the orthodox view touted by ministers and generally accepted by courts, but with an important proviso that received its strongest Australian articulation in an early case before the High Court. In *Marconi's Wireless Telegraph v. Commonwealth* (1913), the Commonwealth relied upon what it claimed was a well-known doctrine: that documents relating to affairs of state were exempt from production if the head of the department having custody claimed that their disclosure would be injurious to the public interest. This privilege extended to anything in the possession of government, it was claimed, and the opinion of the department head was conclusive. A number of judges in that case, however, rejected such a sweeping claim, insisting on limits to such a privilege and on examinability by the court. It was not sufficient simply for a minister or head of department to say something was a state secret. The court would need to determine from examination of the instrument whether it was within the class of state secrets recognizable by law as exempt. With heavy irony, Chief Justice Griffith commented: "The imperfections of Judges, who are not exempt from human limitations, do not justify them in refusing to make inquiry into facts necessary for the exercise of their jurisdiction."

The judiciary's deference to the executive reached its zenith in wartime Britain. In a case involving plans and specifications for a submarine, Viscount Simon enunciated the rule that documents otherwise relevant and liable for production must not be produced if the public interest so required (*Duncan v. Cammell Laird & Co.* [1942]). But who should decide? And if it were the executive, would such ministerial decisions be reviewable by the courts? Not surprisingly, *Cammell Laird* accepted the proposition that assertion by the executive of what the public interest required was conclusive. This was the broadly accepted view at the time and would survive until the 1960s. It had been applied in an earlier Australian case, *Griffin v. South Australia* (1925), in which a majority of the High Court held that the minister or head of department was the exclusive judge of whether department documents should be produced. In a prescient dissent that recognized the growth of government, however, Justice Stark proposed a bolder role for the judiciary (401):

> The commercial activities of Australian Governments are becoming more and more extensive and the sphere of political and administrative action correspondingly wider. . . . May not this be a good reason for submitting the Australian Governments to the jurisdiction of the courts, and imposing upon them the duty of making discovery and inspection of documents according to the ordinary rules of law and practice?

The High Court's judgment was not accepted when the case went on appeal to the privy council where a stronger judicial position was staked out in *Robinson v. South Australia* (No. 2) [1931]. In that case it was held that courts would not simply accept unreasonable claims of privilege against discovery made by a minister. In an action for damages for alleged negligence concerning wheat placed under state control, an aggrieved party sought access to documents containing communications between the state officers involved. Privilege was claimed by the responsible minister in a minute stating that disclosure would be contrary to state and public interests. The privy council held that the minister's claim was insufficient because it was not made on oath, nor based upon his personal consideration of the documents, nor did it indicate the nature of the suggested injury to the public interest. The court made clear that the principle of the rule of privilege was concern for the public interest and that the rule would be interpreted strictly to apply no further than the object required. Hence, it was held that the Supreme Court of South Australia should exercise its power to inspect the documents involved.

This more assertive judicial stance finally triumphed in the landmark case *Conway v. Rimmer* [1968], which overruled *Cammell Laird*. The right of courts to inspect documents subject to claims of public interest immunity was strongly asserted. According to Lord Pearce, it was essential to put aside the broad claims of privilege "and get down to realities in weighing the respective injuries to the public of a denial of justice on the one side and, on the other, a revelation of government documents which were never intended to be made public" (986). Nevertheless, the same judge reserved a special position for cabinet documents, regarding which, he said, "production would never be ordered of cabinet correspondence, letters or reports on appointments to office of importance and the like" (987).

Similarly, Australian judges continued to give the cabinet a wide berth. In *Lanyan v. Commonwealth* (1974), the High Court upheld the claim of privilege for Commonwealth cabinet documents. In that case, Justice Menzies articulated the central problem as being one of deciding whether, without actual examination, the claim for privilege covered a class of documents including cabinet submissions and papers of the cabinet's committees and subcommittees. Except in "very special circumstances," which did not apply in this case, he allowed that such papers did belong to a class of documents "of a nature that ought not to be examined by the court" (653). Even here, however, we can see that judicial scrutiny of cabinet documents is not entirely ruled out but reserved for very special circumstances.

By the 1970s, the broad exemption previously allowed against production of departmental documents on the request of the minister or department head had been discarded by courts. But judges remained deferential to the cabinet and were prepared to give carte blanche exemption to cabinet documents. A subsequent bolder Australian Federal Court that ordered production of cabinet notebooks described this earlier period as one of "self-imposed judicial restraint" *(Commonwealth v. Northern Land Council* 1991, 51).

JUDICIAL ASSERTION OVER CABINET DOCUMENTS

Perhaps it was no coincidence that the tide of judicial thinking had turned decisively by the end of the 1970s, after the stormy period of assertive Whitlam Labor government from 1972 to 1975. There is a certain irony in the fact that in a case concerning cabinet records of the Whitlam government, *Sankey v. Whitlam* (1978), the High Court took advantage of the opportunity to sweep away the doctrine of privilege from immunity that courts had previously accorded such records.

The case arose as follows. Several years after the Whitlam government lost office and Lionel Murphy, attorney-general during the Whitlam period, had been appointed to the High Court, a Sydney solicitor brought an action for conspiracy under the New South Wales Crimes Act against Whitlam and his senior ministers, including Murphy. The charge was one of conspiring for an unlawful purpose of the commonwealth and of deceiving the governor general in "the Loans Affair," an abortive attempt by Whitlam and his senior ministers to outflank the opposition-controlled senate and borrow enormous sums of money allegedly for short-term purposes under the special provisions of section 105A of the constitution. The bungling of this matter and its protracted exposure led to the dismissal of the Whitlam government in 1975 and was a significant factor in its electoral defeat. The subsequent pursuit of Whitlam and his senior ministers through the courts was totally unprecedented and eventually abortive. Before the action was finally terminated by the Fraser Liberal government's decision to wind up proceedings, which led to the resignation of its attorney-general, Robert Ellicott, who supported the action and was eager to make cabinet records available, the High Court was asked to rule on the principle of the immunity from production of such documents.

In *Sankey v. Whitlam*, the High Court decided quite categorically that there was no class of documents exempt from judicial review and, if the balance of public interest as determined by the courts required it, production for judicial proceedings. In this instance the High Court was very conscious of the fact that it was deliberately reworking the law that previous judges had made. As Justice Stephen made clear, judge-made law relating to Crown privilege erected "no immutable classes of documents to which a so-called absolute privilege is to be accorded." On the contrary, he insisted, the essence of such law was the recognition of competing aspects of the public interest that needed to be weighed and balanced in particular instances (63-64). By reformulating the first principles governing disclosure—the need to balance competing claims in order to determine the public interest—the High Court effectively undermined the doctrine of a class of documents to be accorded absolute privilege from production. This was forcefully stated by Justice Mason: "Cabinet decisions and cabinet papers do not stand outside the general rule that requires the court to determine whether on balance the public interest calls for production or nonproduction. They stand fairly and squarely within the area of application of that rule" (96).

What was required, according to the High Court, was a process of balancing conflicting claims of public interest concerning disclosure. On the one hand, there existed a public interest in preventing the curial process from disclosing documents containing sensitive areas of government and administration. On the other hand, the proper adminis-tration of justice required that evidence necessary for particular cases be available to litigants. The only proper resolution when these conflicted, as for example in the case of criminal proceedings against former ministers of the Crown in relation to their conduct in office, was through a sensitive assessment and balancing of such interests. Therefore, blanket Crown privilege could have no justification but would need to be weighed against the interests of disclosure in particular circumstances. And most importantly of all, although this was taken for granted rather than argued, it was the judiciary's role and prerogative to do the assessing and balancing and have the final say.

The sea change effected by the High Court in *Sankey v. Whitlam* was reflected in a number of subsequent Australian cases and paralleled by a somewhat similar, but more incremental, development of doctrine by British courts (in *Burmah Oil v. Bank of England* [1980] and *Air Canada v. Secretary of State for Trade* [1983]). Hence, the *Northern Land Council* case (1991) in which the Australian Federal Court ordered the production of 126 cabinet notebooks was not a radical departure in the doctrine of judicial oversight of sensitive executive documents but the boldest instance of its exercise within the expanded domain of judicial review.

In reviewing the development of judicial doctrine from earlier restraint to vigorous oversight, the Federal Court characterized the earlier concession of public interest immunity as "a self-imposed judicial restraint" (51, 79). The "true position" in Australia was now that of "the balancing of competing interests," as articulated by Peter Hogg:

Every claim has to be considered on its own merits. It involves three judgments: (1) How much injury would be caused to executive interests by disclosing the evidence? (2) How much injury would be caused to the interests of justice by withholding the evidence? (3) Which interests should prevail? A minister can answer (1) but he cannot answer (2) or (3), and therefore his decision should not be treated as conclusive. (Hogg 1989, 68)

In the *Northern Land Council* case, the Northern Land Council, representing traditional owners, sought revision of an agreement, claiming it was made under duress and as a result of breaches of fiduciary duties owed to Aboriginal people by the Commonwealth. The government had sold short Aboriginal interests, it was claimed, in rushing through a settlement with a mining company that gave the go-ahead for the Ranger uranium mine at Jabiru in the Northern Territory in exchange for modest royalties, part of which would be paid to the traditional Aboriginal owners. A Federal Court judge had ordered production of the 126 cabinet notebooks for inspection. The Common-wealth appealed to the full bench of the Federal Court, arguing exemp-tion because of the need to protect cabinet secrecy and collective responsibility.

The Federal Court adopted the role sanctioned in *Sankey v. Whitlam* of recognizing competing aspects of the public interest and took responsibility for weighing these. In deciding whether documents for which public interest immunity was claimed should be produced, it was held that the judge might inspect the documents or if, as in this case, they were too voluminous, allow confidential inspection by the legal advisers to the litigating parties (*Commonwealth v. Northern Land Council* 1991). The Commonwealth government appealed this decision to the High Court and, in the meantime, introduced legislation into Parliament prohibiting disclosure of cabinet notebooks, except those under review in this case, in any court proceedings (Cabinet Notebooks (Access and Protection) Bill of 1992). This legislation was allowed to lapse, however, when the High Court found in the Commonwealth's favor in *Commonwealth v. Northern Land Council* (1993).

In finding in the Commonwealth's favor, the High Court majority in a joint opinion acknowledged that there were strong considerations of public policy militating against the disclosure of cabinet documents regardless of their content. The court said: "It is only in a case where there are quite exceptional circumstances which give rise to a significant likelihood that the public interest in the proper administration of justice outweighs the very high public interest in the confidentiality of documents recording cabinet deliberations that it will be necessary or appropriate to order production of the documents to the court"(415). Moreover, it was necessary for the judge to decide and not appropriate to allow access to the litigant's lawyers before the court had made a ruling, as had been ordered by the trial judge in this case. The High Court envisaged that disclosure of cabinet documents would probably always be unwarranted in civil proceedings and only warranted in cases of allegations of serious misconduct on the part of cabinet ministers. Such generous weighting in favor of cabinet secrecy went somewhat against the grain of recent trends and surprised many observers, with one major daily accusing the court of "overbalancing on cabinet records" (*Canberra Times* Editorial, April 24, 1993).   Nevertheless, the High Court reiterated that it was for the courts to decide and that cabinet documents were not immune from judicial review: "Whatever the position may have been in the past, the immunity from disclosure of documents falling within such a class is not absolute" (413).

CONCLUSION

The modern Australian cabinet is no longer the small and highly secret body that Bagehot described, but a complex organization with routinized processes for submissions, recording of proceedings and decisions, and preservation of documents. Despite such growth and bureaucratization, the cabinet does retain the central features of collective responsibility and secrecy, which remain crucial to its functioning. Until the 1970s, the courts exempted government departments generally and cabinets in particular from judicial
scrutiny, accepting at face value ministerial claims by the minister, or even the department head, of immunity from production of records on the grounds of public interest. As blanket exemption for such a broad class of documents was whittled down through the judiciary's requiring a balancing of aspects of the public interest, the cabinet remained sacrosanct. However, that changed dramatically in *Sankey v. Whitlam* with the High Court insisting that there was no class of exempt documents, not even those of the cabinet. Rather, it was the duty of the courts to balance the competing claims of public interest and decide for

or against disclosure in a particular case. In overturning the Federal Court's ruling on disclosure of cabinet notebooks, the High Court nevertheless reaffirmed the right of the courts to determine such matters. At a time when there is a good deal of concern about increasing executive dominance, particularly among the judiciary, this rather bold extension of judicial oversight to the cabinet itself represents a significant counterbalance. It fits with the larger pattern of the increased judicialization of Australian politics evident in the New Administrative Law.

REFERENCES

BOOKS, ARTICLES, AND PAPERS

Administrative Law Forum. 1991. Papers from the 1991 Administrative Law Conference, *Canberra Bulletin of Public Administration*. No. 66.

Administrative Law Seminar. 1989. Papers from the 1987 Administrative Law Seminar, *Canberra Bulletin of Public Administration*. No. 58.

Bagehot, Walter. 1963. *The English Constitution*. 1867. Reprint Collins/Fontana.

Cabinet Handbook. 1991. Department of Prime Minister and Cabinet, Australian Government Publishing Service, Canberra.

Canberra Bulletin of Public Administration. 1988. "Making the New Machinery of Government Work." No. 54, Special issue.

Codd, Michael. 1990. "Cabinet Operations of the Australian Government." In Brian Galligan and J. R. Nethercote, eds. *Decision-making in Australian Government: The Cabinet and Budget Processes*. Federalism Research Center, Australian National University, Canberra.

Constitutional Commission. 1988. *Final Report of the Constitutional Commission*, Volumes 1 and 2, Australian Government Publishing Service, Canberra.

Crisp, L. F. 1978. *Australian National Government*. 4th ed. Melbourne: Longman Cheshire.

Galligan, Brian. 1987. *Politics of the High Court*. St. Lucia: University of Queensland Press.

――――. 1991. "Judicial Activism in Australia." In *Judicial Activism in Comparative Perspective*, ed. Kenneth M. Holland. Macmillan, London.

Hawke, Robert. 1987. Prime Minister's Media Release. 11 August.

――――. 1988. Sir Robert Garran Oration. Mimeographed. Melbourne.

Hogg, Peter. 1989. *Liability of the Crown*. 2d ed. Toronto: Carswell.

Mackintosh, John. 1968. *The British Cabinet*. 2nd ed. London: Stevens.

Munro, B. 1975. "Law and Conventions Distinguished." *Law Quarterly Review*, 91.

Quick, J. and R. R. Garran. 1901. *The Annotated Constitution of the Australian Commonwealth*. Sydney: Angus & Robertson.

Solomon, David. 1992. *The Political Impact of the High Court*. Sydney: Allen and Unwin.

Cases

Air Canada v. Secretary of State for Trade (1983) AC 394.

Attorney-General v. Jonathan Cape Ltd (1976) 1 QB 752.

Burmah Oil Co. Ltd v. Bank of England (1980) AC 1090.

Commonwealth v. Northern Land Council (1991) 103 ALR 267.

Commonwealth v. Northern Land Council (1993) 112 ALR 409.

Conway v. Rimmer (1968) AC 9 10.

Duncan v. Cammell Laird & Co. Ltd (1942) AC 642.

FAI Insurances Ltd v. Winneke (1982) 151 CLR 342.

Griffin v. South Australia (1925) 36 CLR 378.

Lanyan Pty Ltd v. The Commonwealth (1974) 129 CLR 650.

Marconi's Wireless Telegraph co. Ltd v. The Commonwealth (1913) 16 CLR 178.

Robinson v. South Australia No. 2. (1931) AC 704.

Sankey v. Whitlam (1978) 142 CLR 1.

Whitlam v. Australian Consolidated Press Limited (1985) 73 FLR 414.

7.

The Executive, the Judiciary, and Immigration Appeals in Australia

JOHN POWER

In this chapter I analyze a case of policy development that would prima facie seem to offer support for the global expansion of judicial power. In the space of a decade or so, a traditionally bureaucratized policy field was "invaded" by a new policy community led by judges. The field was subsequently restructured and its decision-making processes considerably changed. It is thus my purpose to assess the extent to which the new judicially led policy community was influential in the shaping of the field that it had invaded.

Between the years 1976 and 1989, the Australian policy field of immigration and deportation appeals and complaints was substantially restructured. For the first three decades of the nation's massive post-World War II immigration program, the field had remained simple and dominated by a single Commonwealth department. The long-standing arrangement could usefully be characterized as one of "politically tempered bureaucracy" (Power 1992). There was no Australian equivalent of either the U.S. Board of Immigration Appeals or the United Kingdom Immigration Appeal Tribunal. The department handled virtually all complaints about and appeals against its decisions through internal bureaucratic mechanisms. However, this system was significantly tempered politically, because successive ministers could review the decisions of these mechanisms, and some were quite active in responding to pressures from their parliamentary colleagues for the reversal of many of these decisions. The program was thus administered in ways that allowed ample scope for discretion, both at the ministerial and the departmental levels. Formal appeals against such discretionary decisions were rare and expensive, as they went to the nation's peak tribunal, the High Court and thus were largely restricted to highly political cases. However, two streams of reform came together in 1977 to begin the process of limiting discretion.

After an initial surge of reform activity in that year, there was a short pause and then another lesser surge in the years 1981-1983. The greatly increased institutional complexity caused by these two reform surges led ultimately to major legislative changes in 1989. As we shall see, the 1989 reforms significantly improved the overall "shape" of the policy field, without much diminishing its institutional complexity.

The period from 1977 to the present may conveniently be divided into three phases, each commencing with significant sets of reforms.

PHASE ONE (1977-1981)[1]

Of the two reform streams that surfaced in 1977, the strongest was that of the New Administrative Law (NAL) (Pearce 1986; Sharpe 1986; Taggart 1986; Allars 1990; Tomasic and Fleming 1991; Thompson and Paterson 1991; *Canberra Bulletin of Public Administration* 1989 and 1991; Power 1992). This produced in the single year of 1977 three important institutions. The first of these was the Administrative Review Council (ARC), which was established to exercise oversight of the systemic functioning of institutions reviewing administrative decision and action and to develop proposals for structural reform.

For some years, review mechanisms had been proliferating in a number of line agencies (but less slowly in the field of immigration), and the ARC was concerned to effect a measure of rationalization through the establishment of the second of the new mechanisms, the Administrative Appeals Tribunal (AAT).

Although the AAT was designed as a generalist review mechanism, it was not initially given a generalized grant of authority. Rather, its jurisdiction was to be expanded gradually, through successive legislative enactments in various policy fields. The most important of these fields, not surprisingly, turned out to be those of social security and taxation, and the AAT's primary responsibility in immigration has continued to be the proffering of advice to the minister on the deportation of convicted criminals, a numerically small but politically sensitive class of cases.

The third mechanism to emerge from the NAL reform stream was that of the ombudsman. The role of this officer, like that of the member of parliament, is to seek the resolution of problems experienced by members of the public in their dealings with public bureaucracies. This is in some senses a residual role, for the ombudsman has attempted to avoid undue overlap with the jurisdictions of other complaints and appeals mechanisms. In particular, the ombudsman is concerned with the identification of and the pursuit of redress for administrative inefficiencies, undue delays, and ill-considered decisions by officials. His powers are advisory, rather than determinative, and appeals and complaints about immigration procedures and decisions did not loom large in his early years, largely because the roles of the parliamentarian and minister for some time remained prominent in this field.

A final mechanism created in 1977 was a product, not of the NAL reform stream, but rather of a stream within the field of immigration policy: the department had begun to be subjected to considerable pressures from the demographically increasingly volatile region of Indochina. A new mechanism was deemed necessary for the determination of policies and practices on the admission of refugees. As this function was one of considerable political—and indeed diplomatic—sensitivity, the Determination of Refugee Status (DORS) Committee contained representatives from a number of interested Commonwealth departments (such as attorney-general's and foreign affairs). In its early years, DORS proceeded very much on a case-by-case basis (although it has recently been reconstituted with a broader review remit as the Refugee Status Review Committee [RSRC]).

Taken together, these new mechanisms initially covered a fairly narrow segment of the field of immigration and deportation complaints and appeals. Further, in this narrow segment—including criminal deportations, refugees and administrative irregularities—the judicial style of appellate review was only lightly in evidence. In the following phase, this was to change, as was the proportion of the field that came to be affected by the two reform streams.

PHASE TWO (1981-1989)

The early years of the decade of the 1980s witnessed a considerable increase in the complexity of the institutional ecology of immigration and deportation appeals. In 1980 the Federal Court gained a significant entree to the field through an amendment to the Migration Act. In the next year the Human Rights Commission (HRC) was established (and was to be reconstituted in 1986 as the Human Rights and Equal Opportunity Commission, HREOC), to be followed in 1982 by nonstatutory, advisory Immigration Review Panels (IRPs).

The first two of these initiatives brought to five the number of NAL institutions with some role in the field of immigration and deportation appeals. Because all five were led either by judges or academic lawyers, with a good deal of cross-membership between them, they may plausibly be claimed to constitute an administrative law policy community (although the HREOC has always been marginal to both the administrative law community and to the field of immigration appeals).

The last of the initiatives belonged in the second of the reform streams and represented the first attempt by the government to provide an extradepartmental mechanism for the review of the great majority of decisions (that is, those concerning relatively straightforward applications for immigration entry permits).

As the decade progressed the judges on the Federal Court and the AAT became increasingly assertive. The attention of the Federal Court was directed most closely to a new paragraph in the act, which required there to be "strong compassionate or humanitarian grounds" if a noncitizen already in Australia were to be accorded the benefit of a permanent entry permit. In administering this provision, the department initially took the view that one of the important compassionate or humanitarian grounds would be provided by the existence of "gross and discriminatory denial of fundamental freedoms and basic human rights" in the applicant's country of origin. As the decade progressed, the court substantially liberalized this policy in a series of decisions that ended in the conclusion that the primary basis for assessing the extent of denial of freedoms and rights was provided by the standards of the average person not in the country of origin but in Australia. As one well-placed observer noted (Arthur 1991), the effect of this series of decisions was the demolition of a small but significant part of the department's policy structure.

During the same phase, the Administrative Appeals Tribunal (led by Federal Court justices) was also asserting itself. The most important part of the niche that the AAT had been given by amendments to the Migration Act was concerned with the making of recommendations to the minister considering deportation of noncitizens convicted of serious crime (especially if it concerned dealing in hard drugs). In this niche, unlike the others that it came to occupy in other policy fields, the AAT did not have the power to override a ministerial decision, though it could, and did, express the view in some cases that a ministerial decision had been inconsistent with the minister's own stated policy (Sharpe 1986). In view of the great political significance of deportations, the AAT's role was restricted to that of tendering advice to responsible ministers, but early recipients of such advice nearly always followed it. The administrative law community soon succeeded in crystallizing this practice into a convention. Thus, as early as 1982 "the then Minister, Mr. Ian McPhee, revealed that in the period from the establishment of the Tribunal until that time there had been thirty cases in which the Tribunal had recommended the revocation of a deportation order. The recommendation had been accepted in twenty-seven of those cases." Further, "on no occasion between 1983 and 1987, did the Minister decline to accept a recommendation by the Tribunal to revoke a deportation order" (Wilcox 1990, 144-45).

There were, however, persisting difficulties with this convention. Both the AAT and the department of immigration had firm and stable positions on deportation, and these were in conflict. The minister, being in the middle, could maintain the convention only at the expense of this department's line.

The convention finally broke in 1987, and in the succeeding two years, the majority of AAT recommendations on deportations were refused by two successive ministers. It is hard to determine the reason why the convention broke at that time, although a substantial part of the explanation may be found in Sharpe's argument that the AAT's understandable sensitivity to the rights of prospective deportees might well have promoted the incremental development of policies that could have seriously impacted on administration overall (Sharpe 1986, 197-98). In view of this experience, it was not surprising that the government was unreceptive to arguments that the powers of the AAT should be widened in the field of immigration policy. Wilcox, for example, had in 1988 put forward a strong case for the reform of the system that had handled the much larger population of potential deportees, those who were not criminals but had simply overstayed the official welcome (Wilcox 1990, 143). Members of this population, he argued, would be much more likely to have their cases determined on their merits by the AAT than by the Federal Court (to whom many had desperate but usually hopeless recourse, unless they succeeded in establishing themselves in the small minority that could plausibly base their cases on compassionate or humanitarian grounds). Fearing the policy consequences of such a reform, the government, as we shall shortly see, moved in 1989 in a different direction.

An even more significant widening of the authority of the AAT had earlier been advocated by both the Human Rights Commission (HRC 1985) and the Administrative Review Council (ARC 1986). After expressing strong criticism of the functioning of the Immigration Review Panel's, both the commission and the council advocated the introduction of a two-tier review system, with the AAT occupying the upper tier. This recommendation, which was subsequently endorsed in the report of the influential Committee to Advise on Australia's Immigration Policies (1988), also proved to be unacceptable to the government.

By the end of the decade, then, pressures for major reform were strengthening. At the macrolevel, the processing of large numbers of applications (running at close to one third million a year) stood in need of an objective and autonomous review mechanism. At the micro-level—in such significant areas as criminal deportations and the granting of permanent-entry permits to noncitizens already in the country—serious disjunctions had opened up between the policies of the bureaucracy, on the one hand, and the determinations of the administrative law policy community, on the other. The minister of the day determined to put together a major reform package, which was eventually incorporated into legislative changes at the very end of the decade.

PHASE THREE (1989-PRESENT)

The central thrust of the 1989 reform was a determined attempt to minimize bureaucratic (and ministerial) discretion and to substitute wherever possible rule-based decision-making. Although this strategy was publicly justified in terms of enhanced equity and effectiveness, it also carried with it the useful political side-benefit of considerably narrowing the scope for future judicial assertiveness.

The centerpiece of this strategy was the introduction of a two-tier review system. The first tier was occupied by an internal departmental unit (the Migration Internal Review Office [MIRO]); the second by an independent statutory body, the Immigration Review Tribunal (IRT). As this body was given the charge of being "fair, just, economical, informal and quick" (O'Neil 1991) it clearly did not fit comfortably into the administrative law policy community, at least as that community had developed in Australia.   Instead, it has devoted great care to the identification of the ways in which it might move away from the adversarial system that has for so long characterized Australian law (and politics!). Its concerns have included, among others, the fashioning of appropriate procedures that, it is claimed, draw significantly from the "Romano-Germanic" tradition (Certoma 1991); creating architectural designs that facilitate informal interaction; and selecting members so that half are from non-English-speaking backgrounds and nearly half are women.

The IRT has been compared by one of its members (Karas 1990) with other similar bodies operating in the different bureaucratic jurisdictions of veterans' affairs and social security. It also bears some close resemblances to some of the state equal opportunity commissions which, unlike their Commonwealth counterpart, have been only partially absorbed into the administrative law policy community. The IRT may thus be fairly characterized as an important new member of an emergent complaints and appeals processing network.

One further initiative in the 1989 package requires attention, if only because it has proven more durable than the government had initially intended. In order to rally parliamentary support for its reforms, the government sponsored the establishment of a Joint Select Committee on Migration Regulations, which was supposed to complete a review of all regulations in the short period of six months. Because this proved infeasible, and because of continuing parliamentary nervousness about the government's strategy of shifting to rule-based decision making, the committee was retained as a standing body. In the succeeding three years, however, the committee has not concerned itself so much with the careful scrutiny of bureaucratic rule making, but instead has to date produced reports on such high-profile policy areas as the effects that marriage and de facto relationships should have on change of immigration status and the establishment of criteria for the determination of refugee status.

NINE INSTITUTIONAL NICHES IN THE POLICY FIELD

In numerical terms, the three largest niches in the contemporary institutional ecology are those occupied by the departmental bureaucracy, the MIRO/IRT system, and the ombudsman. The middle pair are concerned with reviews of the bulk of appeals that have been lodged against the mainstream of bureaucratic decisions on immigration applications; the last is concerned with complaints about the unsatisfactory nature of the procedures used in the making of these mainstream decisions.

Two niches of especial political sensitivity are occupied by the Refugee Status Rights Commission and Determination of Refugee Status Operations Branch—for the making and reviewing of applications for refugee status[2]—and the Administrative Appeals Tribunal, for the making of recommendations on prospective criminal deportations. (This latter function may yet pass to the IRT.)

Two further smaller niches of particular relevance to civil and human rights and entitlements are occupied by the Federal and (occasionally) High Courts, and the Human Rights Commission and Equal Rights and Equal Opportunity Commission. The former pair of institutions are especially concerned to ensure that the minister and his bureaucracy act reasonably within the powers and in accordance with the provisions of their statutes. Even seemingly absolute ministerial discretion have on occasion been deemed to have been limited by the requirements of natural justice. The latter institution is concerned with remedying anomalies not easily addressed through the courts and other review mechanisms (such as that which arose in 1988 when a woman who had been informally adopted had initially been refused the permanent residency accorded the other members of her family).

Finally, we may identify two niches of especial concern to the legislature—that of bipartisan policy development and that of open and democratic scrutiny of the ever-changing and complex sets of bureaucratic regulations. To date, the Parliament's Joint Standing Committee on Migration Regulations, which was intended to occupy the latter of these niches, has preferred to busy itself with the pursuit of issues in the former. To some extent, the function of regulation review has been performed as a by-product of the IRT's activities, but this development cannot in itself suffice to fill the niche of open and explicit review by elected representatives. It may thus unfortunately be the case that there is one significant continuing gap in an institutional ecology that for the most part appears now to be adequately, if untidily, covering its field of policy.

CONCLUSION

The foregoing analysis would suggest that such judicialization as has occurred has been more pronounced in the sphere of administration than in that of politics and has taken the weaker of the two forms identified by Vallinder "the spread of judicial decision-making methods outside the judicial province proper." Despite the relative assertiveness of the New Administrative Law judges, which seems to have been greater than that of their United Kingdom and U.S. colleagues (Legomsky 1987), there has been little expansion in the province of the courts. There can be little doubt, however, that pressures from the NAL policy community have had a significant influence on the reshaping of the field of immigration and deportation appeals and complaints. But how, one might ask, did the NAL community come to develop so influential a reform agenda?

In the absence of an authoritative political history of the NAL movement, this chapter can offer only a most speculative preliminary account (which ends up with a surprisingly anthropological flavor).

The most notable feature of the NAL movement in its early years was the dominance of lawyers trained in a single school—that of the University of Sydney (in the oldest and most populous of the Australian states, New South Wales).

Thus, there were three major committees that in the late 1960s and early 1970s fashioned the set of NAL institutions: the Commonwealth Administrative Review Committee (1968-1971), the Committee on Prerogative Writ Procedures (1971-1973), and the Committee on Administrative Discretion (1971-1973). Among them, these contained eight members[3] of whom all but one were Sydney-trained. As a group, these eight lawyers spanned the spheres of politics, administration, and the judiciary. Six had held senior positions in the Commonwealth public service and, of these, two were former solicitors-general. One (Hon. Robert Ellicott) was to become a Liberal attorney-general and later a Federal Court justice. Another (Hon. Sir Anthony Mason) is the current chief justice of the High Court. The one "outsider" in the group, Mr. Peter Bailey, clearly needed outstanding qualification to compensate for his University of Melbourne qualifications. The son of a former solicitor-general and University of Melbourne law professor Sir Kenneth Bailey, he was soon to become a member of the prestigious Coombs Royal Commission on Australian Government Administration and later to play a central role in the establishment of the Human Rights Commission. The linkages with the Liberal side of politics did not stop with Ellicott, for he was the nephew of another former Liberal attorney-general and the then chief justice, Sir Garfield Barwick, and another member, Sir Henry Bland, was the son of the noted University of Sydney professor of public administration and later Liberal M.P., F. A. Bland. One further member of the group, and the chair of the most important of the three committees, was soon to achieve a central place in Australian political history. This was Sir John Kerr, who in 1975 dismissed the Labor prime minister, Gough Whitlam—yet another, but very different, product of the Sydney Law School (and a son of yet another senior Commonwealth law officer).

Although it would obviously be most improper to associate all eight members of the group with the events of 1975, in which only Kerr and Ellicott (together with Barwick) were publicly involved, it is possible to trace some connections between the underlying tenets of the definition of the role of the governor-general that emerged in 1975, on the one hand, and of the NAL, on the other. Both stressed the values of what one might term liberal constitutionalism, in the face of what was seen as an overweening executive branch. If the protection of a putative public interest brought the primary guardians of that interest (the governor-general and the judiciary) into conflict with the political executive—and even with the House of Representatives in which it was based—so much the worse for that executive.

Although the NAL initiatives were not nearly as spectacular as the 1975 dismissal, their long-term significance for the quality of Australian governance is undoubtedly greater. Thus, Malcolm Fraser, the Liberal prime minister who came to power as a result of that dismissal, considered the installation and consolidation of the full set of NAL mechanisms to have been the greatest accomplishment of his seven years in office.

But why, it may be asked in conclusion, was Sydney so prominent in this reform movement? All that can be suggested here is that the alienation of the liberal establishment from the executive branch has, at the State level, been more severe in New South Wales than elsewhere. Halligan and I (1992) argue that long periods of traditional Labor rule by politicians of overwhelmingly Irish extraction produced in that state a "bureaucratist' regime, in which the interests of subordinate staff and their unions came to predominate in Crozierian public bureaucracies. Decades of such a Bureaucratist regime might well have produced a climate of liberal reform in the Sydney Law School. Having been exposed to that climate in their early training,[4] post-war cohorts of reform-minded law graduates found that the most promising opportunities awaited them in the rapidly expanding "administrationist' regime that was emerging at the Commonwealth level during 23 uninterrupted Anglophile Liberal years from 1949 to 1972. Over a relatively short time span, these reformers generated a momentum that took Australia, in several fields of policy, including that of immigration and deportation, well beyond the practices of the British "homeland."

NOTES

1. Although the purpose of this chapter differs clearly from that of its companion (Power 1992), the discussion of the phases of reform of the policy field has much common ground.

2. At the time of writing, refugee policy had moved to the very center of the political stage. As the result of an emotional prime ministerial intervention in the aftermath of the Tiananmen Square massacre of 1990, the government committed itself to granting 20,000 Chinese students initial four-year residence visas. In April 1992 it was announced that these students were to be accorded permanent residency status (Masanauskas 1992), thus in one stroke consuming the equivalent of a normal year's refugee intake. This announcement came in the midst of a continuing controversy about the government's attempt to repatriate hundreds of Cambodian boat people.

3. Two of these, Professor Harry Whitmore and Hon. Robert Ellicott, served on two of the committees.

4. So far as I have been able to discover, the climate was not created by the forceful teachings of a reform-minded professor. Rather, it may have been the outcome of the particularly strong linkages between the spheres of practice and learning that have themselves been fashioned by an unusual ecology. Uniquely in Australia, the Sydney Law School has for long been located in the downtown legal heartland.

References

Administrative Review Council. 1986. *Review of Migration Decisions: Report to the Attorney-General.* Canberra: Australian Government Publishing Service.

Allars, Margaret. 1990. *Introduction to Australian Administrative Law.* Sydney: Butterworths.

Arthur, Evan. 1991. "The Impact of Administrative Law on Humanitarian Decision-Making," *Canberra Bulletin of Public Administration.* No. 66. October.

Canberra Bulletin of Public Administration. 1989. "Administrative Law: Retrospect and Prospect." No. 58. April.

———. 1991. "Fair and Open Decision-making; Administrative Law Forum." No. 66, October.

Certoma, Leroy. 1991. "The Non-Adversarial Administrative Process and the Immigration Review Tribunal." Unpublished paper.

Committee to Advise on Australia's Immigration Policies. 1988. *Report.* (Chair: S. Fitzgerald.) Canberra: Australian Government Publishing Service.

Halligan, John and John Power. 1992. *Political Management in the 1990's.* Melbourne: Oxford University Press,

Human Rights Commission. 1985. *Human Rights and the Migration Act 1958.* Report No. 13., Australian Government Publishing Service.

Karas, Steve. 1990. "Australia's Immigration Law and the Immigration Review Tribunal: A Synopsis," *The Queensland Lawyer.* 11 August.

Legomsky, Stephen H. 1987. *Immigration and the Judiciary: Law and Politics in Britain and America.* Oxford: Clarendon Press.

Masanauskas, John. 1992. "Tiananmen Students to Stay Permanently." *The Age.* 27 April, 1.

O'Neil, Pamela. 1991. "Do Review Bodies Lead to Better Decision-making?" *Canberra Bulletin of Public Administration.* No. 66. October.

Pearce, D. C. 1986. *Commonwealth Administrative Law.* Sydney: Butterworths.

Power, John. 1992. "The Institutional Ecology of Administrative Appeals in Australia: With Particular Reference to Immigration and Deportation." Paper presented to the 22d International Congress of Administrative Sciences, July, Vienna.

Rhodes, R. A. W. and David Marsh. 1992. "New Directions in the Study of Policy Networks." *European Journal of Political Research* 21:181-205.

Sharpe, Jennifer M. 1986. *The Administrative Appeals Tribunal and Policy Review*. Sydney: Law Book Company.

Taggart, Michael, ed. 1986. *Judicial Review of Administrative Action in the 1980's—Problems and Prospects*. Auckland, Melbourne: Oxford University Press, in association with the Legal Research Foundation, Inc.

Thompson, Ian and Moira Paterson. 1991. "The Federal Administrative Appeals Tribunal and Policy Review: A Re-assessment of the Controversy." *Public Law Review*. December.

Tomasic, Roman and Don Fleming. 1991. *Australian Administrative Law*. Sydney: Law Book Company.

Wilcox, Murray. 1990. "Judicial and Administrative Review." In *Public Administration in Australia: A Watershed*, ed. John Power. Sydney: Hale and Iremonger, in association with the Royal Australian Institute of Public Administration.

Canada

8.

Social Progress and Judicial Power in Canada

W. A. Bogart

"[I]t is simply not true that a politician must lie or intrigue. That is utter nonsense, very often spread about by people who—for whatever reasons—wish to discourage others from taking an interest in public affairs."

—Václav Havel, 1992

There is a certain telling skepticism in Canada about the benefits of litigation. Ironically, these reservations are of often expressed most strongly concerning social reform on behalf of the disadvantaged, the very groups and individuals who it is claimed are most likely to need the courts' protection from insensitive majorities. At stake are two very different models of democracy. The first recognizes the power of the ballot, but a ballot curbed by independent and tenured judges who, removed from the fray, will ensure that rationality and principle are never ejected by impetuous legislatures, rigid bureaucracies, and a dulled citizenry. In this depiction courts will shelter the disadvantaged, who will harness that rationality and principle to prevail. The second places its confidence in those who can claim the power of the ballot. Realistic about democracy's foibles, it is even more reserved about curing them by judicial intervention. In this version judges' independence and tenure make them unaccountable, elitist, and, at present in any event, unrepresentative. The apprehension is that, far from invigorating democracy, judicial review will sap it because of regressive decisions; progressive decisions that, nonetheless, blunt popular responses to societal problems; and barriers to access because of the costs of litigation. In this second construction those seeking social reform may have the most to lose at the hand of the courts.

I might have subtitled this chapter "Speculation," because making hard pronouncements about the differences an entrenched rights document will make, particularly over the long haul, is obviously impossible. But such uncertainty is at least as much a basis for a skeptical attitude as it is for olympian pronouncements about the benefits of judges in our lives. I could have titled it "Speculation" also because to judge the impact of litigation upon any society is to enter the realm of cause and effect, a tricky issue if ever there was one, perhaps particularly in terms of social and political ordering. But if the issue of cause and effect is difficult to measure, its complexities reside on both sides of the debate. Skepticism in the face of such uncertainty is no less reasonable than assured declarations that Canada has been on the road to betterment since 1982.

Meanwhile, the Canadian public is continually bombarded with claims about the importance of the Charter and, indeed, of all litigation in their lives. Within legal circles it is a self-evident proposition that "as the Charter evolves so evolves Canada" (Canadian Bar Association and Federal Department of Justice 1992). But spectacular claims appear in the general media as well. A recent front-page story in a national newspaper included a four-column picture of the present chief justice, entitled "Top Court Becomes Supreme Player," and quoted him as saying that the introduction of the Charter "has been nothing less than a revolution on the scale of the introduction of the metric system, the great medical discoveries of Louis Pasteur, and the invention of penicillin and the laser" (Sallot 1992a, 1992b). It will be noted that no upheaval of less benign consequences made the chief justice's list.[1]

PERSPECTIVES ON LITIGATION:
WE OF THE "PRAGMATIC AND EMPIRICAL"

"We could tear up the goddam country by this action but we're going to do it anyway"

—Pierre Trudeau on the
Constitutional reformulation, 1982

The Charter and the Rise of the Legitimacy Debate

Notwithstanding the extravagance of some of the statements just quoted, in many ways the Charter will forever be a divide. Certainly this is the case in terms of Canadians *thinking* about litigation. Before its coming little effort was expended debating the politics of law, and especially the political consequences of litigation. True, there were notable exceptions,[2] such as Weiler's full length study of the Supreme Court, but even this book focused more on the court's need to be reflective and forthright about the values animating its decisions than on the impact of its activity (Weiler 1974). Only a few, such as political scientists Donald Smiley (1982) and Peter Russell (1975), were focusing upon the implications of judicial power and in doing so warning about its limitations. Russell's article on the occasion of the hundredth anniversary of the Supreme Court (1975, 593) discussed the court's troubled history with civil liberties and warned against extravagant entanglements with Locke and the exaggerated notions about legal rights that could follow:[3]

> [The approach] which is truest to our experience and most in keeping with our capabilities is that of Edmund Burke, not John Locke. Canadians—neither their judges, nor their politicians—are creatures of the Enlightenment. Their forte is not abstract, rationalist philosophising. The American Republic may be built on self-evident principles and universal rights, but Canadian political and legal thought is far more pragmatic and empirical.

We, of course, took a different route, one that has created a paradox for courts: the moment of the greatest increase in the curial function has resulted in their greatest exposure in terms of debate about their role, about the legitimacy of their function. That this legitimacy debate exists is clear as arguments proceed about entrenchment of a right to property; about calls for increased use of the section 33 override, on the one hand, and its dismantling, on the other; about attempts to create a social charter not necessarily administered by judges; and, most prominently, about Quebec's wholesale exclusion/abstention from the 1982 pact and attempts to bring it back that swirl about us as the country is immersed in yet another round of constitutional maneuvering.

The legitimacy debate extends to the very role of the judiciary and the Charter. It is often viewed through its most extreme poles and is often given a stark two-dimensional cast: curial pronouncement is the most principled expression of values; or the judges are marauders oppressing democratic, egalitarian values. But in fact there are several strands to these often heated and frequently complex conversations, and I wish briefly to discuss them. I will not do justice to their richness and variety, but even a cursory analysis can demonstrate that they shed a great deal of light on the spectrum of opinion on the judicial role in Canada.

Before discussing these strands it is important to respond to the assertion that, since Americans have long had discussions about the limits of the judicial role, a legitimacy debate is just part and parcel of any entrenched rights document. But here may be a sharp difference: our debate questions the judicial role itself, whereas the American discussion is essentially about the mapping of that territory and its borders. This is not to suggest that there are not familiar echoes in each debate but there is an essential element to Americans' view of their Bill of Rights and judges as its agents that we may be missing. Unlike us, American have long accepted a vibrant strain of liberal individualism as the guiding ideology in their governance. Such a set of beliefs not only complements an entrenched bill of rights; it may be a necessary precondition for its acceptance: "[J]udicial review as it has worked in America would be inconceivable without the national acceptance of the Lockian creed, ultimately enshrined in the constitution. . . . The removal of high policy to the realm of adjudication implies a prior recognition of the principles to be legally interpreted" (Hartz 1955, 9). It may be too stark, but nevertheless instructive, to suggest that fundamental agreement about ideology ensures fundamental agreement about the judicial role; in its absence, however, the legitimacy debate is assured a long and vigorous existence.

The Strands of the Debate

The Charter, of course, has many champions, and the claims for it of the most unqualified enthusiasts are high indeed. Dubbed "Charterphiles," they "[a]t an abstract level . . . believe that the Charter enshrines Canada's most important political truths and principles and, therefore, ought to be interpreted in the most generous manner" (Morton, Russell, and Withey 1991, 6). Stern warnings are delivered from the group about any tendency on the part of the courts to deviate from a strong interventionist stance to promote progressive—but unswerving liberal—values (Beatty 1990; Beatty and Kenett 1988). Section 33 (the power of the legislatures to override judicial decisions in some instances) is anathema and must go, since it is an affront to courts as guardians of these fundamental precepts, and all issues of justice housed in the Charter should receive responses "ultimately ajudicable" (Whyte 1990; see also Dyzenhaus 1989).

At the opposite end, mostly dominated by self-styled leftists, is a movement excoriating courts at every turn (see Fudge 1987; Glasbeek 1989; Hutchinson 1987; Ison 1985; Mandel 1989; Martin 1991; Petter 1986). The vehemence against the judges arises not from satisfaction with the political process in Canada but rather from the fact that rule by the judges subverts any prospect of the flowering of true democracy, which "means the greatest possible engagement by people in the greatest possible range of communal tasks and public action" (Hutchinson and Monahan 1987, 119). In this conception the Charter is a "reflection of the inherent contradiction of liberal ideology" (Hutchinson and Petter 1988, 283). Such advocates are short on what would occur with this bursting forth of true democracy (Galloway 1988). They have unquestionably contributed to the vigor of the debate with their stark and trenchant criticism, but it is probably safe to suggest that calls by some proponents for "street theater"[4]—in the interim—will provide limited inspiration.

But there are important variants in between that support or at least accept the Charter but with a great deal of apprehension about how lawyers and judges will use it: "The danger of the Charter is not that it results in decisions that run counter to the will of the majority but that it may foster a political process in which ordinary citizens leave questions of justice to lawyers and judges and thereby withdraw from the central activity of human politics" (Russell 1992). In this conception the legislative override in section 33 is essential to maintain balance in the valuing of important social and political issues between popular and legal actors but is accompanied by anxiety about whether "we have the intelligence and courage to use it" (Russell 1992; see also Russell and Weiler 1989)[5] The hope is that a true dialogue will arise, a synthesis, so that we can conclude: "A society that cannot imagine its disadvantaged going to court to achieve reform will have an impoverished sense of justice; one that relies on such Herculean efforts will have an illusory one" (Roach 1991, 247). This is an inspiring statement of balance, in the abstract. The question is, Will our modest reality, "pragmatic and empirical" (Russell 1975), sustain it?

Yet another variant that accepts the Charter but is insistent upon corralling the judge's role would draw the divide between questions of substance and procedure, leaving the former issues to elected representatives unhampered by curial second-guessing (Fairley 1982; Monahan 1986). Fundamental to this view is the assertion that the Charter does not oblige courts "to test the substantive outcomes of the political process against some theory of the right or the good but, instead, its focus is to assure the integrity of politics by buttressing 'the opportunities for public debate and collective deliberation'" (Monahan 1986, 89). This strand does mirror an American theory of judicial review and like its southern relation, has been criticized on many grounds, not the least of which is that the very text of the Charter (and Bill of Rights) seems to speak to substantive entitlements.[6]   Yet, even this perspective in Canada, duly modified, is inspired, at least in part, as an attempt to preserve our tory and social democrat traditions from judicial dilution (see Monahan 1987, chap. 5.3).

The last strand of the legitimacy debate can be characterized, like this chapter itself, as speculative. It is hard to describe exactly the contours of this attitude, but a description of the vital points would go something like this. Embrace of leftism is by no means a requisite of belonging.[7] The issue is not whether Canada ought to be a liberal democracy. The question is What kind of liberal democracy is it and ought it to be? The United States is a liberal democracy but so are Great Britain, Sweden, Holland, and France. Yet these countries evidence substantial differences in their social and political construction, most prominently for discussion here, in the role of judges and litigation.

Further, the members of this last strand are varied, including individuals within public interest groups,[8] politicians present at the creation of the 1982 reconfiguration (Romanow 1986), quite plausibly most of the general population,[9] to say nothing of the people of Quebec in particular, and assorted academics,[10] including myself (see Bogart 1991b). It is not that the frailties of the electoral and representative process are not acknowledged, or that elected representatives and their agents have not committed many sins in our name,[11] or that there have not, at times, been progressive judges and judgments.[12] It is the risks that the judicial exercise brings compared with the achievements of popular politics in Canada that is the focus.

THE CASE AGAINST THE JUDGES

What is the core of the leeriness reflected in these various strands ranging from skepticism to unbridled antagonism? Though presented in different forms, the arguments can be reduced to three. The first concerns substantive outcomes and claims that the elected members of government and their emanations have been the more effective vehicle for improving the lives of most Canadians in most circumstances. The second relates to process and claims that the best chance for a vigorous democracy (quite apart from specific results) that is responsive and respected comes from elected representatives. The third is about the costs of access to the courts, which privilege the powerful and organized and thus will allow them disproportionate use of judicial review either to dismantle legislation and programs or to shield themselves from attack by government or other groups. These three points are comparative.[13] They do not deny that courts have sometimes acted in admirable ways[14] or that there have been some progressive judges.[15] They do not claim that legislatures and their agents have always reached just outcomes by processes beyond reproach. What they do contend is that, relatively, the chance for greatest justice will come from legislatures and their emanations. To expand the scope of judicial review is to take a flyer, and the evidence concerning courts suggests the path is befogged.

The first argument claims that the assisting, not only of the disadvantaged and poor but also of ordinary citizens in their daily existence, has more often happened because of legislative action (Monahan 1987). Whether in health, occupational safety, workers' rights, housing, peace and order in the streets, or other aspects of life, the advancement has come because of the popular support of political will. In this view government, while open to many criticisms about possible waste and inefficiency, has also been the agent of civilizing and progressive change. It has mediated between those who wish laissez-faire and the enrichment of the few regardless of the consequences and those who insist upon a basic claim to entitlement for all.

Conversely, this argument contends that the historical record reveals that courts, rather than aiding in achieving conditions to nurture and protect ordinary people in their everyday lives, have at best been uncaring about them, or worse, actively hostile. The explanation for this lies in an embrace of liberal ideology and an active suspicion of the political process as intrusion upon the purity of the judge-made common law, which did not develop to meet these ends.   State regulation and programs, designed to be responsive to the concerns of such people, have often been cut back and pruned under the guise of interpretation of statutes, but for the purpose of allowing the ideas of the judiciary to hold sway.

It is significant that boosters of the Charter and the judicial role rarely look to the history of courts to buttress their arguments.   Beatty, in his work urging judges to be the agents of progress for the rights of labor, advances what may be some insightful ideas about the conditions of working men and women in this country.   But when he argues that judges should and will be a vital force for implementing these propositions, the record upon which he bases this claim is revealing in its caution and qualifications:

> As with the law the courts contributed to the pre-industrial codes some members of the judiciary were at least sensitive, even in the heyday of laissez-faire liberalism, to the most basic physiological needs workers pursue through their work . . . [T]hey offer some basis to be optimistic that, in our times as well, courts can contribute legal rulings to our labour code that will be equally sensitive to the most important purposes each of us has in our work.   (Beatty 1987, 40, 197, 198)

In contrast, it is history that prompts many skeptics to be wary of judges and to prefer the hazards of the legislative processes to handle the complex social and economic problems of Canadian society.   Arthurs, in discussing the intrusiveness of the courts in terms of review of administrative action, observed:

> [T]o the extent that contemporary claims for judicial pre-eminence are based upon the perceived superior performance of the courts, it is necessary to remind ourselves, by an examination of the historical evidence, that the courts utterly failed to deal with the most significant legal repercussions of the Industrial Revolution in the nineteenth century and with the revolutions of rising expectations in the twentieth.   (Arthurs 1990, 225)

And even commentators who are much more accepting of the judicial role in review of administrative action point out the judicial indifference and awkwardness in responding to the complexities of twentieth-century society (Evans, et al. 1989, 12-17).

What of civil liberties, as traditionally conceived, the protection of minorities? There were a few valiant attempts by some judges in what have been called the implied bill of rights cases.[16] But the list of cases under the actual Bill of Rights (the predecessor to the Charter in the 1960s and 1970s) displayed the Supreme Court's lack of enthusiasm even though it, initially, manifested some promise of vigor. On this point, Allan Borovoy, a prominent civil libertarian, is instructive:

Historically at least, Canadian judges have shown something less than enthusiasm for the principles of civil liberties. Since 1960 there has been a statutory Bill of Rights operating at least at the federal level. The language of the bill could have sustained some far-reaching protections for human rights and civil liberties. Regrettably, that same language could also support a more feeble construction. With few exceptions the senior Canadian courts chose the latter approach. (Borovoy 1988, 208)

So any initial flourishes under the Charter, admirable though they might be, for example, the former chief justice's warning that the Charter must not be a club against the disadvantaged,[17] have to be put in the balance against that record.

The second argument urges that for democracy not to be sapped, but instead invigorated, basic decisions affecting the people must be made by elected representatives. This point does not urge that such a process has not led to mistakes, sometimes horrible ones, as noted previously. Nor does it suggest that there are not major impediments to popular participation (see Monahan 1987, 120). What it argues is that concerted efforts should be exerted to eliminate them and not to rely upon a small, unelected corps. Unlike the first argument, the worry here is less that judges will impose their views on a democratic majority than that critical social and political questions will be translated into legal issues and fall to the workings of judges and lawyers instead of being left with the citizenry to work out acceptable and supportable solutions (Russell 1983; Glendon 1987).

In this view even a cycle of progressive and enlightened decisions, while the results may be desirable, brings costs. There may be benefits, but they come from a small group of judges and lawyers bound together by a limited set of ideas and attitudes, who impose conclusions rather than persuade and build consensus among the electorate. The danger is that the basis for the people's making their own decisions and facing future issues will be eroded and that the resentment felt by having solutions handed down will make future progress even more difficult and may even contribute to regressive backlash.

This process argument is sometimes put in terms so strong as to rob it of some persuasiveness. Adherents are heard to caption it by asserting: "the people should be allowed to go to hell in a hand basket," "the people and their representatives must prevail even when wrong." Others would not put it in such absolute terms but, rather, base it on the particularities of the Canadian political culture. Each country must decide where the risk of error should lie. The argument then becomes specific to the country and is that, because Canada has been a country of moderate politics and social construction, risk should lie with the people.

It is sometimes said that Canada is not an ideological country, and various prominent individuals have taken their self-proclaimed freedom from it as a hallmark. Yet it is not that Canada is ideologically free but that it allows a number of such organizing ideas to shape politics and society.[18] Certainly liberalism with its reverence for a particular conception of individualism is vital. But others make their presence continually felt. Whether to dismay or to applause, Canada has a resilient tradition of social democracy organized politically primarily in the NDP,[19] while from the right has come toryism, with its tolerance of hierarchy and inequality, but also with its call for restraint of the individual for the greater good. As Horowitz has aptly put it: "Here Locke is not the one true god; he must tolerate lesser tory and socialist deities at his side" (Horowitz 1968, 18). Then too, nationalism, cutting across many political lines, has become a focus for debate and discussion about how the country should evolve (Christian and Campbell 1983).

The claim here is that this competition of ideas, along with other factors, has kept the nation moderate and center left. This is a disquieting positioning for some, not a perfect formula for anyone, but a mix with the potential for greater popular accountability but also for hostility to an enhanced role for a legal elite, no matter how well intended.

The third point focuses upon the costs of any court response. The contention is that, whatever meaning is possible in interpreting the Charter, it will inevitably come to be slanted toward the rich and the organized. A number of isolated figures for the costs of litigation

SOCIAL PROGRESS AND JUDICIAL POWER IN CANADA   127

illustrate how expensive it can be (Petter 1986) and the problems this engenders have been recognized by some judges.[20] The successful argument by Southam Newspapers that a search of its offices by anticombine officials should be struck down took over two and a half years and cost about $200,000. The unsuccessful suit by Operation Dismantle to have cruise missile testing declared unconstitutional cost about $50,000 even though the lawyers acting for it charged reduced fees and the action was determined at a preliminary stage.

Though some programs have existed to help the weaker and less strongly organized to engage in Charter litigation, they have been limited both in application and amount (Fox 1989) and, as we shall see at the end of the chapter, the most important one has very recently been eliminated. Meanwhile, richer and more organized parties who not only have greater resources but are also more familiar with the tactics of repeated use of the court system, can better position themselves not only to use the Charter to attack legislation and programs that they resist but also to use it as a shield when sued. Even when they are ultimately unsuccessful, the threat of such costly and delaying procedures can chill the claims of those less able to contend with the expenses of litigation. At the same time, the scarce energies and resources of these groups are deflected away from the branch of government that has historically been receptive, the legislature, and toward the political institution that has been least encouraging and accountable, the courts.

CONCLUSION

Two events occurred in the last week of February, 1992 that seem pertinent. The first was a Supreme Court of Canada decision upholding federal antipornography legislation explicitly recognizing the harmful effects pornography can have, most frequently on women. The second was the federal government's austerity budget as it desperately sought to control the deficit. Many programs fell under the axe, but of note were the Court Challenges Program, the Federal Law Reform Commission, and a commitment to a national day care program.

Are these two events associated with the subject of this chapter? To answer this question is to speculate, no matter how it is answered. But I believe it is plausible to suggest they are further evidence of a turning toward litigation for solutions and a corresponding waning of the influence of legislatures and their agents. They may be symptomatic of a series of small steps, possibly justified on their own, but that in the aggregate may put us on a very different course. In this sense there may be a naïveté among public-interest groups who assure that they know the pitfalls of litigation and who use it only as "a tool" so that both legislatures and courts can be harnessed to reform (Kassel 1992, 2). The danger is that judicialization of social issues may become so strongly entrenched that these groups will become constrained by the very process of litigation they now seek to utilize when other divisions of government resist their claims.

As for these two events, let me start with the *Butler*[21] decision upholding the antipornography law.   The decision was hailed as a breakthrough.   Catharine Mackinnon, the prominent American feminist who helped write an intervenor's brief in support of the law, declared: "This makes Canada the first place in the world that says what is obscene is what harms women not what offends our values" (Lewin 1992). But surely this cheering is misplaced. It was not the Supreme Court that had recognized the linkage between pornography and harm to its victims, but the legislature that had passed the enactment.   True, the court had ratified the statute, but only after a long, hard court battle badly draining and deflecting the reserves of the groups that supported the legislation and preventing them from dealing with other issues.

Meanwhile, the federal government abandoned its support for a national day care policy (better left to the provinces) and cancelled the Court Challenges Program, which had financially supported individuals and groups in language and equality litigation under the Charter (enough supportive precedent had accumulated), and the Federal Law Reform Commission (austerity pure and simple). Could a number of plausible, if discordant, reasons be advanced to explain these cuts? Of course. On the other hand, they can be viewed as quite consistent with a habit of mind that is turning from legislatures toward courts to provide solutions to complex, many-sided and connected issues in which a win-lose solution is no solution at all, especially when only a range of interests have the resources to be there. In this depiction the ending of the Court Challenges Program is not a second thought about the wonders of litigation but a signal to the disadvantaged that lack of access is not a deficiency of this process but an unfortunate side effect for some implicated interests that is, in any event, those interests' problem.

Gerald Rosenberg has recently, in *The Hollow Hope* (1991), detailed with great care why courts are, in the long run, unresponsive to pleas for social reform in the United States. His work is the latest in a growing body of studies written by those who are by no means unsympathetic to progressive social change but all of which arrive more or less at the same conclusions.[22] Courts do, however, produce what Rosenberg calls the "fly-paper" phenomenon, the lure of litigation deflecting groups and organizations from working through the democratic process, with all its tedium, frustrations, and compromises, to effect reform. To end I will quote his concluding remarks, since they provide such an eloquent warning, particularly for those who seek an enlivened and progressive democracy (Rosenberg 1991, 343): "To ask [courts] to produce significant social reform is to forget their history and ignore their constraints: It is to cloud our vision with a naive and romantic belief in the triumph of rights over politics. And while romance and even naivete have their charms, they are not best exhibited in court rooms."

NOTES

1. The following section of this chapter, "Perspectives on Litigation," is drawn from Bogart 1991a.

2. Discussions about judicial review of administrative action contained some echoes of the legitimacy discussion though these quarrels were more abstract discussions about the meaning of the rule of law and the judges' role than they were arguments about the actual impact of judicial review on the administrative state: see, for example, Arthurs 1990.

3. See also Cheffins and Johnson, 1986, 151: "Canada has a much more distinctly European flavour than the United States. Its thinking owes much more to the great philosopher Edmund Burke than to another great English philosopher, John Locke. Locke emphasized the individual. Burke emphasized the community."

There is a point too complicated to make in this chapter, but the excerpt from Russell quoted in the text also makes its way into J. Hagan, *The Disreputable Pleasures* (1991), 225. Full of insight the book explores the relationship between the criminal system and Canadian society.

4. "The ultimate goal must be to promote 'street theater,' the spontaneous involvement of people in everyday situations" (Hutchinson and Monahan 1984, 243).

5. For a defence of section 33 on the ground that it will enable judges to be more vigorous in their protection of rights see Weinrib 1990.

6. See Hogg (1987). Nor has the Supreme Court shown much interest in trying to self-limit on this basis. See: *Re B.C. Motor Vehicle Act (1985)* [1985] 2 S.C.R.

7. One does well to remember that debates over the Charter caused great cleavages within the "left-wing" NDP: Robin Sears, then general secretary of the NDP stated "The '80 to '81 period was the worst political experience of my life. It was as nasty and difficult and painful as it comes in this world short of violence . . ." (Steed 1988, 242).

8. For example, in terms of civil liberties, see Borovoy (1988, 213):

[T]he generalities of the Charter give the courts an abundance of power without the requisite guidelines. As a practical matter, of course, civil libertarians should press for the best Charter judgements they can get. But they should recognize that the Charter is no substitute for specific legislation addressed to specific problems. And they should also be grateful for whatever potential there is in the "notwithstanding" clause to rescue the sovereignty of the people from possible usurpations by the judiciary.

Many of the aboriginal groups are seeking to resolve their claims outside courts at least as traditionally conceived: see Shoalts (1991), in which P. Keenan, an elder of the Teslin Tlingit band of the Yukon is quoted as saying "The Charter puts the rights of the individual ahead of the group . . . [i]n our culture, the rights of the group must come ahead of the individual"; see also Turpel (1989-1990). Many of those representing women's issues have expressed grave reservations about the courts, both historically (see, e.g., Baines, 1989) and under the Charter (see, e.g., Brodsky and Day, 1989).

9. See A. Bryant et al., 1990. This study, as its title suggests, focused on exclusion of evidence. Canadians were asked an initial set of questions (15, Table 1): 75.7% had heard of the Charter, and 77.7% responded affirmatively to the question of whether the Charter was a good thing. However a very interesting set of responses was elicited depending on how a question was posed about the effect of the Charter on the way the system of justice works. Even if respondents were simply asked the question, only 56.1% said it would have a positive effect but when the questioner explicitly indicated it was possible to answer "not sure" ("or are you not sure what effect the Charter will have . . .") those answering "positive" fell to 32.3%, while 52.3% answered "not sure." Indeed, if one takes account of those who have not heard of the Charter (23.6%) then those who both know about the Charter and think it is a good thing "represented only 58.8% of the total population" (14).

10. See, e.g., Cheffins and Johnson (1986, chap. 2). One of the most eloquent warnings about the limits of litigation comes from Mary Ann Glendon's (1988) thoughtful comparison of Canadian and American (and continental) approaches to the abortion issue. Professor Glendon (1987) has studied abortion law in many western countries, and concludes that the judicialization of the issue in the United States has made it much more difficult to achieve an acceptable

solution, particularly compared with many countries in Europe. With refreshing tentativeness she sends this warning to us (32): "Canada, it seems to me, with its traditional concern for social welfare, neighborliness, and future generations, may be legally and politically closer in important respects to the continent than the United States."

Some legal academics have expressed strong reservations about the futility of using litigation to express public values including outside the constitutional context. See, e.g., Glenn, 1986; Weinrib, 1989.

11. For example, our failure to save as many Jews as lay within our power during World War II is an egregious instance of the sins committed in our name (Abella and Troper 1983).

12. For example, the implied bill of rights cases (e.g. *Reference Re Alberta Statutes* [1938] S.C.R. 100 and *Switzman v. Eibling* [1957] S.C.R. 285). Justice Dickson's warning that the Charter must not be a club against the disadvantaged (*Edwards Books and Arts Ltd v. R.* [1986] 2 S.C.R. 713, 779) and the acceptance of the "disadvantage" analysis in equality challenges under s.15 (*Law Society of B.C. et al v. Andrews et al* (1989), 56 D.L.R. (4th)(1).

13. This section of this chapter, "The Case against the Judges," is drawn from Bogart, 1991b.

14. For instance, see Russell's brief but spirited defense of the judiciary and its protection of some civil liberties based on the "pragmatic and empirical" (1975, 576, 592-93): "Our judges have been at their best in the field of civil liberties when, instead of being asked to theorize about such abstractions as 'equality before the law' or 'due process of law', they have been called upon to identify the rights implicit in the working of our basic institutions of government."

15. For example, the courts' liberalization of standing and the recognition that a broader array than traditional legal interests should be protected (Bogart, 1989).

16. For example, *Reference Re Alberta Statutes* [1938] S.C.R. 100 and *Switzman v. Elbling* [1957] S.C.R. 285, though, Cheffins and Johnson (1986, 133) observe: "It is absolutely clear that no Canadian court has ever based a decision on the implied bill of rights".

17. *Edwards Books and Arts Ltd. v. R.* [1986] 2 S.C.R. 713, 779: "In interpreting and applying the Charter I believe that the courts must be cautious to ensure that it does not become an instrument of better situated individuals to roll back legislation which has as its object the improvement of the condition of less advantaged persons."

18. Christian and Campbell (1983, 3): "Canada was in its origins and is still a country of rich ideological diversity. . . . The explicit expression and acknowledgement of these differences gives our country a much greater chance to resolve the question of the kind of social life we wish to share as fellow citizens."

19. Robertson Davies, in New York to publicize *The Lyre of Orpheus*, gave an interview describing Canada. After talking about us as a northern country with a "deep affinity with Scandinavia" he observed: "Canada doesn't have an oppressive Government. It's hard for people in the States to recognize this, but Canada is a socialist monarchy, like Sweden, Denmark and Norway. We have a leg in both camps, a limited welfare state and also a monarchy that causes a kind of clinging to the past" (Mitgang 1988).

20. Petter (1986, 483), citing remarks made by Chief Justice Dickson to the midwinter meeting of the Canadian Bar Association, February 2, 1985, 1.

21. *R. v. Butler* February 27, 1992, S.C.C., unreported.

22. For example, Rocher (1986) on Canada; Griffith (1981) on England; Handler (1978) and Glendon (1991) on the United States.

REFERENCES

Abella, Irving and Harold Troper. 1983. *None Is Too Many*. Toronto: Lester and Orpen Denny.

Arthurs, H. 1990. "Jonah and the Whale: The Appearance, Disappearance, and Reappearance of Administrative Law." *University of Toronto Law Journal* 30:225.

Baines, B. 1989. "Women and the Law." In S. Burt et al., eds. *Changing Patterns: Women in Canada*.

Beatty, David M. 1987. *Putting the Charter to Work*. Kingston, Ont.: McGill-Queens University Press.

―――. 1990. *Talking Heads and the Supremes: The Canadian Production of the Constitutional Review*. Toronto: Carswell.

Beatty, D. and C. Kennett. 1988. "Striking Back: Fighting Words, Social Protest and Political Participation in Free and Democratic Societies." *Canadian Bar Review*. 67:573.

Bogart, William A. 1989. "The Lessons of Liberalized Standing." *Osgoode Hall Law Journal* 27:1.

―――. 1991a. "Ambiguity." Paper prepared for the Yves Pratte Conference: Class Actions in Ontario and Quebec, University of Laval, October.

―――. 1991b. "'And The Courts Which Govern Their Lives': The Judges and Legitimacy." In *Remedies: Issues and Perspectives*, ed. J. Berryman.

Borovoy, A. Allan. 1988. *When Freedoms Collide*. Toronto: Lester and Orpen Denny.

Brodsky, G., and S. Day. 1989. *Canadian Charter Equality Rights For Women: One Step Forward or Two Steps Back?*

Bryant, A., et al. 1990. "Public Attitudes Toward The Exclusion of Evidence: Section 24(2) of the Canadian Charter of Rights and Freedoms." *Canadian Bar Review* 64:1.

Canadian Bar Association and the Federal Department of Justice. 1992. Brochure advertising Conference on the Tenth Anniversary of the Charter, 14-15 April.

Cheffins, Ronald I., and Patricia A. Johnson. 1986. *The Revised Canadian Constitution Politics as Law.* Toronto: McGraw Hill-Ryerson.

Christian, William, and Colin Campbell. 1983. *Political Parties and Ideologies in Canada.* 2d ed. Toronto: McGraw Hill-Ryerson.

Clarkson, Stephen, and Christina McCall. 1990. *Trudeau And Our Times. Vol. 1. The Magnificent Obsession.* Toronto: McClelland and Stewart.

Dyzenhaus, D. 1989. "The New Positivists." *University of Toronto Law Journal* 39:361.

Evans, J. M. et al., eds. 1989. *Administrative Law Cases, Text and Materials.* 3d ed. Toronto: Edmond Montgomery.

Fairley, H. 1982. "Enforcing the Charter: Some Thoughts on an Appropriate and Just Standard for Judicial Review." *Supreme Court Law Review* 4:217.

Fox, M. 1989. "Costs in Public-Interest Litigation." *Advocates' Quarterly* 10:385.

Fudge, J. 1987. "The Public/Private Distinction: The Possibilities of and the Limits of the Use of Charter Litigation in Further Feminist Struggles" *Osgoode Hall Law Journal* 25:485;

Galloway, D. 1988. "No Guru, No Method . . ." *Windsor Yearbook of Access to Justice* 8:304.

Glasbeek, H. 1989. "Some Strategies For An Unlikely Task: The Progressive Use of Law." *Ottowa Law Review* 21:387

Glendon, Mary Ann 1987. *Abortion and Divorce in Western Law.* Cambridge: Harvard University Press.

———. 1988. "A Beau Mentir Qui Vient-Du Loin: The 1988 Canadian Abortion Debate in Comparative Perspective" Legal Theory Workshop, Faculty of Law, University of Toronto, (January).

———. 1991. *Rights Talk: The Impoverishment of Political Discourse.* New York: Free Press.

Glenn, P. 1986. "The Dilemma of Class Action Reform." *Oxford Journal of Legal Studies* 6:262.

Griffith, J. A. G. 1981. *The Politics of the Judiciary*. London: Fontana.

Hagan, John. 1991. *The Disreputable Pleasures*, 3d ed. Toronto: McGraw Hill-Ryerson.

Handler, Joel P. 1978. *Social Movements and the Legal System: A Theory of Law Reform and Social Change*. New York: Academic Press.

Hartz, Louis. 1955. *The Liberal Tradition in America: The Interpretation of American Political Thought since The Revolution*. New York: Harcourt Brace.

Havel, Václav. 1992. "Paradise Lost." *The New York Review of Books*, 39 April 9, 6-7.

Hogg, P. 1987. "The Charter of Rights and American Theories of Interpretation." *Osgoode Hall Law Journal* 25:87, 104-111.

Horowitz, Gad. 1968. *Canadian Labour in Politics*. Toronto: University of Toronto Press.

Hutchinson, A. 1987. "Charter Litigation and Social Change: Legal Battles and Social Wars." In *Charter Litigation*, ed. Robert J. Sharpe. Toronto: Butterworths.

Hutchinson, A., and Patrick Monahan. 1984. "Law, Politics, and the Critical Legal Scholars: The Unfolding Drama of American Legal Thought." *Stanford Law Review* 36:199-243.

———. 1987. "Democracy and the Rule of Law." In A. Hutchinson and Patrick Monahan, eds., *The Rule of Law: Ideal or Ideology*. Toronto: Carswell.

Hutchinson, A., and A. Petter. 1988. "Private Rights/Public Wrongs: The Liberal Lie of the Charter." *University of Toronto Law Journal* 38:278.

Ison, A. 1985. "The Sovereignty of the Judiciary." *Adelaide Law Review*.

Kassel, J. 1992. "Courts Not Only Solution to Fighting Inequality." *Law Times*. March 2-8, 2.

Lewin, T. 1992. "Canada Court Says Pornography Harms Women and Can Be Barred." *New York Times*, February 28, A1.

Mandel, Michael. 1989. *The Charter of Rights and Legalization of Politics in Canada*. Toronto: Thompson Educational.

Martin, R. 1991. "The Charter and the Crisis in Canada." In David E. Smith, Peter Mackinnon and John C. Courtney, eds., *After Meech Lake-Lessons for the Future*. Saskatoon, Sask: Fifth House

Mitgang, G. 1988. "Robertson Davies, a Novelist of the North." *New York Times*, December 29, 11.

Monahan, Patrick. 1986. "Judicial Review and Democracy: A Theory of Judicial Review." *University of British Columbia Law Review* 21.

———. 1987. *Politics and the Constitution*.

Morton, F. L., Peter H. Russell and Michael Withey. 1991. "The Supreme Court's First One Hundred Charter of Rights Decisions: A Statistical Analysis." Research Unit for Sociolegal Studies, The University of Calgary, Occasional Papers, Research Study 6.1.

Petter, A. 1986. "The Politics of the Charter." *Supreme Court Law Review*. 8:473-79ff.

Roach, K. 1991. "Teaching Procedures: The Fiss/Weinrib Debate in Procedure." *University of Toronto Law Journal* 41:247-86.

Rocher, G. 1986. "Canadian Law: Sociological Perspective." In Ivan Bernier and Andre Lajoie, eds., *Law, Society and the Economy*. Toronto: University of Toronto Press.

Romanow, R. 1986. "Courts and Legislatures in the Age of the Charter." *Parliamentary Review* 6.

Rosenberg, Gerald. 1991. *The Hollow Hope: Can Courts Bring About Social Change?* Chicago: University of Chicago Press.

Russell, Peter H. 1975. "The Political Role of the Supreme Court of Canada in its First Century." *Canadian Bar Review* 53:577.

———. 1983. "The Political Purposes of the Canadian Charter of Rights and Freedoms." *Canadian Bar Review* 61:30.

———. 1992. "The Politics of Law." *Windsor Yearbook of Access to Justice*.

Russell, Peter H. and Paul C. Weiler. 1989. "Don't Scrap Override Clause—It's a Very Canadian Solution." *The Toronto Star*, June 4, B3.

Sallot, J. 1992a. "Top Court Becomes Supreme Player." *Globe and Mail*, April 6, A1.

———. 1992b. "How The Charter Changes Justice." Interview with Chief Justice Lamer. *Globe and Mail* April 17, A11.

Shoalts, D. 1991. "Natives Value Justice Differently." *Globe and Mail*, September 9, Al.

Smiley, Donald V. 1982. "A Dangerous Deed: The Constitution Act, 1982." In Keith Banting and Richard Simeon, eds., *And No One Cheered*. Toronto: Methuen.

Steed, Judy. 1988. *Ed Broadbent: The Pursuit of Power*. Toronto: Carswell, Methuen.

Turpel, M. F. 1989-1990. "Aboriginal Peoples and the Canadian Charter: Interpretive Monopolies, Cultural Differences." *Human Rights Yearbook* 66:3.

Weiler, Paul C. 1974. *In the Last Resort: A Critical Study of the Supreme Court of Canada*.

Weinrib, L. Eisenstat. 1989. "Adjudication and Public Value: Fiss' Critique of Corrective Justice." *University of Toronto Law Journal* 39:1.

Weinrib, L. Eisenstat. 1990. "Learning to Live with the Override." *McGill Law Journal* 35:541.

Whyte J. 1990. "Not Standing for Notwithstanding." *Alberta Law Review* 28:347.

9.

Canadian Constraints on Judicialization from Without

PETER H. RUSSELL

This chapter focuses on Canada's recent experience with what Torbjörn Vallinder terms "judicialization from without," even though "judicialization from within" in Canada as elsewhere may be the more pervasive, though less spectacular, aspect of the global expansion of judicial power. As an example of judicialization from within, Vallinder refers to the expansion of courtlike decision making within Britain's administrative tribunals. There has certainly been plenty of that in Canada. The insistence on judicial-style due process in ever-widening realms of public administration is part and parcel of the ever expanding catalogue of justiciable rights that has been a hallmark of modernizing societies as they have moved from *gemeinschaft* to *geselleschaft* (Tönnies 1965). The adoption of national and international bills of rights, the primary foundation of judicialization from without, reflects and reinforces this tendency.

Since 1982, when Canada adopted a constitutional bill of rights, called the Canadian Charter of Rights and Freedoms, it has experienced a heavy new dose of judicialization from without. Judicial review of legislation and executive acts based on the Charter has undoubtedly expanded the Canadian judiciary's sphere of activity and in that sense has increased the judiciary's power. However, this expansion of judicial power has not necessarily been "at the expense" (to use Vallinder's phrase) of the legislative or executive branches. The main impact of a constitutional bill of rights on the political system, if Canada's experience is a guide, may be less a transfer of power to the judiciary than a general transformation of the nature of political life.

When Canadians were debating whether to adopt a comprehensive constitutional bill of rights, I was one of a relatively small number of academics who drew attention to such a measure's tendency to expand judicial power. Indeed, at the time the Charter was adopted I wrote that its main effect on the governmental process in Canada would be "a tendency to judicialize politics and politicize the judiciary" (Russell 1983, 51-52). It may seem ironic that after the Canadian Charter has been in force ten years I am writing on the limits to judicialization in Canada. I am doing so not to recant my prediction but in the hope that an examination of Canadian constraints on judicialization might illuminate some of the key variables that impinge on the process and shape its consequences.

A constraint on judicialization that has *not* been very effective is the one built right into the Canadian Charter—section 33, the legislative override clause. Canada's constitutional bill of rights is one of the few in the world that expressly permits legislatures (federal or provincial) to pass legislation notwithstanding certain specific rights.[1] The rights against which the override can be used include virtually all of the Charter's universal rights: political freedoms, due process rights, and protection against discrimination. Its use requires only a majority vote of the legislature. An override dies after five years but can be renewed.

The legislative override was inserted in the Charter at the insistence of politicians, mainly provincial premiers, who wanted an accountable, democratic check on judicial review (see Weiler 1984). To those who believe fundamental, constitutional rights are being taken seriously only when the judiciary can uphold them against the majoritarian decisions of the political branches, the legislative override contradicts the very purpose of the Charter (see Whyte 1990). For those who see judicial review as another form of fallible policy-making, the override is a prudent fail-safe device (Russell 1991). In practice, the legislative override is hardly ever used. The fact that outside of Quebec it is, politically speaking, almost unusable tells us much about how constitutionalizing rights can affect the nature of politics.

The override has been used only once outside of Quebec. That was in the Charter's early years, when Saskatchewan's legislature used the override in legislation ordering striking civil servants back to work. As it turned out there is no need to immunize that kind of legislation from judicial review, because in subsequent cases the Supreme Court of Canada ruled that the Charter's right to "freedom of association" does not embrace the right to strike (Russell, Knopff, and Morton 1989, 5). Quebec, however, used the legislative override in a massive way, applying it to all past legislation and all new legislation. It did this for symbolic reasons as a way of protesting the fact that the Charter and the other 1982 constitutional changes were imposed on Quebec without the consent of its National Assembly. But in 1988, after a Liberal government led by Robert Bourassa had replaced a separatist government and the override's five-year period had run out, Quebec's National Assembly used the override clause to counter a Supreme Court decision. The court had ruled that a section of Bill 101, Quebec's charter of the French language, requiring French-only advertising signs, violated the Charter's guarantee of "freedom of expression."[2]

The court's decision provoked the largest nationalist rallies in Quebec since the 1980 referendum. "Ne toucher pas la loi 101" ("Don't touch law 101") was their slogan. Responding to this pressure, the Bourassa government, which in its election campaign had promised to restore bilingual signs, decided now to use the override to restore French-only commercial signs outdoors but allow multilingual signs indoors.

All this occurred during a major round of constitutional politics based on the Meech Lake Accord, a set of constitutional proposals primarily designed to win Quebec's support for the constitutional changes imposed on the province in 1982. By December 1988, when the Supreme Court rendered its decision, ratification of the Meech Lake Accord was almost complete: the federal Parliament, Quebec's National Assembly, and the legislatures of all but two of the other provinces had approved the accord. But so great was English Canada's furor over Quebec's use of the override to protect its "visage linguistique" that from this point on "there was virtually no chance that the Meech Lake Accord would be ratified" (Monahan 1991). The Meech Lake Accord indeed died and with it, perhaps, the chance of maintaining the unity of the Canadian federation. A constitutional bill of rights designed to unify the country may turn out to be the final instrument of the country's breakup.

That this could happen shows, at least in the Canadian case, that the impact of constitutionalizing rights on civic consciousness can be far more significant than any shifts it brings about in the balance of power between the branches of government.   For opinion-leaders among English Canadians the Charter had become an icon, its rights fundamental and absolute.   Although I had been concerned about the way a rights discourse may impede social consensus on divisive community interests, I had not fully appreciated the extent to which "[T]he rhetoric of constitutional rights invests political discourse with a deep sense of moral rectitude" (Russell 1990, 246).   English Canadians had never cared very much for the French-only sign policy, which had been in place since 1977, but now that they viewed that policy as a violation of a fundamental constitutional right, their opposition could be mounted on a high moral plane.   No longer was there any need to consider French Quebecers' beliefs about what is necessary for their cultural survival. The individual's freedom to advertise in the language of choice was so fundamental, so absolute that it should not make room for any other value or interest.

In taking this position English Canadian opinion was less moderate than the Supreme Court's.   The court's opinion on the sign law acknowledged that Quebec was justified in abridging freedom of expression in order to maintain a French "visage linguistique" but held that a law requiring *predominantly* rather than *exclusively* French signs is all that was needed for this purpose.   Bourassa's outdoor-indoor compromise was potentially consistent with the Supreme Court's ruling, and might have survived judicial review.   But the use of the override by Quebec, just like the opposition it provoked, was a political imperative in Canada's constitutional struggle.   By using the override, Quebec's National Assembly asserted its determination to maintain sovereign authority over the means needed to preserve and promote Quebec's distinctive culture.

After the Quebec sign-law incident, the legislative override became, from a political standpoint, virtually unusable outside of Quebec.   Even before the signs case the popularity of the concept of a Charter of Rights would make legislators very reluctant to use the override.   Now the override was tainted in English Canada by its use to secure the language policy of Quebec's French majority.   The very existence of the legislative override so disgusted Brian Mulroney, the Canadian prime minister, that he was moved to declare that the Canadian Constitution was "not worth the paper it was printed on" (*Toronto Globe and Mail* 1989).   Normally politicians are not reluctant to use constitutional powers that are important to them.   The key to understanding the willingness of Canadian governments other than Quebec's to forsake use of the override power is that the Charter, as it was being interpreted and applied by the courts, did not threaten their vital policy interests.

Here we encounter the most important constraint on the Canadian Charter's tendency to promote "judicialization from without": the limited policy scope of Canada's Charter of Rights and Freedoms. The policy area most frequently affected by Charter litigation is criminal justice. At least 80% of court cases involving Charter-based judicial review fall in that area. Criminal justice is undoubtedly an important field of state policy, but it is a field in which the judiciary, throughout the common-law world, has always been an active policy maker. Also, criminal justice is not normally a high-priority policy area in the policy objectives of governments in Canada. Outside of criminal justice, the only program of major importance to a government that has been mauled by judicial review under the Charter is Quebec's language policy. At the federal level probably the most important Charter hit is the Supreme Court's ruling in the *Singh* case, requiring judicial-type hearings (that is, judicialization from without forcing judicialization within) in settling claims for refugee status.[3] Even here, the government, quite independently of the *Singh* case, was already planning to introduce such a change in refugee proceedings. None of the key economic and social policy interests of governments—monetary and fiscal policy, international trade, resource development, social welfare, education, labor relations, environmental protection—have been significantly encroached upon by judicial enforcement of the Charter.

The limitations on the Charter's policy impact stem both from the Charter itself and from its interpretation by the judiciary. Although the list of rights and freedoms included in the Canadian Charter is relatively comprehensive, one notable omission is property rights. This omission is no accidental oversight. It was insisted upon by Canada's social democratic party, the NDP, as a condition for its support of the Charter. The absence of property rights reduces the Charter's impact, especially its due-process-of-law guarantees, on social, economic, and environmental regulation. Of more fundamental importance is the fact that the Charter applies only to governments and legislatures. Charter rights and Charter freedoms can be claimed only against actions of governments or legislatures. However, the main barrier to full enjoyment or exercise of some rights, particularly equality rights, is not government action but government inaction in responding to problems emanating from the private sector and the very structure of society. This, I believe, is the main reason the Charter has been a disappointment to those who expected it be a major vehicle for social reform.

The Charter's limited scope has not deterred lawyers representing social action groups from trying to use the Charter as a vehicle for social change, thereby arousing the ire of critics on the right who fear that a "court party" of Charterphile lawyers will use Charter advocacy as an undemocratic means of advancing the objectives of special-interest groups (Knopff and Morton 1992) and critics on the left who fear that Charter litigation will fritter away the resources available to progressive social forces (see Mandel 1989). There is not much empirical evidence to support either of these concerns. The right-wing critics can point to few instances where judicial review under the Charter has forced elected politicians to initiate policies or spend money against their wishes. Nor is there any evidence that feminists, antiracists, the labor movement, environmentalists, and other groups working for social reform in Canada have decided to forsake direct political action while some of their lawyer-members flail about in the courts with the Charter.

Although the Charter has not judicialized Canadian politics in the sense of bringing about a major transfer of policy-making power to the courts, it could have a long-term impact on policy by shaping how Canadians think about political values. I have already commented on how the Charter has influenced, in a highly divisive manner, attitudes toward constitutional politics. The Charter could also have a potent effect on policies concerned with the distribution of wealth and power in the Canadian variant of welfare-capitalism if "its concern about restrict-ing government activities [came] to be identified in the public mind with social progress" (Russell 1990, 256). In other words, if most Canadians in English Canada come to believe that their Charter rights are more fundamental than any other rights or interests they might have, then the direction of policy and the entire political spectrum might well shift to the right. Some would argue that the emergence of a new right-wing Reform Party in Canada with policies resembling those of the American Republican Party is evidence that this shift is occurring.

The Charter's built-in limitations have been augmented by a cautious performance on the part of its most authoritative interpreter, the Supreme Court of Canada. After a rollicking barrage of initial decisions in which the court, citing John Marshall, expressed its determination to take Charter rights seriously and upheld three-quarters of the Charter claims brought to it, the court settled down to a relatively moderate approach (see Russell 1988, 385). In its first 100 Charter decisions, the percentage of successful Charter claims—35%—was just one percent below the success rate of Bill of Rights claims in the United States Supreme Court during the same period (Morton, Russell, and Withey 1992). The Canadian Supreme Court's moderate performance has not been well received in the academy—it is far too restrained for proponents of judicial activism and not nearly deferential enough for advocates of judicial self-restraint. But it has probably kept the court in line with the mainstream of political opinion in the country. That, it has been argued, may be the underlying, if somewhat instinctive, rationale of the court's Charter performance (see Pond 1992).

Whatever the motive, there can be no doubt that the Supreme Court's jurisprudence has significantly restricted the scope of the Charter's impact and thus the ambit of judicialization. In a 1986 case, *Dolphin Delivery*,[4] the court narrowed the realm of state action to which the Charter applies by removing from that realm judicial decisions applying common-law (in this case a common-law rule against secondary picketing) in actions involving private parties. In a trio of 1987 cases, the court denied that the right to strike and other collective bargaining rights could be included within the Charter's guarantee of "freedom of association." Having rebuffed organized labor's efforts to use the Charter to expand its power, the Supreme Court was at pains to rebuff parallel efforts of the business class. In *Edwards Books*, the court upheld Ontario Sunday-closing legislation designed to give retail workers a common day of rest. Chief Justice Dickson justified this decision by arguing that in interpreting the Charter "the courts must be cautious to ensure that it does not become an instrument of better situated individuals to roll back legislation that has as its object the improvement of the condition of less advantaged persons."[5] In *Irwin Toy*, Dickson made it clear that the right to liberty guaranteed in section 7 was not to be used to protect corporate commercial rights.[6]

The Supreme Court's treatment of the Charter's section 15, setting out equality rights, has shown a similar limiting tendency. That section, as written, was potentially wide open. It inscribes a general right to equality "before and under the law" as well as "equal protection and equal benefit of the law without discrimination" and then gives as particular examples of unconstitutional discrimination "discrimination based on race, national or ethnic origin, color, religion, sex, age or mental or physical disability." In interpreting this section, the Supreme Court has in effect reduced section 15's coverage to laws that harm or prejudice groups covered by or analogous to the section's enumerated categories.[7] This immunizes a great many discriminatory laws—for instance most areas of business regulation—from judicial review. And even to laws that discriminate on the explicitly prohibited grounds, the court applies no doctrine of "strict scrutiny." Under the Charter's "reasonable limits" clause, the court can defer to legislative judgment on the balance to strike between constitutional equality rights and other important societal interests. It did just that, for instance, in dismissing a challenge by university professors to policies requiring mandatory retirement at age 65.[8]

The target of most of the Supreme Court's Charter's activism has been the criminal law and police practices. In a number of areas of criminal justice the court's treatment of due process rights has been more liberal even than the Warren Court in the United States. Examples are extending the right to counsel to noncustodial situations and excluding evidence based on a nonconsensual blood sample as a violation of a right to privacy.[9] But here too, in the criminal justice field, where the courts have always been relatively active, constraints on judicialization are operative. Enunciating liberal rules of criminal procedure is one thing; securing police compliance with these rules is another matter. Until the appropriate kind of empirical research is carried out, we will not know the extent to which the Supreme Court's Charter jurisprudence is actually modifying police behavior, particularly in the treatment of suspects. But even at the level of constitutional doctrine, the court has not pushed its activism so far in the criminal justice field as to overturn highly popular law-enforcement programs. For example, it invoked the reasonable limits clause to uphold gun-control provisions of the Criminal Code[10] and random roadside tests aimed at apprehending drunk drivers.[11]

So far the court's Charter activism has not undermined criminal justice policies to which elected governments are strongly attached. A major exception may seem to be the court's decision in *Askov*, which through its interpretation of the Charter's speedy-trial rule put at risk thousands of criminal charges in Ontario.[12] The principal policy impact of this decision was to strengthen the position of Ontario's attorney general in securing more resources for Ontario's justice system and making management changes in a very badly administered judicial region. Besides, when the media made a hullabaloo about dangerous criminals going free because they were not brought to trial within eight months, the Supreme Court justice who authored the opinion was moved to comment (off the bench) that he had not meant his judgment to be interpreted so rigidly. In a subsequent decision the court clarified its *Askov* ruling to make it clear that it did not support a rigid eight-month rule.[13]

What we see, then, in the Canadian experience with a new constitutional bill of rights is a judiciary constraining the growth of its power. Most of the members of the country's highest court are conscious of the political reasons for exercising this constraint. This is very evident in the following passage from an interview with the current chief justice, Antonio Lamer, published in a leading national newspaper on the tenth anniversary of the Charter of Rights: "In 1982 when the Charter came in, governments were watching the courts to see what they would do. I think now they realize we haven't gone berserk with the Charter and we aren't striking down laws right and left. They know how far we'll go and how far we're not going to go because we've said so" (*Toronto Globe and Mail* 1992). Lamer reflects the desire of most members of the court not to push their power of judicial review so far as to antagonize leaders in other branches of government or the mainstream of public opinion.

Of course sometimes it is impossible to avoid controversial outcomes. Some Charter cases raise "moral issues" on which there are sharply opposed political interest groups and no strong or clear public consensus. Abortion, Sunday closing, anti-hate propaganda, prostitution, and pornography are examples. For most politicians these are "lose-lose" issues, which they would be happy to off-load to the courts. A legislative override could really be an embarrassment here if it encouraged those who lost in the courts to bring the issue back to the legislature.

The clearest examples of this pattern of judicial interaction with the legislative process are the Supreme Court's decisions on abortion and sexual assault. In *Morgenthaler*, the court struck down restrictions on abortion in Canada's national criminal code,[14] and in *Seaboyer*[15] it struck down "rape-shield" provisions of the criminal code preventing the use of evidence of a complainant's sexual conduct in prosecuting sexual assault cases. *Morgenthaler* aroused the right-to-life movement, while *Seaboyer* aroused feminists—evidence in itself of the court's weaving around the center lane in areas of social controversy. In both cases, the aroused and losing group went immediately to the parliamentary lobby to press for legislative redress. In neither case was there any inclination on the part of the politicians to use the override, but in both cases the government agreed to bring in new legislation designed to accommodate the Supreme Court's jurisprudence.[16]

In cases dealing with antihate propaganda,[17] restrictions on Sunday shopping,[18] prostitution[19] and pornography,[20] the Supreme Court invoked the Charter's reasonable limits clause to uphold legislation encroaching on Charter freedoms. Here, as with cases where it overturned legislation, the court's decisions did not remove the issues from politics. Judicialization in these cases is best analyzed not as transferring decision-making authority from one branch of government to another but as judicial processing of social controversy. We should trace the political consequences of this judicial processing along two lines: its effect on the political resources of the contending sides and its tendency to inject a rights discourse into the political debate.

Though a court decision upholding legislation against a constitutional challenge may increase the legislation's legitimacy and thereby enhance the resources of those interested in maintaining the legislative policy, it will not make legislation invulnerable to a determined political attack. A good example is the provincial Sunday-closing legislation upheld by the Supreme Court. Sunday closing has continued to be under siege by commercial interests and the strength of consumerism. These political and societal forces in one way or another will bring about a different outcome from that sanctified by the Supreme Court. There are clear examples of judicial decisions injecting a rights discourse into disputes. I have already commented on that consequence of the Supreme Court's decision in the Quebec signs case. The passionate sense of righteousness that characterizes both sides of the abortion issue in Canada (and the United States) has been intensified by judicial processing. To the extent that judicialization has this effect it may make social consensus on such issues more difficult to obtain.

As Canada has settled into life under a constitutional bill of rights, judicial review has not provoked a legitimacy crisis. There is no popular hue and cry—even in Quebec where Charter decisions appear to be most obviously countermajoritarian—against appointed judges making decisions on important questions of public policy. The constraints flowing from structure of the Canadian Charter of Rights and Freedoms plus the self-imposed constraints of the Canadian judiciary, especially the country's highest court, in interpreting the Charter, may have something to do with the absence of a legitimacy crisis. Even more fundamental, I suspect, is a general disillusionment with representative democracy: in Canada, as perhaps in other industrial democracies, it is elected politicians, not judges, who are experiencing a legitimacy crisis. The "Citizens' Forum," which in 1990-91 heard from over 400,000 Canadians on their concerns about the country, reported that the most common concern of forum participants was that they "have lost faith in both the political process and political leadership." (*Toronto Globe and Mail* 1991, A9) Even though judges are in better odor in Canada than politicians, there is a good deal of resistance to giving the judiciary a major role in applying some new constitutional provisions that are now being considered in Canada. Among the constitutional proposals under discussion in the current round of constitutional politics are a stronger guarantee of free trade within the Canadian federation and a social charter establishing social policy and environmental standards to be maintained by all governments in the federation (see Russell 1992, chap. 10). The supporters of both proposals are of the opinion that "the courts are not the appropriate forum in which to settle disputes on such complex issues of law and public policy" (Beaudoin-Dobbie Report 1992). For the free-trade guarantee they propose a dispute-settlement mechanism with a specialized trade tribunal, and for the social charter they recommend political monitoring by an intergovernmental commission instead of judicial enforcement.

It is, of course, politicians in the elected branches of government who favor these constraints on the growth of judicial power in Canada. Nonetheless, the reluctance of political leaders to deal the judiciary into a vast expansion of discretionary decision making in the field of socioeconomic policy has not stirred up much public controversy. There are some on the left who say that they would like to see the courts enforcing positive entitlements to such things as "comprehensive health care," "high quality education," "adequate social services and benefits," "the integrity of the environment," "full employment," and a "reasonable standard of living."[21] But it is most doubtful that a majority of Canadians, left, right, or center, could come to believe in such judicial fairy tales. In Canada, judicialization of politics from without is not likely to exceed its modest expansion under the Charter of Rights.

NOTES

1. The other constitution with a clause most resembling Canada's is the Jamaican Constitution. However, it requires a two-thirds majority of both houses of Jamaica's Parliament. For further comparisons see Letourneau 1991.

2. *Quebec v. Ford et al.* (1988) 2 S.C.R. 712.

3. *Singh v. Minister of Employment and Immigration* (1985) 1 S.C.R. 177.

4. *Retail, Wholesale and Department Store Union v. Dolphin Delivery Ltd.* (1986) 2 S.C.R. 573.

5. *Edwards Books and Art Ltd. v. The Queen* (1986) 2 S.C.R. 713, 779.

6. *A.G. Quebec v. Irwin Toy* (1989) 1 S.C.R. 927.

7. The key case is *Andrews v. Law Society of British Columbia* (1989) 1 S.C.R. 143.

8. *McKinney v. University of Guelph* (1990) 3 S.C.R. 229.

9. For a full discussion of these and other cases see Harvie and Foster (1990).

10. *The Queen v. Schwartz* (1988) 2 S.C.R. 443.

11. *The Queen v. Hufsky* (1988) 1 S.C.R. 621; *The Queen v. Thomsen* 1 S.C.R. 640.

12. *The Queen v. Askov* (1990) 2 S.C.R. 1199.

13. *Deepak Kumar Sharma v. The Queen* (judgment rendered March 26, 1992).

14. *Dr. Henry Morgentaler et al v. The Queen* (1988) 1 S.C.R. 30.

15. *The Queen v. Seaboyer; The Queen v. Gayme* (1991) 2 S.C.R. 577.

16. The new criminal code provisions on abortion were blocked by the Senate. The new "rape-shield" law was just at the drafting stage at this writing (see Sallot, 1991).

17. *The Queen v. Keegstra* (1990) 3 S.C.R. 697.

18. *Edwards Books and Art Ltd. v. The Queen* (1986) 2 S.C.R. 713.

19. *The Queen v. Skinner* (1990) 1 S.C.R. 1235.

20. *Butler v. The Queen* (February 27, 1992).

21. These are some of the social policy standards to be included in the social covenant and economic declaration proposed in the Beaudoin-Dobbie Report. For an attack on the social charter proposal for its failure to empower judges to help the disadvantaged, see Jackman 1992.

REFERENCES

Beaudoin-Dobbie Report. 1992. *Report of the Special Joint Committee of the Senate and the House of Commons on a Renewed Canada (Beaudoin-Dobbie Report)*. Ottawa: Supply and Services Canada.

Harvie, Robert, and Hamar Foster. 1990. "Ties That Bind: The Supreme Court of Canada, American Jurisprudence and the Revision of Canadian Criminal Law Under the Charter." *Osgoode Hall Law Journal* 28:729.

Jackman, Martha. 1992. "When a Social Charter Isn't." *Canadian Forum*, April, 8.

Knopff, Rainer, and F. L. Morton. 1992. *Charter Politics*. Toronto: Nelson.

Letourneau, Stephane. 1991. *The Legislative Override Power: Section 33 of the Canadian Charter of Rights and Freedoms*. M.Litt thesis, University of Oxford.

Mandel, Michael. 1989. *The Charter and the Legalization of Politics in Canada*. Toronto: Wall and Thompson.

Monahan, Patrick. 1991. *Meech Lake: The Inside Story*. Toronto: University of Toronto Press.

Morton, F. L., Peter H. Russell, and Michael J. Withey. 1992. "The Supreme Court of Canada's First One Hundred Charter of Rights Decisions: A Statistical Analysis." *Osgoode Hall Law Journal* 30.

Pond, David. 1992. "The Supreme Court of Canada and the Politics of Public Law." Ph.D. dissertation, University of Toronto.

Russell, Peter H. 1983. "Political Purposes of the Canadian Charter of Rights and Freedoms." *Canadian Bar Review* 61:30.

———. 1988. "Canada's Charter: A Political Report." *Public Law* 1988:385.

———. 1990. "The Charter and the Future of Canadian Politics." In Alain-G. Gagnon and James Bickerton, eds. *Canadian Politics: An Introduction to the Discipline*. Peterborough, Ont.: Broadview Press.

———. 1991. "Standing Up for Notwithstanding." *Alberta Law Review* 1991:293.

———. 1992. *Constitutional Odyssey: Can Canadians Become a Sovereign People?* Toronto: University of Toronto Press.

Russell, Peter H., Rainer Knopff, and F. L. Morton. 1989. *Federalism and the Charter: Leading Constitutional Decisions*. Ottawa: Carleton University Press.

Sallot, Jeff. 1991. "Political Battle Rages over Sex-Assault Bill," *Toronto Globe and Mail*, December 13.

Tönnies, Ferdinand. 1965. *Community and Association.* Trans. and supplemented by Charles P. Loomis. London.

Toronto Globe and Mail. 1989. April 8.

———. 1991. "Citizens Forum on Canada's Future." Condensed version, July 2, A9.

———. 1992. April 17.

Weiler, Paul C. 1984. "Rights and Judges in a Democracy: A New Canadian Version." *University of Michigan Journal of Law Reform* 51.

Whyte, John D. 1990. "On Not Standing for Notwithstanding," *Alberta Law Review* 1990:347.

PART III

EUROPEAN ROMANO-GERMANIC DEMOCRACIES

Cross-National Analyses

10.

Training the Legal Professions in Italy, France and Germany

ANNA MESTITZ AND PATRIZIA PEDERZOLI

In democratic regimes the education and training of judges, public prosecutors, and lawyers assume a special relevance at least for two main reasons: first, because the different ways of recruitment represent a significant variable, among others, determining the degree of independence granted to the judiciary; and second, because in such political systems citizens' rights and expectations increasingly rely upon the professional qualifications of all legal experts (Di Federico 1989). In this chapter we shall deal with this second issue, taking into consideration only the most relevant elements that have emerged from wider field research we have undertaken in Italy, France, and Germany[1] in recent years.

Actually, liberal-democratic countries are experiencing changes in the substance and method of law that seem to undercut the identity of legal institutions and legal professions (Unger 1976, 200). Such transformations gradually modify both the scope and actual behavior of judges and lawyers, visibly strengthening their participation in the political process: the judiciary has acquired, or is in the process of acquiring, growing political significance,[2] and lawyers have been performing a wider range of functions, which more and more highlight "the inherently political character" of their role (Larson 1988, 472).

Being deeply entangled with welfare-state policies (Unger 1976; Nonet and Selznick 1978), these phenomena have been detected throughout the common-law and the civil-law world, notwithstanding some differences in their actual dimensions and intensities:[3]

> The growing participation of the judiciary in the "authoritative allocation of values" . . . is a necessary and unavoidable consequence of the increasingly extensive and penetrating regulation of economic, social and political relations between individuals, groups, public agencies and citizens. This "law explosion" is reflected in the ever more numerous and frequent occasions of recourse to jurisdiction requiring direct intervention in delicate areas such as those concerning our liberty, our property, our access to public services, to work, etc.; it is also reflected in an increasing resort to courts for the defence or assertion of rights which, even when promoted by individuals, raises problems requiring a judicial solution which is often crucial for the defence of wider interests and often of great importance for the entire community. (Di Federico 1987b, 3-4)

Such a significant evolution of legal experts' roles and the peculiar relevance of the "human factor" in the administration of justice suggest the need of updating the education and training of judges, public prosecutors, and lawyers in order to guarantee their personal and professional qualifications (Di Federico 1987a). The main problem at stake is obviously how to accomplish it.

The relevance of this issue is demonstrated by the attention it is receiving from scholars.[4]   Furthermore, it is confirmed by several reforms recently introduced in some European countries, providing new, complex structures aimed at improving the education, selection, and training of judges and lawyers. Among them we can note the cases of Spain, Portugal, France, and Germany; unfortunately, Italy cannot be included in this list. Though such reforms differ in content, all of them stress the importance nowadays attached to selection, training, and continuing education and clearly represent an attempt to cope more effectively with the growing complexity of legal practice.

Research Background

Let us briefly explain the starting point of this research and the reasons that have led us to choose the cases of Italy, France, and Germany.

The "Italian way" of legal education is clearly marked by an ongoing stagnancy, with effects on the professional qualifications of magistrates[5] and lawyers so troubling as to become a major issue. The widespread dissatisfaction with the present situation has provided the starting point of this research, carried out in the period 1986-1990 and aimed at widening our knowledge concerning the socialization process of the legal professions in France and Germany, supplying in the meantime a memorandum for promoting reforms in Italy. In other words, our choice was partly due to the problems experienced in Italy and partly due to a specific interest in understanding which qualifications are granted and which training methods and contents are adopted abroad.

Information on France and Germany has been gathered first through a systematic overview of the available literature on this subject.[6] The kind collaboration of the Ministries of Justice of both countries allowed us to complete the collected material with legislative acts and statistical data. Further explanations of real work, reform plans, and unsolved problems have been gathered through several interviews granted by executives of Ministries of Justice and administrative managers of professional schools, as well as by judges, lawyers, and law professors.[7]

In treating the concept of the legal profession, it must be remembered that while in the common-law world this refers to a category that is essentially unitary, its core being "historically, numerically and ideologically" private practice (Abel 1988, 5), in civil-law countries this category is generally parceled out into distinct professional subsets in which career patterns have little or no de facto connection with each other. The subsets include magistrates (judges and prosecutors), private practitioners, civil servants, law professors, law graduates in commerce and industry, and people without specific legal training performing other activities elsewhere (such as notaries). This is the very reason why, referring to civil-law countries, we speak of legal professions, as the singular form in those contexts is nonsense or, even worse, misleading.

We chose to focus our research efforts on France and Germany mainly because they represent the two alternative patterns of socialization for the legal professions, which in various ways have influenced other European countries: the "separate" and the "unitary" models. In the

Federal Republic, judges, public prosecutors, lawyers, notaries, and higher civil servants are selected and trained in the same way. But France, like Italy, provides two distinct recruitment and training patterns, qualifying successful candidates respectively for forensic and judicial practice. Notwithstanding this basic divergence, our comparison can rely on several common features shared by Italy, France, and Germany that should allow us to overcome some obstacles often occurring in cross-national analysis.

First, all are democratic regimes, grounded on nearly common constitutional values, with constitutional arrangements concerning the judicial branch that are very similar (at least for our purposes). All belong to the same family of law, that is, the civil-law tradition. As a result they share many similarities in the uses they make of law and legal experts.

Second, they do not seem to differ greatly in their social, political, and economic structure, which represent notable variables in defining lawyers' functions (Abel and Lewis 1988, 479), and they are now experiencing a common expansion of the political significance of the judiciary. Thus, they now have to cope with similar problems concerning the changing roles of magistrates and lawyers.

Third, the selection and training of magistrates in these three countries follow a bureaucratic model, with major traits that can be briefly summarized:

1. applicants for the judiciary, generally possessing a law degree, are selected through written and oral examinations aimed at testing their general knowledge in various branches of law;

2. candidates enter the competition soon after graduation, when they are about 30 years old or less, and start from the bottom of the career ladder;

3. professional training and experience are acquired mainly within the judicial organization, where judges and prosecutors are expected to remain until their retirement (Di Federico 1976, 1987a).

Selection of lawyers, whether carried out in common with or separate from that of judges, takes place traditionally on the same basis, that is, through written and oral examinations.

Finally, France, Germany, and Italy share a similar, though not identical, understanding of the very concept of legal profession(s). Their concepts are not identical because, as noted, all the German legal professions rely on a common education and training background.[8] While this might seem to contradict what we have just said about the meaning of this concept in civil-law countries, data on the distribution of German law graduates in different professional subsets reveal that mobility rates are very low, and that mobility is usually limited to a short period soon after graduation (Kötz et al. 1982). This phenomenon can be explained when considering the actual relevance of training on the job. The longer a legal professional stays within a career hierarchy, the fewer are the turnover opportunities, and any such opportunity would require a basic reconversion of one's professional knowledge and abilities. Moreover, one must keep in mind that in many European countries the examinations to enter the higher ranks in the civil service usually test subject matter similar to that tested for admittance to the judiciary (Di Federico 1976). From this point of view it could be said that Germany has only formalized a general feature detectable in the development of the modern state in continental Europe: the move toward extending the so-called bureaucratic model of recruitment to the judicial branch (Poggi 1990, 30-32).

FRENCH, GERMAN, AND ITALIAN MODELS

To make further discussion easier, we have summarized in table 10.1 the main characteristics of the French, German, and Italian models. We can now briefly describe each model, mentioning the most significant reforms that have been recently introduced.

In France until the end of the 1950s law graduates were selected by means of different examinations for judicial careers and private practice, but the subsequent training on the job in courts and in lawyers' offices was quite similar. In the last three decades many transformations have occurred. These began in 1958, when a wide reform of the judicial selection system created the Ecole Nationale de la Magistrature (ENM) to improve the professional qualifications of magistrates through a more structured training, carried out both in the school and in the courts. Then, in 1971, the first step of a slow reform process concerning private practice began. This reform was aimed at unifying different groups of lawyers[9] and at improving their selection and training. Undoubtedly, its most important achievement was the creation of several schools, inspired

Table 10.1: Education, Training, Selection and Continuing Education of Legal Practitioners in Italy, France, and Germany

	Education and Training		Means of Selection	Continuing Education
	University[a]	Post-University		
Country	JUDGES AND PUBLIC PROSECUTORS			
Italy	4 years	15 months (on the job)	1 exam (before post-university training)	CSM[c] programs (occasionally organized)
France	3 years	27 months (ENM[b] + on the job)	2 exams (before and after post-university training)	ENM program
Germany	3.5 years	30 months (on the job + seminars and work groups)	2 exams (before and after university training)	Federal and state programs
Country	LAWYERS			
Italy	4 years	24 months (on the job)	1 exam (after post-university training)	-
France	4 years	36 months (CFPA[d] + on the job)	2 exams (before and after post-university training)	CFPA programs
Germany	together with judges and public prosecutors			Federal and state programs[e]

[a]Official duration
[b]Ecole Nationale de la Magistrature
[c]Consiglio Superiore della Magistratura
[d]Centres de Formation Professionelle d'Avocat
[e]Continuing education programs for lawyers are separated from those for judges and public prosecutors

by the ENM model, but spread all over the country: the Centres de Formation Professionelle d'Avocats (CFPA). The reforms began to work effectively only at the beginning of the 1980s, when further law modifications were made. As we noted, until that time the training of lawyers was carried out on the job, in courts, and in lawyers' offices, and ended with a final examination. Subsequently, law graduates no longer have to take examinations to enter their professions, but, rather, are admitted to the ENM or the various CFPA, depending on their planned career path.

French law graduates may enter their professions only after a long training period and final evaluations carried out by these schools. For some time lawyers' training has been fixed at three years. In 1990 the training period for magistrates was lengthened from 24 to 27 months. Several adjustments have been continuously introduced in the training programs and methods of these professional schools.[10]

As already mentioned, legal education in Germany is unitary: the same law degree (the *Befähigung zum Richteramt*) enables graduates to serve in all legal professions: as judges, public prosecutors, lawyers, and notaries. In addition, it qualifies them for the higher ranks of public administration. The prescribed curriculum consists of two steps: the first, devoted to theory, takes place in a university law faculty; the second, a practical training period of 30 months, is aimed at establishing contacts with various legal activities.[11] Both phases end with a state examination in two parts, called "first" and "second" state examinations, testing substantially the same subject matter, though at different levels of difficulty.

It would be hard to sum up in a few lines the twenty-year debate on legal education in Germany as well as the many reforms that have followed in the wake of the controversies associated with it. We can note that in 1971 the widespread dissatisfaction with the traditional two-step pattern, mainly due to the lack of a close, significant linkage between theory and practice, led the federal legislature to adopt an "experimental clause" aimed at merging the two phases and introducing the study of nonlegal matters. These objectives have been pursued by means of very different structural solutions in eight university law faculties randomly distributed throughout the country. In spite of the many positive results, this experiment was substantially abandoned in 1984. At present new reform plans, which in various ways take this experience into account, are under discussion in order to improve the suitability of legal education for the "rendezvous with Europe" begun in 1992.

In Italy the recruitment and training of magistrates are separated from those of lawyers and still follow the model that France abandoned in the late 1950s (Mestitz 1991). Law graduates who wish to enter the judicial career are recruited through a national competition and then trained both in courts and public prosecutors' offices. This multipurpose training, based on a job-rotation pattern, lasts at present about fifteen months, though it has been modified several times in the last decades (ranging from six to 18 months). Private practitioners have to serve at least a two-year apprenticeship in a lawyer's office and then pass a state examination qualifying them for professional practice.[12]   This pattern also clearly follows the one adopted in France before the creation of the various CFPA. Even though recent years have witnessed an escalation of reform claims, neither model has ever undergone any substantial change: the only postuniversity training still is apprenticeship.

We can now focus our attention on the main steps taken by magistrates and lawyers in the process of socialization: education and training, selection, and continuing education.

EDUCATION AND TRAINING

We here consider university and post-university education and training, emphasizing the three major issues arising from the comparison: purely legal versus interdisciplinary education, multipurpose versus specialized training, and theory versus practice.

Traditionally, in civil-law countries, universities have been entrusted with those gatekeeping and training functions that, in the common-law world, are mainly performed by apprenticeship with a private practitioner (Abel 1988, 15). But one of the distinctive features of legal education in continental Europe has traditionally been, and to an extent still is, the overwhelming weight given purely theoretical learning. In recent years the need to put the students in touch with "law in action" seems to be more clearly perceived in France and Germany: lectures or seminars given by lawyers and magistrates, oral and written exercises approaching the American case study, and resort to specific didactic methods such as role playing are just a few examples of practical training with no parallel at all in Italy.

Legal culture in continental Europe has long been influenced by the myth of the judge as "*la bouche de la loi* totally aloof from the socio-political context" (Di Federico 1976, 45). Such a myth rested also on the "insularity" of a "legal science" claimed to be self-sufficient and autonomous.[13]   Indeed sociopolitical agnosticism is but one of the factors that can explain the minor role traditionally played in legal education by nonjuridical matters. Such a cultural bias is going to be overcome in France and Germany, though gradually. Reforms introduced either in law faculty programs[14] or in postuniversity schools[15] provide law graduates with some useful knowledge of economics and finance, psychology, criminology, and sociology. These countries seem more likely to recognize that magistrates and lawyers are increasingly required to rely on some basic notions related to the social and political context at large, as well as to the various topics dealt with by welfare legislation.

By contrast, even if some Italian jurists agree in principle with this point of view, the majority still appear to be bewitched by the myth of "legal science," placing emphasis on purely legal disciplines and rejecting the nonlegal ones.[16]   Before commenting further, we shall pause to consider one particular aspect of the education of lawyers.

It has been observed that in Western industrialized countries, characterized by a trend toward the concentration of economic units, legal experts are securing a hold on corporative agreements, thus taking part in decisions that often cross national boundaries (Larson 1988). This supranational dimension of lawyers' work seems likely to require basic knowledge of comparative law as well as of foreign languages. On these grounds the French ENM and CFPA are now running courses devoted to English legal jargon and comparative law. Moreover, future lawyers may choose to carry out their training on the job in lawyers' offices abroad. In Germany federal and local statutes offer law students the chance to devote the last six months of their training to visiting foreign law firms and courts, so as to improve their acquaintance both with other legal systems and with foreign languages. Once again, we must note the total lack of similar projects in Italy: all initiatives in this field are dependent on the willingness (and personal estate) of individuals.

The broadening scope of legal education is not progressing without serious problems, mainly because of an implicit strain between two opposite goals: the need to provide future magistrates and lawyers with a sound legal and nonlegal background and the conflicting need to supply them with a specialized professional knowledge in a reasonable period of time. In Germany the attempt to privilege the first aim has contributed to lengthening education and training, since the same curriculum must shape a wide range of professional competencies and provide a minimum amount of nonlegal knowledge. In fact, though formally fixed at six years, it takes, de facto, about ten years to complete.[17] On the opposite side we find the French choice of a dual system (deeply rooted in a long-established tradition) supporting the specialized, thus separate, training of lawyers and magistrates. Yet by providing two different patterns, which clearly pursues the second of the above-mentioned goals, such a choice gives rise to cultural cleavages among professional groups and "can cause problems of communication between them" (Abel 1988, 8). Actually, France has experienced not only "problems of communication," but also such difficult interactions between lawyers and magistrates that they have episodically reached overt conflict. Very similar controversies have been recurrently observed in Italy, too, but not in Germany, where a common "internal legal culture" (Friedman 1975, 222) seems to represent a powerful connective tissue among different professional subsets.

A comparison of experiences in these countries clearly suggests that common postuniversity training can be a suitable tool for filling cultural cleavages between professional groups. Nevertheless, such all-purpose education fails to build up specific professional abilities, which must be acquired on the job, further delaying full role performance. Reform plans now under discussion in France and Germany seek to find a balance between these two goals. A bill recently presented in Germany insists on specialization as an essential means for coping with the growing complexity of each profession. French observers (Terré 1987) and even the Ministry of Justice now stress the need to face the dysfunctional consequences of the separate model and suggest continuing education programs for both magistrates and lawyers as an attempt to improve their professional relationships.

The third issue we want to underline here relates to the *ratio* between theory and practice during training. According to Freidson, "the actual substance of the knowledge that is ultimately involved in influencing human activities is different from the formal knowledge that is asserted by academics and other authorities. . . . Down at the level of everyday human experience . . . formal knowledge is transformed and modified by the activities of those participating in its use" (1986, xi). The creation of special professional schools in France, as well as the required thirty-month training in Germany, seems to rely on a substantial agreement with this opinion, emphasizing the need for anchoring academic knowledge in practical experience. In other words the mainly theoretical university knowledge is recognized to be a necessary though not sufficient condition for the practice of a legal profession. In both countries training on the job is integrated with phases of study (through seminars or working groups), where trainees have the opportunity to prepare for practical experience and to discuss it.

In Italy newcomers' apprenticeships take place under the supervision of magistrates and lawyers; generally, seminars or working groups are not provided. A fifteen-month training on the job after recruitment is deemed sufficient to build up the skills of the judges and public prosecutors. From a comparative perspective this period is not long enough to form and enhance the professional abilities of magistrates.[18] Its length does not represent the only shortcoming of the training. Among other faults one might remember here the overcrowding of trainees in some judicial offices, which makes it very difficult for each of them to get his/her own supervising magistrate, and the lack of reliable assessment of actual performance, since evaluations are almost invariably positive (Di Federico 1978). The training of lawyers has also undergone severe criticism: it has been remarked that it depends on the willingness of private practitioners to accept trainees in their offices, and their acceptance mostly rests on "family relationship or friendship rather than merit" (Olgiati and Pocar 1988, 345). Moreover, apprenticeship to a single lawyer often means exposure to a narrow experience, the character and quality of which may vary from excellent to deplorable, depending on the work the trainee is asked to do and how she/he is supervised.

SELECTION

Moving on to consider the selection of magistrates and lawyers we shall confine ourselves to the issues that in our view appear most relevant: the evaluation of professional skills, the quantitative efficacy of selection, and the reliability of the verifications of legal knowledge and skills.

To repeat, selection traditionally takes place through national or local competitions consisting of written and oral exams. But if the selective means are by and large the same, or nearly the same, their aims in the three countries appear to be quite different. In France and Germany exams *select candidates to be admitted to training*. Moreover, the selection process does not rely only on entry competitions but functions also during and after apprenticeship. As the entry into the legal professions takes place when training is over, final exams[19] are intended to determine whether the trainees have enhanced their professional skills and ability to apply the law in a decision-making context. In Italy, by contrast, national competitions *select candidates to enter the judicial career directly*, with no further verifications. No value is placed on previous legal experience; it is not considered in the process of selecting magistrates.

As a consequence, most candidates sit for exams soon after graduation, and selection cannot and does not take into account the "practical side" of their future profession.[20] The selection of lawyers, too, is affected by this same shortcoming and fails to evaluate their professional skills and abilities. This may seem a paradox when one considers that examinations to enter private practice take place after a two-year compulsory on-the-job training period. Though written exams consist of legal opinions and of a legal act in procedural law (either civil or criminal), the evaluating criteria end up de facto relating, principally or entirely, to theory. It should come as no surprise that candidates actually devote their efforts (and time) to study, often disregarding their apprenticeships.

We can now briefly consider the quantitative efficacy of the selection means for the judiciary. In tables 10.2, 10.3, and 10.4 we have collected figures on the screening of Italian, French, and German candidates in the period 1981-1989, pointing out the pass rate per year in each country.

For Germany, we must once more note that state examinations qualify successful candidates to practice all legal professions; thus, the figures in table 10.4 refer to the total number of successful candidates, and not specifically to future magistrates. It must also be noted that while table 10.2 shows the results of national competitions to enter the judicial career in Italy, table 10.3 reports on competitions to enter the French ENM, which can be said to represent the most important moment of the whole selective process for judicial recruitment in that nation.

It appears, in table 10.2, that the winners in Italy have always been fewer in number than the places offered, except in the two competitions

Table 10.2:   National Competitions to Recruit Magistrates in Italy, 1981-1989

Year	Places Offered	Candidates (w.e.)		Winners	% Winners
1981	415*	3,343	‖	344	13.30
1982	260	2,390	‖	198	8.29
1983	—	—	‖	-	—
1984	480*	5,152	‖	425	8.25
1985	380*	3,888	‖	274	7.05
1986	418*	4,865	‖	388	7.98
1987	98	2,469	‖	88	3.56
1988	492*	7,571	‖	508	6.71
1989	600*	8,338	‖	493	5.91

w.e. = written exams.   *total of two competitions.

Table 10.3:   National Competitions to Enter the Ecole Nationale de la Magistrature, 1981-1989

Years	Places Offered	Candidates (w.e.)		Winners	% Winners
1981	210**	896	‖	10	23.44
1982	320**	1,260	‖	20	25.40
1983	230*	1,092	‖	30	21.06
1984	230*	1,144	‖	30	20.10
1985	230	1,268	‖	15	16.96
1986	245*	1,414	‖	45	17.33
1987	245*	1,401	‖	21	15.77
1988	245*	1,336	‖	86	13.92
1989	190*	1,223	‖	70	13.90

w.e. = written exams.   *total of two competitions.
**total of four competitions.

undertaken in 1988, but that the pass rate, except in 1981, has never exceeded 9%.[21]   Table 10.3 shows that in France the pass rate has diminished over the years from a high of 25.40% in 1982 to 13.90%; the Italian pass rate is thus significantly lower. Observers in both countries agree that this phenomenon is mainly due to the worsening quality of university education.

In Germany the selective effects of two subsequent screenings are further reinforced by a noteworthy circumstance: among all the successful candidates, only those with higher marks have a real chance of entering the judiciary.[22]   In all three cases examinations seem to fulfill their selective aims, at least with respect to the quantitative screening of candidates.

Table 10.4:   First and Second State Examinations to Enter All Legal Professions in Germany, 1981-1989

Year	First State Examination				Second State Examination		
	Candidates	Winners	% Winners		Candidates	Winners	% Winners
1981	8,189	6,158	75.20	||	4,591	4,152	90.44
1982	7,714	5,592	72.49	||	5,166	4,600	89.04
1983	7,586	5,535	72.96	||	5,679	5,097	89.75
1984	8,084	5,854	72.41	||	4,508	4,004	88.82
1985	8,400	6,015	71.61	||	5,273	4,710	89.32
1986	9,657	7,082	73.34	||	5,527	5,017	90.77
1987	9,436	6,951	73.66	||	6,029	5,260	87.24
1988	10,892	7,927	72.78	||	6,382	5,648	88.50
1989	10,725	8,020	74.78	||	6,867	6,129	89.30

Broadly speaking, the reliability of selective assessment seems unquestioned both in France and Germany, while in Italy strong criticisms have been raised. The results of the examinations for the selection of future lawyers appear not to be homogeneous in the 26 courts of appeal where they take place. In some the percentage of successful candidates is very high, but elsewhere it is very low. According to Olgiati and Pocar, "The pass rate varies from 13 percent to 70 percent" (1988, 346).   As a result, competitions to enter the judiciary are deemed highly unreliable, even in evaluating mere theoretical knowledge of law.

To clarify this statement we can cite the results of research by Di Federico (1978) on national competitions for judicial careers. Since in Italy it takes from two to three years to complete the evaluation of each exam, it may happen that candidates winning a given competition sit also for the written exams of the following one, as the previous results are not yet known.

Examining about 500 cases of candidates who have undergone such an experience, Di Federico found a rate of failure of 59.9 per cent in the second competition, thus giving evidence of the significant role played by chance in the outcomes of the examinations.   These candidates, notwithstanding their failure on the second examination occasion, became, and still are, judges or public prosecutors. Given these results, it is no wonder that these verifications of professional skills in Italy are deemed unreliable.

CONTINUING EDUCATION

Coming now to continuing education, we shall limit ourselves only to considering whether and how it takes place in each country and whether there are specific institutions providing courses for this purpose.

First, it will be important to bear in mind that in civil-law countries magistrates are recruited mainly (or solely) for the lowest levels of the organizational hierarchy (Guarnieri 1991). Thus, promotions are the most important way to reach the higher rungs in the career ladders.   In France and Germany appointments to the higher echelons rest on two effectively working criteria, that is, seniority and merit. Conversely, the *cursus honorum* of Italian magistrates depends, at least de facto, only on the former criterion. As the evaluations of professional performances are always positive—and thus a pure formality--magistrates' careers appears to be exclusively regulated by the mere passing of time. In fact, "after an initial entrance examination of little reliability aimed at ascertaining only whether the applicant has a general knowledge of law, magistrates remain in their career for some forty-five years without undergoing any further screening or any significant verification of professional capacity" (Di Federico 1989, 35). As a consequence individuals are personally responsible for preserving and further developing their knowledge and skills.

This premise can explain the reason why in Italy the substantial lack of permanent continuing education programs has come to be a serious matter in recent years. Actually, from time to time the Higher Council of the Judiciary,[23] which is also responsible under the law for guaranteeing the professional qualifications of magistrates, does run courses or seminars aimed at discussing new laws or specific items. However, these seminars cannot be compared to the French and German experiences in this field, because they depend on the willingness and sensitivity of each council. Reforms concerning continuing education have not yet found favor because of an attitude, rather widespread among magistrates, that the adoption of such programs would damage the public image of the whole judiciary by implicitly admitting the professional deficiencies of its members. Also the updating of the professional skills of lawyers gives rise to significant problems because continuing education is provided neither by specific institutions nor by professional associations.

In Germany 10 percent of all federal and state magistrates attend the approximately 50 courses or seminars given every year by a teaching staff of about 500 jurists, under the auspices of the Deutsche Richterakademie, created in 1973 to fulfil this specific task. A similar institution (Deutsche Anwaltsakademie) has been established by the lawyers' professional association in order to take care of the continuing education of private practitioners.

French magistrates and lawyers may choose among the continuing education programs organized by the ENM and the CFPA, which include both theoretical courses in specialized areas and *stages* in various institutions or organizations in France and abroad. These programs seem to respond to demand, as a number of professionals attend them. Furthermore, as already mentioned, recent reform proposals have suggested setting up common continuing education programs for lawyers and magistrates in order to mitigate some of the negative consequences of the separate training. According to our interviews, the executive staffs of both professional schools agree on the need to overcome the rigidly separate framework, at least as far as continuing education is concerned. Hence, at present efforts seem to be concentrating in this direction. To sum up, in France and Germany the continuing education of both lawyers and magistrates is provided by special institutions, which are quite absent in Italy, where continuing education takes place only episodically for magistrates and is not provided for lawyers.

CONCLUDING REMARKS

Reforms adopted or experimented with in France and Germany seem to rest on a common assumption: that the growing complexity of legal practice, the marked evolution of the roles of magistrates and lawyers, and the increasingly different needs and expectations of the community require new responses from educators. We chose the French and German models primarily because in the civil-law world they represent two alternative approaches to legal education and training. However, even though these countries have given different institutional answers, they seem to evidence the following common features:

1. long or very long post-university training periods are provided for, in order to fill the gap between theory and practice;
2. interdisciplinary knowledge is supplied during either the university or post-university training in order to face the widening scope of legal practice, the growing complexity of issues with that the judicial process has to deal, and more;
3. selection tests are provided before, during and after training in order to guarantee as much as possible the personal and professional qualifications of all robed participants in the administration of justice;
4. continuing education programs are offered by professional schools or specific institutions in order to ensure professional updating.

Although the French and German experiences have yielded overall positive results, we cannot disregard that they have also had some dysfunctional consequences related to the choice between specialized and multipurpose education. The separate training adopted in France pursues the aim of specialization, but it does not allow the development of a common cultural background facilitating relationships between magistrates and lawyers. The unitary model adopted in Germany, though supplying this kind of background, takes too much time to provide the specific skills and abilities needed to perform any professional role (Wassermann 1989). Specialization—which is an instrument to rationalize the legal practice and to guarantee professional competence (Kötz et al. 1982)—represents a suitable alternative to the long training period carried out in Germany. But Italian and French experiences show that separate patterns can and do lead to professional conflicts between magistrates and lawyers.

Broadly speaking, in civil-law countries reforms concerning legal education have had to struggle with the legacy of an academic culture that has often privileged the theoretical side of learning and rejected nonlegal disciplines. Such cultural biases still exert a notable influence in Italy, where it is very hard to change legal education. Various groups that are active among magistrates, lawyers, scholars, and legislators agree on the need to revise the present model, but little agreement on what to do has been reached so far. Indeed, critics have come to realize that reforms in this field are facing apparently intractable difficulties (Di Federico 1989; Guarnieri 1991), as all of them potentially clash with cultural prejudices or with widespread corporative interests. Conversely, changes occurring in France and Germany (and we could mention Portugal as well) point out the actual concern of these countries for a more thorough training of the legal professions and suggest that cultural biases can be gradually overcome. The French experience in particular shows that the attempt to mix theory and practice in order to find a balance between these two components of the learning process can be more profitably pursued by institutions charged with this specific task. In Germany purely legal education has been challenged during a fourteen-year process of trial and error, and today nonlegal matters are present in university curricula. In these countries the increasing number of successful projects concerning continuing education have had to break down widespread resistances often based on the idea that such programs may be perceived as an implicit admission of low levels of professional competence.

NOTES

Financial support for this research was provided by the Italian National Research Council.

1. See preliminary results in the report by Di Federico (1987b) for the Italian Ministry of Justice and in Di Federico and Mestitz (1988). See also Mestitz (1988, 1989, 1990), Mestitz and Pederzoli (1991), and Pederzoli (1992).

2. According to Becker (1970, 345) the concept of political significance points out both the "influence" and the "impact" of courts' decision making on the political system. Influence is defined as "the judged utility of the courts by the various (or separate) sets of political actors," whereas impact "consists of attitudes and reactions attributable to the operation of the courts" (347).

3. For analytical studies on the political relevance of the judiciary in liberal-democratic countries, see Murphy (1964), Murphy and Tanenhaus (1972), Shapiro (1981), Guarnieri (1981, 1984, 1989), Cappelletti (1984), Waltman and Holland (1988). Although the essays of Chayes (1976) and Horowitz (1977) refer to the U.S.A., they assume general relevance with respect to western democracies. See further bibliographic references in Pederzoli (1990). Peculiarities of the Italian setup have been widely described by Di Federico (1968, 1976, 1989), Freddi (1978), Zannotti (1981, 1989) and Guarnieri (1991). On the evolution of lawyers' functions, see Rüschmeyer (1973), MacCormick (1976); Friedman (1985), and Abel and Lewis (1988, 489-494).

4. See Lonbay (1988) and Abel and Lewis (1988). Recently the topic was discussed at the Joint Meetings of the International Conference of Law and Society (Amsterdam, June 26-29, 1991). Moreover, one of the workshops of the ninth World Congress of the International Association of Procedural Law (Coimbra-Lisbon, August 25-31, 1991) was devoted to "The Education and Training of Judges and Lawyers" (Carpi and Di Federico, 1991).

5. "Magistrates" is the translation for the Italian *magistrati* as well as the French *magistrats*, including both judges and public prosecutors, so that it indicates a professional group quite different from the English one. This is so because in Italy and France judges and public prosecutors share the same career and form a unitary body. Although in Germany they belong to two separate groups, we shall here refer to them shortly as magistrates.

6. For detailed references on France, see Mestitz (1990), and on Germany, see Pederzoli (1992).

7. For Italy, we relied on the vast, rich documentation gathered by Giuseppe Di Federico at the *Centro Studi e Ricerche sull'Ordinamento Giudiziario* of the University of Bologna during his twenty years of research activities on the administration of justice.

8. In fact all their members are qualified as *Volljuristen* (full jurists).

9. By contrast with other civil-law European countries, private practice in France was traditionally divided into many groups exercising different tasks (*avocats, agrées, avoués, conseils juridiques*, etc.). The last step in the process of merging the various subsets of private practitioners was accomplished in 1990 by a reform unifying the *conseils juridiques* and the *avocats* (Mestitz 1990, 362-363). At present lawyers (*avocats*) are going to become the most representative group.

10. The high costs of magistrates' training are supported by public budget, while lawyers' training is mainly paid for by the whole profession itself, as the public contribution is almost irrelevant (Mestitz 1990).

11. Since successful candidates are qualified for all legal professions, they serve their apprenticeship through job rotation in courts, public prosecutors' offices, lawyers' offices, and public administration offices. The high costs of training are supported by federal and state budgets.

12. Magistrates' training is financially supported by the public budget, while the costs of lawyers' training are supported by the trainees themselves.

13. "Legal scientists deliberately focus their attention on pure legal phenomena and values. Hence the data and theories of the social sciences are excluded as non-legal. . . . The result is a highly artificial body of doctrine that is deliberately insulated from what is going on outside, in the rest of the culture" (Merryman 1969, 69). On the concept of "legal science," see also Merryman (1965, 45).

14. Since the beginning of the 1970s various nonlegal subject matters have been introduced in the eight German law faculties that took part in the experiments discussed previously. The most interesting one, but also the most controversial, was adopted at the University of Bremen, whose syllabus provided a year of study in common with the sociology faculty. Nowadays students are generally offered courses in philosophy and sociology of law, criminology, economics, and finance.

15. In the 1970s the ENM began to include the social sciences in its programs. Although several debated phases have characterized this difficult integration (Billard 1986), today many problems have been overcome: psychologists and sociologists give some seminars on specific issues and collaborate with the teaching staff of magistrates in the case study and the role playing methods.

16. In fact, neither social sciences nor other nonlegal disciplines (among them languages) are provided by the Italian university law programs. However, after obtaining the faculty's approval students are allowed, but not encouraged, to present personal study plans including other subject matters taught outside their faculty (Mestitz 1991).

17. The increasing age of successful candidates in state examinations is a major handicap of German jurists in comparison with their European colleagues. German law graduates enter the judiciary when they are about 30 years old and

have to undergo a period of trial employment (ranging from three to five years) before becoming full judges. By contrast, in Italy and France magistrates are appointed when they are about 27.

18. It has to be stressed that newcomers can be assigned to various quite different tasks, dealing for instance with civil, criminal, juvenile, labor, or financial matters. Moreover, "by law magistrates enjoy a monopoly on all executive positions in the ministry of justice, including those in minister's cabinet and legislative office" (Di Federico 1989, 37).

19. The German second state examination and the final exams provided by the CFPA and the ENM in France.

20. On this subject Di Federico remarks that "applicants for the judiciary are selected on the basis of their general institutional knowledge of several branches of the law as tested by written and oral exams and guaranteed by a university degree in law. Professional training and experience are to be acquired within the judicial organization starting from the bottom of the career ladder. The recruiting system is such that candidates for the judiciary enter the competition soon after graduation and in any case before 30 years of age. . . . Practical professional training acquired in other branches of the legal profession is in no way considered valuable for the judicial career." (1976, 117-118)

21. The law provides that if the number of winners exceeds the number of places offered, there can be a 10% increase in the number of recruits, with the only condition that vacancies in the judicial offices have had to occur in the interim.

22. This same circumstance becomes a shortcoming when seen from the lawyers' point of view, because graduates who cannot enter the judicial career often turn to private practice, thus contributing to the phenomenon of "lawyers' wave" (Blankenburg and Schultz 1988).

23. The Higher Council of the Judiciary, the governing body of magistrates, became operative in 1959. It is totally renewed every four years and is composed of 33 members: 20 magistrates elected by their colleagues, 10 representatives elected by Parliament, and three ex officio members (the president of the republic, president and procuratore generale of the Court of Cassation).

REFERENCES

Abel, R. L. 1988. "Lawyers in the Civil-law World." In R. L. Abel and P. S. C. Lewis, eds. *Lawyers in Society*, Vol. 2, 1-51. Berkeley, University of California Press.

Abel, R. L., and P. S. C. Lewis. 1988. "Putting Law Back into the Sociology of Lawyers." In R. L. Abel and P. S. C. Lewis, eds. *Lawyers in Society*. Vol. 3, 478-526.

Becker, T. L. 1970. *Comparative Judicial Politics: The Political Functioning of Courts*. Chicago, Rand McNally.

Billard, P. 1986. Magistrats, *Informations Sociales* 7:85-88.

Blankenburg, E., and U. Schultz. 1988. "The Legal Profession in Germany." In R. L. Abel and P. S. C. Lewis, eds. *Lawyers in Society*. Vol. 2, 124-159.

Cappelletti, M. 1984. *Giudici legislatori?* Milan: Giuffrè.

Carpi, F., and G. Di Federico. 1991. "The Education and Training of Judges and Lawyers." Paper presented to the 9th World Conference on Procedural Law, 25-31 August, Coimbra and Lisbon.

Chayes, A. 1976. "The Role of the Judge in the Public Law Litigation." *Harvard Law Review* 89:1281-1316.

Di Federico, G. 1968. *Il reclutamento dei magistrati*. Bari: Laterza.

———. 1976. "The Italian Judicial Profession and its Bureaucratic Setting." *The Juridical Review*, Pt. 1:40-57.

———. 1978. "Il reclutamento dei magistrati: caratteristiche, affidabilità degli strumenti di selezione, efficacia del concorso." In *Il reclutamento del personale del Ministero di Grazia e Giustizia*, 38-77. Rome: Ministero di Grazia e Giustizia.

———, ed. 1987a. *Preparazione professionale degli avocati e dei magistrati: Discussione su una ipotesi di riforma*. Padua: CEDAM.

———. 1987b. *La preparazione alle professioni legali nella Repubblica Federale Tedesca e in Francia*. Rome: Ministero di Grazia e Giustizia.

———. 1989. "The Crisis of the Justice System and the Referendum on the Judiciary." In R. Leonardi and P. Corbetta, eds. *Italian Politics: A Review*, 25-49. London and New York: Pinter.

Di Federico, G. and A. Mestitz. 1988. "La psicologia nella formazione delle professioni legali in Francia e nella Repubblica Federale Tedesca." In *La giustizia penale e la fluidità del sapere:*

Ragionamento sul metodo, ed. L. de Cataldo Neuburger, 233-248. Padua: CEDAM.

Freddi, G. 1978. *Tensioni e conflitto nella magistratura.* Bari: Laterza.

Freidson, E. 1986. *Professional Powers: a Study of the Institutionalization of Formal Knowledge.* Chicago: University of Chicago Press.

Friedman, L. M. 1975. *The Legal System. A Social Science Perspective.* New York: Russel Sage Foundation.

————. 1985. *Total Justice.* New York: Russell Sage.

Guarnieri, C. 1981. *L'indipendenza della magistratura.* Padua: CEDAM.

————. 1984. *Pubblico ministero e sistema politico.* Padua: CEDAM.

————. 1989. "Magistratura e sistema politico." In *Scienza dell'amministrazione e politiche pubbliche*, ed. G. Freddi, 243-279. Rome: La Nuova Italia Scientifica.

————. 1991. "Magistratura e politica: il caso italiano." *Rivista Italiana di Scienza Politica* 21:3-32.

Horowitz, D. L. 1977. *The Courts and Social Policy.* Washington, D.C.: Brooking Institution.

Kötz, H., W. Paul, M. Pédamon and M. Zander. 1982. *Anwaltsberuf im Wandel: Rechtspflegeorgan oder Dienstleitungsgewerbe.* Frankfurt: Metzner.

Larson, M. S. 1988. "The Changing Functions of Lawyers in the Liberal State: Reflections for Comparative Analysis." In R. L. Abel and P. S. C. Lewis, eds. *Lawyers in Society.* Vol. 3, 427-477.

Lonbay, J. 1990. *Training Lawyers in the European Community.* Birmingham: The Law Society.

MacCormick, D. N., ed. 1976. *Lawyers in their Social Setting.* Edinburgh: W. Green and Son.

Merryman, J. H. 1965. "The Italian Style I: Doctrine." *Stanford Law Review* 18:39-65.

————. 1969. *The Civil Law Tradition.* Stanford: Stanford University Press.

Mestitz, A. 1988. "La formazione professionale dei magistrati in una prospettiva comparata." *Documenti Giustizia* 9:40-80.

————. 1989. "La socializzazione professionale dei magistrati nella Repubblica Federale Tedesca, Francia, Spagna, Portogallo, Italia: aspetti comparativi." In *Psicologia e processo: lo scenario di nuovi equilibri*, ed. L. de Cataldo Neuburger, 275-319. Padua: CEDAM.

————. 1990. *Selezione e formazione professionale dei magistrati e degli avocati in Francia*. Padua: CEDAM.

————. 1991. "Education and Training of Magistrates and Lawyers in Italy." Paper presented to the 9th World Conference on Procedural Law, 25-31 August, Coimbra and Lisbon.

Mestitz, A. and P. Pederzoli. 1991. *The Socialization of the Legal Professions in Western Europe: the Cases of Italy, France and Germany*. Paper presented at the Joint Meetings of the International Conference of Law and Society, 26-29 June, University of Amsterdam.

Murphy, W. F. 1964. *Elements of Judicial Strategy*. Chicago: University of Chicago Press.

Murphy, W. F., and J. Tanenhaus. 1972. *The Study of Public Law*. New York: Random House.

Nonet, P., and P. Selznick. 1978. *Law and Society in Transition. Toward Responsive Law*. New York: Octagon.

Olgiati, V., and V. Pocar . 1988. "The Italian Legal Profession: an Institutional Dilemma." In R. L. Abel and P. S. C. Lewis, eds. *Lawyers in Society*. Vol. 2, 336-368.

Pederzoli, P. 1990. "Il giudice nei regimi democratici." *Rivista Italiana di Scienza Politica* 20:293-323.

————. 1991. "La formazione alle professioni legali nella Repubblica Federale Tedesca." *Rivista Trimestrale di Diritto e Procedura Civile* 45:1203-1227.

————. 1992. *Selezione e formazione delle professioni legali in Germania*. Padua: CEDAM.

Poggi, G. 1990. *The State. Its Nature, Development and Prospects*. Cambridge: Polity Press.

Rüschmeyer, D. 1973. *Lawyers and their Society. A Comparative Study of the Legal Profession in Germany and in the United States*. Cambridge: Harvard University Press .

Shapiro, M. 1981. *Courts. A Comparison and Political Analysis*. Chicago: University of Chicago Press.

Terré, F., ed. 1987. *Magistrats et avocats: formation, carrière, activité professionelle*. Paris: La Documentation Française.

Unger, R. M. 1976. *Law in Modern Society*. New York: The Free Press.

Waltman, J. L., and K. M. Holland, eds. 1988. *The Political Role of Law Courts in Modern Democracies*. Hong Kong: MacMillan.

Wassermann, H.   1989.   "Deutsche Juristen: Schlechte Karten für Europa. Die überlange Juristenausbildung steht erneut zur Diskussion." *Recht und Politik* 25:155-157.

Zannotti, F. 1981. *Le attività extragiudiziarie dei magistrati ordinari*. Padua: CEDAM.

———. 1989. *La magistratura, un gruppo di pressione istituzionale*. Padua: CEDAM.

11.

The Judicialization of Judicial Salary Policy in Italy and the United States

FRANCESCA ZANNOTTI

The judicialization of politics is a well-known and wide-spread phenomenon in liberal-democratic countries, but it is particularly present in countries going through rapid social evolution and carrying out an extensive program of welfare policies. With the growth of public regulation of private behavior in many spheres, the judge's potential range of intervention, his or her capacity to influence social behavior, and the actual means of carrying through public policies have also increased considerably. The institutional consequences of this phenomenon and the levels it has reached are affected by three main interrelated factors.

The first factor is the way the judge sees his/her role and the consequent choice of self-restraint or activism in response to social demands (Nonet and Selznick 1978). The second is the increasing incapacity of decision makers to determine the "public interest" when they are forced to make choices among growing and conflicting social demands. As a result of this incapacity, representative bodies are often no longer able to satisfy needs in the various sectors of society and to resolve conflicts of interests. The third is the increasing effort to lobby the judiciary, for example, through test cases, to obtain what it was impossible to get from legislative or executive powers because of the multiple vetoes available to the holders of conflicting interests. One result of this activity is growing litigation and judicial lawmaking.

The interaction of these three factors is affected by the institutional features of each political system and its judicial subsystems (Friedman 1975, 267ff.), such as the degree of independence of judges and the political significance of the judiciary (Becker 1970, 347). The internal legal culture shared by the legal personnel in each country has the task of transforming social demands into rights protected by the various legal systems. The external legal culture (people's attitudes toward the law) also influences both litigation and judicial lawmaking (Friedman 1975, chaps. 8-9).

The result of the judicialization of politics can be positive if the judicialization works as an alternative channel for the conveyance of social demands when other institutional channels are overloaded or clogged, thus safeguarding pluralism (Ely 1980; Zemans 1983). For instance, in the U.S.A. fundamental rights such as freedom of speech (Shapiro 1966) and the enjoyment of civil rights by minorities have been enlarged by the U.S. Supreme Court. U.S. judges sensitive to the pressure of organized groups have taken the social responsibility of protecting minority or fundamental rights well beyond the capacity or willingness of the majority to do so.

The courts' contributions to innovation in the law in a pluralist society can be positively evaluated because they have been instrumental in guiding or pushing the legislature towards decisions on social and economic behavior in a rapidly changing society. Courts have taken the place of the other two powers both in civil-law and common-law countries.

In contrast, the judicialization of politics can be negative in civil-law countries in which there is a rigid separation of powers. In these countries courts may be politically irresponsible, but they enjoy an indirect democratic legitimacy. The "consensus model" suggests that such courts should not create law to respond to unsatisfied social needs (Bell 1983, 184ff.). Nevertheless, to satisfy corporate interests—quite often only economic ones—many pressure groups have used courts that have upheld their demands, so that citizens have been discouraged from using the traditional instruments of democratic representation. Neocorporativist pressures, which are widespread in many Western countries, can be encouraged by the judicialization of politics. When courts satisfy these demands they determine not only the implementation of many public policies, but also their design, both at local and central levels (Shapiro 1968). This practice often leads to extra public expenditures, increasing the national deficit in unplanned or unforeseen ways.

In the liberal democratic countries, the negative effects of the judicialization of politics are different, depending on both the structure characteristics and the political significance of the judicial subsystems. In the U.S., for instance, both the political significance and guarantees of independence of the judiciary are considerable, but the hierarchical structure of the jurisdiction (embodied in the stare decisis doctrine) allows the U.S. Supreme Court to secure a consistent judicial law-making policy. Both the monopoly over criminal initiative and the discretionary powers related to it allow for a sufficient control of criminal policies on the part of the executive branch.   Federal judicial recruitment is carried out by the executive with senatorial consent. It is based both on transparent political evaluations and tough professional ones, implemented, for example, through the ratings of the American Bar Association. These features of the judicial subsystems have led scholars (Dahl 1957, 279-295) to argue that the judicial creativity of the U.S. Supreme Court has never been in conflict with the dominant political forces, because the court is part of the same national coalition. This is also possible because a powerful, effective, and efficient mechanism of checks and balances induces the judges' self-restraint at least on some issues.

In countries like Italy, where both the political significance of the judicial subsystems and judicial independence are considerable, the lack of institutional checks and balances makes the judges' lawmaking and consequently the judicialization of politics so strong as to cross the border to "government by the judges." The problem of the democratic legitimacy of judicial lawmaking exists in Italy because the bureaucratic recruitment system and a career structure based only on seniority lead to politically irresponsibility on the part of judges and prosecutors. Moreover, higher courts are not able to develop a consistent judicial policy because of the fragmentation of the jurisdictions. Judges have a monopoly on the initiative in criminal proceedings, without any coordination by the executive power. Judges are also the gatekeepers to the Constitutional Court, through the instrument of the "appeal to constitutionality brought by a judge during trial" (*ricorso incidentale di costituzionalità*).

The judicialization of politics in Italy is neither positive nor limited to only certain issues because the constitutional provision, according to which the judge is subject only to law, seems too weak to impose real limits. A judge's ideology and personal values, which are impossible to eliminate in any political system (Murphy and Pritchett 1986), often become in Italy the only guide to his or her creativity.

The judicialization of judicial salary policy can be a useful tool to focus on the different behavior of judges in Italy and in the U.S., two similar political systems[1] that have produced radically different results in salary policy, results that appear to arise from the different features of their judicial subsystems.

The pay of judges and magistrates, and especially the increases in that pay that may occur over the years, may have some considerable influence on their independence. In fact, in all modern political systems with a liberal-democratic regime the responsibility for establishing judges' salaries is assigned to other authorities than judges (parliaments or governments or both).

The problem may only be one of image, but the independence of the judiciary, as a guarantee of the impartiality that legitimates its authority, is also based on the citizens' perception of such characteristics. Thus, while periodic negotiations over pay increases for all other civil servants are seen as a normal means of protecting their interests, such negotiations can strongly damage the magistrates' image of impartiality and independence. Both positive and negative outcomes in negotiations of this kind may be interpreted as reflecting positive or negative evaluation of the judges' performance, as assessed by the other powers. Such salary negotiations might be perceived as a means of illicit interference with their independence and impartiality.

It is for this reason that some national legal systems have established specific guarantees in this field. For example the U.S. Constitution (art. 3, sec 1) has forbidden the reduction of active judges' salaries while they are in office. In Italy magistrates' salaries can be changed only by Parliament through the enactment of statutes. In England, the Act of Settlement guarantees that judges' salaries are "ascertained and established," that is, they are not subject to suspension or reduction; and until the present, English judges' salaries have been included in the "consolidated fund," a special fund that secures their payment even if Parliament is not in session (Lederman 1956; Spreacher 1976; Smith 1976).

Despite these safeguards, the problem of protecting or increasing judges' pay—even if it is only a matter of guaranteeing the amount established at the moment of recruitment from erosion by inflation—still remains an unsolved problem that must be faced periodically. It is particularly aggravated in civil-law systems such as Italy, where judges are recruited on a bureaucratic basis and where salary increases follow a career pattern based on seniority.

RELEVANT FEATURES OF EACH JUDICIAL SUB-SYSTEM AND SALARY SETTLEMENT IN ITALY AND THE UNITED STATES

In every liberal-democratic regime, and particularly in the United States and Italy,

> an ideal-typical characteristic of the judicial system is its passivity, in the sense that its activation depends on external inputs. This passivity has its origins in the triadic mechanism of conflict resolution, where the third usually intervenes if requested by the parties in conflict. The way in which the judicial system, and consequently the judge, may be activated is extremely important for the evaluation of its influence on the political system (and precisely to evaluate its significance). (Guarnieri 1981, 111)

We therefore have to identify the characteristics of each legal system, the means of access, the procedures courts have to follow, the kind of disputes they can deal with, who can bring them, and what kind of solutions are possible (Sarat and Grossman 1975, 1207ff.; Shapiro 1975; Eckhoff 1965, 11-48). Through the analysis of the limits set on the courts' inputs, it is possible to evaluate the political significance of a judicial subsystem. The relevant factors to consider are (1) the dimensions of the courts' jurisdiction, in particular its vertical and horizontal fragmentation; (2) the structural characteristics affecting the ability of all citizens to have equal access to justice, independent of their financial resources; and (3) whether gatekeepers exist within or at the borders of the judicial system to reduce the number of demands or to modify their content.

The same kind of analysis may be applied to the outputs of the courts. Since the courts' decisions are not immediately executory, the most relevant aspects here are the extent to which their pronouncements require and receive the collaboration of the other powers and are subject to review by other powers, and the autonomy enjoyed by and instruments available to the judge in conducting a trial.   All these structural characteristics influence the political significance of each judicial subsystem, making it more or less influential in the political system.

Having laid this groundwork, let us now turn to the characteristics of the recruitment and careers of American federal judge and Italian magistrates. The American federal judges are appointed by the President of the United States with the consent of the Senate, hold office for life on condition of good behavior, and are recruited from the legal profession at large.   American federal judges' career are not of a bureaucratic nature: they are, in fact, appointed to exercise their function in a specific court of first instance or of appeal. This does not mean that a federal judge of first instance may not be appointed as an appellate judge, but only that progress up the judicial hierarchy is not automatic nor determined by seniority. If such a promotion does occur, the procedure for confirming the judge to the appointment does not differ from that which would apply to a lawyer who has not served as a judge.

Ordinary Italian magistrates, on the other hand, are recruited on a bureaucratic basis at an early age through a public competitive exam, without having any previous work experience or job training in the judicial field. They hold office until the age of seventy and during their tenure in the judiciary—usually for more than forty years—their career progress depends almost exclusively on seniority. In twenty-eight years this allows them to achieve the highest echelons of the judicial hierarchy, to become magistrates of the Supreme Court of Cassation with directive functions. Advancement up the career ladder corresponds, at least formally, with a parallel increase in professional competence.

Nevertheless, the judicial hierarchy (tribunal, court of appeal and supreme court of cassation) does not correspond to a hierarchy among the actors undertaking these specific functions. Under the Italian Constitution, the judge is subject only to the law (art. 101). The Higher Council of the Judiciary (*Consiglio superiore della Magistratura* or *CSM*) is responsible for making all the decisions relating to the magistrates' status. The CSM is composed of twenty magistrates elected by their colleagues and ten members appointed by Parliament in plenary session from among university professors of law and senior lawyers. The first president of the Court of Cassation and the general prosecutor of the same court are also members of this council. The chairman of the CSM is the president of the Italian republic.

If we analyze the salary systems in Italy and in the United States we can easily see that the Italian pay mechanisms are much more complex than those of the U.S. because of the existence of a career pattern. American federal judges' salaries are established by the executive and ratified by Congress. The American Constitution (art. III, sec 1) does not allow the salaries assigned to the judges to be diminished during their continuance in office. Moreover, there are no mechanisms that provide the American judges with increases in salary determined on the mere basis of years served in office, since judicial service is not a bureaucratic career.

The Federal Salary Act of 1967[2] established that federal judges' pay increases would be proposed by the president and ratified by Congress. The president's proposal arises from plans submitted to him by an ad hoc commission. The president, having modified the commission's proposal as he thinks appropriate, submits his proposal to Congress together with his annual message on the budget. Congress has thirty days to approve a contrary motion; after that period, the president's proposal is automatically effective. This process is repeated every year.

The Italian magistrates' salaries are provided for by statute (art. 108, Constitution), like any other measure that concerns their status, and increases must be approved by Parliament. The fragmentation of the Italian judicial system into ordinary, administrative, public accountability (Corte dei Conti), and military jurisdictions requires different bodies of judges, who are recruited separately and who have, on the basis of historical inheritance, different seniority ladders.

Nevertheless, there is a horizontal equivalence established among the different judicial positions. For example, a magistrate of cassation is equal to a councillor of state and to regional administrative tribunals councilors, and also to councilors of the court of account and to military cassation magistrates. Until 1983 this functional equivalence corresponded to a common salary, different only in the specific allowances attributed to each body. By tradition, the State lawyers, an autonomous group that represents the state in all judicial cases, had the same salary as the cassation magistrates.

To obtain raises, the associations of the various categories of magistrates, behaving like a real pressure group (Zannotti 1989, chaps. 1-3) in Parliament, have traditionally adopted two different strategies, shifting from one to the other. The first consisted of taking advantage of the civil servants' trade union's negotiations, since the trade unions represented so many more people; this allowed them to protect their image of independence by avoiding awkward direct negotiations with the executive and the Parliament. The second strategy consisted of separating themselves from the higher civil servants, claiming their uniqueness and the superiority of their functions. This occurred especially in negative economic circumstances, when it was much easier for a body composed of a relatively limited number of members (approximately 8,000) to be dealt with separately. The mechanisms for determining the amounts of the salaries have undergone four different modifications through time. After the breakdown of the fascist regime Italian magistrates' salaries were put on a par with those of the higher civil servants. But by 1951 the magistrates had already pressured Parliament into separating them from the civil service in order to have higher salaries, claimed on the basis of the high quality of their functions. In 1968, following a reorganization of the State administration and a readjustment of the civil servants' salaries, the magistrates' pay was once again linked to those of the higher civil servants. Finally, with two further statutes passed in 1979 and 1981, the magistrates obtained the separation of their salaries from other categories of civil servants, thereby achieving higher pay and a mechanism for automatic salary realignment to avoid trade-union negotiation over their compensation. This realignment allowed an automatic upgrading of the magistrates' salaries every three years on the basis of the average percentage increase achieved cumulatively by all categories of civil servants in the previous three years. From 1981 to 1991 this mechanism led to a 105% real increase in the magistrates' salaries. Moreover, magistrates, like any other civil servants, are entitled to receive cost-of-living allowances that partially protects their salaries' real value from inflation. Besides career progression, which brings with it higher qualifications and salaries, the Italian magistrates enjoy within their current positions automatic salary raises every two years, that increase their salary in percentage terms.

This particularly favorable treatment, compared to other professional employees, was obtained by magistrates because of Parliament's recognition of their merits in having defended the nation's democratic institutions against the subversive actions of terrorism. For this reason, in 1981 ordinary magistrates were also given a further allowance, a "risk indemnity," which was applied to all of them, regardless of whether their actual specific functions were civil, criminal, or investigatory.

The Italian Parliament and government thought that by granting these further benefits to the magistrates they were going to stop them from claiming higher salaries, but this was not true!

THE JUDICIALIZATION OF JUDICIAL SALARY POLICY: THE ITALIAN CASE

The high rate of inflation in the early 1980s (approximately 20-22% a year) led the magistrates of ordinary, accountability, administrative, and military courts and the state lawyers to start new negotiations with the executive and Parliament, in order to achieve further salary increases. The economic crisis, the increasing deficit, and the awareness that many other civil servant categories had not received any salary raises led the executive and Parliament to deny a further raise in magistrates' salaries. The leaders of the various magistrates' associations, who are themselves organized into the *Coordinamento delle magistrature* (Zannotti 1989, chap. 2), decided to adopt the strategy of litigation.

The 1982-83 operative strategies of the magistrates' associations were based on test cases filed to Regional Administrative Tribunals (TAR), who were competent to pass judgment on the matter. As noted above, Italian magistrates, beside having a common basic salary, enjoy various rates of pay, since their economic treatment is fixed by different statute provisions according to the judicial body to which they belong. In their suits, the members of each jurisdiction requested that the different structure of the salaries of the various judicial bodies granting this request result in a substantial salary increase for each group. The claimants stated that equal functions must be provided with equal salaries. The TAR upheld the appeal and also recognized the overdue arrears, the inflation linked to monetary revaluation with interest matured from January 1979.

The executive appealed to the Council of State, sitting in plenary session, but the council, having consolidated the various appeals, awarded significant economic increases dating from December 1983. The executive, attempting both to avoid the effect of the decision and to allow Parliament time to legislate in this field, appealed the Council of State's decision to the Court of Cassation, the only constitutional body available to prevent a decision of the Council of State from passing into a judgment beyond recall. At the same time it also brought a bill before Parliament providing new economic treatment of the magistrates and state lawyers. The bill's main institutional purpose was once again to regulate the economic treatment of these officials by statute, and not by the administrative extension of the council's decision, as the magistrates' association had asked. In a political situation characterized by cuts in public expenditure, the statute had a further aim: introducing into the public budget an expenditure not previously foreseen.

This new statute was necessary because more than 3,000 magistrates had appealed to the TAR. They would in any case have obtained the salary increases, the outstanding back payments, the inflation linked to monetary revaluation, and the interest, in open violation of parliamentary prerogatives.

It is important to underline that the judges both of the TAR and of the Council of State, unlike their American counterparts, did not consider in their decisions the problem of being a party to a case, taking for granted that, for them, just as for any other citizen, the legal protection of their interests was a constitutional guarantee.

While Parliament was at work on the approval of the new economic plan for the magistrates and the state lawyers, the Court of Cassation, more rapidly than usual, announced its decision on the appeal brought by the executive, denying the government's claims. The Court of Cassation applied the status "not recallable by law" to the decision of the Council of State. The executive temporarily suspended the execution of the decision, which was valid only for the claimants, waiting for Parliament to enact the statute concerning the magistrates' new economic treatment, and denying the administrative extension of the decision to all interested parties. The magistrates' and state lawyers' new economic treatment was established by law in August 1984.

The mechanisms adopted to determine the new economic treatment, which ensured that the mechanisms of automatic realignment and career progression were still in effect, were completely new and very complex. Briefly, they provided that each salary would be determined on the basis of the actual years served in office by each magistrate. The result was that each magistrate's salary would be differentiated.

To fully understand the effects of the new statute, a further explanation is required. The complexity of the law and its vague formulation, which lead to different interpretations, have been used by the magistrates in further litigation to avoid the implementation of the parts of the statute that they did not favor (Zannotti 1989, chap. 6).

Although I will not make reference to all these appeals that have been upheld, one seems of particular importance to understanding how the institutional checks and balances do not work in Italy. The new statute, beside providing for the new economic package (which was more favorable than the one obtained with the Council of State decision), has also pronounced the extinction of the appeals still pending concerning this subject. The intention of the lawmakers was to avoid further burdening the treasury with the judicial cost of the cases, the arrears, and other supplemental payments specified by the Council of State.

In response, the judges appealed to the Constitutional Court. The fundamental questions were whether Parliament, as the supreme representative of the community's will, could (1) extinguish pending judgments that had been rendered obsolete by new legislative provisions, and (2) issue an interpretative statute in contrast with a judgment beyond recall. Through the instrument of the "appeal to constitutionality brought by a judge during trial" (*ricorso incidentale di costituzionalità*), the judiciary and the state lawyers forced the Constitutional Court to solve once and for all an institutional conflict among political powers.

The Constitutional Court in its April 7, 1987, decision considered Article 10.1 of the challenged statute as damaging the constitutionally granted right of action. According to the court the extinction of a trial could occur because the parties either give up their rights to action or remain inactive. Decisions reached on the merits during a trial have to be carried out. Article 10 "claims the ineffectiveness of all provisions not yet passed in judgment. This underlines the intention of the law maker to deny the possibility of having justice done in relation to controversial matters, even when a sentence has been passed."

The Constitutional Court ruled that Parliament had the power to enforce an interpretative statute by providing the judges with the intended meaning of specific provisions. Nevertheless, it could predetermine the effects of the interpretative statute on pending judgments by directly extinguishing them. Since the interpretative law was introduced when various concordant judicial provisions had passed—one of which had the status of res judicata—it is evident that the lawmaker, foreseeing the extinction of the pending cases, intended to put an end to this practice, using his prerogative as interpreter of the law, and therefore violated the provisions contained in Article 24 of the Constitution. Moreover, in Article 10 the lawmaker intended to exclude the judges' decision on the merits, making them officially declare the extinction of the pending judgments.

On institutional grounds the court went beyond the repeal of Article 10 since with this decision it set a limit to the effectiveness of the community's will, which Parliament represents. Briefly, the law maker cannot enforce new statutes of interpretation concerning the provisions that he himself has previously enacted where there is a contrasting judicial interpretation passed into a definitive judgement.

In proclaiming the constitutional illegitimacy of what Parliament had done, the Constitutional Court indirectly declared that the citizens' rights to obtain a judgment of merit cannot be evaded by parliamentary extinction through statute, without incurring constitutional illegitimacy. But this only happens when the new parliamentary interpretation of the previous provision endorses a continuous judicial interpretation. Following this decision, the demands of the claimants were endorsed, and both the arrears and raises were recognized.

THE JUDICIALIZATION OF JUDICIAL SALARY POLICY: THE CASE OF THE UNITED STATES

In 1977 a group of 140 district federal judges presented a claim to the U.S. Court of Claims to get the court to recognize their right to receive salary increases that in the period 1969-1975 had been proposed by the President, but rejected by Congress. The requests of the claimants were based on the fact that the inflation rate in the U.S. in the period taken into consideration had been 34.4% while the salaries of the claimants had been more or less the same ($40,000). On the basis of 1969 dollars, the real value of their salaries had fallen below $30,000. In the same period seven federal judges had been obliged to resign because of the freezing of their salaries.

The claimants emphasized that in this period both private and public salaries had increased even more than the cost of living. Thus the claimants asserted that such a situation violated Article 3 section 1 of the Constitution, since it resulted in a substantial decrease in their salaries *during* their continuance in office. They also claimed a supposed unconstitutionality in the legislative provision allowing rejection of the president's proposed salary increases, since Congress had taken the place of the executive, assuming prerogatives that were exclusively reserved to the president. The claimants claimed that the presidential proposal became effective from the moment it was transmitted to the Congress, and, furthermore, that a veto posed by only one House was not sufficient to invalidate the president's proposal.

The government's answer to these requests was that the federal judges had already been broadly compensated for their services in office and that they did not have any right to claim increases in their salaries since Article 3 section 1 did not intend to guarantee any kind of realignment of nominal salaries to the rate of increase in inflation.

Moreover, the executive claimed that this case was not suitable for judicial decision because of its political nature, since an eventual endorsement of the decision relating to the judges' requests would have represented an illegitimate interference in legislative and executive prerogatives. In other words, it would have led to self-determination of the salary levels and would have involved the court in a subject that could not be dealt with by judicial instruments.

The Court of Claims in May 1977 rejected the request of the claimants. The reasons it gave to support this judgment seem relevant to the working of the institutional checks and balances between the judicial power and the two other powers.

The court asserted its own competence in dealing with the case. Noting that since the Constitution limits the legislative and executive by stopping them from diminishing the judges' salaries during their continuance in office, the court was the appropriate body to control the observance of such a limit in a system of checks and balances. The court further asserted that it lacked neither rules nor experience to guide it in dealing with the problem. Nevertheless, the court rejected the appeal on the merits.

The protection of the judicial system's prerogatives from the other two powers asserted by the court in its legal reasoning is in itself an emblematic example of how strongly the working of checks and balances is felt at all levels of government in the U.S. The opinions expressed by the court in rejecting the appeal on the merits are astonishing and demonstrate a sense of self-restraint that is not common in Italy: it is important to remember that in this case the court is judge of itself.

The court did not accept the grounds of unconstitutionality stated by the claimants, ruling that the law provides the Congress with full powers as to the determination of the salary increases proposed by the President, including the power to diminish or to repeal them, that the proposal presented by the president before the Congress does not have legal value ab initio, but only after thirty days, if Congress had not in the meantime made different provisions; and finally that the veto by one house is not unconstitutional.

According to the court, the aim of the Constitution was to protect the independence of the third power from political interference. In guaranteeing that the judges' pay should not be diminished while holding office, it did not intend to guarantee that the real value of salaries would remain the same through time. Thus the decision whether periodically to realign judges' salaries to adjust for inflation falls fully within the discretion of the executive and legislative powers. A decision not to realign the salary levels would produce a violation of the Constitution only if it were discriminatory.

After this decision, thirteen federal district judges took legal action in a federal district court demanding that the Legislative Branch Appropriation Acts of 1976 and 1977 should be declared unconstitutional because they were in conflict with Article 3 section 1. With regard to the 1976 Act, which the president had signed on October 1, Congress repealed the pay increase (4.8%) that the president had proposed and with regard to the 1977 Act, which the president signed on July 12, Congress once again repealed the proposed pay increases (7.1%). The federal district court endorsed the judges' claim.

On October 19 the same thirteen judges, having obtained this favorable result, conveyed to the same federal district court a claim that was similar to the previous one but with reference to the Legislative Branch Appropriation Adjustment Act of 1978 and to the Executive Salary Cost of Living Adjustment Act of 1979. The federal district court recognized the unconstitutionality of the 1978 act but not that of the 1979 act, since it generically referred to executive personnel. The U.S. government appealed both decisions to the Supreme Court.

On December 15, 1980, the Supreme Court ruled that there was a violation of the constitutional principle that did not allow the diminishing of the federal judges' salaries during their continuance in office in the 1976 and 1979 laws, but not in the 1977 and 1978 laws. The opinions expressed in the decision are highly significant for the evaluation of the institutional checks and balances between the government, Congress and the judiciary in the U.S.

The court explained its competence in deciding on the case on the basis of a rule that extends the Supreme Court's competence to civil appeals in which the U.S. government is a party and in relation to the constitutionality of federal rules. Moreover, the court assessed that in the case at issue it was not possible to apply the rules that call for the judges' abstention when his impartiality or financial interests may be in question because in the case at issue all the judges—including those of the Supreme Court—would be forced to recuse themselves. The court assumed that in the case in point the rule of necessity mandated that it proceed lest the controversy remain unresolved, leading to a denial of justice.

In endorsing only part of the judges' requests, the Supreme Court followed reasoning strictly based on legitimate legal criteria. It asserted that the 1976 and 1979 statutes violated the Constitution because they were signed by the president when the salary increases were already to be considered effective, that is, after the fiscal year had begun. In the 1979 statute the court assumed that the generic reference to the "executive personnel" could not be used to exclude the judges from its application, for it clearly intended to extend this provision to the judges as well. In contrast, the 1977 and 1978 statutes did not produce a violation of the Constitution because they were signed by the president before the proposed salary increases became effective. Finally, the court emphasized that the possibility of repealing or diminishing the periodic realignments due to the cost of living is fully included in the powers of Congress.

THE FLOATING OF JUDICIAL COMPENSATION: FURTHER ITALIAN SALARY INCREASES

The new Italian statute on magistrates' salaries has provided further increases, including one not previously foreseen. The highly complicated mechanisms for determining salaries on the basis of seniority have introduced two different ways of calculating them, depending upon whether the magistrate's current rank was achieved before or after July 1, 1983. This has resulted in disparities in the treatment of different magistrates holding the same position, making the salaries of magistrates who had just acquired a specific rank exceed those of magistrates who had already developed real seniority within the same rank. The system also tended to disproportionately reward magistrates whose career progress was slower than normal, whether for good or bad reasons (for example, career stagnation due to disciplinary sanctions or negative evaluations of their merits), thus providing a disincentive to those who had ostensibly performed well and progressed normally through the ranks of their respective judicial corps.

Without going into the complex patterns of salary inequity that resulted from the workings of the new law, it is quite clear that these disparities were illogical. They eliminated any kind of sanctioning or rewarding element to induce magistrates to adopt more responsible behavior and provided a disincentive to those who had undertaken a regular career. The solution to this problem reconfirmed the judicialization of the policy on judicial salaries. It is also an example of how the fragmentation of the judicial corps, which usually decreases the political significance of the judiciary (Guarnieri 1981, 112), actually reinforced that significance in the Italian context when the administrative and ordinary judiciary adopted the same strategy to promote increases in their own salaries.

The expedient they adopted, known as the floating of compensations (*galleggiamento delle retribuzioni*) was sanctioned by decisions of the Court of Accounts handed down in 1984 and 1985. It provides that each time the compensation of those already in a given rank turns out to be inferior to the compensation of those who have been lately promoted to that rank, the salary of the newly promoted is also given to those magistrates who, having a different seniority within the rank, receive a lower compensation for their services. The pay increase obtained in this way is calculated on the basis of a fictitious seniority. The floating mechanism was applied to correct both of the disparities just described. Since it requires a reevaluation of judicial salaries every time a magistrate is promoted to a new rank, possibly receiving thereby a salary that may be higher than those of some already in the rank, it leads to frequent judicial salary increases: for example, there are magistrates now at the top of their career who have had salary realignments from three to six times because of the floating of compensations.

One of the most unfortunate aspects of the floating mechanism is that this phenomenon presents itself every time the Higher Council of the Judiciary promotes to a new qualification a magistrate who has experienced a delay due to obstacles met with in his career. This is in open violation of the constitutional provision that states that questions of the status of magistrates can be dealt with only by Parliament. This perverse mechanism was stopped only through a radical legislative intervention in 1991. But even this intervention was able to avoid its only most macroscopic effects.

Parliament was obliged to enact such an interpretative law because of flagrant cases of floating that occurred in 1991, well illustrated by the following case. A magistrate, suspended from service for serious disciplinary and penal reasons from December 1973 to November 1979, was later acquitted because of an amnesty issued while he was still appealing his sentence to the Court of Cassation, reinstated in his functions, and then promoted to the position of cassation magistrate on October 5, 1985. For salary purposes the calculation of his seniority by the control section of the Court of Accounts included those years in which he was suspended from service. He was thus able to take advantage of the salary floating of a colleague in the same rank to reach a fictitious seniority of forty-two years in rank as a cassation magistrate, as of January 10, 1990. The delay in promotion of six actual years implied a salary realignment for as many as 2,013 magistrates and preliminary costs of approximately $55.3 million, according to data from the Ministry of Justice. All these costs were incurred through a judicially-created mechanism without the constitutionally mandated approval of Parliament.

CONCLUSIONS

The difference between the American federal judges' behavior and that of their Italian colleagues in the appeals made to obtain judicial pay increases is so significant that it requires an explanation. A factor that may be very important in evaluating the two kinds of judicial behavior manifested in the matter of judicial compensations is the different political-legal cultures of the two countries. Friedman emphasizes that there are no comparative studies of legal culture supported by systematic data. This of course limits us to an essentially impressionistic analysis. Nevertheless, Friedman argues that it is possible to identify different features in the legal culture of two countries, and that in particular the American one is outstanding for its uniqueness. "One of the aspects of the American legal culture is the fragmentation of power. . . . The 1787 Constitution highlights the obsessive necessity of having checks and balances. . . . In the United States the checks and balances philosophy is so deeply shared that it has become a distinctive feature of this legal culture" (Friedman 1975, 349-350). Shonfield (1965, 318-319) emphasizes this trait, making reference to a "national instinct that leads to a fragmentation of the political and governmental power." The Americans consider their political system as "a confederation of bodies, more or less mutually hostile, which enter in competition to obtain more money and power." All those who are in charge of a formal power are limited by some other counterpower. For example, the greatest value attributed to a jury resides in the fact that it balances the judge's power and, through the judge, the power of the state (Friedman 1973, 134-137).

Another distinctive aspect of the American legal-political culture is the spirit of "self-consciousness in demanding" which, for modern national cultures, "is among the highest since it tends to stimulate aggressiveness in asserting its own rights. . . . Very obstinate litigants who are conscious of their rights bring suits to judges who are in turn very reactive and active" (Friedman 1985, 352). Given these characteristics of the American legal culture, it is evident that the U.S. federal district judges' attitudes, and particularly the way they see their roles, differ from those of the Italian magistrates.

In the context of their history and customs, the peculiarities of the judicial political-legal culture in every country depend on the structural characteristics that society expects to be taken into consideration by the judicial system and the kind of professional recruitment and socialization processes undergone by the judges.

The mechanisms of recruitment have strongly shaped the American federal judges' perception of the judiciary's role. This and the legal culture previously described highlight one initial difference between their and the Italian magistrates' behavior in the salary disputes. Since the judicial systems are functionally equivalent, it is not possible to ascribe the differences in behavior to the increased political role of the courts in the two countries, because this increase occurred similarly in both countries (Zelditch 1971, 273-288). These differences must be ascribed instead to the variations in impartiality and independence of the judges of the two sub-systems.

In both systems the main purpose for trying to guarantee independence to judges is "to ensure the judge's impartiality, making him independent from the contending parties and creating an independent judicial power enabled to limit and control the power exercised by the other governmental structures" (Guarnieri 1981, 70). Enabling the judges to exert a certain degree of control over the actions of the other authorities gives them a participative role in the policy-making process. The degree of the actual independence enjoyed by the judicial subsystem fundamentally shapes judicial power and establishes the kind of relations it has with the political system.

One must evaluate the degree of the judges' independence from the other political authorities in order to understand their different behaviors in the case of the salary increases.

The safeguards set on the American judges' independence are undoubtedly quite remarkable. . . . Once the American Federal judge has been appointed he or she is completely independent from the executive and legislative power. . . . [H]e or she does not have any kind of problem related to internal independence because career patterns are not based on bureaucratic and hierarchical principles. However the main characteristic of the American considerable situation is the political significance of the judiciary. It is not only with reference to institutional conditions—the system does not control except in a very limited way its own input and even less its output—which in any case foresee constitutional control and make the system conform internally due to the *stare decisis* rule. The judiciary's self-perception of its role however leads the judges to participate actively in policy-making functions and in particular in forming the rules. Moreover, the recognition of the policy-making role of the American judges is a constant feature of the American political system. . . . The weakness of the political aggregation function in the United States . . . has led the courts—in a system characterized by numerous and active pressure groups—to carry out the function of transmitting political demands when not answering them directly. From the institutional point of view, the American judicial system also has strong ties with its own political environment, especially through the process of recruitment. It is mainly this mechanism which allows the maintenance of a certain equilibrium between the needs to have democratic legitimation and the judges' activism (Guarnieri 1981, 173-175).

Independence assumes major importance as an instrument to guarantee the presence of a judicial power in a constitutional framework of checks and balances, while the recruitment mechanism assures that the ties with the bodies through which the community's sovereignty expresses itself are not broken. What seems to make the federal judges conscious of their roles and of the political consequences of their behavior is the fact that the constitutional review of laws has been the judicial system's prerogative for 200 years. The fact that the Supreme Court acts as a tribunal of last resort, and the stare decisis mechanism, imply that such a final revision is made by the latter. Nevertheless, the mere fact that he or she is vested with the power of revising the laws has induced the federal judge to assume an attitude of great respect toward the principles of legality and of protection of the legitimacy of his function. This attitude is facilitated also by the institutional checks and balances that are placed on its power.

Indeed, the factor that most distinguishes the American judicial system from the Italian one is the limitation set on the judge's prerogatives by the other powers, that is the provision of institutional checks and balances. As a matter of fact the judicial system (and therefore the subsystem's input) may be contained through external limitations before these demands become a judge's prerogative. The jurisdiction of the Supreme Court is exercised "with such exceptions and under such regulations as the Congress shall make." As underlined by Guarnieri, "Congress, in some cases, has made use of this possibility of regulating, in a restrictive sense, the Supreme Court's jurisdiction, particularly during and immediately after the civil war. Afterwards, in 1914 and in 1931 Congress denied the federal courts the competence of enforcing decisions in cases relating to conflicts over questions of work" (1981, 156).

In practice, however, there are some limitations imposed on the outputs of the judicial system. In fact, in the U.S., maybe more than anywhere else, the judicial system's output is influenced by the actions of the other structures of authority. Many researchers have pointed out that Congress has frequently enforced regulations with the aim of repealing, or in any case modifying, the effects of judicial decisions. It often takes part in matters of merit, modifying law in order to avoid the repeating of certain decisions made by the courts (Goldman and Jahnige 1976, 212-258).

This interaction with Congress has induced self-restraint in the behavior of judges that contrasts with that of the Italian magistrates, who do not have any limitation on the inputs of the judicial subsystem, and rarely have experienced parliamentary intervention in the way mentioned above. This is because in the Italian system there is entrusted to either Parliament or government no mechanism for balancing the judiciary's power. Even when Parliament tried to introduce a statute providing an interpretation of a previous decision concerning the magistrates' salaries—as we have seen before—the Constitutional Court repealed it because such a decision was in contrast with a sentence that was beyond recall.

In fact the Italian magistrates enjoy an autonomy and independence that are probably greater than those of judges in any other liberal-democratic country. They recruit themselves (through bureaucratic exams); they determine their won career pattern, through the Higher Council of the Judiciary and they are irremovable. The magistrates are politically "non-responsible" (Di Federico 1988) and the minister of justice has no chance of influencing their performance, even in an indirect way. They have a monopoly of prosecution and through it they determine criminal policies, with no control provided by the executive. The judges determine the inputs of the constitutional review of laws to the Constitutional Court. The only indicator of minor political significance is represented by the fragmentation of the jurisdiction, which—as we have seen—has been overcome in the case of the salary increases because of the coordination carried out by the different categories of magistrates in the forming of a pressure group.

With these structural features, how is it possible to imagine self-restraint on the part of the Italian judiciary that places limitations on its creative activity as policy maker?

NOTES

1. The following comparison may be considered a "most similar systems comparison" (Przeworski and Teune 1970; Smelser 1976) since it analyses very similar judicial systems that, despite their specific characteristics, are marked by the prevalence of a legal-rational authority.

2. Now superseded by the provisions for an 11-member "Citizens' Commission" in the Ethics in Government Act of 1989. The commission consists of two members appointed by the President, two appointed by Congress, two by the Supreme Court, and five chosen randomly from voter registration rolls by the General Services Administration. Still being formed, the commission has not yet acted.

REFERENCES

Becker, T. 1970. *Comparative Judicial Politics*. Chicago: Rand McNally.

Bell, J. 1983. *Policy Arguments in Judicial Decisions*. Oxford: Clarendon Press.

Dahl, R. 1957. "Decision-Making in a Democracy: The Role of The Supreme Court as a National Policy Maker." *Journal of Public Law* 6.

Di Federico, G. 1985. "Il trattamento economico dei magistrati: Decide il giudice o il Parlamento?" *Rivista Trimestrale di Diritto Pubblico* 2.

————. 1988. "La crisi del sistema giudiziario e la questione della responsabilità civile dei magistrati." In *Politica in Italia. I fatti dell'anno e le interpretazioni*, ed. P. Corbetta and R. Leonardi. Bologna: Il Mulino. Translation "The Crisis of the Justice System and the Referendum on the Judiciary." In *Italian Politics: A Review*, ed. P. Corbetta and R. Leonardi. Volume 3. London: Pinter.

Eckhoff, T. 1965. "Impartiality, Separation of Powers, and Judicial Independence." *Scandinavian Studies in Law* 9.

Ely, J. 1980. *Democracy and Distrust*. Cambridge: Harvard University Press.

Friedman, L. 1973. *A History of American Law*. New York: Simon and Schuster.

————. 1975. *The Legal System: A Social Science Perspective*. New York: Russel Sage.

————. 1985. *Total Justice*. New York: Russell Sage.

Goldman, S. and T. Jahnige. 1976. *The Federal Courts as a Political System*. New York: Harper and Row.

Guarnieri, C. 1981. *L'indipendenza della magistratura*. Padua: Cedam.

Lederman, W. 1956. "The Independence of the Judiciary." *Canadian Bar Review* 34.

Murphy, W. and C. Pritchett. 1986. *Courts, Judges, and Politics*. New York: Random House.

Nonet, P. and P. Selznick. 1978. *Law and Society in Transition: Toward Responsive Law*. New York: Octagon.

Przeworski, A. and H. Teune. 1970. *The Logic of Comparative Social Inquiry*. New York: Wiley.

Sarat, A. and G. Grossman. 1975. "Courts and Conflict Resolution: Problems in the Mobilization of Adjudication." *American Political Science Review* 69.

Shapiro, M. 1966. *Freedom of Speech: the Supreme Court and Judicial Review*. Englewood Cliffs, N.J.: Prentice Hall.

———. 1968. *The Supreme Court and Administrative Agencies*. New York: Free Press.

———. 1975. "Courts." In *Handbook of Political Science*, ed. F. Greenstein and N. Polsby. Vol. 5, *Governmental, Institutions and Processes*. Reading, Mass.: Addison Wesley.

Shonfield, A. 1965. *Modern Capitalism: The Changing Balance of Public and Private Power*. London: Oxford University Press.

Smelser, N. 1976. *Comparative Methods in the Social Sciences*. Englewood Cliffs, N.J.: Prentice-Hall.

Smith, J. 1976. "An Independent Judiciary: The Colonial Background." *University of Pennsylvania Law Review* 74.

Spreacher, R. 1976. "Threats to Judicial Independence." *Indiana Law Review* 51.

Zannotti, F. 1989. *La magistratura, un gruppo di pressione istituzionale*. Padua: Cedam.

Zelditch, M., Jr. 1971. "Intelligible Comparisons." In *Comparative Methods in Sociology*, ed. I. Vallier. Berkeley: University of California Press.

Zemans, F. 1983. "Legal Mobilization: The Neglected Role of the Law in the Political System." *The American Political Science Review* 77.

12.

Complex Coordinate Construction in France and Germany

ALEC STONE

Complex coordinate construction refers to a condition in which both public policy and constitutional law are the products of sustained and intimate judicial-political interaction. Such interaction is an increasingly important fact of government in France and Germany. Where this condition obtains, the constitutional environment constitutes, in large part, the policy-making environment, and legislative processes structure the creative development of constitutional law. Where it obtains, parliamentarians behave judicially—debating and determining constitutionality—not unlike the way constitutional judges behave. Constitutional courts, for their part, behave legislatively—amending, vetoing, and even drafting legislation—not unlike the way legislators do.

This chapter focuses on the politics of coordinate construction. I begin with a general discussion of the sources and dynamics of judicialization. Selected case studies of judicialized policy-making are then employed to ground a discussion of constitutional politics in France and Germany. I want to stress at the outset that my argument is neither an attack nor a defense of constitutional review. My concerns are analytical and conceptual: to offer a framework for the study and understanding of how European constitutional courts function in their political enviroi ents and interact with other governmental actors.

THE JUDICIALIZATION OF POLITICS:
A POLICY-MAKING PERSPECTIVE

The judicialization of politics refers to the general process in which legal discourse—norms of behavior and language—penetrates, and is absorbed by, political discourse. I mean to distinguish legal from political discourse only minimally—the two have always been interdependent. Legal discourse, that of judges and lawyers, *tends* to be rule laden, and is structured by doctrinal norms and the demands of exegesis. Political discourse, that of politicians and political scientists, *tends* to be interest laden, and is conducted in the language of power or ideology. Judicialized politics are politics pursued at least in part through the medium of legal discourse. While many of us may quibble with aspects of these definitions, I suspect that there is broad agreement on fundamentals, at least at this high level of abstraction.

At lower levels, consensus ends. One important macropolitical effect of evolving judicialization has been to close off reform routes that would otherwise be open to reform-minded governments. As levels of judicialization rise, the web of constitutional obligation and constraint facing legislators becomes increasingly close-meshed. Some see the phenomenon negatively.

Because judicialization preempts policy-making space while removing accountability from representative institutions, Christine Landfried, a German political scientist, has argued that it is "dangerous for democracy" (Landfried 1985). Proponents of this view tend to reject certain tenets of modern constitutional ideology, namely, that constitutional review itself is a central requisite of democracy. Others see only virtues. Louis Favoreu, a French law professor, claims that judicialization moderates radical tendencies, encourages "centrism," and ultimately succeeds in its "pacifying" politics. In the pacified parliament, political "quarrels" that, in the absence of judicialization, would have been fought in ideological-partisan terms, are "appeased" and worked out more reasonably—in constitutional terms. For Favoreu, judicialized politics are pacified politics (Favoreu 1986; Favoreu 1988). The argument significantly underestimates the provocative nature of constitutional lawmaking and cannot account for those (not uncommon) instances when the intervention of the court itself leads to an escalation of ideological-partisan conflict (see Stone 1992a, chap. 7).

Normative debates like these are important and useful. But their settlement need not preclude research on and the evaluation of judicialization.

THE JUDICIALIZATION OF THE LEGISLATIVE PROCESS

Policy processes can be described as judicialized to the extent that constitutional jurisprudence, the threat of future constitutional censure, and the pedagogical authority of past jurisprudence alter legislative outcomes. This definition is sensitive **both** to direct impact (a ruling of unconstitutionality is a veto) and indirect (policy outcomes may be altered by anticipatory reactions). We now know a great deal about the origins, development, and effects of judicialization, at least in France and Germany (Landfried 1984, 1985, 1989; Stone 1989, 1990, 1992a). Four general points deserve emphasis.

First, judicialization is an empirically verifiable phenomenon. While a court's direct impact is obvious, indirect influence can be observed and to some degree measured by tracing legislation through the policy process to determine how and why it is altered as a result of constitutional argument. With the specter of court intervention hovering over deliberations, governments may choose to compromise with the opposition rather than suffer constitutional censure. This effect is called *autolimitation:* the exercise of self-restraint on the part of the majority in anticipation of an eventual negative decision of the constitutional court. Governments may also use constitutional arguments as convenient pretexts, and constitutional courts as convenient scapegoats, to deflect blame for abandoning measures once promised to party activists.

Second, judicialization is neither permanent nor uniform. Disaggregating constitutional court impact along sectoral lines shows that each policy area manifests its own dynamic of constitutional possibility and constraint, conforming to the intensity of judicial-political interaction and the development of constitutional control. Legislative processes are more or less judicialized as a function of this variation. In France, nationalization, privatization, media policy, criminal law, and electoral law are examples of highly judicialized policy areas; the same can be said for the criminal justice, campaign finance, education, and broadcast media sectors in Germany. Moreover, the perceived political legitimacy of constitutional review also appears to vary across issue area.

Third, constitutional courts and political oppositions are connected to one another by a kind of jurisprudential transmission belt. Oppositions judicialize legislative processes in order to win what they would otherwise lose in "normal" political processes. Their referrals provide courts with crucial opportunities to construct constitutional law, to extend jurisprudential techniques of control, and (in other words) to make policy. As constitutional jurisprudence grows more dense and technical, so do grounds for judicial debate and the potential for higher levels of judicialization.

Fourth, creative techniques of control, which constitutional courts have developed in part to cushion their impact, have strengthened their dominance over policy outcomes. Courts have asserted the power to attach *strict guidelines of interpretation* (SGI) to otherwise constitutional legislation; this occurs when the court rules that a bill is constitutional only if it is interpreted as the court has done. Enabling control while avoiding (potentially dangerous) outright annulment, the pronouncement of SGIs often results in unambiguous constitutional lawmaking. Courts may also accept the principle of a reform but not the means; courts then may be led to tell legislators how they ought to have written the law in the first place. A second legislative process is generated, which I call a *corrective revision process:* the reelaboration of a censured text in conformity with constitutional jurisprudence in order to secure promulgation. Corrective revision processes lead to court-written legislation, with governments copying the terms of decisions directly into beleaguered legislation.

Accepting these commonalities, there are also important cross-national differences in the conduct of constitutional politics. Table 12.1 compares certain structural aspects of the principal French and German constitutional courts, the *Conseil constitutionnel* or Constitutional Council (the Council) and the *Bundesverfaßungsgericht* or Federal Constitutional Court (FCC). Most important, both institutions are enabled or required by jurisdiction to intervene in legislative processes. Politicians have the power to refer legislation directly to the courts for rulings on constitutionality; this process is called "abstract review" because it is not dependent on "concrete" case or controversy. The initiation of abstract review lengthens the legislative process to include what is in effect a final, definitive "reading" of the bill by the constitutional court. The Council exercises only abstract review, while the FCC also hears cases

Table 12.1: Structure and Mandate of the French and German Constitutional Courts

	France (1958)	W. Germany (1951)
Composition and recruitment:		
Number of members	9	16
Appointing authorities	President (3) President of the National Assembly (3) President of the Senate (3)	Bundestag (8) Bundesrat (8)
Length of terms	9 years	12 years
Requisite qualifications	None	40-68 Years of Age; 6/16 = federal judges; all qualified to be judges
Constitutional review authority:		
Abstract review	Yes	Yes
Concrete review	No	Yes
Power to refer constitutional controversies to the court possessed by:		
Politicians (abstract review)	President President of the National Assembly President of the Senate 60 Deputies or 60 Senators	Federal Government Land Government 1/3 of Bundestag
Judiciary (concrete review)	No	Yes
Individuals (concrete review)	No	Yes

on appeal from the judiciary, as well as complaints submitted directly by individuals.

Originally created to guarantee executive supremacy over the legislative process, the Council today functions as an important constraint on the government and its parliamentary majority.   Table 12.2 summarizes the Council's constitutional review activity.

Table 12.2: Constitutional Review and the Council: 1958-1990

	1959-73	1974-80	1981-87	1988-90
Referrals*	9	66	136	47
President	0	0	0	0
Prime Minister	6	2	0	2
President, National Assembly	0	2	0	0
President, Senate	3	0	2	0
Parliamentarians	-	62	134	45
Decisions	9	46	92	31
Censuring text	7	14	49	17
Favorable to text	2	32	43	14

* Due to multiple referrals, the number of referrals since 1974 is larger than the number of decisions.

Most striking in table 12.2 is the dramatic increase in the number of referrals, decisions, and rulings of unconstitutionality beginning in 1974. This increase is related to two general factors. First, a 1974 constitutional amendment granting the right of referral to parliamentarians radically expanded the system's capacity to generate review. Given the executive's mastery over parliament, *constitutional threats and referrals to the Council are by far the most efficacious weapons possessed by the opposition.* Since the late 1970s, virtually every major bill (and every budget since 1974) has been referred by parliamentary minorities. Their efforts have been rewarded: since 1981 more than half of all referrals have resulted in annulments.

A second factor has been the Council's own activism. As originally conceived, the Council was denied control over the content of legislation (beyond confirming that parliament had not preempted executive prerogatives).   In the 1970s the Council incorporated three texts contained in the preamble of the 1946 constitution, opening up an unexplored area of *substantive* constraints on policy-making.   These texts—the 1789 Declaration of the rights of man, the "fundamental principles recognized by the laws of the Republic [FPRL]," and the list of "political, economic, and social principles particularly necessary for our times" (the 1946 principles) today constitute higher law binding upon the legislature.

The 1946 preamble has a history too complex and convoluted to address adequately here (see Stone 1992a, chap. 1).   What is clear is that: (1) the 1789 Declaration, an expression of classic liberalism, generally embodied the Right's version of rights; (2) the Left accepted the 1789 rights of due process and legal equality but opposed, along with centrists and Gaullists, the "sacred" right to property (not least because all three were committed to nationalization policies); (3) the 1946 principles, an expression of social collectivism, constituted the Left's version of rights; and (4) the FPRLR, left totally unenumerated, referred to rights to Catholic education.   Had the constitutional assemblies of 1946 foreseen the preamble's incorporation by the Council in 1971, *only* the 1946 principles would have stood a chance of being granted such status.

In Germany, the bargains struck by political elites in establishing constitutional review have held firm.   The FCC was granted wide-ranging jurisdiction (perhaps more wide-ranging than that of any other court anywhere) and clear status as the guardian of constitutional rights and order (Kommers 1989, chaps. 1, 2).   Table 12.3 summarizes the court's review activities.   In contrast to the Council, the great bulk of the FCC's caseload involves review of legal disputes brought before it either by courts or by individual litigants.   The court's activities are thus anchored in what are undeniably judicial processes, even though the legal order it is asked to defend, that of higher law, is inherently a political order.   The Council, detached from the judiciary and exercising only abstract review,[1] can be argued to perform less a judicial than a legislative function (Stone 1992b).   In Germany, scholars and even some FCC judges have argued for the abolition of abstract review, on the ground that it is needlessly provocative, since unconstitutional laws will come before the court eventually anyway (for example, Landfried 1984; Interview with Judge Martin Hirsch 1978).

Nonetheless, in comparison with the French case, the comparatively small number of instances of German abstract review is noteworthy.

Several factors account for the difference. First, in contrast to the French practice, opposition parties have traditionally worked not to obstruct but to cooperate in lawmaking (Kirchheimer 1966; Lepsius 1982). Controversial laws that are adopted are most often sent to the FCC by governments controlled by Länder wings of the national opposition party. Second, the German policy-making process is heavily veto-laden, that is, multiple structural impediments serve to filter out

Table 12.3: The Constitutional Review Activity of the German Federal Constitutional Court, 1951-1991

	Referrals	Decisions
Abstract review*	112	63
Referrals leading to a decision by:		
Federal Government	0	5
Bundestag Deputies	0	14
Land Governments	59	
Concrete review	2,619	897
Constitutional complaints	82,253	3,689

*Due to multiple referrals and the consolidation of cases, the number of abstract review decisions rendered does not equal the number of referrals.

Source: Data compiled from FCC decisions and FCC statistical office.

audacious or nonincremental legislation (Scharpf 1977). The requirements of coalition government have allowed the small Free Democratic Party to reorient policy toward the center (Schmidt 1983; Pulzer 1978); and the absolute veto of the Bundesrat (the upper chamber, whose consent is required for about 55 percent of all legislation) structures bargaining in the service of cooperative federalism (Lehmbruch 1978). The FCC is only the third filter of legislative ambition and thus receives few "radical" reforms. Virtually all commentators agree, however, that the FCC has exhibited increasingly high degrees of "judicial activism," beginning at least in the 1970s (Landfried 1989; Biehler 1989; Johnson 1982). In France, where the Senate's veto is merely suspensive, the Council is the *only* policy-making institution that can impose its will on the government and its majority.

THE COORDINATE CONSTRUCTION OF LEGISLATION

The case studies that follow focus on the constitutional fate of six high-profile legislative initiatives: nationalizations (1982), antitrust for the press industry (1984), and reform of the penal codes (1986) in France; and decriminalization of abortion (1975), industrial codetermination (1976), and university reform (1976) in Germany. Dozens of other examples could be used to tell much the same story. Each of these sets has the advantage of (1) providing a range of constitutional issues and lawmaking behavior, and (2) occupying relatively narrow time frames, eliminating problems associated with institutional development. Each of these initiatives, with one exception, was promulgated after a highly judicialized legislative process capped by a constitutional court decision. In several instances, corrective revision processes were necessary to secure promulgation, and in all cases, the impact of the constitutional court on final outcome was extensive.[2]

Judicialized Policy-Making in France: Selected Case Studies

The Constitutional Council's 1982 decision on the nationalization law is a defining moment in the evolution of French constitutional politics. As a complex annulment of the centerpiece of the newly elected Socialist government's program, it touched off an extended judicial-political confrontation (Keeler and Stone 1987), that lasted through the end of the first year of the neoliberal Chirac government (Stone 1989). Perhaps even more important, the decision harmonized the conflicting principles enshrined in the different texts of the preamble.

The nationalization of France's largest banks and industrial conglomerates raised these conflicts unambiguously (the following is based on the case study in Stone 1992a, chap. 6). Each stage of the legislative process—deliberations within the ministries, the Assembly, and the Senate—was dominated by tortuous, polarized debate of constitutional law, history, and doctrine.[3] Discussion focused on the respective status of three texts. Article 34 of the 1958 constitution grants to Parliament the exclusive, sovereign authority to legislate in a number of substantive areas, including nationalization and privatization. The 1789 Declaration proclaims, in article 17, that property rights are "inviolable and sacred." The constitutional incorporation of the 1789 text was rejected 429-119, largely because the Communist and Socialist left, much of the center, and even the Gaullists were committed to nationalization policies. The 1946 principles, which were removed from the second and final version of the 1946 constitution and placed in a preamble after the first version had been rejected in referendum, declares an *obligation* to nationalize in certain circumstances (line 9). Had the Council not bestowed by constitutional status to the preamble in 1971, of course, judicialization would not have occurred. The fate of nationalization would have hinged on a simple majority vote of Parliament.

The Council, while accepting Parliament's power to nationalize in principle, vetoed the bill on the ground that the compensation formula did not meet the constitutional requirements of "fair payment" mandated by article 17 (1789); it then went on to elaborate its own detailed compensation formula.[4] The government, once it had decided not to legislate by referendum, had the choice of either copying the Council's compensation policy directly into new legislation or foregoing nationalizations entirely. It chose a corrective revision process, mechanically incorporating the Council's formula into those sections of the law that had been vetoed.

In policy-making terms, the Council's decision held the reform hostage until stockholders had received sufficient ransom. The ruling raised the cost of nationalizing by 25 percent; indeed, no stockholder who has ever been bought out in any major nationalization has received terms as good as those in France in 1982. In jurisprudential terms, the decision harmonized the discordant terms of the preamble. The Council ruled that the property rights proclaimed in 1789 had neither been eroded nor superseded, and then went on to declare that the 1946 principles could never weaken but only supplement the rights contained in the 1789 text. The decision, as one commentator put it, "is a condemnation of the whole of socialist doctrine"; in another's words, "[the French] republic . . . can never be a socialist republic" (Favoreu 1982, 41).

After nationalizations, the 1984 press law was the most controversial bill adopted during the first Socialist government (the following is based on Stone 1992a, chap. 7). Its purpose was to establish an enforceable antitrust policy to counter increasing concentration in the newspaper industry. The rules then in place—a one person/one paper standard—had never been enforced. Indeed, the rules had been openly flouted by the Rightist deputy, Robert Hersant, who had built a press empire of 19 dailies, seven weeklies, and 11 periodicals in a series of shady deals. After the 1981 elections, Hersant mobilized his papers to oppose the Socialist government, and to promote the Right's emerging neoliberal agenda. While the government could justly claim that its bill was designed to protect "press pluralism" and to restore respect for law, its partisan aspects were obvious.

The legislative battle was waged in the language of constitutional law, but arguments were no less recognizably pro- or anti-Hersant. For Socialists, freedom of the press was conceived as the right of readers to choose from offerings representing the diversity of opinion existent within society. This right could no longer be guaranteed, claimed a minister, because "certain men" had engaged in "fraud, cheating, and embezzlement." The opposition argued that talk of rights only obscured the government's true motive, to take revenge on Hersant. Freedom of the press was conceived in terms of ownership and free enterprise, what Jacques Chirac called, the "inseparable principles of the freedom of expression, the right of private enterprise, and the rights to property."[5] The bill, under the threat of referral, lost much of its teeth in a massive autolimitation process: 26 of the bill's 41 articles were rewritten; the most important amendments resulted from worries about constitutionality. In its final form, Hersant would still have been forced to choose between his regional papers and the national *Figaro*.

In one of the most complex decisions in its history, the Council annulled parts of ten different articles of the law.[6] Most important, the Council declared that the antitrust rules could not be applied to "existing situations" unless: (1) these situations had been illegally acquired; or (2) pluralism was actually threatened. The Council then declared that neither condition had been met, thus destroying the bill and saving the Hersant empire; further, the decision had the perverse effect of freezing Hersant's dominance, since the ant-trust rules applied in full to competitors. In so ruling, the judges willfully ignored the lengthy parliamentary discussions of (1) the illegality of Hersant's situation (then pending in several courts); and (2) the evolution of concentration in the industry. It apparently arrived at this conclusion without reference to any objective criteria. We know only that at least five members of the

Council had agreed that this point had not yet been reached and that they voted to overrule the contrary opinion expressed by the government and parliament. At no point in the decision did the Council explain on what basis it had determined that pluralism was not threatened or why it had judged Hersant's situation to have been legally acquired.

In the case of the nationalization and press laws, prior jurisprudence did not meaningfully structure the deliberations of Parliament (since the Council had never before been asked to rule on the matters at hand). But because the threat of referral to the Council had been made explicit, judgments about constitutionality were also judgments about how the Council would ultimately decide the matter. In the presence of relevant constitutional jurisprudence, the potential for lawmakers to be placed under the tutelage of the constitutional court is very high.

The Pasqua laws (named for the minister in charge) provide an example of policy-making under such tutelage. The Chirac government sought to make good on a central campaign promise, the tightening of the penal codes. A package of legislation was produced restricting the rights of accused, lengthening sentencing requirements for certain crimes, and expanding the discretionary powers of the police, immigration, and security forces. At first resistant to compromise, the Chirac government allowed the reforms to be gradually but substantially rewritten. Crucial to this change of heart was the fact that by 1986 the Council had largely "constitutionalized" penal law.[7]   That is, its pre-1986 rulings on legislative amendments of the penal codes added up to a relatively coherent and knowable jurisprudence, particularly with respect to rights of due process. Left to a small group within Parliament, each bill was discussed with regard to its constitutionality and to relevant Council decisions. "Judicial pointillism" was how one deputy characterized the process[8]: the deliberate, almost bipartisan effort to rewrite and improve the texts line by line, point by point with respect to constitutional jurisprudence. In a striking example, Michel Sapin (Socialist) congratulated the majority on its good sense after the 1986 law expanding police powers to demand personal identification cards was amended to the Socialist's satisfaction. This led to the following exchange:

Sapin: From the first examination of the bill in committee, we emphasized that if you had refused to modify your position [by accepting a Socialist amendment] on this point, your text would be unconstitutional.

Jean-Louis Debré: Mr. Sapin claims authorship a little too easily. Let's just say that there is a confusion about paternity.
Bernard Dérosier: We would need a blood test.[9]

In one decision the Council even expressed its appreciation of the effort, citing with approval an amendment that required police to obtain a writ before photographing and fingerprinting subjects.[10]

Judicialized Policy-Making in Germany: Selected Case Studies

Compared with their French counterparts, government ministers possess far less control over the outcome of policy processes and outcomes. By the time the FCC receives a piece of important legislation it has most likely been through a time-consuming and tedious exercise in bargaining and compromise. The complex series of initiatives that ultimately led to the University Framework Law of 1976 is a well-documented illustration (Katzenstein 1987, chapter 7). The law was promulgated after five years of debate and punctuated by several crucial FCC decisions and successive vetoes by the Bundesrat. The most controversial aspect of the original bill was the provision to expand participation in university governance by giving to three groups—teachers (both nontenured and full professors), staff, and students—voting parity on university councils. The reform was designed to break up the monopoly of power possessed by full professors, a monopoly that had led to inflexible university structures and the obstruction of other democratization reforms (Tilford 1981). The CDU/CSU (Christian Democratic Union/Christian Social Union) opposition labored to block any change in the status of professors and to retain, as much as possible, state (*länder* or provincial) control over the domain of education.

In May 1973, while final touches were being put on the bill in cabinet, the FCC ruled on a similar 1971 education framework law of Lower Saxony.[11] That law, adopted by an Social Democratic Party (SDP) government impatient with the glacial progress being made on the reform in Bonn, was subsequently referred to the court by 398 professors in a constitutional complaint. The court ruled that the law violated a provision of article 5 of the Basic Law, which states: "Art and science, research and teaching shall be free." This provision, the FCC decided, required the state to maintain the "special position" of university professors in research and teaching. It then went on to declare that professors must always retain at least 50% of the votes in decisions concerning teaching and must possess "a decisive influence"—"to assert themselves against the combined opposition of other groups"—in decisions pertaining to research broadly conceived. The dissent of the two SDP judges accused the FCC of "exceeding its function and placing itself in the position of the legislature."

The decision, by arming the opposition with detailed constitutional arguments, fundamentally altered the debate on the federal bill. The government, while claiming that its bill as introduced conformed to the FCC's ruling, nonetheless sought to maintain control over how that ruling would be translated into law. This it was not able to do. In the original bill, for example, seats allocated to "teachers" included reference to assistant professors; this group was then given an absolute majority of votes on decisions pertaining to teaching and research.[12]   The opposition, strengthened by the Bundesrat's veto, was able to delete mention of nontenured professors and then require a majority vote within the group of professors to ratify certain decisions.[13]   The law not only enshrined the FCC's preferred policy but (as a federal law) forced the policy on several states that had delayed compliance with the FCC's Lower Saxony decision (Blair 1978, 362). This legislative outcome, and many others in the education sector, can only be understood by taking account of constitutional politics.

The attempt to decriminalize abortion provides another example of an intensely judicialized debate leading first to an FCC veto and then to a corrective revision process implementing the court's policy. The rank and file of both the Social SDP and the FDP (Free Democratic Party) supported the total decriminalization of abortion in the first trimester of pregnancy, and afterward on medical and other grounds. At the November 1971 SDP conference, delegates supported such a solution by a vote of 638-59, and polls showed public support hovering at about 75% (Braunthal 1983, 250-52).   After intense two-year negotiations with critics (especially the Catholic church), the minister of justice decided only to relax penalties for abortion in cases of medical necessity, rape, and other social emergencies. The bill, which the minister knew would be fiercely opposed by the church for going too far and by SDP and FDP deputies for not going far enough, was approved by the cabinet in early 1972, but by only a slim majority. It died with the dissolution of Parliament. When the new parliamentary session opened, the government lost control of the legislative process to SDP deputies, who rewrote the bill in conformity with party resolutions. The law was referred by 193 deputies and five Länder.

The FCC annulled the bill on the ground that the legislature had violated "right to life" protections contained in article 2 of the constitution.[14] The court (with the two SDP appointees writing strong dissents to the effect that the court had again exceeded its competence and usurped legislative authority), ruled that because post-Nazi Germany had a special obligation to protect human life, including the embryonic, abortion could not be decriminalized; it would nonetheless not be punished when justified by certain health and social considerations. The FCC then went on to propose detailed draft legislation that a corrective revision process ratified. In what appears to be the only high-level public protest of any FCC decision, the vice president of the Bundestag protested that women "would not accept or abide by the decision"; but she was overridden by the minister of justice, who stated that the government would, with regret, respect the FCC's ruling.[15]

Like the abortion case, the Industrial Codetermination Law of 1976 provides another example of an intense judicialization of parliamentary deliberations without the aid of a prior guiding decision. The strengthening of industrial codetermination constituted the principal socioeconomic structural reform in the SDP government's program when it came to power in 1969. Backed by the unions, the party hoped to extend "parity codetermination" (equal representation with management on supervisory boards), which existed in the coal and steel sectors, to the rest of industry (Katzenstein 1987, chap. 3). The debate within Parliament focused on the proper balance between two aspects of property: the constitution (article 14) guarantees the right to property, but it also states that property must serve the public good. Existing jurisprudence could not easily settle the matter, but seemed to favor the government: in a landmark case in 1954, the judges had declared that the Basic Law was "neutral" with respect to the economic system and that political authority enjoyed broad powers to shape and reshape the system.[16]

A special committee heard testimony from eleven constitutional lawyers called in to predict the FCC's future ruling on parity. This group split between those (five jurists) who argued that property rights were absolute and thus could not bear parity, and those (six jurists) who argued that property rights in the context of large corporations must be balanced by the interests of society and workers. In the end the committee recommended that Parliament err on the safe side and renounce parity. Politicians agreed, whereupon the bill was adopted all but unanimously. According to Landfried, this autolimitation process was a disturbing case of excessive "obedience in advance" of an FCC ruling (Landfried 1984, 47-63). It is also true that the probusiness FDP, lobbied fiercely by business organizations, opposed parity. Biehler, while agreeing that constitutional arguments were important, disputes that they were decisive, arguing that parity would not have been supported by a majority of the Bundestag (Biehler 1989, 57). In either case the judicialized process allowed the government an excuse for reneging on a promise while keeping peace within the coalition.[17]

An Evaluation

I have argued elsewhere that, for students of policy-making at least, constitutional courts ought to be conceptualized as specialized third legislative chambers, specialized because their legislative powers are meaningfully restricted to decisions on constitutionality (Stone 1990, 1992b). To this I would add the following: *the more any given legislative process is judicialized, the less that restriction matters.* In highly judicialized processes, constitutional debate tends to overwhelm all other aspects of debate. Once aired in both chambers of Parliament, the debate is transferred to constitutional courts for a third, authoritative judgment.

In traditional separation-of-powers schemes (common to both anglo and continental theory), legislatures differ from courts in that the former make law generally and prospectively. In contrast, judicial lawmaking is said to be particular and retrospective, since it is a by-product of case-by-case adjudication and applies to past or existing situations. In abstract review processes, courts make law outside of the judicial process and according to law-making techniques more "legislative" (prospective) than "judicial" (retrospective). In the French press pluralism case, the Council overrode Parliament's judgment that press pluralism was threatened and then went on to specify how pluralism should be protected in the event that a threat might develop. In the German abortion case the FCC ruling is indistinguishable from draft legislation (with constitutional commentary attached). Abstract review processes regularly lead courts to behave unambiguously as third chambers. The effects of concrete review of legislation, however, are not necessarily less legislative or prospective. Management's legal attack on codetermination, for example, was animated not by expectations of annulment, but by hopes that the

FCC would fix limits on future attempts to extend codetermination (Markovitz 1986, 140). In corrective revision processes, the distinction between parliamentary and constitutional court lawmaking breaks down entirely. In these, policies that have been laid down by constitutional courts (how stockholders shall be paid, how the penal code must treat the crime of abortion) are sent to governments and Parliament for ratification. Finally, once policy space has been preempted by relevant jurisprudence (German university reform and the Pasqua laws), there may be no need for new decisions: existing jurisprudence, given agency through the medium of judicialized legislative politics, determines general outcomes.

THE COORDINATE CONSTRUCTION OF CONSTITUTIONAL LAW

In judicialized environments constitutional courts behave legislatively. But the following is also true: the degree to which any legislative process is judicialized is equivalent to the degree to which parliament behaves judicially. In France and Germany the building of constitutional law, like the making of public policy, is participatory.

This simple truth is fiercely resisted by the doctrinal community. European academic lawyers labor continuously to separate law from politics and, by extension, to distinguish what constitutional courts do from what "political" institutions do. This distinction functions to insulate doctrinal activity (and to some extent courts) from the vagaries of politics, providing a stable setting for the scholarly synthesis of doctrine and law. While something of a disciplinary article of faith, the distinction is supported by a number of concrete arguments (see Luchaire 1979; Gusy 1985). According to the most important of these, constitutional courts are particular institutions in that (1) they are charged with determining constitutionality; (2) they "function" to protect fundamental rights; and (3) their review authority is determinative and final.

The first argument is most often invoked, by doctrine and the courts themselves, to counter charges of usurpation: because the constitution provides for constitutional review and locates its exercise in a constitutional court, attacks on the conduct of review are easily dismissed as attacks on the constitution itself (and thus illegitimate). The next step, the assertion that the constitutional court's power to determine constitutionality is exclusive, comes easily. But it cannot be accepted. In judicialized settings legislators, too, determine constitutionality. The court's monopoly on constitutional interpretation exists only with respect to the judicial system.

The point can be pushed further. In France, deputies and senators are required to behave as constitutional judges whenever a *Motion of Unconstitutionality* is raised. Such motions—which are written in the form of a judicial decision—are debated "in order to determine if the proposed text is contrary to one or more constitutional provisions."[18] During these debates, legislators cite constitutional provisions, original intent, past Council decisions, and the work of respected law professors. If the motion is adopted by a majority, the bill is declared unconstitutional and it dies. The Senate, declaring itself to have a special role in the protection of public liberties, has adopted a number of such motions. Table 12.4 shows the remarkable increase in their popularity on the floor of the Assembly. Although the argument has now been forgotten, it was once widely accepted by doctrine that Parliament constituted a constitutional court whenever it debated such motions (see Waline 1928).

Table 12.4: Motions of Unconstitutionality* in the French National Assembly

	1967-73	1974-80	1981-87	1988-90
Motions Raised	2	35	203	35
Average per Year	0.29	5.0	29.0	11.7
Motions Voted	1	35	93	23
Average per Year	0.14	5.0	13.2	7.7

*Motions of Unconstitutionality are allegations that a bill is unconstitutional. If a majority supports such a motion, the bill in question is rejected. Motions are virtually always raised by the opposition, and the vote is virtually always along party lines.

Source: *Statistiques, Bulletin de l'Assemblee nationale, numero speciale* for each of the years cited. The statistical bulletin does not present figures for the pre-1967 period, probably because no such motions were raised.

German parliamentarians possess no such procedural manoeuvre. Nonetheless, constitutional debates can be highly structured. Bundestag committee hearings regularly invite legal experts and former constitutional judges to advise them as well as to engage in "Karlsruhe--astrology"[19]—attempts to predict the future position of the court (Landfried 1989). The concern for constitutionality is, however, not generated by fear of FCC censure alone. As observers of German politics unanimously agree, political elites share a deeply rooted commitment to *rechtsstaat* ideology, a commitment that has been at the heart of state theory for more than a century. In consequence, legislators are unusually willing, even anxious, to rely on law to guide their work (Blair 1978; Brinkman 1981; Johnson 1982, 1978; Dyson 1982). Because of the consolidation of constitutional review in the Federal Republic, the *rechtsstaat* is today a *constitutional rechtsstaat,* and legislators naturally draft legislation according to their understanding of it.

The second argument—that constitutional courts "function" to protect individual rights—should not obscure another reality of constitutional politics: under judicialized conditions, the work of parliament, too, is dominated by the question of how best to protect and to balance rights claims. In the cases examined here, for example, legislators at no point denied the constitutional status of such principles as "due process," "free education," "fair compensation" for expropriation, or the "right to human life." On the contrary, they worked to uphold and even to extend these principles, as they understood them. They also sought to establish others for the first time (worker's participation, press pluralism). In each case, the opposition countered with rights arguments of its own. Once settled by Parliament, these *constitutional debates*—about the *legislative* applicability of rights—were transferred to constitutional judges for yet another constitutional deliberation.

Do judges protect rights better than do parliamentarians? No structured, systematic research on this question exists, in spite of its obvious importance.[20] My own view is that in *judicialized environments, courts do not protect rights better than do legislators.* There are few (I doubt that there are any) constitutional rulings under judicialized conditions that unambiguously indicate the contrary. Leading decisions do not normally force legislators to pay attention to rights that would otherwise be ignored and do not normally raise issues that had not already been raised in legislative debate. Leading decisions are legislative *choices* replacing those of the parliamentary majority, about how constitutional rights must be protected.

Partly because rights are neither self-evident nor self-actualizing, constitutional courts are at times led to balance contending rights claims, and therefore to legislate. In the German abortion case, the balancing act was a subtle one. The dissenting opinion nevertheless focused on the fact that the FCC's ruling would force Parliament to renounce a liberalization of the penal code, and to require a more repressive law. Courts, the dissenters wrote, fulfill their duty to extend liberties only when they require the state to liberalize. The 1981-1985 period in France (the first Socialist government) is an extraordinary example of what can be done by a government committed to the extension of fundamental rights and liberties (see Safran 1988). It did so on its own, largely outside of the requirements of constitutional politics. In contrast, it can easily be demonstrated that many of the Council's most important decisions during this period served not only to consecrate the opposition's version of rights, but to protect those in privileged social and economic positions (see Keeler and Stone, 1987). The same can be said for several key decisions of the FCC during the SDP-FDP governing period (1969-1983).

My point is not to belittle the role of constitutional courts. The FCC and the French *Conseil d'état* protect, in individual complaints and administrative review processes, the constitutional rights of individuals in interactions with the state; the protection is often unambiguous and can be observed and measured. My argument is that constitutional review processes under judicialized conditions do not necessarily function to protect rights in the same unambiguous way. Constitutional judges and legislators are partners—in cooperation or rivalry—in the development of constitutional rights.

The third argument, essentially that constitutional courts have "the final say" on constitutional matters, is more structural than ideological and unassailable. But the argument cannot in itself distinguish what constitutional courts do from what legislators do. Indeed, one might respond as follows: when legislators behave judicially, constitutional courts constitute their appellate jurisdiction. During the process of adopting the industrial codetermination law, eleven different constitutional lawyers and former FCC judges testified on the constitutionality of worker-management parity. After months of debate, one such expert told the Bundestag, "[B]y now you have heard more or less everything which could be defended . . . ; absolute opposition, absolute support, and everything in between. You'll have to form your own opinion about how legal science ought to be put to work" (quoted in Landfried 1984, 54). In its decision on the matter, the FCC refused to speculate on the constitutionality of parity. But it pointedly praised legislators for their debates on constitutionality—which the FCC studied in, great detail—leaving the impression that the absence of parity may have been crucial to the ruling. This at least is what business celebrated and the political left and the unions feared (Markovits 1986, 141).

In France, parliamentarians recognize that their decisions at times constitute distinctly separate acts of judicial authority. Here is how Etienne Dailly put it during the Senate's debate on a motion of unconstitutionality against the nationalization bill: "I repeat: I have never said that we would refer this bill [to the Council]. I have limited myself to arguing that it is unconstitutional. . . . Personally, I consider that we [in parliament] are judges of the first instance. But we are under the control of the Council, just as judges of first instance are under the control of the Court of Appeal and the *Cour de cassation.*"[21]

CONCLUSION

Judicialization is in essence the formalization of an extensive and intimate form of what in American parlance has been called "coordinate construction" (Fisher 1988). More than simply "negative legislators," constitutional courts possess creative legislative powers: to recast policy-making environments, to encourage certain legislative solutions while undermining others, and to have the precise terms of their decisions written directly into legislative provisions. Ministers and parliamentarians deliberate in the language of constitutional law and make reasoned decisions about the constitutionality of legislation; these deliberations and decisions structure the building of constitutional jurisprudence. If I have pushed the argument too far, there are sound reasons. Students of public policy, and especially comparativists, all too often ignore the crucial role of law and courts. Legal scholars all too often assume that constitutional interpretation is the exclusive prerogative of judges. In France and Germany, at least, the making of public policy and the development of constitutional law are often one and the same thing.

NOTES

Portions of this paper have been published in Stone 1994.

1. In 1990 President Mitterrand proposed a constitutional amendment that would have enabled the Council to receive referrals from individuals through the court system. The opposition-controlled Senate killed the initiative, stating, among other motives, that a codification of rights would have to come first.

2. Drawing off the dependent variable is necessary to the extent that judicialization itself is the focus of the analysis.

3. Within weeks of assuming office, the Mauroy government retained the services of the law professors François Luchaire (a former Council judge) and Jacques Robert (whom Mitterrand would appoint to the Council in 1989). They were asked to draft a report on the constitutionality of nationalizations in principle and on compensation in particular. The opposition commissioned a report from three other law professors. These reports, which came to radically opposed conclusions (each in favor of the position of their client), helped to polarize debate. Both are published in Favoreu 1982.

4. Council (1982, 81-132).

5. National Assembly *Debates* December 15-16, 1983, 6547-48, 6605.

6. Council (1984, 84-181).

7. Especially Council (1981, 80-127).

8. National Assembly *Debates* June 26, 1986, 2546.

9. National Assembly *Debates* July 3, 1986, 2854.

10. Council (1986, 86-211).

11. FCC 1973, 35, 79; translation in Kommers (1989, 437-43).

12. Bundestag *Drucksache* 7/1328, 64-65.

13. Bundesrat *Debates*, February 21, 1975; Bundestag *Drucksache* 7/4462; Bundestag *Debates*, December 12, 1975.

14. 14 FCC 1975, 39, 1; translation in Kommers (1989, 348-59).

15. Bundestag *Debates,* November 7, 1975.

16. FCC 1954, 4, 7; translation in Kommers (1989, 249-52).

17. The law was referred to the FCC by employers and business associations. The FCC rejected the complaint, ruling that share ownership differs from "tangible property," since "its use requires the cooperation of employees" whose rights are also involved. (FCC 1979, 50, 290; translation in Kommers [1989, 278-282]).

18. *Règlement de l'Assemblée nationale* (Bureau de l'Assemblée, April 1986, 7th ed.), 94. The Senate's standing orders are similar.

19. The FCC is located in the town of Karlsruhe.

20. One would be faced with a range of exceedingly complex ideological issues.

21. Senate *Debates,* November 20, 1981.

REFERENCES

Blair, Philip M. 1978. "Law and Politics in West Germany." *Political Studies* 26 (3): 348-362.

Braunthal, Gerard. 1983. *The West German Social Democrats: Profile of a Party in Power.* Boulder, CO: Westview.

Brinkman, Gisbert. 1981. "The West German Federal Constitutional Court: Political Control through Judges." *Public Law* (Spring): 83-104.

Dyson, Kenneth. 1982. "West Germany: In Search of a Rational Consensus." In *Policy Styles in Western Europe,* ed. J. Richardson. London: Allen and Unwin, 17-46.

Favoreu, Louis. 1988. *La politique saisie par le droit.* Paris: Economica.

———. 1986. "Europe occidentale." In *Le contrôle juridictionnel des lois.,* ed. L. Favoreu and J. A. Jolowicz. Paris/Aix-en-Provence: Economica, 17-68.

———. 1982. "Une grande décision." In *Nationalisation et Constitution,* ed. L. Favoreu. Paris, Aix-en-Provence: Economica, pp. 19-55.

Fisher, Louis. 1988. *Constitutional Dialogues: Interpretation as Political Process.* Princeton: Princeton University Press.

Gusy, Christoph. 1985. *Parlamentarischer Gesetzzeber und Bundesverfaßungsgericht.* Berlin: Duncker und Humbolt.

Interview with Judge Martin Hirsch. 1978. *Der Spiegel* 48 (27 November): 38-49.

Johnson, Nevil. 1982. "The Interdependence of Law and Politics: Judges and the Constitution in Western Germany," *West European Politics* 5: 236-52.

———. 1978. "Law as the Articulation of the State in Western Germany: A German Tradition Seen from a British Perspective." *West European Politics* 1: 177-92.

Katzenstein, Peter J. 1987. *Policy and Politics in West Germany: The Growth of a Semisovereign State.* Philadelphia: Temple University Press.

Keeler, John T. S., and Alec Stone. 1987. "Judicial-Political Confrontation in Mitterrand's France: The Emergence of the Constitutional Council as a Major Actor in the Policy-Making Process." In *The Mitterrand Experiment*, ed. S. Hoffmann, S. Malzacher, and G. Ross. New York: Oxford University Press, 161-81.

Kirchheimer, Otto. 1966. "Germany: The Vanishing Opposition." In *Political Oppositions in Western Democracies.*, ed. R. A. Dahl. New Haven, Yale: Yale University Press, 237-59.

Kommers, Donald P. 1989. *The Constitutional Politics of the Federal Republic of Germany.* Durham, N.C.: Duke University Press.

Landfried, Christine. 1989. "Legislation and Judicial Review in the Federal Republic of Germany." In *Constitutional Review and Legislation: An International Comparison*, ed. Christine Landfried. Baden-Baden: Nomos, 147-68.

———. 1985. "The Impact of the German Constitutional Court on Politics and Policy-Outputs." *Government and Opposition* 20: 522-41.

———. 1984. *Bundesverfaßungsgericht und Gesetzgeber.* Baden-Baden: Nomos.

Lehmbruch, Gerhard. 1978. *Parteien wettbewerb im Bundesstaat.* Stuttgart: Kohlhammer.

Lepsius, M. Rainier. 1982. "Institutional Structures and Political Cultures." In *Party Government and Political Culture in West Germany*, ed by H. Doring and G. Smith. London: MacMillan, 116-29.

Luchaire, François. 1979. "Le conseil constitutionnel: est-il une juridiction?" *Revue du droit public* 95: 27-52.

Markovits, Andrei S. 1986. *The Politics of the West German Trade Unions.* Cambridge: Cambridge University Press.

Pulzer, Peter. 1978. "Responsible Party Government and Stable Coalition: The Case of the German Federal Republic." *Political Studies* 26 (2): 181-208.

Safran, William. 1988. "Rights and Liberties Under the Mitterrand Presidency: Socialist Innovations and Post-Socialist Revisions." *Contemporary French Civilization* 12 (1): 1-35.

Scharpf, Fritz. 1977. *Politischer Immobilismus und Ekonomische Krise: Afsätze zu den politischen Restriktionen der Wirtschaftspolitik in der Bundesrepublik Deutschland.* Kronburg: Athenium.

Schmidt, Manfred G.   1983.   "Two Logics of Coalition Policy: The West German Case." In *Coalition Government in Western Europe* ed. V. Bogdanor. London, Sydney: Croom Helm, 38-57.

Stone, Alec.   1994.   "Judging Socialist Reform: The Politics of Coordinate Construction in France and Germany." *Comparative Political Studies* 26:443-69.

————. 1992a.   *The Birth of Judicial Politics in France*. New York: Oxford University Press.

————. 1992b. "Where Judicial Politics are Legislative Politics: The Impact of the French Constitutional Council." *West European Politics* 15:29-49.

————. 1990. "The Birth and Development of Abstract Review: Constitutional Courts and Policy-Making in Western Europe." *Policy Studies Journal* 19:81-95.

————.   1989.   "In the Shadow of the Constitutional Council: The 'Juridicisation' of the Legislative Process in France." *West European Politics* 12: 12-34.

Tilford, Roger.   1981.   "The State, University Reform, and the 'Berufsverbot,'" *West European Politics* 4: 149-65.

Waline, Marcel.   1928.   "Elements d'une Théorie de la jurisdiction constitutionnelle." *Revue du droit public* 45: 441-462.

The Italian Case

13.

Italy: A Peculiar Case

GIUSEPPE DI FEDERICO

In dealing with the global expansion of judicial power and the Italian experience, it would be almost natural—and in general terms relatively easy—to analyze the Italian case following a pattern that seems to be recurrent in the analysis of the subject in the existing literature. In spite of the limited amount of empirical research, one could describe in general terms, and with reference to decisions of Italy's constitutional, administrative and ordinary judges, the increased relevance of judicial discretion in sensitive political areas. One could relate such a phenomenon to the so-called "law explosion" in Italy; to the ever increasing specificity in legal regulations of economic social and political relations; to the ensuing and ever increasingly numerous occasions for recourse to the judge for the definition of the actual rights of the citizen vis-a-vis one another and vis-a-vis governmental agencies, resulting in a growing dependency of the citizens' well-being on judicial decisions.

Comparing and contrasting such phenomena and analogous phenomena in other countries, one could further specify that in Italy, too, the regulatory influence of judicial decisions often goes far beyond the single case being decided (for example, in the field of labor relations). One could note that Italy also has an increasing number of judicial decisions that determine substantial increments in public expenditures, displacing into the hands of the judiciary a relevant part of the power of the purse. In other words, one could make a summary presentation of the many and multifaceted ways in which judicial decisions are attaining increased relevance in Italy, detailing the growing participation of the judicial subsystem in the political function of defining "who gets what, when, and how" in the community.

Such an account, though certainly pertinent and perhaps also interesting, would fail to bring out the most peculiar contribution of the Italian experience in the judicialization of politics: the increasing political relevance of the Italian judicial subsystem, deriving from the atypical institutional setup of public prosecution in Italy.   This institutional setup is atypical with regard not only to common-law countries, but also to other continental European countries of the civil-law tradition.

In fact, in Italy public prosecutors are as much a part of the judicial subsystem as judges are.   They are just as independent as judges from outside influence in making decisions.   Their independence from outside influence is protected just as much as that of the judges.   Furthermore, each individual member of the prosecutor's office is, de facto, largely free from internal hierarchical supervision.   I will try to show that such an institutional arrangement, which I will describe in more detail shortly, opens up avenues to judicial activism that are different from and far more ample than those we find in other democratic countries.   To put it in more correct terms, such an arrangement gives a different, and far greater, political relevance to the Italian judicial subsystem.

Any foreigner with a minimum of knowledge of the general characteristics of the judicial system of his or her own country, or of democratic countries in general, would be rather puzzled if he or she were to review the recent content of the Italian media, for example, the front pages of newspapers and magazines, the headlines of TV news shows, and so on.   She or he would find, day after day and in great abundance, headlines and articles reporting that various "judges" are directing or supervising large police operations, questioning suspects of corruption, conducting extensive interrogations of witnesses or suspects, deciding to throw them in prison under preventive detention, ordering and conducting their direct confrontation in jail, and deciding to free them or to confine them to house arrest, often as a recognition of their willingness to collaborate through confessions of their own crimes or by providing the names of their accomplices.   Our foreign observer would realize that many of the initiatives and investigative activities of these "judges" concentrated on cases of corruption of public officials, local administrators and politicians, members of Parliament, and industrialists: as of this writing, there have been nearly fifty arrests and seven requests for authorization to investigate members of Parliament, including one minister, with the concrete prospect of a substantial increase of such phenomena in forthcoming months.[1]

He or she would also have noticed several other interesting things:

1. that the whole thing was started in Milan by "Judge Di Pietro" just before the general political elections held April 5, 1992, and that initially only members of the Socialist Party were involved in his initiatives, one being caught while actually receiving money;

2. that thereafter representatives of the other parties were involved in a great "crescendo" of investigative activity, still going on;

3. that "Judge Di Pietro" was meanwhile acquiring national fame and being proclaimed a public hero.

The foreign observer would also have observed that, as days went by, more and more "judges" of other cities throughout Italy (Venice, Trapani, Genoa, Naples, Varese, Rome, Verona, Foggia, Florence, etc.) were following in the wake of "Judge Di Pietro" and joining his fight against political corruption, starting their own investigations and deciding on their own arrests, sometimes in cases that newspapers claimed to have revealed several months or years before, but on which no effective investigation had been conducted by those "judges" until 1992. Our foreign reader would further perceive a general agreement among political commentators in attaching political consequences of the greatest magnitude to the initiative daily taken by those "judges." Electoral results suggested an evident penalization of those parties whose members were involved in judicial investigations. Thereafter, day by day and in many ways, the initiatives have conditioned the political process, even effectively limiting the discretionary powers of the president of the Republic in designating the prime minister.

While reading Italy's press, our foreign observer, whether American, German or French, would certainly be more and more puzzled and intrigued by the nature of the activities of the "judges" and by the immediate impact and repercussions that their initiatives—publicized widely and in great detail—have in the political arena. But looking deeper into the matter and resorting to sources other than the media, he or she would discover that, in spite of the title attributed to them, those judges actually are public prosecutors, or, more accurately, "substitutes" for public prosecutors. She or he will realize that the general public no longer perceives the difference between the two roles, and that the terminology of the newspapers is generally adopted also by learned jurists and members of the judiciary.

Should our foreign friend be a member of the legal professions, say an American lawyer or judge, he or she would immediately cry: "Don't they have the separation of powers in this country?" Should the observer be a less naive person, let us say a political scientist, she or he would at least hypothesize that the theory of the division of powers is far less tenable in this country than in others. I will try to provide an answer to these and other questions of our foreign reader, first by sketching the peculiar characteristics of public prosecution in Italy and its most visible implications. I will thereafter refer to other features of the Italian judicial and political system that facilitate and actually bolster the special case of judicial activism made possible by those features. I will finally submit some research ideas on public prosecution that we are cultivating at present and that, to be productive, have to be pursued at a comparative level.

In preparing the text of its Constitution after World War II, Italy's founding fathers devoted a great deal of attention to public prosecution. To avoid the possibility that the powers of public prosecution could be used in a politically discriminatory fashion, as during the previous fascist period, they felt it necessary to sever the traditional link that had until then made public prosecutors hierarchically dependent on the Ministry of Justice.[2] Italy's constitutional fathers did not deem it necessary, however, to divide judges and prosecutors into different corps. "Magistrate" is the term that indicates them both, and the rules provide that both be selected through public competition as a guarantee of nonpartisan recruitment. As a consequence, once a magistrate begins his or her career—generally around the age of twenty-six, with no previous professional experience in law practice—he or she may be assigned to either of these two activities and can switch, even recurrently, from one function to another during his or her career.

To further ensure the actual independence of judges and prosecutors, the constitutional assembly decided on a wide-ranging self-government for the judiciary by providing that all decisions concerning the magistrates (judges and prosecutors) from recruitment to retirement, should be concentrated in the hands of the Higher Council of the Judiciary, and that a two thirds majority of that body should be composed of magistrates elected by their own colleagues.[3]

The constitutional assembly also decided that magistrates should have a monopoly over initiating criminal proceedings. It specifically wanted that monopoly to be exercised in full independence, that is, without any of the direct or indirect political responsibility typical of other constitutional democracies. Somewhat naively, it also decided, in order to avoid a discretionary or arbitrary, and therefore politically relevant, use of the criminal prosecution power, that it would be sufficient to prescribe that penal action should be mandatory for all criminal violations.

To our knowledge, none of the framers of Italy's Constitution doubted that such a provision could be observed de facto; none doubted that all penal violations could be actually and equally prosecuted. They firmly thought, furthermore, that independence and a compulsory criminal initiative—two faces of the same coin—would be the safest guarantee of the constitutional precept of the equality of all citizens before the criminal law.

For years my colleagues and I have concentrated our research efforts, among other things, on analyzing the consequences of these decisions for the evolution of Italy's judicial subsystem. Of course, it would be impossible to report here even summarily on our findings.[4] All we can do is indicate some of those findings that can further illustrate the peculiar political importance of Italy's judicial subsystem, omitting all the relevant and often important nuances that ordinarily characterize scholarly presentations.

The first clear element that emerges from our research is that, in spite of the constitutional provision that requires Italian magistrates to prosecute all criminal violations, penal action in Italy is de facto largely discretionary—just as much, and perhaps more, than is the case in other countries. The magistrates to whom this task is assigned initiate proceedings not only on incoming requests from "outside" (from police, other public authorities, citizens, etc.), but also on their own initiative. In other words, it is quite legitimate for them to start and carry out, with the greatest independence, investigations of any kind, on any citizens, using the various police forces to verify whether the offenses they (more or less justifiably) assume to exist have actually been committed. In pursuing such activities they have available to them a very large array of preventive measures to restrict the personal liberties, privacy, and use of personal properties of suspects.[5]

The second relevant finding is that in the course of the last 25 years the criminal initiative has tended to become more an attribute of the individual prosecutors than of the office to which they belong, in spite of the hierarchical power formally vested in the head of the office. Various factors have contributed to this evolution, among them the orientation of the Higher Council of the Judiciary toward undermining the hierarchical powers of the heads of prosecutors' offices as a means of promoting an unfettered development of compulsory criminal action. This policy even has been given a name: the "personalization of prosecutorial functions."

Such a policy complicates the concrete difficulties of reconciling the de facto unattainable, but still formally valid, principle of compulsory criminal action with the hierarchical power of coordination. After all, any directive or order regarding priorities, how to deal with single cases, or whether to restrict the personal liberties of suspects could be represented as a malicious interference in the full-fledged application of the constitutional duty of every prosecutor to pursue compulsory criminal action. The hierarchical powers of the chief prosecutors have recurrently been challenged by their "substitutes" in front of the Higher Council of the Judiciary. As a consequence the chief prosecutors have tended to use such powers less and less.

A third aspect of our research findings is that the extensive exercise of individual judgment that actually characterizes the criminal initiatives and the investigative activities of Italian public prosecutors and the possibility of exercising those powers on a personal basis, has had, at least to a large extent, a series of notable consequences:

1. It has made it easy for public prosecutors to play the role of problem solvers for the great political, social, and economic issues of society. As public fashions have dictated from time to time, these have included safety in the workplace, environmental pollution, tax evasion, bank frauds and other economic crimes, corruption of public officials and politicians, terrorism, organized crime, and so on.

2. It has allowed great differences to develop among public prosecutors, both in their preference for this or that sector of criminal activities and in their ways of conducting investigations.

3. It has more and more promoted an image of a judiciary involved not so much in judging as in fighting against society's evils.

Individual magistrates, through the wide publicity often given to their initiatives by the media, have often acquired national fame regardless of the results that their initiatives achieved, years later, at the trial level. Often fame has also bestowed on them more concrete gratifications in terms of extrajudicial appointments to various positions. They have even recurrently acquired seats in Parliament while remaining members of the judiciary on "temporary leave." During the 1970s the inclination of various public prosecutors to be visibly active and in search of fame through their criminal initiatives spread and was given the name "protagonismo." Their visible freedom to act arbitrarily and their frequent lack of consideration for either the damage that their initiatives would inflict upon innocent people, or the long periods of preventive detention suffered by citizens found innocent at the trial level years later, have frequently resulted in the accusation that public prosecutors are politicized; that they used their powers for partisan ends; that they choose for their initiatives the times best suited to produce maximum political damage; and that they act to promote their personal image and interests in utter contempt for procedural guarantees safeguarding citizens' liberty and dignity.

Such accusations became quite widespread in the mid-1980s. They resulted in a 1987 referendum on the civil responsibility of magistrates: 80% of the voters requested of public prosecutors—in vain as it turned out afterwards—that the magistrates be made accountable for the irreparable damage caused to citizens in the frequent cases of unsubstantiated accusation, unjust preventive detention, lack of diligence in conducting investigations, and so on.

As years have gone by, it has become increasingly clear that the independent use of ample discretionary power in initiating criminal action and in conducting investigations has largely placed in the hands of the prosecutors the (often personal) definition and implementation of the country's criminal policy. It has become clear that this discretionary power, however great its political relevance in a modern state, however profoundly it impinges on the rights of the citizens, is not accompanied by any form of accountability or responsibility. Paradoxically, the preservation of the unattainable constitutional provision for mandatory criminal initiatives, far from protecting the equality of citizens before the law, frequently promotes unequal treatment because of the different orientations of the various public prosecutors.

In spite of all this, no reform in this sector is in sight. The only attempt made recently has been to create a national office for the coordination of the activities of public prosecution against organized crime and the mafia. Even that has encountered great resistance on the part of the judiciary. At present there is a widespread conviction that, in spite of the negative aspects of the current setup of public prosecution, its preservation is the only means available to keep under a minimum of control the grave phenomenon of public corruption. It is felt that the introduction of any form of accountability for the activities of public prosecutors, their subjection to any form of policy directives, would undermine their initiatives in that very crucial sector.

It would be of no avail to observe that the recurrent initiative of "Judge" Di Pietro and his many imitators against corruption follows a long period (several years) in which no initiatives on serious cases of corruption were undertaken. It would do little good to suggest that the most relevant question in Italian democracy is not so much whether Di Pietro and his imitators are doing the proper thing, but rather whether there is any authority that we can hold politically responsible for the long period of inactivity of the public prosecutors in the area of political corruption. It would be useless to argue that if things are left unchanged in the organization of public prosecution, the omissions and inefficiencies that have allowed the development of such a widespread system of corruption might reproduce themselves again in the future in the same or in other sectors of criminal activity. Anybody uttering such opinions would at best be considered a very naive person, and at worst suspected of deviously and maliciously proposing to undermine the only existing bulwark against political and administrative corruption.

I have conducted a very brief and incomplete review of some of the factors that make Italy a peculiar case for those interested in analyzing the various ways in which the judicial subsystem may acquire political relevance. Let me add that the analyses we have conducted have stimulated in us a great deal of interest in acquiring detailed empirical knowledge of other countries' solutions to at least two relevant problems that greatly condition the effectiveness of criminal justice, problems that in our view have not received enough attention in Europe.

The first concerns the regulation and actual operative relation between two conflicting values. On the one hand there is the need to protect the autonomy of public prosecutors so that they can effectively and correctly perform their delicate function as gatekeepers of the criminal justice system.   On the other hand, there is the need to maintain democratic control of the basic choices and policies in the criminal justice sector.

The second question concerns the relationship between public prosecution and the police, which varies greatly from country to country in Europe.   Such working relations have great relevance for the effective and correct conduct of investigations and for the assessment of their reciprocal responsibilities.   On these and other aspects of public prosecution we have already conducted a substantive amount of field research in Germany, France, and England,[6] and in the future we certainly want to extend and make more analytical our studies in this sector.   We hope that the important topic of public prosecution will attract the interest of researchers.

NOTES

This chapter was originally presented as the Keynote Address at the opening session of the conference on "The Judicialization of Politics" hosted by the *Centro Studi sull'Ordinamento Giudiziario* of Bologna at the University of Bologna's campus in Forlí, Italy, June, 1992. Professor Di Federico is founder and Director of the *Centro*.

1. As this paper went to press (December, 1993), more than one-third of the members of the Italian Parliament were being investigated.   Furthermore, the requests to investigate members of Parliament have caused numerous resignations of cabinet members and heavily conditioned the process of forming new cabinets.

2. They eliminated by the same step the only existing mechanism capable of coordinating the investigative activities of public prosecutors at the national level.

3. Such a body actually became operative only at the very end of the 1950s.

4. For a summary view of the most relevant research results in the area as of 1989, see Di Federico (1989).

5. To be more precise on this point, it would be necessary to discuss some relevant differences between the old code and the new code of criminal procedure enacted in 1989.

6. In England the setup of public prosecution has, of course, changed greatly in the last seven years.

REFERENCE

Di Federico, Giuseppe. 1989. "The Crisis of the Justice System and the Referendum on the Judiciary." In *Italian Politics: A Review*, ed. P. Corbetta and R. Leonardi. Vol. 3. London: Pinter, 25-69.

14.

Judicial Independence and Policy-Making in Italy

CARLO GUARNIERI

Since the end of World War II, the institutional setting of the Italian judiciary has been radically transformed in an attempt to make it as independent as possible of the political environment. As a result the position now held by the judiciary in the Italian political system seems to be, on many counts, rather peculiar. In order to correctly estimate the extent of this peculiarity, its origins, and its implications, we shall take a brief look at the role of the judiciary in democratic systems of government in general and then compare the present institutional setting of the Italian judiciary with those of the judiciaries in other democratic countries.

THE JUDICIARY IN DEMOCRATIC REGIMES

The judiciaries of major democratic regimes—England, the United States, France and Germany—are characterized, notwithstanding their peculiarities (See Guarnieri 1981, 1984; Dechênes and Shetreet 1985; and Waltman and Holland 1988), by some common features:

1. The process through which judges are recruited is always more or less directly influenced by the political environment; the ways in which this influence is exercised are different. The greatest difference is seen

between civil-law countries, where the process normally is run, through some kind of public competition, by the ministry of justice, and therefore by officers or magistrates more or less answerable to the executive branch, and common-law countries, where the political branches of government are directly involved in the appointment process. This is the case in England, where the lord chancellor, and the prime minister, have a prominent role, and in the U.S., where, at the federal level, appointments are made by the president with the advice and consent of the Senate, and in many states judges are elected by local voters, often for limited terms of office.

2. The function of prosecuting is entrusted to magistrates or officers directly or indirectly responsible to other governmental bodies, if not to the voters themselves. Existing prosecuting systems include the classic ministerial structure, either in its centralized (France) or federalized (Germany) version; a semi-autonomous governmental organization (the Crown Prosecution Service in England); the peculiar setting of the U.S. federal prosecution (more or less under executive control); and direct election of the chief prosecutor, as is the case in many American states. Only in France do prosecutors and judges belong to the same corps, even though French prosecutors are directly responsible to the minister of justice.   Elsewhere, judges and prosecutors belong to separate organizations, although they may under certain conditions cross over from one branch to the other.

In all these countries, despite significant variations, these institutional traits act as checks on judicial power: they are institutional means through which the other branches of government—or, in some cases, the voters themselves—can indirectly influence the behavior of judges and the political significance of the judicial system.   The influence on the process of recruitment, even when only indirect, assures, at least to a certain extent, that the values of the individuals who perform judicial functions will not be too much out of step with those prevailing in the political system.   The position of the prosecuting branch guarantees the passivity of the judicial system, that is, that it lacks a self-starter, allowing the political environment to regulate to some extent the demands for action placed upon the judicial system.   This was already underscored by Hamilton in the *Federalist* (no. 78) and, according to Cappelletti (1989), the respect of procedural rules is essential to the democratic legitimation of an independent judiciary.

However, the cases analyzed involve systems enjoying different levels of institutional independence. Judicial guarantees of independence of the political system seem to be stronger in common-law countries. Moreover, in civil-law countries judges tend to enjoy a lower degree of internal independence, vis-à-vis other judges, since the organizational setting within which they operate is different.   In contrast to what happens in common-law judicial organizations, in the judiciary of civil-law countries (Di Federico 1976, Freddi 1978):

1. The selection of judicial personnel is made through examinations at a youthful age, and no consideration is given to the candidates' previous professional nonjudicial experience.

2. The professional training of the judge takes place in large part within the judicial body.

3. Organizational roles are ordered according to a hierarchy of ranks. Advancement up the career ladder is competitive and promotions are granted according to formal criteria combining seniority and merit, merit being assessed with a great latitude for discretionary judgment by hierarchical superiors.

Generally speaking, in all the judicial organizations we have here considered there is a felt need for checks designed to ensure that the institutional goals are pursued by their members.   Anglo-Saxon judiciaries, which tend to employ individuals trained outside the organization, usually with lengthy apprenticeship, rely less upon internal controls.   In continental Europe, where the personnel are recruited without significant professional experience, young judges are placed at the bottom of the pyramid-like structure, and their organizational socialization is constantly monitored through a career based on a hierarchical ladder (Freddi 1978; for details on France and Germany see Mestitz 1990; and Pederzoli 1991).

THE ITALIAN CASE: PECULIARITY OR DEVIATION?

Traditionally, the Italian judiciary was structurally very similar to that of the continental European judicial organizations. During the Unification (1859-1870) the influence of Napoleonic models of governmental organization was especially strong, and, notwithstanding some minor adjustments, the basic structure did not change very much, at least until the end of World War II.

The guarantees of judges and public prosecutors vis-à-vis the executive were somewhat reinforced immediately after the war (in 1946). This strengthening was a reaction to abuses that had occurred, with different intensities, during both the liberal and the fascist regimes. Nevertheless, the hierarchical character of the judiciary was left untouched. The Constitution of 1948 envisaged the establishment of a self-governing body of judges—the Higher Council of the Judiciary, two-thirds composed of magistrates elected by their colleagues and one-third of lawyers or law professors elected by Parliament. All decisions concerning the status of magistrates were assigned to this council by the Constitution, which also provided special guarantees for public prosecutors. To help ensure these guarantees, the principle of compulsory prosecution of criminal offenses by public prosecutors was written into the Constitution.

The consolidating phase of Italian politics demonstrated at first a substantial evasion of the constitutional design. Only after 1959 did things began to change, leading to a great increase in both the internal and external independence of Italian judges. In that year, the constitutionally mandated Higher Council of the Judiciary was finally instituted, and began progressively taking away the powers of the executive in the administration of judicial personnel, both judges and public prosecutors.

The second major modification in the organizational setup of the judiciary concerned the system of promotion. Under pressure from the majority of lower-ranking magistrates, strongly organized by their professional association (see Freddi 1978; Guarnieri 1976). Between 1963 and 1973 Parliament passed a series of laws that dismantled, step by step, the traditional system of promotions. As a result, today the evaluation of candidates possessing the seniority to compete for promotion at the different ranks of the judicial hierarchy is no longer based, as it was until the 1960s, either on written and oral exams or on the consideration of their written judicial works. Instead, there is a global assessment of candidates' judicial performance. What this means in actuality is that all candidates who fulfill the seniority requirements are promoted to the highest ranks (Di Federico and Guarnieri 1988).

As a general result of these processes, a peculiar judicial setting has emerged in Italy, at least in comparison with that prevailing in other democratic regimes. First, some of the traditional features of Italy's judicial organization have been modified. The most notable change is that the internal hierarchy of the judiciary has been completely dismantled. The model of recruitment—exclusively from the bottom, with the categorical exclusion of any lateral entry, allowing into the corps only young graduates without any professional experience—has not changed substantially. Training is handled internally, even though the instruments that once allowed the judicial elite to control and influence this process are no longer working.   At present, after a short apprenticeship, the young magistrate is entrusted with judicial (or prosecutorial) functions, and his or her professional competence is not subject to later evaluations. From this point of view, it could be said that the Italian judiciary combines *in an original way* features typical of continental systems with elements found in Anglo-Saxon judiciaries.

Thus Italy stands out because of the unusual relationships that exist between the judiciary and the other governmental branches. The latter are almost completely devoid of institutional means of influence over the former. As we have seen, there are within democratic regimes two basic types of judges. The common-law judge is usually an established professional, recruited at a mature age, who is granted extensive guarantees of independence. The civil-law judge enters the judiciary through public competitive examinations right after graduating from the university and usually spends his entire working life there, going through the stages of a long career, but subject to continuous evaluation by higher ranking colleagues and, in certain cases, by the minister of Justice. In the first case, the political branches of government intervene only at the time of the judge's recruitment or in the rare case of serious breach of conduct. As a result there is not a judicial career as such: the judges are called to fill specific positions, and promotions to higher levels are not routinely foreseen, at least institutionally. A civil-law judge, however, perhaps because the initial examination is not believed to be sufficiently reliable, remains subject to various forms of control that limit his or her independence.

Against this context, Italy seems to be in a unique position. Italian judges today enjoy guarantees of both internal and external independence higher than those found in any other democratic country. Both in the process of recruitment and professional socialization and in administering the guarantees of their status, Italian judges—and Italian public prosecutors—are subject only to limits that are unquestionably less constricting than those found elsewhere, since all decisions relating to them are made only by a body, the Higher Council of the Judiciary, two-thirds of whose members are magistrates elected by their colleagues. The Italian judiciary is thus not subject to the external controls still prevalent in France—which remains most faithful to the hierarchical traditions typical of a bureaucratic setting, with a judiciary strongly conditioned by the executive branch—and even in Germany, whose judiciary is influenced to a certain extent by both the executive and the legislative branches. Yet the recruitment and socialization of Italian judges, in contrast to what occurs in common-law countries, is also completely removed from any intervention on the part of the political environment.

The uniqueness of the institutional setting of the Italian judiciary becomes even more clear if we consider the position of public prosecutors. In all the principal democratic countries there exist institutional ties between the prosecuting officers and the political system (also see for Canada, Grosman 1969 and Baar 1988; for the Netherlands, Austria, Switzerland, and Norway, Jenscheck and Leibinger 1979; for Spain, Grenados 1989). Despite country-to-country variation, specific mechanisms are always in place that allow the prosecution to be influenced by the political environment, at least along general lines. Only Italy shows a different setup: the institutional means at the disposal of the political system are few and, at any rate, hardly used. The status of public prosecutors is identical to that of the judges. In fact, prosecuting magistrates and judges are part of the same body that governs itself through the Higher Council of the Judiciary.

THE ROOTS OF THE PRESENT-DAY SETTING

The transformations that have characterized the Italian judiciary in the postwar period have been accompanied and supported by the growing conflict that developed inside the judicial corps through the 1950s and the 1960s. The reasons for this conflict lie mostly in the structure of the judicial career, which did not seem to allow a balanced distribution of professional rewards, in the political and unionization liberties guaranteed by the new democratic regime; and in the emergence, after 1959, of a new institutional player, the Higher Council of the judiciary (Freddi 1972). Certainly in the postwar era many of the bureaucratic judiciaries of continental Europe have experienced a certain level of internal conflict. The Italian Judiciary stands out, if at all, because of the particular harshness of its conflict and especially because of the reactions of the political system (Mancini 1980; Guarnieri 1991).

The conflict within the judicial body drove the "progressive" magistrates—those proposing a "democratic" reform of the traditional setting, leading, among other things, to a dismantling of the career—to seek allies elsewhere, in face of opposition from the higher-rank magistrates and of the lack of sensitivity on the part of the government. Their search was directed to public opinion, where on the whole they found support, albeit without concrete consequences, and, more strategically, to the political parties. But in the late 1950s an important change occurred in the relationship between judiciary and politics. Prior to that time the Italian judiciary was governed mainly by the higher-ranking magistrates, acting very often in full agreement with the minister of justice, since magistrates were and are in charge of all important positions within the Ministry of Justice (see Di Federico 1976). Direct interventions by the executive in judicial affairs was rare, since the hierarchical setting allowed more discrete intervention through senior magistrates.

Since the early 1960s, new and increasingly more important relationships have evolved between the political parties and the representatives of the magistrates' association. The parties of the opposition, for example, the Communist party, or those that were slowly moving from opposition to government roles, like the Socialists, were obviously interested in developing contacts with a strategic body such as the judiciary and, above all, in strengthening its guarantees of independence from an executive branch they did not expect to fully control. The party traditionally in government, the Christian Democrats, found itself under pressure from new and dangerous competitors. Its internal fragmentation, with competition among its various factions, and the growth of socialist and, above all, communist influence on the decision making of the Parliament (Di Palma 1977), resulted in the approval of reforms that satisfied the demands of the magistrates' association and created an attitude of general acquiescence toward the demands of the judiciary (Di Federico 1989).

While other elements, such as the involvement of the judiciary in the fight against terrorism in the 1970s, could have supported such an evolution, the above-mentioned factors seem without doubt the most relevant, as the different outcomes in the cases of France and especially Spain show. In these countries, not only have different parties alternated in power, but the legislative process has been, at least until today, solidly in the hands of the government. Let us turn briefly to consider these cases.

The institutional setup of the Spanish judiciary under Franco well exemplified that of an authoritarian regime (Toharia 1975). The Spanish judiciary was characterized by a relatively high degree of independence but by a low political significance, since special courts were in charge of all politically sensitive matters. The process of transition to democracy in Spain has been marked by a higher degree of continuity (Huneuus 1982). No purges were carried out within the judiciary (Toharia 1987), although the instauration of the new democratic regime brought about some significant changes in the judicial organization: the abolition of the special courts; the strengthening of the jurisdiction of the ordinary courts; and the introduction in the Constitution of 1978 of a self-governing body for the judiciary, the Consejo General del Poder Judicial. Modeled on the Italian example, the Consejo was placed in charge of administering the guarantees of the independence of the judicial corps (Andres Ibañez and Movilla 1986). In Spain public prosecutors have always been separated from the judiciary and are, in contrast to those in Italy, connected with the executive (see Grenados 1989).

In 1980, the first Consejo General began to function. It was composed of twelve judges elected by their colleagues and by eight lay members representing Parliament. The period that followed was characterized by a factionalization of the judiciary, more or less into three groups, but with conservatives apparently in the majority (Anon et al. 1988), and by growing tensions between the judiciary, represented in the Consejo General, and the executive, especially after the rise to power of a Socialist government in 1982 (Andres Ibañez and Movilla 1986). The judiciary was among all political institutions the one least affected by the regime change, and its actions seemed to be influenced by this failed renewal (Porras Nadales 1986). The consequence of the conflict between the government and the Consejo General was the enactment in 1985 of a new Ley Organica del Poder Judicial. This law decreased the prerogatives of the Consejo General and drastically changed its membership selection procedures by providing that its judicial members would be selected by Parliament. Despite strong political opposition in Parliament and a jurisdictional battle fought before the Constitutional Court, the law survived all challenges. Its implementation has so far brought about a sharp decrease in the degree of independence of the Spanish judiciary (Andres Ibañez 1991).

The French case is also interesting. As we have seen, France has always been the country more faithful to the traditional, bureaucratic, executive-dominated model of judicial setting (Merryman 1985; Radamaker 1988). In 1981, before acceding to power for the first time under the Fifth Republic, the Socialist Party promised to increase strongly the independence of the French judiciary. Notwithstanding this promise and, later, the work of a study commission, nothing has changed in the setting of the French judiciary (see Perrot 1989 and Bodiguel (991), although President Mitterrand in 1992 did envisage a reform of the 1958 Constitution, providing, among other things, a strengthening of guarantees of judicial independence.

. . . AND THE CONSEQUENCES

The unique pattern of institutional relationships between the judiciary and the Italian political system allows Italian magistrates to have a great effect on the political environment and, especially, on the other structures of government (for examples, see Di Federico 1981, 1989 and Zannotti 1989). It clearly can be said that an expansion of judicial power is well under way in Italy. The political significance of the magistrates, supported by their strong guarantees of independence, is remarkable in the criminal field. Prosecuting magistrates can influence the requests addressed to the criminal justice system in a decisive way, regardless of the principle of compulsory prosecution described by Di Federico in chapter 13 (also see Di Federico 1989 and 1991; Guarnieri 1984, esp. 125-52). It is difficult to determine the extent to which such institutional conditions have been employed in concrete interventions (but see Guarnieri and Pederzoli 1988). It must be underscored, however, that these conditions make politically incisive interventions more possible.

Such interventions are more likely to occur today than in the past. In part, this reflects the pressure of interested political actors. But it is due also to the apparent inability of the present-day Italian judiciary to uphold the traditional definition of the judicial role, even making allowances for the general transformations that have occurred in the judicial role in democratic regimes (Cappelletti 1989; Pederzoli 1990). Traditionally, the judge in civil-law systems (Freddi 1978, Merryman 1985) was seen as a technical, passive executor of options previously processed by the legislator and expounded by academic doctrine.

We have already seen how the influence of higher-ranking judges has been reduced in the Italian system. The influence of academic doctrine has also lessened because it appears today much more diversified than before—many academics are advocating a more activist posture by the judges—and because the organizational mechanism that once supported its importance, the evaluation of written judicial rulings as a base for career advancement, is no longer effective. As a result there is no incentive for the judges to conform to the dictates of academic doctrine (Di Federico 1976, 1985; Rebuffa 1986).

The Italian institutional setting seems to be positively related to two important phenomena already discussed: the development of organized factions (correnti) inside the judiciary and the dismantling of the hierarchical controls, that allowed some evaluation of and control over the performance of magistrates. The professional association of the Italian magistrates (ANM) is officially divided into factions, each with a stable, even if small, organizational structure. The main factions are, from left to right: Magistratura Democratica, Unità per la Costituzione, and Magistratura Indipendente. The organized factions are born from conflicts that develop within the judiciary over a specific theme: the career. They become the instrument through which, very effectively, the magistrates articulate their demands to Parliament and to the government, even though their strength is due mainly to the influence they exert on the Higher Council. The changes in that body's electoral rules, especially those of 1975, which introduced the proportional system with competing lists of candidates, contribute to making the *correnti* even stronger. Through proportional representation, all the main factions are virtually guaranteed representation in the council.

The role of the factions cannot be understood without taking into account the dismantling of the hierarchical structure, which has deprived the council of criteria with which to evaluate magistrates in order to make appointments to higher positions or to decide on transfers. Since the council finds itself in the position of choosing among candidates of the same official rank in these cases (Di Federico 1985; Rebuffa 1986, 62-68), the tie of a candidate to a faction or a party becomes highly relevant. In other words, when a transfer or promotion to a given position occurs not on the basis of the simple seniority, it occurs as a result of a bargain among the factions and the parties, which often support one another with reciprocal exchanges: remember that the Higher Council presently consists of ten lawyers or law professors chosen by Parliament, usually along strict party lines, in addition to twenty magistrates elected by the corps. In this way the magistrates, at least the substantial number interested in these personnel decisions made by the council, cannot fail to take into account the logic of its decision making and of the complex configuration of factional and party forces that play a role in it.

In this context, a strong tendency has emerged toward the development of connections between the judiciary and the political environment. Personal ties are difficult to document in full, but they have been often reported and are based, above all, on the flourishing of extrajudicial duties assigned with remarkable frequency to many magistrates by the political and social environment (Di Federico 1981; Zannotti 1981). Personal ties often support more complex relationships among groups, or factions, of magistrates and parties (Zannotti 1989). In the latter case, there are naturally some connections of an ideological nature. Perhaps the most visible, but not the only, one is that between Magistratura Democratica and the parties of the left (Pappalardo 1987). But there are also different ties of an "opportunistic" nature.

Regardless of their nature, such connections tend to produce the exchange of favors between magistrates and parties as the main, if not their only, outcome. They might explain, for example, the long and—at least until recently—often ineffective investigations of political corruption, as well as parliamentary generosity in setting judicial salaries (on the connections between politicians and magistrates at the local level see della Porta 1992). Such exchanges find a useful institutional seat in the Higher Council, where representatives of the magistrates' factions continuously interact with the representatives of both government and opposition political parties (Rebuffa 1986). Because of this role, the significance of the Higher Council has steadily increased in recent years, progressively eroding the traditional position of the Court of Cassation as the apex of the judicial system.

Further signs of the development of these connections and of their ramifications in other institutions are the growing number of magistrates elected to Parliament, and the not-so-rare cases of rapidly rising political careers achieved by magistrates: The twelve magistrates in the previous Parliament (Zannotti 1989, 201-2), became thirteen in the April 1992 elections and there have been cases of magistrates becoming ministers or deputy ministers. Above all, the consequences brought about by these connections serve in some way as checks on the power of the judiciary, since they affect its actions, even though they were not institutionally foreseen.

POLITICS AND JUSTICE: THE ITALIAN CASE

No political institution, including the judiciary, can be made wholly autonomous from its environment:

> The "disconnectedness" of the judicial process from the political system . . . is only relative. Changes in the rest of the system affect the nature of the decisions that will be made. Like all who make decisions affecting the fate and fortunes of the community, judges exercise their discretion not only within the confines of the requirements of the judicial process itself but within the context of the political system of which it is a part. What distinguishes judicial from other kinds of political actors is not that the judges are outside the system but that they are related to it in a different fashion than are the other decision makers. (Peltason 1968, 287)

The judiciary will be inevitably subjected to influence attempts, especially if its political significance is high (Shapiro 1981).

Generally speaking, the pressures coming from the political environment can be channelled and regulated, but not canceled or made completely ineffective. After all, according to the traditional dictates of liberal constitutionalism, the guarantees of judges' independence are designed, first, to protect their impartiality--and thereby to defend the rights of citizens—and in some cases to make the judiciary a check on the power of other governmental structures (Weiler 1968; Guarnieri 1981). In the civil-law tradition of continental Europe, judicial independence has been aimed mainly, if not exclusively, toward the first objective. Perhaps only in the U.S. has the judiciary been charged for any substantial period of time with the task of balancing the power of the political branches. Thus, in the first case, the guarantees of independence are normally limited, while in the second, where the contribution of the judicial body to the equilibrium of the constitutional system is far greater, the guarantees are stronger. However, these guarantees and the judicial power they foster are matched by a system of checks and balances in a political regime of limited government (Murphy and Pritchett 1986, 598ff.). Each tradition has its own logic, even if the U.S. seems better able to fill the needs of modern democratic regimes in facing a phenomenon that, like it or not, is more or less present in all political systems: expanded judicial creativity with the inescapable growth of judicial power (Cappelletti 1989). In fact, it is clear that the dangers arising from a judge-law-maker are higher where there are no institutional checks on his actions, but that is another very complicated theme, whose development would need at least another, and much longer, paper.

The peculiar features of the institutional setting of the Italian judiciary—probably the byproduct of a consensual political regime (Lijphart 1984) together with the traditional bureaucratic setup—influence in a more general way its relationships with the political system, characterized by the development of checks institutionally neither foreseen nor regulated. The importance of these restraints has to be understood in connection with the lack of effective institutional channels of influence. In fact, in this case it is likely that other, formally unforeseen channels will emerge, maybe as a result of the configuration of the institutional setup: consider, for example, the growing role played in the last few years by the Higher Council and the development, even through the assignment to extrajudicial duties, of "new" careers. In this process, the traditional character of Italy's political system cannot be neglected: the power of the parties should not surprise anyone.

Thus, the case of the Italian judiciary seems to be characterized by a paradox: it enjoys a very high degree of institutional independence, but its autonomy of action is rather limited, at least in the context illustrated above. This result can be concisely interpreted as the consequence of the attempt to insert elements typical of the professional judiciaries of common-law countries into a bureaucratic setting, without properly taking into proper account all the implications of such innovations. The scarcity of channels of institutional influence and the increased political significance of the judicial body in Italy drive the political environment to utilize every resource at its disposal to try to condition the judiciary. But the unchanged bureaucratic mode of recruitment and the dismantling of the traditional controls exercised by the hierarchy do not facilitate the acquisition of professional competence and values by the magistrates (Di Federico 1981). Instead, they stimulate their affiliation with factionalized unions and makes them more subject to co-optation by external forces.

The most important consequence of the whole process analyzed in this chapter is that the Italian judiciary, more than forty years after the first reforms, is still characterized by limited autonomy: it tends to act according a logic not of its own, but highly conditioned by the political environment. However, while once its low level of autonomy was mainly due to the limited guarantees of independence from the executive branch, today, given the complex network of relationships that we have outlined, the influence of the political environment is certainly more pervasive, if not more powerful. It is exercised not so much and not only by the executive, but by a whole series of resourceful political actors.

REFERENCES

Andres Ibañez, P. 1991. "Il modello e i suoi frutti: cronaca di cinque anni del Consiglio Generale del Potere Giudiziario spagnolo." *Questione giustizia* 10:211-22

Andres Ibañez, P., and C. Movilla Alvarez. 1986. *El poder judicial*. Madrid, Tecnos.

Anon, M. J., et al. 1988. "Las asociaciones profesionales en el ambito de la Administracion de Justicia (jueces, magistrados y fiscales)." in *Anuario de filosofia del derecho* 5:155-93.

Baar, Carl. 1988. "The Courts in Canada." In *The Political Role of Law Courts in Modern Democracies*, ed by J. Waltman and K. Holland. London: Macmillan, 53-82.

Bodiguel, J. L. 1991. *Les magistrats un corp sans ame?*. Paris, P. U. F.

Cappelletti, M. 1989. *The Judicial Process in Comparative Perspective*. Oxford: Clarendon Press.

Dechênes, J., and S. Shetreet, eds. 1985. *Judicial Independence: The Contemporary Debate*. Dordrecht: Nijhoff.

della Porta, D. 1992. *La corruzione politica in Italia. Tre casi di governo locale*. Bologna: Il Mulino.

Di Federico, G. 1976. "The Italian Judicial Profession and Its Bureaucratic Setting." *The Juridical Review*. 1976, I, pp.40-57.

———. 1981. "Gli incarichi extragiudiziari dei magistrati." Introduction to Zannotti. *Le attività extragiudiziarie dei magistrati ordinari*.

————. 1985. "Le qualificazioni professionali del corpo giudiziario: carenze attuali, possibili riforme e difficoltà di attuarle." *Rivista trimestrale di scienza dell'amministrazione* 31:21-60.

————. 1989. "The crisis of the Justice System and The Referendum on the Judiciary." In *Italian Politics: A Review*, ed. R.Leonardi and P.G. Corbetta. Vol. 3, 25-49. London, Pinter.

————. 1991. "Obbligatorietà dell'azione penale, coordinamento delle attività del pubblico ministero e loro rispondenza alle aspettative della comunità." In *Accusa e ruolo del p.m. nell'evoluzione del sistema italiano.* Naples: Jovene.

Di Federico, G., and Guarnieri, C. 1988. "The Courts in Italy." In *The Political Role of Law Courts in Modern Democracies*, ed by J. Waltman and K. Holland. London: Macmillan, 153-180.

Di Palma, G. 1977. *Surviving without Governing.* Berkeley: University of California Press.

Freddi, G. 1972. "La magistratura come organizzazione burocratica." *Politica del diritto.* 3:325-339.

————. 1978. *Tensioni e conflitto nella magistratura.* Bari: Laterza.

Grenados, F. 1989. *El Ministerio Fiscal (del presente al futuro.* Madrid: Tecnos.

Grosman, B. A. 1969. *The Prosecutor: An Inquiry into the Exercise of Discretion.* Toronto, University of Toronto Press.

Guarnieri, C. 1976. "Elites, correnti e conflitti fra magistrati italiani: 1964-1976." *Politica del diritto.* 6:653-82.

————. 1981. *L'indipendenza della magistratura.* Padua: Cedam.

————. 1984. *Pubblico ministero e sistema politico.* Padua: Cedam.

————. 1991. "Magistratura e politica: il caso italiano." *Rivista italiana di scienza politica* 21:3-32.

Guarnieri, C., and P. Pederzoli. 1988. "Judicial Activism in Italy." Paper presented to the ECPR Joint Workshop, Rimini.

Huneuus, C. 1982. "La transicion a la democracia en Espana. Dimensiones de una politica consociational." In *Transicion a la democracia en el sur de Europa y America Latina*, ed. J. Santamaria, 243-86. Madrid: Centro de Investigaciones Sociologicas.

Jenscheck, H.H., and R. Leibinger, eds. 1979. *Funktion und Tätigkeit der Anklagebehörde im ausländischen Recht.* Baden-Baden: Nomos.

Lijphart, A. 1984. *Democracies. Patterns of Majoritarian and Consensus Government in Twenty-One Countries.* London: Yale University Press.

Mancini, G. F. 1980. "Politics and the Judges—the European Perspective." *The Modern Law Review* 63:1-17.

Merryman, J.H. 1985. *The Civil Law Tradition*. 2nd ed. Stanford, Stanford University Press.

Mestitz, A. 1990. *Selezione e formazione professionale dei magistrati e degli avocati in Francia*. Padua: Cedam.

Murphy, W. F. and Pritchett, C. H. 1986. *Courts, Judges, and Politics*. 4th ed. New York: Random House.

Pappalardo, S. 1987. *Gli iconoclasti Magistratura Democratica nel quadro della Associazione Nazionale Magistrati*. Milan: Franco Angeli.

Pederzoli, P. 1990. "Il giudice nei regimi democratici." *Rivista italiana di scienza politica* 20:293-329.

———. 1991. "La formazione alle professioni legali nella Repubblica federale tedesca." *Rivista Trimestrale di Diritto e Procedura Civile* 65:1203-27.

Peltason, J. W. 1968. "Judicial Process: Introduction." In *International Encyclopedia of the Social Sciences*. Vol. 8, 283-291. New York, MacMillan.

Perrot, R. 1989. *Institutions judiciaires*. Paris: Montchrestien.

Porras Nadales, A. J. 1986. "Conflictos entre organos constitucionales del estado y principio de division de poderes." *Revista de estudios politico* 52:19-46.

Radamaker, Dallas. 1988. "The Courts in France." In *The Political Role of Law Courts in Modern Democracies*, ed by J. Waltman and K. Holland. London: Macmillan, 129-52.

Rebuffa, G. 1986. *La funzione giudiziaria*. Turin: Giappichelli.

Shapiro, M. 1981. *Courts: A Comparative and Political Analysis*. Chicago: The University of Chicago Press.

Toharia, J.J. 1975. "Judicial Independence in an Authoritarian Regime: The Case of Contemporary Spain." *Law and Society Review* 9:475-496.

———. 1987. "*!Pleitos tengas!*" *Introduction a la cultura legal espanola*. Madrid: Centro de Investigaciones Sociologicas.

Waltman, J. L. and Holland, K. M., eds. 1988. *The Political Role of Law Courts in Modern Democracies*. London, Macmillan.

Weiler, P. 1968. "Two Models of Judicial Decision-Making." *Canadian Bar Review*. 46:406-71.

Zannotti, F. 1981. *Le attività extragiudiziarie dei magistrati ordinari.*
Padua: Cedam.
———. 1989. *La magistratura, un gruppo di pressione istituzionale
L'autodeterminazione delle retribuzioni.* Padua: Cedam.

15.

Legal Politics Italian Style

MICHAEL MANDEL

The bitterly contested Canadian constitutional developments of the past decade point strongly to a theory of constitutional rights and constitutional courts that is the opposite of the one found in most textbooks on the subject. These generally celebrate the advent of judicial constitutionalism as the dawn of a new era of human rights and democracy after a long, dark night of oppressive government (for example, Cappelletti 1989). The Canadian experience, on the other hand, supports a theory of constitutional judicial review as politically conservative. But no theory is worth very much until "replicated" in other contexts. For reasons outlined below, Italy presents as good a proving ground as any. Furthermore, the Italian constitutional system is interesting enough in its own right to make study worthwhile; and posing the fundamental questions about judicial review arising from one's own national experience seems a good way of trying to grasp the nature of the Italian system.

THE CANADIAN EXAMPLE

It is easy for a Canadian of my generation to be cynical about constitutional rights and constitutional courts. In Canada the Charter of Rights was introduced to defeat a nationalist movement in the province of Quebec that had the popular support of the great mass of the working class, almost entirely French, in a province where the French constituted approximately 80 percent of the population. In an attempt to protect the unequal status quo of economic power represented by the province's wealthy English minority (a minority in Quebec, but the majority in Canada as a whole, not to mention North America), the federal government wrapped itself in the banner of individual rights and unilaterally changed the rules of confederation, limiting the power of the Quebec provincial government by imposing upon it the Charter of Rights and Freedoms, which applied only to government and restricted any interference with the status quo of market power. Using the Charter, federally appointed judges struck down legislation that, though seeking to break the economic stranglehold of English in Quebec, in fact scrupulously respected minority human rights. In other words, the Canadian federal government relied on a quintessentially deregulatory device to delegitimate popular public power and thus to give free reign to private economic power. Since the entrenchment of the Canadian Charter, its general deregulatory effect has also been felt in contexts far removed from the struggle between French and English, for example in labor relations and business regulation. Even in the realms of criminal procedure and women's rights, where socially weak groups seem to benefit, the benefits are not only precarious but are also of the deregulatory sort. Abortion has been removed from the Criminal Code, but access depends on class in those parts of the country where the anti-choice point of view is dominant. Powerful corporate criminals have had much more success with the Charter than the great mass of socially marginal criminals, whose record levels of incarceration seem merely to be legitimated by Charter activity.[1]

THE GENERAL IDEA

This unhappy experience with charters of rights led to a general hypothesis that sees judicial review under constitutional bills of rights as, contrary to appearances, an attempt to protect private social-economic power from the claims of democracy. Parliamentary sovereignty is the battle cry of the bourgeoisie so long as the suffrage is restricted to property owners. But property owners and constitutional theory both lose confidence in parliaments the moment they threaten property. Then it is the conceptual turn of "the tyranny of the majority" and the necessity of a bill of rights, which, in its classic form, applies only to government and thus protects private power. The idea is that the exceptionally wide suffrage and great inequality in 1780s America called forth judicial review, which spread to Europe in the twentieth century as a constitutional antidote to universal suffrage. A particularly complicated and tragic version of the same thing can be seen in Southern Africa right now. Charters of rights provide even more ideological reinforcement for private power than they do concrete reinforcement, by legitimating the status quo in the great mass of cases where laws are given the judicial stamp of approval, by delegitimizing democracy, by alienating people from politics, and by repeating that the solution to the lack of democracy in our representative institutions and in our everyday lives is to be found, not in more democracy but in less democracy, namely in an undemocratic check on representative institutions.

I prefer the term *legalization* of politics to *judicialization* of politics because I want to emphasize the partial, indeed mercenary, nature of the legal profession, as opposed to the myths of impartiality surrounding the judicial role. On the other hand, in Canada and elsewhere, constitutional politics have gone beyond both legal and judicial politics to a new form of legitimation with only a tenuous, formal relationship to the legal/judicial realm. Recently, in an attempt to legitimate a concrete deregulatory program, the Canadian federal government also proposed the "entrenchment" in the constitution of unenforceable statements of ideals and (idealized) characteristics of Canada. Not to be outdone, the New Democratic Party (NDP) government of Ontario, representing organized labor and most of the Left, proposed a "social charter," not to deregulate, but to protect public sector social programs. The Social Charter was not intended to be enforceable, and as such was greeted warmly by the political and business establishments. This posed a potential challenge to the thesis that constitutional politics are conservative, deregulatory politics. However, it seems to me more accurate to view this development as an attempt by the NDP to legitimate its own failure to provide any real concrete obstacles to the retreat of the public sector, indeed to legitimate the NDP government's own participation in the decline of public services and working-class living standards and its various contributions to the increasing sway of market power. Furthermore, when it entered the final constitutional deal reached by the premiers in August 1992, the Social Charter also helped to legitimate the government's concrete, enforceable business program. Of course, the whole scheme went up in smoke in a resounding defeat in the October

26 referendum, which just goes to show that you can only fool most of the people some of the time, but it does not, it seems to me, detract from the part the Social Charter played and was intended to play in the whole debate.

THE ITALIAN CASE

The original purpose of my investigation of legal politics was to determine the role that charters of rights play in the struggles between rich and poor, that is, in the socialist politics of capitalist societies, to determine whether legal politics are congenial, neutral, or inherently uncongenial to socialist politics. The North American experience pointed strongly to the inherently uncongenial conclusion, but it was always possible that things only appeared that way because of the notorious weakness of socialist politics in North America. The idea, then, was to test the thesis in Europe, where socialist politics are stronger. Italy was chosen both for its important similarities with and its important differences from the North American experience.

In the constitutional field, the similarities, and apparent support for the thesis, were very strong. As in Canada, judicial review under a constitutional bill of rights was unknown before the Second World War and was adopted while Italy operated under the strong economic and cultural influence of the U.S.[2] Furthermore, the relationship with universal suffrage was also very strong in Italy. At unification in 1861, only the richest 1.9% of Italians had the right to vote, and by 1909 this percentage had only reached 8.3%. Universal male suffrage with the "uninominal" system (the English riding system of "first-past-the-post," that still obtains in Canada) enlarged the suffrage to 23.2% in 1912 (Ghisalberti 1978, table II). In 1919, the suffrage went up to 27% but the key innovation was the introduction of proportional representation. As prophesied by Marx (1973, 56, 71, 127), granting such full suffrage to the working class (if only to the male element) led to a period of great instability, the *biennio rosso*, followed by the rise of Fascism and the destruction of parliamentary democracy.[3] With the defeat of Fascism in 1945 and the triumph of universal adult suffrage (male and female) and political liberties, we also find a new type of constitutional arrangement under which Parliament is fettered, for the first time, by a "rigid" constitution policed by a constitutional court acting under the authority of a Bill of Rights. In the words of the opponents of the Constitutional

Court in the Constituent Assembly (led by the Communists and Socialists, but with some conservative adherents to the old system included):

Nenni [Secretary of the Socialist Party]: You could say that the secret vice of this constitution is the same one to be found at every stage of our history, from the Risorgimento on: a lack of faith in the people . . . the necessity of putting as many obstacles as possible between the expression of the popular will and the execution of that will. . . (Constituent Assembly, March 10, 1947, 304-5)[4]

Togliatti [Secretary of the Communist Party]: Why have these norms been introduced? The honorable Nenni has given an answer that seems to me to be the right one. All of this is inspired by fear: the fear that tomorrow there might be a majority that is the free and direct expression of those working classes that want to remake profoundly the political, economic, and social structure of the country; and against this eventuality they want to have guarantees and to place impediments: from this we get the heaviness and slowness of the legislative procedure and all the rest; from this we get that bizarre creature the Constitutional Court. (Constituent Assembly, March 11, 1947, 330).

But it was the Christian Democrat Bertone who put the matter of the relationship of judicial review and universal suffrage in its clearest form: "Are we not, thoughtlessly, going to undermine the parliamentary sovereignty of this Parliament of the first Republic to represent the people?" (Constituent Assembly, November 28, 1947, 2606)

On the other hand, the differences from the Canadian situation were also very great. The fundamental one was the presence of a powerful Marxist Left, which, as I just noted, unlike the Canadian Social-Democratic Left, at first opposed judicial review as a potential fetter on fundamental change, and then, when forced to bow to the inevitable, played an important role in shaping both the Constitution and the court.

The Left's main impact on the Constitution itself was to ensure the presence of what are now called social rights. Unlike the American and Canadian constitutions, whose fundamental rights sections are brief and apply only to prevent government from interfering in the "private sphere" (that is, the sphere of private economic power), the Italian

Constitution is long and detailed; and, while not neglecting the traditional guarantees of private power, it also contains many limits on its exercise and even, in one clause, commits the government to its elimination, by an express obligation to end social inequality. These social rights are written in terms as obligatory as those that require the government to respect the traditional negative constitutional freedoms. Nor is the Constitution restricted in its terms to the public sphere. Here are a few examples:

> 3. All citizens have equal social dignity and are equal before the law, without distinction of sex, race, language, religion, political opinion, or personal or social condition.
>
> It is the duty of the Republic to remove those obstacles of an economic or social nature, that, limiting in fact the freedom and equality of citizens, impede the full development of the human person and the effective participation of all of the workers in the political, economic and social organization of the nation.
>
> 36. The worker has the right to a salary proportionate to the quantity and quality of his work and in every case sufficient to assure him and his family a free and dignified existence.
>
> 41. There is freedom of private economic initiative. It cannot be pursued in a manner contrary to social utility or in a way that causes harm to security, freedom and human dignity.
>
> The law shall determine the appropriate programs and controls so that public and private economic activity can be directed and coordinated for social ends.

The Left parties in the Constituent Assembly also left their imprint on the composition of the court. Unlike North American courts, appointed by the government of the day for life, Italian constitutional review was "democratized" by the creation of a special court with limited tenure (12 years in the original constitution, shortened in 1967 to nine years) and election procedures that ensured a close relationship to the political sphere (equal representation of three constituencies, the president, Parliament, and the magistracy), and that also ensured a measure of pluralism by providing that the Constitutional Court judges elected by Parliament were to be elected by an enhanced majority of 3/5 (Constitution, article 135; L.11, March 1953, n. 87), which in practice guaranteed a measure of representation on the court for the large Left-wing opposition.

The initial activity of the court, its initial mission, one might say, was also sensibly different from the North American experience. Instead of entering the fray against popular movements (for example, the U.S. Supreme Court against the debtors' movement of the 1780s, or the Canadian Supreme Court against the independence movement [Beard 1913; Galloway 1991; Mandel 1989]), its major activity was the dismantling of the Fascist legal order, not only left intact by the Christian Democratic governments of the early 1950s, but also vigorously used by them to repress workers' agitation.

The modern role of the court in everyday political life is also very different. In the first place, constitutional litigation in Italy has a very low political profile. The "test case" system does not exist, and rarely does constitutional litigation become the symbol of a political movement or cause. This may be due partly to the style of the court. The decisions are many and, by Anglo-Saxon standards, very short, consisting of only one (the majority) opinion. The judges generally have a low profile as judges, which is not to say that they are unknown or that the job lacks prestige. On the contrary, in the presidential elections of May 1992, which turned into a desperate attempt to find a depoliticized yet prestigious president, fully three of the serious candidates were currently or had recently been Constitutional Court judges: Giuliano Vassalli, Ettore Gallo, and Giovanni Conso. The major difference is that the job of Constitutional Court judge is, in effect, a part-time job. It is not the pinnacle of a legal career, but a stop—and not always the last one—in the course of what may be a very prominent career in public service. Vassalli was much better known (and distrusted) as the former Socialist minister of justice and a too loyal supporter of the controversial Socialist secretary Bettino Craxi than as a judge of the Constitutional Court. Conso went from president of the court to unsuccessful candidate for president of the republic to the sensitive post of minister of justice in the both the Amato and the Ciampi governments formed after the elections of 1992.

On the other hand, the Constitution is often invoked outside of the litigation context; for example, the pacifist Article 11 ("Italy repudiates war . . . as a means of resolving international controversies") became the symbol of opposition to the Gulf War of 1991, complete with pamphlets signed by long lists of jurists (Allegretti et al. 1991) and antiwar stickers reading "I, too, repudiate war," though nobody seems to have thought of going to court over it.

All considered, the Italian experience offered a challenge to the thesis that charters of rights tend to legalize and undermine democracy, in both its social-class and participatory senses. Here we had a constitution full of social rights that purported to limit private and not only public power, a court tied firmly to the political realm, and a functioning system of review that did not seem to replace or undermine traditional forms of politics.

Though much work remains to be done before firm conclusions can be drawn, results so far tend to confirm the theory of the "conservative constitution," that is to say that constitutional rights and the Constitutional Court seem to play basically the same antidemocratic role in Italy that they do in North America. Indeed, not only does the theory seem to be confirmed, but it actually seems to be strengthened and enriched. It is strengthened by the many political and institutional differences outlined above that logically could have, but actually did not, result in a different basic role for the court. It is enriched by the rather different ways in which the court is conservative in the Italian context. On the other hand, it must be added that the negativity of the court's role seems to have been attenuated somewhat (so far) by the peculiarities of both the constitutional and the political systems, which are products of the different historical context. This would mean that the social-political context, though not able completely to overcome the negative tendencies of the institution, can at least mitigate them.

These points can be illustrated by looking at some key areas of Constitutional Court activity: (1) the general conflict between the public and private spheres; (2) criminal procedure; and (3) the relationship between the Constitution and Italian political life.

The Private Sphere versus the Public Sphere: Deregulation and Social Rights

The Protection of Property

Despite the explicit social limitations on economic rights and property found in the various articles of the Constitution (for example in article 41, cited earlier, but also in articles 42-46), the Constitutional Court has been able to nullify a number of important regulatory initiatives. These include the clear cases of the radical agrarian laws of the 1950s, the urban planning laws of the 1960s and 1970, and the more arguable, but in my view equally conservative, contribution of the Constitutional Court to the television fiasco of the 1970s and 1980s.

Not long after the court was inaugurated it issued its sentence against the *imponibile di mano d'opera* (Sentence no. 78/ 1958). The *imponibile* (literally the "labor levy") was a job-creation policy instituted by the Federation of Italian Trade Unions in the desperate conditions of the rural south immediately after liberation by the Allied forces. It entailed "a contract which obliged landowners to employ a certain number of laborers in strict proportion to the size of their estates" (Ginsborg 1990, 61). The transformation of this policy into law in 1947 was one of the fruits of the immediate postwar Communist Party participation in the government when the Calabrian Communist Fausto Gullo was minister of agriculture. With the Communists safely in opposition, the court struck down the law as an interference with free enterprise. According to Ginsborg, the decision of the court was part of a general "worsening in the conditions of rural laborers" and "removed one of the most important props to rural employment. For example, in the winter of 1956-57 alone, the *imponibile* had ensured more than 186,000 laborers regularly paid work for more than two and a half months each." (Ginsborg 1990, 221). The decision moved Togliatti to claim vindication for his opposition to the court in the Constituent Assembly in a famous article in *Rinascita* in 1959 (Togliatti 1959).

In the 1960s and 1970s, the court struck down several planning laws meant to regulate development with an expansive reading of Article 42. These, too, were generally the fruits of the increasing strength of the Communist Party and the consequent increasing participation of the Left in the government, first the Socialists in the 1960s and then, for a brief period, the Communists in the late 1970s. While upholding the theoretical legitimacy of restrictions on property, the court decreed that not only full expropriations, the kind mentioned in Article 42, had to be compensated, but indeed so did all nontemporary legislative limits on development that reduced the market value of a given property holding. Furthermore, not only did there have to be compensation, but it had to be at full market value (Sentence no. 55/1968). Similar deregulatory decisions can be found in the 1970s and 1980s (Sentences no. 260/1976 and no. 5/1980).

Of course, the court has also upheld state regulation such as the nationalization of the energy industry in 1964 (Sentence no. 14/1964); but, to my knowledge, it has never *required* the government to nationalize anything to counterbalance the cases in which it has effectively prohibited expropriation. The closest it has come is in the series of cases on television, the recent aspects of which have been celebrated by the left-wing magistrates as a defense of the public sector against the current powerful pressures for privatization (Ippolito 1988, 647). I would argue that the court's overall contribution in this area ought really to be placed in the privatization category. It is worth some special attention.

Television

Virtually since the beginning of its existence, the court has been at the center of the struggle over television broadcasting rights. This is a well-traveled area and for reasons of space I cannot give it much attention here, but I would argue that it fits the thesis of the conservative constitution.

When the Christian Democrats were firmly in control of the machinery of state, the court not only upheld the government monopoly but celebrated it as being in the interests of democratic free expression. The court's argument was that television had an inherent tendency to monopoly, and that the best guarantor of broad access was a public as opposed to a private monopoly. "As opposed to any other monopolist, the State as monopolist finds itself institutionally in conditions of objectivity and impartiality more favorable to pursuing the overcoming of the difficulties posed by the natural limits of the medium for the realization of the constitutional precept aimed at assuring individuals the possibility of disseminating their opinion by any medium" (Sentence no. 59/1960). The court also exhorted the government to respect pluralism but did not in fact hold it to account for its manifest failure to do so.

However, in the 1970s, just as the Christian Democrats began to lose their grip on the state apparatus, the court allowed some crucial leakage in local broadcasting. In a bombshell decision of 1976, it struck down the government monopoly at the local level. Though the court exhorted the government "to establish . . . every other condition necessary to ensure that the exercise of the right . . . does not give rise to forms of concentration or situations of monopoly or oligopoly," Italian private television remained completely unregulated for more than a decade. This led to the growth of the empire that would come to dominate Italian media in general and television in particular: the Fininvest empire of Milan entrepreneur Silvio Berlusconi (known in Italy as sua emittenza—his transmittance to rhyme with sua eminenza—his eminence).[5] In 1985, with the Socialist Bettino Craxi as prime minister, a temporary law (L.10, February 4, 1985) was finally passed that was immediately dubbed the "Berlusconi Decree" because it legalized the Berlusconi empire exactly as it was.

In Sentence number 826/1988, a challenge to the Berlusconi law, the Constitutional Court once again made a strong statement in favor of the public monopoly in the absence of regulation of competition in the private sphere, but it did not declare the Berlusconi law unconstitutional for its lack of control on competition. Instead, it concentrated on the provisional nature of the law and provisionally upheld it in the expectation of a more complete regulation. This caused some discomfort among commentators (for example, Roppo 1990, 260) for its lack of appropriately constitutional detachment, but ultimately the law did come in 1991. Though it placed some new regulations on private television networks (for example, limits on advertising, and a requirement to broadcast news), its limits on media concentration were very mild, requiring only that Berlusconi sell one of his newspapers, but not preventing his selling it to his brother: "Altogether, Berlusconi was not seriously impacted, but was given the opportunity of extending the attractiveness of his three channels and operating in a more stable legal environment" (Noam 1992, 160).

To sum up, there has been a massive privatization, commercialization, and concentration of television and the court has played a major role in this development. The only thing that might possibly qualify this as an exception to the thesis that constitutional law is deregulatory would be the completely ineffective statements by the judges in favor of public television and against private monopoly. Though supporters of the court would argue that, in its reasoning at least, the court has stressed the value of democratically administered public broadcasting and the virtues, indeed the necessity, of regulation of the private sphere (Roppo 1990; Ippolito 1988, 603, 647), on closer examination, even the rhetoric of the court has supported the development of a mixed system. The court has never distinguished between a democratically run public sector and a private sector with a competition law; its jurisprudence has completely blurred the distinction as well as blithely underestimated the dominant influence the private has on the public.

The Social Rights in the Constitution

As noted earlier, the Italian Constitution differs from the U.S. and Canadian ones not only in placing express limits on the protection of property (limits that have nevertheless been unable to eliminate the deregulatory/privatizing tendency we have just seen exhibited), but also in "entrenching," to use a Canadian word, social rights that appear to impose a duty on the state to intervene in the private sphere and to mitigate, even eliminate, social inequality. Despite these important textual differences, the jurisprudence of the Italian Constitutional Court has been remarkably similar to that of its North American counterparts: it has declawed the social rights provisions by various interpretive techniques. Prominent among these has been their treatment as "programmatic" norms: that is, provisions that do not impose immediately enforceable legal obligations on the government, but rather nonenforceable goals, or at least indefinitely delayed-action entitlements, that the government is obliged (morally or politically or constitutionally—anything but legally) to seek to fulfill by its policies (see generally, Crisafulli and Paladin 1990, 29-35). The difference is not entirely unlike the Dworkinian distinction between principle and policy, except that in the Italian case it requires something more than the usual inventive jurisprudence in the face of vague constitutional provisions, namely a radical rewriting of a detailed text.

An important example is found in Article 4, according to a recent text "one of the most paradigmatic examples of a programmatic norm contained in the Italian Constitution" (Crisafulli and Paladin 1990, 34). It provides as follows: "The republic recognizes the right to work for all citizens and promotes the conditions that render this right effective. Every citizen has the duty to follow, according to his or her own possibilities and choice, an activity or a function that contributes to the material or spiritual progress of society."

Despite its wording, this provision has been repeatedly held not to provide an enforceable right to a job, even against the state, for anyone willing and able to work, much less the enforceable right to have the Constitutional Court supervise the economic policies of the government to see whether it is sincerely pursuing full-employment policies. The clause has not even been held to require job-security legislation. According to the court these questions are left to the legislator's discretion (for example, Sentences no. 45/1965 and no. 15/1983).

Much has been made of a recent tendency on the part of the court to interpret some social rights as not programmatic but immediately enforceable. The most famous example is the 1987 decision of the Constitutional Court on access to education by disabled persons. But there is nothing unfamiliar to North American constitutionalists in the substance of this decision; it merely held that a public sector good (access to education) had to be distributed without discrimination. Like its North American counterparts, the Italian Constitutional Court has, since the late 1960s, been quite activist in its defense of public-sector equality, despite an initial hostility (yet more evidence that it is never the constitutional provisions themselves, but rather the changing historical context that determines the outcome of a case). A well-known about-face involved the law of adultery; after upholding a criminal law that punished adultery on the part of women but not men in 1961 (Sentence no. 64/1961), in 1968 the court struck the law down, citing a "substantial change in the collective sentiment in recent years" (Sentences no. 126 and no. 127/1968). Not only did the court uphold Italy's first divorce law (Sentence no. 169/1971), but it actually led the way in abortion rights in 1975 by striking down the blanket prohibition in a law dating from the Fascist period (Sentence no. 127/1975), though the decision was obviously influenced by the well-known and much-discussed decision of the U.S. Supreme Court in *Roe v. Wade*, which would later have its Canadian counterpart in *Morgenthaler v. The Queen* (1988).[6] In the 1980s the court entered the realm of public-sector spending by establishing equality requirements for pension rights not only between men and women (Sentences no. 6 and no. 105/1980) but also between different categories of pensioners. A recent example is Sentence number 1/1991, in which the court ordered the government to make a pension increase more retroactive (applicable to those who had retired before a given cutoff date) than it had originally planned. Sentences requiring extra public expenditure by the government are not unknown in Canada either. An instructive example is *Silano v. B.C.* (1987),[7] where a provincial government was held to have unconstitutionally discriminated on the basis of age in welfare payments. The government responded by reducing payments for the privileged recipients so that its total expenditures remained the same (Mandel 1989, 266). Similarly, the president of the Italian Constitutional Court recently responded to criticism by saying that nothing in the court's judgments require more spending, only *equal* spending (Saja 1990). The government of Italy has since undertaken a massive cut in pension spending, and no amount of constitutional equalizing will be able to disguise the fact that there will be less for everyone.

Application of the Constitution to the "Private" Sphere

Besides imposing what appear to be express obligations on the government, the Italian constitution differs from the Canadian one in applying to both nongovernmental and governmental behavior, the so-called private sphere as well as the public. In Canada, the constitution applies only to government (section 32) and the Supreme Court has read this very restrictively as excluding the common-law as made by judges. Many of the building blocks of private power, such as contract law, are thus beyond the scope of the Canadian Charter. Practically speaking, this means that the Charter can operate only to limit government and does nothing about private power. In Italy, not only does the constitution have no such limited application, but in this case it has not been interpreted that way. Nor is there any such obvious line of demarcation, such as between common-law and statute law: all of the law is contained in statutory codes. Interestingly enough, this has not resulted in radicality of decision making, but merely different strategies on the part of the court to uphold the status quo. While accepting jurisdiction over private disputes, the court has read into the provisions the conventional wisdom of bourgeois economics. While a Canadian court might say that questions of inequality in contract law were common-law questions beyond its jurisdiction, Italian courts readily accept jurisdiction, but deny that legal "freedom of contract" operates to "perpetuate situations of economic privilege and predominance" (Sentence no. 256/1974).

An even more striking application of the Constitution to the private sphere, and one with unmistakable class implications, is found in Article 36, which, it will be recalled, provides: "The worker has the right to a salary proportionate to the quantity and quality of his work and in every case sufficient to assure him and his family a free and dignified existence."

Retained by the left-wing magistrates association as having extremely radical implications (Ippolito 1988, 637), this clause is astonishing to North Americans because it is clearly an invitation to the judiciary to reopen wage contracts and reexamine them for their fairness. On the other hand, one is inevitably reminded of Marx's Critique of the Gotha Program in which he ridiculed a weak German Workers Party demand for the "fair distribution of the proceeds of labor":   "Do not the bourgeois assert that the present-day distribution is 'fair'? And is it not, in fact, the only 'fair' distribution on the basis of the present-day mode of production? Are economic relations regulated by legal conceptions or do not, on the contrary, legal relations arise from economic ones? (Marx 1977, 566).

And indeed, this is how the Constitutional Court, even while holding it applicable to private wage relations, has read the provision: as a guarantee of fair wages only in the capitalist sense of the going market rate and not in the remotest socialist sense (to each according to their work or contribution).

A clear example of this capitalist reading of the Constitution is in the decision on wage indexing in collective agreements (Sentence no. 34/1985).   The unions claimed that an antiinflation law that altered cost-of-living arrangements in collective agreements was an infringement of Articles 36 and 3.   As far as Article 36 was concerned, the court merely repeated the governmental justifications of the law: that antiinflation measures, even though they cut wages, had a long-run effect of protecting them by maintaining their purchasing power, as well as by favoring economic recovery.

But the more radical challenge was on the basis of Article 3 of the Constitution.   The unions complained not only that the program was unequal in its treatment of different levels of salary earners, but that it was discriminatory in a class sense by only applying to wage earners ("by the imposition of a sacrifice only on wage earners and not on the self-employed or the beneficiaries of income from capital"). The court here employed a two-pronged argument: first the somewhat paternalistic idea, a version of the Article 36 argument, that the law could also be understood as being in the workers' interests (even though the unions before the court were apparently unable to see this) because inflation was everybody's concern.   More fundamentally, the court argued that interclass comparisons were inapt for constitutional purposes, applying a kind of presumption that class struggles are political, and not constitutional:

> Nor is it of use to compare—for the purposes of the present judgment—the condition of wage-earners with those receiving other income. Such comparisons lend themselves to being made and discussed on the political level (and have already formed, in this sense, the material of vivid polemics), but are not enough to determine the constitutional illegitimacy of the impugned law for violation of the principle of equality. From the point of view of the containment of inflation, the mechanisms of indexing of the "sliding scale" type cause particular difficulties, which are not homogeneous in respect of those concerning categories for which the same mechanisms do not operate. If anything, the proper comparison would be with the system of controlled rent increase . . . ; but it is no accident that this mechanism was also blocked for the past year. (Sentence no. 34/1985)

The implication is clear, then, that interclass politics are intrinsically nonconstitutional; or better, that, notwithstanding the words of the Constitution, they cannot be read so as to challenge the basic assumptions of capitalist social and economic relations.

To sum up, the Constitutional Court, while displaying many of the privatizing tendencies found in North American constitutionalism, has adopted a variety of strategies to ensure that the potentially radical elements of the Italian Constitution, those that differentiate it from North American ones, have not challenged the social and class power inequalities characteristic of advanced capitalism.

Criminal Procedure

In Canada, defenders of the egalitarian nature of the Charter usually cite as their main example the realm of criminal procedure. They point out that the criminal accused who benefit from Charter guarantees are generally those with the least social power, the poorest classes and ethnic groups. It's true that the criminal accused generally represent the most marginalized social classes by many indicators. What is not clear is that they benefit from Charter guarantees. I argue that constitutionalized criminal procedure provides few obstacles to the prosecution of street crime. Indeed, the era of the Charter has been the most repressive in Canada's history, in terms of the per capita use of imprisonment and other criminal sanctions. This may be mere coincidence, because of the delay in constitutionalization that took place in the United States in the 1960s during a period of lightening repression, but the general formula of judicial review was certainly no obstacle to the massive increases that followed. It is also no secret that the United States, where constitutionalized criminal procedure was invented, has the highest prison population in the Western world as well as an increasingly frequently exercised death penalty unknown in Italy since the fall of Fascism and, before Fascism, since unification. I argue that the role of a high level of procedural due process in such a context is to legitimate high levels of repression. Furthermore, I argue that constitutionalized criminal procedure is much more advantageous to powerful corporate criminals and contributes to the class bias in the criminal justice system.

In Italy, too, criminal procedure makes up a large part of the constitutional repertoire. In the 1960s the Constitutional Court, with very little constitutional text to go on, but under the weighty influence of the Warren Court developments, not to mention the very popular American television show "Perry Mason," started to issue judgments that contributed to the transformation of the Italian system from what has been described as a mixed system, into a more accusatory one. By the mid-1970s these judgments had rendered the system very difficult to operate and had necessitated fundamental reforms (Neppi Modona and Violante 1978, 333).

The tortuous reform process took until 1989 when a new Code went into force that not only changed the system into a basically accusatory one, where "instruction" was abolished and the trial became the center of the proof process, but also went far beyond North American models in protecting the rights of the accused, for instance in the almost complete inadmissibility of prior statements by the accused. This was added to some already guarantistic features of the inquisitorial system, such as the automatic right to two full appeals and the extraordinary independence of the prosecutors from the government. But it is clear that the idea of protecting the rights of the accused was seen mainly as a means to the end of an efficient process capable of more rapidly and legitimately processing a growing number of charges, even if the efficiency had to do partly with protecting the process from constant constitutional challenge. Even those supporters of the Code who stressed the requirements of the Constitution (Andò 1990, 3) or the more symbolic side of instituting "a superior juridical culture" (Jacobelli 1990, vii) and "a political choice to guarantee the fundamental values on which rest the order of a modern society" (Andò 1990, 4) also stressed the importance of efficiency,"that justice be more rapid" (Jacobelli 1990, vii), and the reduction of the number of trials, through such devices as plea bargaining (Andò 1990, 9), "facilitated" by a mechanism well known to North Americans, a discount of one-third off the prescribed punishment (article 442.2 of the Nuovo Codice di Procedura Penale; Scisciot 1990). The connection between accusatory procedure and efficient procedure has been made by Stefano Rodotà, who importantly modifies Churchill's dictum to read, "the criminal trial *and its efficiency* are sure indications of a nation's level of civilization" (Rodotà 1990, 138, emphasis added), and by the Calabrian prosecutor Antonio Scopelliti who, shortly before his assassination by the Mafia, defined the hopes for the new Code as "finally a transparent procedure that is more respectful of the rights of the honest and, above all, a procedure more modern and more rapid" (Scopelliti 1990, 147).

What this means is that the new procedure was expected to cater to and to be accompanied by a rising level of prosecution, very similar to that witnessed in Canada and the United States. The new procedure was supposed to make this technically possible and at the same time to legitimate it as modern and civilized in its respect of the rights of the accused.

Levels of repression in Italy do not show the same pattern as they do in North America. They exhibited a descending pattern from the end of the Second World War to a historic year-end low in 1970 of about 35 prisoners per 100,000 population (the comparable Canadian figure was about 90 [Mandel 1991]). Clearly, the early initiatives of the Constitutional Court took place in the context of very low levels of repression; but the next two decades saw a rising trend in prison populations, which in 1984 brought levels to heights they had not seen since the early 1950s (about 70 per 100,000). There was a falling off in the late 1980s (42 per 100,000 in 1990), but this can be attributed to the New Code itself which, according to some observers, virtually paralyzed criminal justice because the necessary resources were not available. These were more or less rapidly obtained and the result in 1991 was the largest increase in prison population in postwar history—more than one-third in one year. The figures for the first six months of 1992 showed a rise of 28.4% to a count of 45,577 prisoners on June 30 (*Il Manifesto* November 4, 1992, 10), a rate of 78 per 100,000 population, the highest since 1952, suggesting a return to the "hard years" of the early 1950s.

It is clear that the period of the great reform of the criminal procedure has coincided, as in Canada, with rising prison populations and may have paved the way for record highs. This is the reality that will be made possible by the new Code's efficiency and legitimated by its modernity.

As in Canada, there is also the sense that the due process elements of procedure are of greater advantage to powerful criminals, such as the Mafia and the powerful objects of the recent investigation into the massive system of political and business corruption (the so-called tangenti scandal). Unfortunately, I do not have the space to explore this complicated issue here. Suffice it to say that the constitutional rights of the criminal accused have become a central element in the debate over crimes of power, and the Constitutional Court is right in the thick of it. In one interesting twist, the Constitutional Court struck down a provision of the new Code that actually appeared to *favor* the accused, obliquely referring to the importance of decreasing obstacles to the fight against organized crime (Sentence no. 255/1992). The court's sudden about-face cannot be separated from the national revulsion at recent Mafia killings and what appears to have been a breakdown in the hitherto solid relationship between the ruling elites and organized crime. If anything, it shows the flexibility of a system based on constitutional procedural rights rather than on codified rights: the moment they become bothersome, constitutional rights can be reversed. It is not the rights but their constitutional nature that renders them mere legitimation.

ROLE OF THE CONSTITUTION IN POLITICAL LIFE

As I mentioned earlier, one cannot fail to notice the lower political profile of the Constitutional Court in Italy compared to North American courts. This may be due to the high degree of political participation of the Italians and the method of nomination of court members with a consequent strong party identification, both of which prevent the court from replacing political debate with the supposedly depoliticized abstract debates of North American courts. This lower profile is also reflected in the form of judgment mentioned earlier. The court is important; it is just that it is not *as* important and its role is more material than ideological.

One of the court's material roles is to set limits on the referendum power. In Italy, there is a right to referendum in the Constitution on the demand of 500,000 citizens (Article 75), but it took almost a quarter of a century to activate that right. In the law on referendum, the Constitutional Court is given a veto power, which it has interpreted broadly and paternalistically to include not only the natural constitutional questions (for example, whether the referendum would result in an unconstitutional law) but also questions of coherence and clarity. The court has also added the requirement of pure negativity, disallowing referendums that propose "a new discipline" as opposed to merely repealing a part of an old law (for example, Sentence no. 47/1991). The jurisprudence developed by the court gives it complete control over what questions will be asked, and many proposals with the required number of signatures do not get to the electorate.

It is also possible to argue that the court's positive reforming role, visible especially in the early years, when it dismantled much of the old Fascist apparatus, but also in its (as we have seen, limited) equality decisions of the 1970s and 1980s, may have contributed to one of the most enduring negative features of Italian politics, namely its lack of "alternation" between political parties. Despite the many crises, Italy has had basically one government since 1946: a Christian Democrat-dominated coalition, which effectively excluded the country's second largest and main opposition party, the Communists, from ever forming a government. The court has often been congratulated for delivering the modest necessary reforms that this government, with its fragile coalitions and heavy conservative support, could not manage. But it is probable that the court's delivery of these reforms contributed to the stagnation in Parliament, because it made it unnecessary to vote Communist in order to get change. This hypothesis requires a lot more research, but it is consistent with the use frequently made by Canadian governments of Charter litigation to avoid responsibility for controversial political policies.

It should be pointed out, though, that though the *court's* ideological role is much reduced, the Constitution itself, apart from litigation, is enormously important in political debate. This has a lot to do with the relatively radical constitutional language the Left was able to get into the constitutional text at the Constituent Assembly. This phenomenon is worth pausing over because it has become so much a part of modern politics outside of Italy, with social charters figuring prominently in political debates from Canada to Europe to South Africa.

As I pointed out earlier, though the court has interpreted them as "programmatic" or otherwise nonbinding, provisions such as the social rights and antiwar Articles in the Constitution are frequently invoked in Italian political life as part of left-wing discourse. The question of the role of nonbinding, nontraditional constitutional rights was actually raised in the Constituent Assembly in 1946 in terms of great value to today's debates. There was substantial resistance to their introduction, only the Communist Party wholeheartedly supporting them. But in order to get them passed, the Communists had to concede that they would be treated differently from other rights. It was Togliatti himself who used the word "programmatic" to characterize these new constitutional rights, thus legitimating in advance the court's subsequent differential treatment of them. In arguing that, despite their judicially unenforceable character, they should still be included in Articles of the Constitution as opposed to the Preamble, Togliatti outlined a constitutional strategy repeated frequently today all over the world:

> The Constitution . . . if it sanctions only that which exists today in Italy, would not correspond to what the majority of the people want from the Constitution. Our Constitution must say something more, must have a programmatic character, at least in some of its parts, and particularly in those parts in which is affirmed the necessity of giving a new content to the rights of the citizens, as has been said, a social content, with the affirmation of the right to work, of the right to rest, etc., with the affirmation of guarantees of these rights. The Soviet Constitution, after having affirmed a right, can then, in the same paragraph, fix a complex of real conditions that permit its realization, because these conditions in fact exist. In Italy, these factual conditions have to be created. . . The right to work will be guaranteed only when one has an economic organization of the Nation different from the existing one, in which those capable of working would have the possibility of joining the labor force.
>
> If this new content is relegated to the Preamble, we will be making affirmations that can be the grandest and most generous, but everyone will understand that this is something that was done

to give a part of public opinion a satisfaction of form, and in substance to wash hands of it. These affirmations become instead something constitutionally and therefore juridically important when they are placed in determinate Articles, even if these Articles can have a form that does not correspond to the old articles of the Civil Code or of a preceding constitutional law. Therefore, . . . the social rights must be affirmed in concrete Articles in the Constitution, which will have a normative character, but at the same time a programmatic character, as a beginning, as a commitment, as an orientation to the creation of a new social order and therefore a new legality. . . . The legislator will have a directive that will inform the entire legislative activity. The Constitution will be something new when the social rights are affirmed in specific articles, with an obligatory formula, and not only declarations of principle that do not minimally commit the future legislator. (Constituent Assembly, October 25, 1946, 47-48)

As we have seen, the social rights went into the Constitution on equivalent textual footing with the more familiar constitutional rights against the state, but that did not prevent the court from reading them differently on the basis of the assumptions in Togliatti's address. We could take this all at face value and say that the Communist Party's initiative and its acceptance by the other parties in the Constituent Assembly were legitimate attempts to advance social rights that were defeated by subsequent historical events, or we could take the contemporary view of the leading constitutionalist, Piero Calamandrei. He opposed the inclusion of social rights in the Constitution as an exercise in dishonesty by both the Left and the Right in terms that resonate strongly today when social-democratic governments like Ontario's seem to be trying to legitimate their failure to do anything concrete for their supporters by advocating unenforceable social charters:

While at one time, it had been maintained that the Constituent Assembly, before dissolving, should deliberate, together with the Constitution, some fundamental reforms of a social character that would mark the beginning of a real transformation of the current economic system and of a radical renewal of the directing class (that renewal which, especially in Northern Italy, was, at a certain period, a founding principle in the revolutionary work of the

Committees of National Liberation), in reality not only did the Constituent Assembly not have time to examine such reforms, but it did not even think of introducing any new mechanisms into the constitutional structure through which the exigencies of social renewal could find a direct outlet, nor did it translate into juridical institutions having any practical value the vague affirmations of principle with which in numerous dispositions were promised the redemption and the preeminence of the working classes. In reality, however much Article 1 affirms that "Italy is a democratic republic founded on labor," the idle in this republic have the same rights as all of the other citizens who work: and what is more they have the right, remaining in idleness, to take advantage of their riches. . . .
In the impossibility of immediately actuating the social reforms dreamed of by some progressive parties of the Constituent Assembly, they contented themselves with inserting in the Constitution at least the preannouncement, holding that tomorrow the political struggle to transform into law these reforms already preannounced will be easier when one can find a foothold in some constitutional provision, which will function thus, even if inefficient in the purely juridical camp, as an argument of propulsion and political propaganda; nor did the conservative parties refuse to play this game: in order to avoid making these social reforms in the heat of the revolutionary spirits (more feared than existing) of the Constituent Assembly, they let pass in the formulas of the Constitution large promises of social renewal, on the understanding that these would be actuated only in the future. Thus to compensate the forces of the Left for the missed revolution, the forces of the Right did not oppose the gathering up in the constitution of a *promised* revolution. Only the future will be able to tell which of the two parties in this skirmish had clearer foresight: those who considered certain dispositions of the Constitution as a launching platform to achieve in concrete the social reforms vaguely promised, or those who were not alarmed by the promises of social renewal registered in the generic formulas of the Constitution, well knowing that, once the moment of crisis had passed, the reforming impulses would lose their urgency, and, once they had ceased to boil, could remain in waiting for another century.   (Calamandrei 1950, 461-462, emphasis in original)

NOTES

The author wishes to thank the European University Institute for its generous support of his research through the provision of a Jean Monnet Fellowship in 1990-1991, as well as the following colleagues, who have provided invaluable assistance in his attempt to understand the Italian constitutional system: Professors Carlo Amirante, Brian Bercusson, Antonio Cassese, Sabino Cassese, Enzo Cheli, Giuseppe Di Federico, Luis Marìa Diéz-Picazo, Carlo Guarnieri, Guido Neppi Modona, Sergio Ortino, Massimo Pavarini, Alessandro Pizzorusso, Ugo Rescigno, Roberto Toniatti, Luciano Vandelli, Sara Volterra, and Gustavo Zagrebelsky.

1. The full story of Canada's Charter can be found in many sources, including Mandel (1989).

2. In Canada, the movement for a Bill of Rights was basically a postwar development when American influence was at its strongest. Even though the Charter of Rights was not adopted until 1982, there was wide acceptance of the concept by 1950. The delay was due to the issue of Quebec-Canada relations, which were determinative of the timing and of the details of the Charter, but not of the fundamental idea.

3. For which much responsibility must be placed in the hands of the national and international property-owning classes (Procacci 1968; Harper 1986; Corner 1990; Woolf 1981; Schmitz 1988).

4. This and all other translations in the text are my own.

5. Berlusconi has many other financial interests besides the Italian media: advertising, finance, film, soccer, computer software, department stores, theaters, transportation, 25% of the television channel La Cinq in France, and 20% of the German channel Tele-5 (Noam, 1992: 155-56).

6. The full citation is *Morgenthaler, Smoling, and Scott v. The Queen.* 37 C.C.C. [3d] 449 [Supreme Court of Canada] 1988.

7. *Silano v. B. C. (Govt.)* 5 W.W.R. 739 [Supreme Court of British Columbia] 1987.

REFERENCES

All references to sentences of the Constitutional Court are to the series *Giurisprudenza Costituzionale*, unless otherwise indicated.

Allegretti, Umberto, et al. 1991. "L'Italia ripudia La Guerra. ONU, costituzione, obiezione: Documenti su un conflitto fuorilegge." *Avvenimenti*, March 6, 1991.

Andò, Salvo. 1990. "Non si torna indietro." In *Processo al nuovo processo*, ed. Jader Jacobelli. Bari: Laterza.

Beard, Charles A. 1935. *An Economic Interpretation of the Constitution of the United States*. 1913. Reprint, New York: Macmillan.

Calamandrei, Piero. 1966. "Cenni introduttivi sulla costituente e sui suoi lavori." In *Piero Calamandrei, Scritti e discorsi politici*, Vol. 2, ed. Norberto Bobbio. 1950. Reprint, Firerize: La Nuova Italia.

Cappelletti, Mauro. 1989. *The Judicial Process in Comparative Perspective*. ed. Paul J. Kollmer and Joanne M. Olson, eds., Oxford: Clarendon Press.

Corner, Paul. 1990. "Italy." In *The Working Class and Politics in Europe and America, 1929-1945*, ed. Stephen Salter and John Stevenson. London: Longman.

Crisafulli, Vezio, and Livio Paladin. 1990. *Commentario breve alla Costituzione*. Padua: CEDAM.

Galloway, Russell W. 1991. *Justice for All? The Rich and Poor in Supreme Court History 1790-1990*. Durham, N.C.: Carolina Academic Press.

Ghisalberti, Carlo. 1978. *Storia costituzionale d'Italia 1848-1948*. Rome: Laterza.

Ginsborg, Paul. 1990. *A History of Contemporary Italy: Society and Politics 1943-1988*. London: Penguin.

Harper, John Lamberton. 1986. *America and the Reconstruction of Italy, 1945-1948*. New York: Cambridge University Press.

Ippolito, Franco. 1988. "Un Magistrato per i cittadini (giurisdizione e valori costituzionale)." *Questione giustizia* 7:603.

Jacobelli, Jader. 1990. Introduction to *Processo al nuovo processo*, ed. Jader Jacobelli. Bari: Laterza.

Mandel, Michael. 1991. "The Great Repression: Criminal Punishment in the Nineteen-Eighties." In *Criminal Justice: Sentencing Issues and Reform*, ed. Les Samuelson and Bernard Schissel. Toronto: Garamond.

———. 1989. *The Charter of Rights and the Legalization of Politics in Canada*. Toronto: Thompson Educational Publishers.

Marx, Karl. 1977. "Critique of the Gotha Program." In *Karl Marx: Selected Writings*, ed. by David McClellan. New York: Oxford University Press.

———. 1973. "The Class Struggles in France: 1848 to 1850." In *Marx: Surveys from Exile*. Harmondsworth: Penguin.

Neppi Modona, Guido, and Luciano Violante. 1978. *Poteri dello stato e sistema penale*. Editrice Tirrenia Stampatori.

Noam, E. 1992. *Television in Europe*. New York: Oxford University Press.

Procacci, Giuliano. 1968. *Storia degli italiani*. Bari: Laterza.

Rodotà, Stefano. 1990. "I giudici alla prova." In *Processo al nuovo processo*, ed. Jader Jacobelli. Bari: Laterza.

Roppo, Enzo. 1990. "La politica surrogate: quindici anni di giurisprudenza televisiva della Corte Costituzionale." *Democrazia e diritto* 30:253.

Saja, Francesco. 1990. "La giustizia costituzionale nel 1989." *Giurisprudenza costituzionale*. Part 2, 564.

Schmitz, David F. 1988. *The United States and Fascist Italy, 1922-1940*. Chapel Hill, N.C.: University of North Carolina Press.

Scisciot, Francesco. 1990. "Il rodaggio di una riforma." In *Processo al nuevo Processo*, ed. Jader Jacobelli. Bari: Laterza.

Scopelliti, Antonio. 1990. "Le urgerize della giustizia." In *Processo al nuevo Processo*, ed. Jader Jacobelli. Bari: Laterza.

Togliatti, Palmiro. 1959. "La Corte contro l'imponibile." *Rinascita* 1:4.

Woolf, Stuart J. 1981. "Italy." In *Fascism in Europe*, ed. Stuart J. Woolf. London: Methuen.

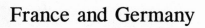

France and Germany

16.

France

JACQUELINE LUCIENNE LAFON

The judicialization of politics in France is a topic that has aroused important controversies. To comprehend the ins and outs of the matter, it is necessary to look back at the principles emerging from the Revolution of 1789 and the institutions established during the Consulat and the First Empire.

In 1789, a majority of deputies in the Constituante, the first national assembly, intended to reject all that had characterized the Ancien Régime. The confusion of powers was one of the main objects of criticism. The king held in his hands what would be considered today the legislative, executive and judicial powers. He could delegate these powers to officers. In such a system, the courts of justice—particularly the upper courts (*parlements*)—assumed judicial functions and when necessary established rules in the form of statutory decisions (*arrêts de règlement*), thus creating law.

During the last years of the Ancien Régime, philosophers and jurists criticized this system and feared the overwhelming power of the judges in *parlements*. Among the opponents was Montesquieu, who developed the theory of the separation of powers (see Pigacé-Mudry 1992).

The principle of separation of powers was affirmed in the Declaration of Rights of Man and Citizen of 1789, and the decree of August 16-24, 1790, forbade the *arrêts de règlements*. This second text was aimed very precisely at the limitation of the judicial power: the judge's sole function was to apply the law, even if he thought it was unconstitutional. He was not to criticize the law, he was not to interpret it. Should he consider it not precise enough, he had to refer it to the legislative power, that is, the national assembly, by means of the legislative reference instituted in the decree. Hence, the judge was not to create law.

Napoleon Bonaparte's restructuring of France during the First Empire made three changes in the field of law that are relevant to our subject. First, Napoleon ordered great initial codifications of French private law: the *Code civil* (1804), the *Code de commerce* (1807), the *Code de procédure civile* (1807), the *Code d'instruction criminelle* (1809), the *Code pénal* (1810). Second, he established the two jurisdictional hierarchies that are still a part of the French system, the "regular" or civil jurisdiction to judge all cases involving nongovernmental legal citizens and the administrative jurisdictions to decide disputes between citizens and the administrative authorities of the state. Third, Napoleon maintained the principle of the separation of powers, even though he neglected it in practice on occasion.

In this setting, in no way favorable to judges inclined to develop rules, a French jurisprudence creative of law appeared as soon as the early nineteenth century and has flourished throughout the years. This phenomenon aroused critics. According to the classical theory, a distinction should be made between political and nonpolitical organisms. Political organisms exercised creative and regulating functions, whereas nonpolitical organisms stood in a subordinate position and applied rules affirmed by the political organisms. In this analysis, judges did not constitute a third power in the state, an organism regulating society. They could not create law and had only a jurisdictional function.[1]

Many arguments in opposition to judicial lawmaking were developed. If judges created law, what became of the separation of powers? Wasn't there a risk of undergoing the imperialism or the government of judges? If the principle of judge-made law were admitted, different initiatives could rise from one or another jurisdiction, requiring an effort to harmonize them. The rules deriving from a judgment would be retroactive if reversed, and retroactivity was contrary to French principles. Furthermore, such rules were not necessarily stable: the courts could change their position and initiate a sudden change in jurisprudence. Would the rule always be easy to comprehend? Wouldn't nonspecialists find it difficult to be informed on this part of the law? There was one more major critique: judges only created law only when a case came up. Thus their role as a source of law depended entirely on chance!

Given these criticisms, could it be reasonable to stand for judge-made law?   From a practical point of view, there is one major advantage: suppleness and adaptability in the law, because the rule is initiated by everyday facts or is modified according to the evolution of society, to which the judge must be attentive.   From a legal point of view, there is also one determinative argument: judge-made law avoids the miscarriage of justice (*déni de justice*) that can occur when a judge refuses to act because of the vagueness of the law.[2]   Over the years, the arguments in favor of judge-made law finally outweighed the others.

Of course judge-made law is delicate to handle: it involves a continual compromise between the consciousness of the necessity of change and the preoccupation with maintaining a relative stability—a stability to which litigators are entitled lest, they feel insecure.

This equilibrium is a constant preoccupation of all judges.   Indeed, today a jurisprudence creative of law exists in the different branches of French law.   But it will be instructive to focus on the two main law-creating jurisprudences, the civil jurisprudence and the administrative jurisprudence.   The civil and administrative jurisprudences developed from sharply contrasting bases.   The civil jurisprudence was elaborated on the basis of the *Code civil* of 1804; it was developed as an addition to written law.   The administrative jurisprudence developed ex nihilo because there was no administrative codification, no written law.

A JURISPRUDENCE CREATIVE OF LAW IN ADDITION TO WRITTEN LAW: THE CIVIL JURISPRUDENCE

Since civil jurisprudence is rooted in legislation, it would seem that when a judge has to solve a case, all he has to do is to apply the law.   But this may be easier said than accomplished.   The judge may be obliged to interpret the text.   His duty may even lead him to assume a creative function.   The authors of the civil code knew it was impossible to anticipate every circumstance and formulate a corresponding rule to handle it.[3]   Therefore, they decided to give the judge a general framework, the main principles of which would serve as reference points and enable him to solve the case.   In a way, they had anticipated the judge's creativeness.

Judge-Made Civil Law: The Technical Approach

There are certain reasons, methods and conditions that explain why civil judges create law. First, the terms of the law are not always precise enough. When a judge has to apply such a text, he must explicate it. For example, article 1382 of the *Code civil* proclaims that one is responsible for the damage he that is his fault, but it does not define the notion of fault. As a result, judges had to take the initiative of determining, in each case, whether there was a fault. In doing so over and over again, they have specified the notion of fault.

At other times, judges consider the text they have to apply to be incomplete or out of date. Sometimes the legislature has difficulty in keeping up with actuality, especially in private law. Then the path seems open to judges. They use the pretext of clarifying a meaning to serve their cause and work out a rule. Thus article 1384, section 1 of the *Code civil* was "interpreted" to facilitate the recognition of responsibility when damages were caused by inanimate things.

On rare occasions, there may be no text to govern a decision. Then the judges have to innovate: they elaborate a "praetorian" jurisprudence.

These explanations are closely linked to the methods used by judges to develop their decisions. Most of the time, judges work on the basis of legislative texts. When a law is not clear, they are induced to intervene. Their search for a better regulation proceeds by methods that appear to be almost automatic reflexes. Nevertheless, it is possible to determine these methods. Judges do their best to apprehend the contents of the law. If the text is particularly obscure, they refer to the draft and preliminary papers to try to discover the intent of the legislature. These working papers do not bind the judge. In either case, judges always base their decisions on the law when they settle a case.

It can happen that the law is silent on a point. Judges then refer to general principles affirmed throughout the years, principles that are founded on the notion of equity. This last method is dangerous, because it could be an invitation to decide merely according to equity, which has not been accepted in the French legal system since the Revolution. Under such circumstances, the judge must find the means to apply the rule without standing against equity, that is, to harmonize the two.

Even if a judge follows these methods, he does not necessarily create law. Certain other conditions must first be fulfilled. When a judge thinks that the case submitted to him requires an "interpretation," he analyzes the facts, follows one or another method previously discussed, and tries to find a solution considering the legal, economic, and social context of the moment.

But judges are only the initiators of the rule. The higher the level of their court, the greater the chances that they will see the rule accepted. Of course the *Cour de cassation* has great authority, but even its rules are not accepted ipso facto. A legal solution reached by a court of appeal or by the *Cour de cassation* becomes a jurisprudential rule only after it is accepted by the other jurisdictions and repeated.

Finally, a judge-made rule is affirmed by the mechanism of appeal and *cassation*. Indeed, a lower-level court is attentive to the position of the court of appeal in similar cases previously judged. If it did not follow the solution adopted by the court of appeal, no doubt the litigant's lawyer would entice him to appeal, and there he would obtain satisfaction. Similarly, on an upper level, a court of appeal is attentive to the decisions of the *Cour de cassation* for identical reasons. Of course a court can take the risk of not respecting a precedent if it seems ill adapted to the present case and if the court wants to initiate a change in the applicable law. While such happenings are not frequent, under such conditions the precedent can acquire considerable authority if confirmed on appeal.

In France, such a rule is applied all over the country. This uniformity is possible because of the control exercised by the *Cour de cassation* on the decisions of the courts of appeal. When the different sections of the *Cour de cassation* pronounce what appear to be contradictory principles, the first president of this supreme court can convoke a "plenary civil assembly to resolve such an issue.

Today, the technique by which judge-made rules are created is accepted. The debate on the appropriateness of judicial decisions as a source of law belongs to the past.

Judge-Made Civil Law: Content

Civil jurisprudence is relatively abundant, although not by comparison with administrative jurisprudence. Every now and then, the legislature finds inspiration in a judge-made rule and sanctions it into law. But the amount of uncodified civil jurisprudence remains considerable. Judges are supposed to know it, but it is not easy to become informed because of the restricted scope of the collections of civil-law decisions. Research is time-consuming and is not always fruitful, particularly research on the decisions of the lower jurisdictions. Nevertheless, a brief survey of several areas of civil jurisprudence may give a useful idea of its nature and scope.

The domain covered by creative civil jurisprudence is vast and merits a rapid description before examining the creation of two specific types of jurisprudential rules. Family law is a domain of constant preoccupation. In this area, courts have provided a right to claim an allowance for necessities to an unacknowledged illegitimate child and to a child of an adulterous or incestuous union in which paternity has not been established. In the antenuptial settlement rules, judges have managed to protect the property in the wife's dowry.

The law of contracts has benefitted greatly from creative civil jurisprudence. Limitations on the liberty of contracting have been established. Article 1134 of the *Code civil* affirms that the conventions have the force of law for the contracting parties. The courts have limited the consequences of this article by invoking the notion of general interest. The courts have also intervened with regard to the principle that each party had to stand on an equal basis and one was not to be advantaged in comparison to the other: judges limited the principle of the autonomy of will and sanctioned a burdensome contract in a certain number of cases.

The cases in which one must assume responsibility for damages have also been considerably extended by judge-made civil law. Individual liberties (for example, the right to habeas corpus) have been guaranteed by the theory of acts of violence. This can be considered as praetorian jurisprudence, since there is no basis for it in written law.

It would be tedious to enumerate all the domains influenced by creative civil jurisprudence. But it may be instructive to give examples of the two principal methods through which civil judges have created jurisprudence. The first is an amusing and classical example of the interpretation judge-made law can give to a legal text. The other is a famous illustration of a praetorian creation.

Interpretation of a legal text. Article 544 of the *Code civil* affirms that "the right of property appears absolute; therefore the proprietor can do what he wants on his estate as long as he is not in contradiction with laws or regulations."

This way of understanding article 544 was limited by a decision of the Requests Chamber (*Chambre des requêtes*) of the *Cour de cassation* of

February 20, 1849: "The right of property is limited by the natural and legal obligation not to cause damage to the property of another." The court of appeal of Colmar confirmed this interpretation on May 2, 1855. In this second case, a man had built a huge chimney on the roof of his house with the sole intention of annoying his neighbor. The court insisted that this was an abusive use of his right of property and condemned his willful malicious action. The limitation of the right of property has never been contested since then.

Praetorian rules. The Roman principle of bona fides was affirmed in a judgment of the *Chambre des requêtes* of the *Cour de cassation* on July 3, 1817: "fraud is an exception to all rules." From then on, the position of the judge-made law was constant. The court of appeal of Dijon, on July 24, 1885, declared the adage *fraus omnia corrumpit* (fraud corrupts all) a rule of law and order that it was not necessary to transcribe into law. The principle of bona fides has ever since been considered as a general principle in French law although it still is not inserted in a legal text.

These examples demonstrate that there is an important civil jurisprudence creating legal rules. Judges hesitate to affirm such a power and the *Cour de cassation* will never accept a petition on the basis of violation of judge-made law: it requires that there be—in one way or other—a violation of code or statutory law.

This prudent attitude is quite remarkable, and one can say that civil judges use their power with moderation. It seems they interfere when it is absolutely necessary in the circumstances previously discussed. Judges have worked to actualize the law, mainly the *Code civil*, which is 188 years old! Mazeaud (1970, 1:133) has found a wonderful expression to summarize their action: "Judge-made law is the fountain of youth for the law." Administrative jurisprudence has quite a different character, as we shall see.

A Jurisprudence Creative of Law Ex Nihilo: Administrative Jurisprudence

Administrative law is fundamentally recognized as being judge-made law. Indeed, some jurists, such as René Chapus (1987) have not hesitated to speak in this context of "jurislation" and "jurislator." The reality is not quite that extreme. Even at the beginning of the nineteenth century, there were some laws that served as a basis for administrative law: for example, the law of *Pluviôse* 28, Eighth year of the Republic (February 17, 1800) established the powers of the prefecture councils that were to become in the twentieth century the administrative tribunals.

Nonetheless, it is true that during the entire nineteenth century and the beginning of the twentieth century, administrative law was essentially praetorian, that is jurisprudential or judge-made. Today the situation has changed. Between 1963 and 1973 normative power of the administrative judges declined in favor of legislative and regulatory rules. This phenomenon established a new, more harmonious, equilibrium in which the administrative judges have tended to leave aside their creative jurisprudential function and assume a more interpretive or declaratory function.

Administrative Jurisprudential Creativity at Its Height

When reviewing the administrative judges' work over a century and a half, one finds that they exercised a creative or normative function in three different types of circumstances. In the first, they created a rule or affirmed a principle when there was no specific text applicable to an administrative matter. The question of responsibility is a famous example. Between 1873 and 1905, the Tribunal des Conflits[4] and the Conseil d'Etat rejected all reference to the *Code civil* and elaborated the theory of administrative responsibility: the responsibility of the administration is based on fault—personal or service fault—or risk. It was in the same state of mind that judges created a jurisprudence to adapt rules to political or social changes when the legislature had neglected to do so. For example, in the Dehaene decision, pronounced on July 7, 1950, the Conseil d'Etat recognized legal authority in the preamble of the Constitution of 1946, thus admitting, indirectly, the right of civil servants to go on strike.

In the second circumstance, judges had to control administrative acts and decide whether they were legal or not. To do so, they analyzed the inserted rules and eventually transformed them into general principles of law to protect the citizens. In the last type of situation, texts existed, but judges interpreted them, even the Constitution, very freely. Administrative judges have always exhibited great independence toward written law. Therefore, it will be worthwhile to comment on the administrative judges' proceedings as well as on the rules they establish.

Administrative judges intervene in delicate situations. They must act with tact, considering the various possible sources of information before starting to elaborate a jurisprudential rule. Judges are conscious of the threshold of jurisdictional tolerance (*"seuil de tolérance juridictionnelle"*—Gaudemet 1972, 189) they cannot trespass. The Conseil d'Etat plays an important role here because of its double nature as supreme court for administrative procedures and counselor of the executive. Administrative courts and the *Conseil d'Etat* in particular have been considered as hierarchical superiors of the bureaucracy by a long tradition. Administrative cases were regarded as occasions to exercise administrative control in judicial form, rather than to settle a conflict or dispute.   But there must be no misunderstanding.   The administrative judge knows his limits: he cannot give an injunction to the administration. It may even happen that his decision will not be respected. For example, on May 10, 1961, the Conseil d'Etat annulled (in *arrêt Fédération nationale des Malades, Infirmes et Paralysés*) part of a decree of June 1955 concerning social security. However, a note of the minister of labor and social security of July 3, 1961, enjoined the different agencies to refer to the decree of 1955 in its initial version, without taking heed of the decision of the Conseil d'Etat.

On the other hand, members of the Conseil d'Etat have the opportunity of working with the executive and developing relations with the political class. Contacts are easily established between the administrative courts and the legislature. This is the distinctive character of the administrative judge when compared to the civil judge. It produces two consequences.

First, the administrative judge knows when to stop so as not to interfere with the activity of the political power. This is very evident in the theory of the acts of government. For the same reason, administrative judges refuse to pronounce on the significance of international engagements. In contrast, the *Cour de cassation* does not hesitate to interpret dispositions in international treaties as long as they concern private interest. Second, the Conseil d'Etat participates in the elaboration of written law. In such conditions, it is not surprising to discover that a law often includes jurisprudential solutions affirmed years before. Outstanding examples include the General Administrators Law of 1946 and later the ordinance of February 4, 1959 establishing the General Public Functions Law: both appear mainly as codification of the jurisprudence elaborated by the Conseil d'Etat.   If administrative jurisprudence is a source of inspiration to the legislature, one can wonder where the judges find theirs.

Sources of inspiration. The field of references is very wide for administrative judges. Legal theory is a classical source of inspiration. In the two decisions Laruelle and Delville pronounced on July 28, 1951, the Conseil d'Etat sanctioned a solution proposed by Marcel Waline in an article published in the *Revue de droit public* in 1948. It amended the theory of administrative responsibility in admitting that the administration could take against a civil servant if it was he who had committed a personal fault. Until then, civil servants had been considered irresponsible. In this case, it was easy to make the connection between doctrine and jurisprudence, but the link is not always as evident.

Administrative judges are attentive to the jurisprudence elaborated by other types of courts. They refer first to civil jurisprudence because of its seniority and its relative stability. It had a strong influence during the nineteenth century, though perhaps more because of its methods than its solutions. But at the end of the century, administrative judges reacted against the influence of civil jurisprudence and affirmed their autonomy, generating diverse rules. So in the last forty years, there have been efforts to rejoin administrative and civil jurisprudence on many points.

In applying the Constitution of October 4, 1958, a new agency has been established that must be taken into consideration: the Constitutional Council (*Conseil constitutionnel*). It has a constitutional power to make decisions having the authority of res judicata that cannot be contested by Parliament, government, the administration, or any other judge. At its very beginning, the Constitutional Council regarded the Conseil d'Etat as a model, which was not surprising, since six out of seventeen persons designated to sit in the Constitutional Council from 1959 to 1965 had been members of the Conseil d'Etat. In these early years, it seemed that the decisions of the Constitutional Council were not regarded as a reference. The Conseil d'Etat insisted on their relativity, declaring that their authority could invoked only in the specific case being judged, and was therefore strictly limited. The Conseil d'Etat even refused (in 1969-1970) to admit as general principles of law those that had been sanctioned by the *Conseil constitutionnel*.

Today the situation has completely changed. The Constitutional Council exercises its influence in all the domains of law—not only constitutional law, but also civil law, criminal law, procedure, and international law. Administrative judges have developed the habit of referring to the jurisprudence of the Constitutional Council.

Finally, in the European context, it is important to mention the relationship between the top French court, the Conseil d'Etat, and the Court of Justice of the European Community (E.C.) The mission of the European court is to survey the application of the treaty by Community agencies and by the member states. Respect for the treaty is to be secured by the national courts. Hence, administrative judges can eventually refer to a decision of the Court of Luxembourg if they have difficulty in finding a solution in a case. They must necessarily refer to it if the validity or interpretation of a disposition of Community law is discussed, according to article 177 of the Treaty of the E.C. In such a case, the Conseil d'Etat recognizes the authority of the European court.

After envisaging all the legal references possible, it is important to mention the other elements to which administrative judges pay attention. They consider phenomena of every day life: the economical and social context, family ways, and religious beliefs and behaviors. They are also attentive to ethical principles as long as they are relatively old and stable. The most common reference in this category is the principles of the French Revolution. The Conseil d'Etat stands as their guardian, even though the content of equality has evolved with the years.

One can say, then, that administrative judges work in total liberty. They choose whatever elements of reference they prefer in order to create a jurisprudential rule. Once they have found the general idea, they must work on its elaboration.

The phases of elaboration. Since the judge perceives the imperfection of the law on some point or its contradiction with common sense and equity, he feels the necessity of creating a better jurisprudential solution. Thus after the Poursines decision (Conseil d'Etat, March 28, 1924) established the total irresponsibility of civil servants, when it appeared that this principle could be unfair, administrative judges worked with different sources of inspiration and came up with the rule discussed above.

A new jurisprudential rule is not affirmed without precaution. It must fit with the other rules concerning the matter. Then it is "tried out," perhaps by inserting it into the conclusions of a government commissioner or by publishing an article in the review *Etudes et Documents* (Studies and Documents). Reactions to such trials are awaited anxiously; If no one protests, the rule is incorporated into positive law through a single decision or, if the question is delicate, through the method of "timely concordant decisions": as several decisions are made with concordant consequences, a new judge-made law is developed. This method was used for the very important theory of improvidence that lasted over fifty years (1855-1916).

Administrative law derives more or less totally from judge-made law. This jurisprudence has elaborated general theories concerning the administrative activity, the responsibility of the public authority, and the rules for the execution of administrative contracts. It has also defined such essential notions as administrative act, public service, public authority, public agent, public works, and public domain. It has established general principles of law, aiming to assure liberty, equality and security to all the citizens in their relations with the administration. It is therefore essential to be able to consult the administrative law decisions. Unfortunately, while some private collections endeavor to provide access to administrative law, the collections and their contents are limited. Research is thus probably more difficult to carry out in administrative than in civil jurisprudence.

The authority of administrative jurisprudence. The specificity of administrative law (especially when compared to civil law) raises the question of the nature of an administrative jurisprudential rule. Some jurists, like Chapus, consider the terminology of the Conseil d'Etat and affirm that the jurisprudential rule has legislative value, the authority of a statute. Others have gone further still, affirming that the general principles have a constitutional character. Some base their argument on the fact that many general principles of law affirmed by the Conseil d'Etat are identical to those inscribed in the preamble of the Constitution and recognized as having constitutional authority by the Constitutional Council But these arguments are weakened by the different nature of the sources: the principles stated by the Conseil d'Etat, even though identical, must not be confused with those established by the Constitutional Council.

Another interesting theory was based on the dichotomy introduced in the Constitution of 1958 in articles 34 and 37, specifying the domains of laws and decrees. From this was developed the idea that since decrees are administrative acts that can be controlled by the Conseil d'Etat, its decisions must be superior to a mere decree and therefore constitutional in nature. This reasoning has been criticized because a decree, even if proclaimed as a substitute for a statute, remains a decree.

One last specification must be given concerning the authority of an administrative jurisprudential rule. Some such rules are imperative: the administration is bound to respect them; otherwise it would commit an illegal act. The rules establishing general principles are always imperative. For other rules, the judge will indicate whether or not they are imperative. A rule that is not imperative is applied unless it is reversed by a formal rule. Judges decide the character of the rules they announce. If there is no precision in the law, there is a presumption that the rule is imperative, though the presumption is not irrefutable. These last specifications reinforce the parallel between a judge-made administrative rule and a statute. They enable one to perceive fully the importance of administrative jurisprudence.

Even though administrative judges have practiced a sort of autolimitation, refusing to go too far in establishing new rules, their creative power has been severely criticized. For example, Olivier Dupeyroux (1960) has called it an abusive source of law. These criticisms should fade in the future because of the recent evolution toward a more formal, "jurisdictional" function for administrative judges.

The Evolution toward a More Jurisdictional Function

Two developments denote this evolution: the contents of the decisions have become more statute-based, and administrative legal texts have been created. In recent years administrative judges, those belonging to the Conseil d'Etat in particular, have tended to react more as civil-law courts having to "solve" a case, than as jurislators. This evolution has even influenced their working methods: local visits and investigations are ordered more frequently now. Is this a logical evolution due to continue? Yes, according to Georges Vedel (1979-1980) who thinks that administrative law cannot continue forever to be judge-made. If this is so, then there will have to be a counterpart development of the legal texts to support the evolution.

The development of legal texts can occur broadly through a codification or more narrowly through specific laws or regulations. A global codification would produce a more accessible administrative law and would certainly be appreciated by those who have to apply it. As already noted, one of the difficulties when studying administrative law is merely finding the decisions. Moreover, once found, these decisions are not always easy to interpret because of their elliptical form. Articles inserted in a code would constitute a safer reference, and the idea has received some support.[5] Curiously, this idea of codification has never found an enthusiastic echo among the specialists in administrative law. Indeed, Gaston Jèze (1952, 347) has contended that the development of administrative law would not have been possible except for the absence of an administrative code. Critics object that a codification of administrative law would never be up to date.

These criticisms explain why French administrative law is still not totally codified. Nevertheless, in the past forty years, timely texts have been created. In 1948 the gigantic task of assembling laws, decrees and decisions topically was begun. The result has been the publication of numerous codes destined to be practical references to the law in such areas as taxes, public health, rural and urban affairs, the domain of the state, posts and telecommunications, eminent domain, and forests.

All these codes are the concrete manifestations of the development of legislation and regulations, a rapid development due to economic, social, and technical evolution. For the first time in more than 150 years, legislation and regulation have taken the preeminent position in administrative law previously occupied by judge-made law. The legislation and regulations have established specific sets of statutory rules at the fringe of general jurisprudential administrative law. Such sets of rules can give greater guidance concerning the principle to apply in certain specific circumstances and can serve as a complement to the general judge-made administrative law. But more often, the adopt rules totally opposed to the general principles, thus creating a derogatory statute.

Thus in recent years legislation and regulation have progressively intervened in general administrative law and reformed some judge-made rules: these more "traditional" sources of law are taking over administrative legal decision making. Many scholars (for example, Linotte 1980) approve this evolution because it tends to harmonize the forces present in administrative law.

This study has reviewed the work accomplished by French judges for more than 180 years. Their goals were multiple: to assure the continuity of fundamental principles, to contribute to perfecting legal texts, to adapt the law to social evolution, to elaborate a rule when there was none. Undoubtedly, judges created law through these activities and will continue to do so. In civil law, they developed prudently a judge-made law based on the *Code civil* and affirmed the importance of their contributions at the end of the nineteenth century. In administrative law, judges started ex nihilo in the early nineteenth century and quickly built up its principal theories, while adopting more recently a more reserved position relying more heavily on legislation and regulation.

These opposite evolutionary patterns of civil and administrative jurisprudence put them now on an equal footing. Each has now realized a harmonious equilibrium, a sort of balance between statutory law and judge-made rules. This way of proceeding in civil and administrative jurisprudence, backed by the rule of precedent, reminds one of a totally different legal system, that of case law. Has French law evolved unconsciously in the direction of the English system? In the years to come, especially in a European perspective, could it be possible, could it be desirable, to envisage a harmonization in the process of creating law?

NOTES

1. Carré de Malberg (1920, I:691) wrote "The jurisdictional function may never be envisaged as a third principal power of the state, as a power equal to the two other organs and irreducibly distinct from them." One could also refer to article 5 of the *Code civil*: "It is forbidden for judges to pass judgment by way of a general, regulative order on the causes which are submitted to them." [This and all subsequent translations are by the editors.]

2. This *déni de justice* is condemned in article 4 of the *Code civil*: "The judge who refuses to make a judgment under the pretext of the silence, obscurity, or insufficiency of the law may be prosecuted for miscarriage of justice." Even Carré de Malberg (1962, I:701) commented on this article in explaining: "Speaking the law sometimes consists also of creating a new law, when on a particular question, there is no rule established by the law itself."

3. In the preliminary discourse on the *Code civil*, Portalis, one of the authors of the *Code civil*, exposed the perspective from which they had worked: "To foresee all is an aim that is impossible to attain. . . . We saved ourselves from the dangerous ambition to wish to regulate all and foresee all. Whatever one does, positive law can never entirely replace the use of natural reason in the affairs of life" (Fenet 1968, I:467ff.).

4. The *Tribunal des Conflits* decides which jurisdiction is competent when there is a conflict between the judicial hierarchy and the administrative hierarchy.

5. Two eminent members of the *Conseil d'Etat* were very favorable: "The proliferation of legislative texts and regulations has become such in France that one can no longer invoke the old principle: nothing can excuse ignorance of the

law. It is quite the contrary that seems true: everyone ignores it and the specialists find themselves rather ill at ease in the middle of this situation." (Michel and Canet, 1952).

REFERENCES

Belaid S. 1974. Essai sur le pouvoir créateur et normatif du juge, L.G.D.J., *Bibliothèque de philosophie du droit*, vol. 17. Paris.

Carré de Malberg, R. 1931. *La loi, expression de la volonté générale.* Paris: Sirey.

——. 1962. *Contribution à la théorie générale de l'Etat*, 2 vols. 1920. Reprinted by CNRS. Paris: Sirey.

Chapus, René. 1987. *Droit administratif général.* 2 vols: vol. 1, 3d ed., vol, 2, 2d ed. Paris: Editions Montchrestien.

Dupeyroux, Olivier. 1960. La jurisprudence, source abusive du droit. In Mélanges Maury, 349.

Favoreu, Louis. 1986. *Les cours constitutionnelles.* Paris: Presse Universitaire Français.

Favoreu, Louis, and Philip Loïc. 1985. *Le conseil constitutionnel.* 3d ed. Paris: Presse Universitaire Français.

Fenet, P. 1968. *Recueil complet des travaux préparatoires du Code civil.* 15 vols. 1827. Reprint, Osnabrück: O. Zeller.

Gaudemet, Yves. 1972. *Les méthodes du juge administratif*, Paris, L.G.D.J.

Jèze, Gaston. 1952. Collaboration du Conseil d'Etat et de la doctrine dans l'élaboration du droit administratif français. In *Livre jubilaire du Conseil d'Etat*, 347.

Lafon, Jacqueline Lucienne. n.d. *La Révolution française face au système judiciaire d'Ancien Régime.* Forthcoming.

Linotte, Didier. 1980. Déclin du pouvoir jurisprudentiel et ascension du pouvoir juridictionnel en droit administratif. *Annuaire Judiciare de Droit Adminstratif*, 632-639.

Long, M., P. Weil, and G. Braibant. 1984. *Les grands arrêts de la jurisprudence administrative.* With the assistance of Sylvie Hubac. 8th ed. Paris: Sirey.

Marty, Gabriel, and Pierre Raynaud. 1972. *Droit Civil*, Vol. 1, *Introduction générale à l'étude du droit.* 2d ed. Paris: Sirey.

Mazeaud, Henri, Léon Mazeaud, and Jean Mazeaud. 1970. *Leçons de droit civil*. Vol. 1, *Introduction à l'étude du Droit*. 4th ed. Paris: Editions Montchrestien.

Michel, G., and L. Canet. 1952. *Le Conseil d'Etat et la codification*. In *Livre jubilaire du Conseil d'Etat*, p. 467-471.

Pigacé-Mudry, Christiane. 1992. Les Racines del la Judiciarisation. Paper presented to the Interim Meeting of the Research Committee on Comparative Judicial Studies, International Political Science Association, *Centro Studi e Richerche Sull'Ordinamento Giudiziario*, June 14-17 at University of Bologna, Forlí.

Vedel, Georges. 1979-80. *Le droit administratif peut-il être indéfiniment jurisprudentiel?* E.D.C.E., no. 31.

Volcansek, Mary and Jacqueline Lucienne Lafon. 1987. *Judicial Selection: The Cross-evolution of French and American Practices*. Westport, Conn.: Greenwood Press.

Waline, Marcel. 1948. *Revue de droit public* 65:5, 537.

17.

Germany

CHRISTINE LANDFRIED

In Germany the Federal Constitutional Court (Bundesverfaßungsgericht or FCC) can especially be characterized as a policymaker. Of course, other courts also take part in judicial policy-making, for example, the Federal Appellate Court (Bundesgerichtshof) or even district courts such as the one in Memmingen that ruled on a key abortion decision. But it is the Constitutional Court that is most involved in policy-making, and it is this court on which I will concentrate. First I will describe the ways in which the court gains influence on policy-making. Second, I will analyze the impact of the expansion of this court's power on politics and on societal change. Third, I will outline what could be a proper balance of power between Parliament and the Constitutional Court. It is the thesis of this chapter that judicial review that leads to the expansion of judicial power is not always and should not be in the interest of the political power elite (contra Preuß 1987).

To answer the cui bono question of judicial review, one has to differentiate according to policies. While it is an inadequate simplification of reality to claim that judicial review always serves the interests of the political elite, the real danger of judicial review lies in the process of judicialization of politics. The more political questions are decided by the Constitutional Court, the more political alternatives are reduced. Members of Parliament contribute to this development by giving too much consideration to legal arguments in legislation and judges contribute by sometimes exceeding their proper competencies.

THE FEDERAL CONSTITUTIONAL COURT AS POLICYMAKER

From its beginning in 1951 through 1990 the Federal Constitutional Court declared invalid or incompatible with the Constitution 198 federal laws, out of a total of 4,298 laws passed by the Bundestag during the same period. Thus, the Court has invalidated roughly 5 percent of all federal laws. Yet the Constitutional Court has a much greater impact on policy-making than these data on invalidated laws suggest.

The most important powers supporting the court's participation in policy-making are its powers of abstract and concrete judicial review and of "constitutional complaint." Even important disputes between the federal government and the state governments have arisen under the abstract judicial review procedure, and not as a result of the relatively small number of direct federal-state conflicts.

In case of doubts about the compatibility between a federal and a state law or between these laws and the Constitution, the abstract judicial review procedure may be initiated by the federal government, by a state government, or by one-third of the Members of the Bundestag. This procedure enables the court to examine the constitutionality of a law without reference to any specific case. Only 110 cases requesting abstract judicial review were filed between 1951 and 1990. More often, the Constitutional Court has influenced policy-making by concrete judicial review and the constitutional complaint. The concrete judicial review procedure arises out of an ordinary lawsuit, when a court is convinced that a federal or a state law, on the basis of which the case must be decided, is unconstitutional. Between 1951 and 1990, 2,529 such cases were filed. A constitutional complaint, provided for in the Basic Law in 1969, may be filed by any person who claims that one of his basic rights has been violated by a public authority. The 78,449 constitutional complaints filed through 1990 (FCC 1991, 1) show that the Constitutional Court has been accepted as the "Court of the Common Man." While the proportion of successful complaints is not high (only 2.25 percent), they have been of great importance for social life in Germany.

An overview of the invalidated federal laws classified by policies shows that the court invalidated the greatest number of norms in social policy, followed by financial policy and legal policy (see table 17.1). Thus, most of the invalidated laws belong to a policy area in which the Constitution is open to a variety of interpretations.

Besides invalidating laws there are other ways in which the Constitutional Court takes part in policy-making. The court has developed several types of sanctions to escape the simple choice of declaring a law constitutional or unconstitutional. These "weapons of limited warfare against unconstitutionality" (Cappelletti 1979, 94) are not reflected in the above statistics. One of these forms is "interpretation in conformity with the constitution" (*verfaßungskonforme Interpretation*), a declaration that a particular interpretation of a law is the only constitutional one. Such declarations often entail precise prescriptions for the implementation of a law and result in significant policy-making by the Constitutional Court. In Germany and in France (Favoreu 1988, 100-101), these interpretations in conformity with the constitution have increased in number.

Table 17.1: Federal Laws Declared Invalid or Incompatible with the Basic Law Classified by Policies 1951-1990

	Number	%*
Social Policy	61	31
Fiscal and Financial Policy	35	18
Legal Policy	29	15
Regulatory Measures within and between Federal Organs	25	13
Economic Policy	12	6
Traffic Policy	9	5
Educational Policy	7	4
Labor Market Policy	6	3
Health Policy	4	2
Military Policy	2	1
Environmental Policy	1	0
Others	7	4
Total	198	102

*Total not = 100% due to rounding.

Source: Up to 1980, Klaus von Beyme, "Verfaßungsgerichtsbarkeit und Policy Analysis," in *Festschrift für Rudolf Wassermann*, ed. Broda, et al. (Darmstadt/Neuwied: Luchterhand 1986), S. 268. From 1980 to 1990, volumes of the decisions of the Constitutional Court, including vol. 82.

While the clear-cut invalidation of a law gives the legislature room for political maneuvering because a new law can be enacted, the interpretation in conformity with the constitution reduces the policy-making power of Parliament. By interpreting norms of the Constitution that are open to different meanings and by applying derived norms like the principle of proportionality (*Verhaltnismäßigkeitgrundsatz*) (Benda 1979, 20), the Constitutional Court influences policy-making. Sometimes the judges also have to deal with questions that are difficult to relate to specific provisions of the Constitution. With this kind of judicial review the court also reduces the possibilities for policy-making and curtails the openness of the Constitution. This development is inherent in a political system that has institutionalized judicial review, and that is why there has to be a certain balance of power between court and Parliament.

One of the areas in which the Constitutional Court has been most involved in policy-making is the protection of the basic rights of the individual (*Grundrechte*) (von Brünneck 1988, 237). For example, the court has developed principles aimed at the protection of the freedom of opinion under Article 5 of the Basic Law. The organization of radio and television also has been influenced by decisions of the Constitutional Court. In its four broadcasting decisions of 1961, 1971, 1981, and 1986 the court has enforced regulations to guarantee a minimum amount of political and cultural pluralism in radio and television. Judicial review proved to be a barrier against consequent deregulation and commercialization of broadcasting. The privatization of radio and television, a development that occurred in Great Britain under the government of Margaret Thatcher, was impossible in Germany because of judicial review. In its decision of 1986, the Constitutional Court (BVerfGE 73, 118) ruled that there had to be a dual broadcasting system. Public radio and television had to provide a comprehensive spectrum of political and cultural information. If public broadcasting thus guarantees basic pluralistic information, then private radio and television need not meet the same standard of pluralism. Some commercialization of radio and television had to be accepted. The court ruled that 20 percent of the private programming time may be dedicated to advertising.

The message of the decision is that private radio and television may give priority to economic interests as long as public radio and television guarantee a certain degree of pluralism. By not demanding from private radio and television high standards of political and cultural information the Constitutional Court chose one specific interpretation of what is meant by a diversity of opinions (*Meinungsvielfalt*) and neglected the interaction between private and public systems.   If private radio and television may give priority to economic interests, this will not be without consequences for public programming.   To a large degree judicial review rather than legislation has determined the future course of radio and television policy.   The court gained this influence not by invalidating laws but by issuing prescriptions.

As long as the Judges do not exceed their proper competencies, judicial policy-making has to be accepted as part of the existence of judicial review.   The judges themselves have become conscious of this aspect of their work.   When the judges of the Constitutional Court were asked in a survey in 1972 if the main load of their work involved norm enforcement or the development of law, and thereby policy-making, a majority answered that it was norm enforcement (see table 17.2).

Table 17.2: Consciousness of Policy Making by the Judges of the Constitutional Court

Question: "Do you think that your work as Judge of the Constitutional Court primarily consists of norm enforcement or of the development of law?"

	1972 %	1983 %
Norm Enforcement	63.0	37.5
Development of Law	7.4	25.0
Both	22.2	37.5
No Answer	7.4	-
Total	100.0	100.0

Sources: For 1972 Manfred Riegel, Raymund Werle, and Rudolf Wildenmann, *Selbstverständnis und politisches Bewußtsein der Juristen* (Mannheim 1974), table Hl.   For 1983 Christine Landfried, *Bundesverfaßungsgericht und Gesetzgeber* (Baden-Baden: Nomos 1984), S. 25.

In 1972, only 7 percent of the judges held the opinion that judicial review means the development of law. When they were asked the same question 11 years later, a much larger proportion (25 percent) interpreted their work as policy-making.

While it is legitimate for a court that has to interpret the provisions of a Constitution to influence policy-making, there have been cases in which the court has exceeded its competencies. One of these cases was the decision on abortion in 1975. Since the 1970s there has been a broad discussion in the Federal Republic of Germany on a reform of abortion, because it had become questionable whether prenatal life could be protected by criminal law. In 1974 the social-liberal government passed a law permitting abortion within the first three months of pregnancy. The Christian Democratic Union/Christian Social Union (CDU/CSU) opposition filed an abstract judicial review procedure, and the First Senate of the Constitutional Court ruled that the state had to protect prenatal life to the utmost by criminal law. The court in its majority opinion gave the legislature a precise prescription for a constitutional regulation of abortion. According to the judges, it was not the pregnant woman who could decide on abortion, but a medical doctor or an advisory board. If the medical doctor or the advisor held the opinion that there was no reason to end the pregnancy through an induced abortion, then an abortion that was nonetheless implemented was a crime.

The legislature, however, had had good reasons to doubt the appropriateness of criminal law for the protection of prenatal life. The question of whether a certain remedy is suitable for the realization of a basic right—in this case the right of life under Article 2 of the Basic Law—is a political question that should be decided by Parliament (Böckenförde 1974, 1536). Without taking into consideration the social problems of abortions, the majority of the First Senate of the Court had exceeded its competence by deciding a question that was definitely within the competence of Parliament. Judges Rupp-von Brünneck and Simon, who wrote a dissenting opinion, emphasized exactly this point: it was up to Parliament to find a solution as to how to protect prenatal life most efficiently (BVerfGE 39, 1[89]).

The decision of the Constitutional Court very much influenced the implementation of the abortion law. After the law had been changed by the interpretation of the Constitutional Court, it soon became clear that the court's demand for criminal law was detrimental to the advisory dialogue with pregnant women. Women were not open to discussion about their pregnancies because of the specter of a criminal sanction (*Bundestags-Drucksache* no. 8/3630, January 31, 1980, 143). Thus the central assumptions of the court, that criminal law and compulsory consultation are ways to protect prenatal life, have proved to be wrong (BVerfGE 39, 1[62]). Nevertheless, the decision of the court continued to influence the process of passing a new bill on abortion even in 1991. The unification treaty of 1990 provided (art. 31, *Vertrag zwischen der Bundesrepublik Deutschland und der Deutschen Demokratischen Republik über die Herstellung der Einheit Deutschlands* vom 31.8.1990 *BGB*1. II, 889) that the German Parliament had to find a regulation for abortion by the end of 1992 in order to end the strange situation that allowed abortion in the former Democratic Republic states, but required it to be punished under certain circumstances in the former Federal Republic - states.

In the present debate on this law the decision of the Constitutional Court of 1975 plays a decisive role. The CDU/CSU has drawn a bill that maintains criminal sanctions in cases of abortion when a medical doctor has declared himself against it. The FDP advocates that women can decide for themselves during the first three months but may be punished if they did not consult an advisory board. Many politicians of these parties argue that a liberalization of abortion is not possible because of judicial review (*Stenographische Berichte der Verhandlungen des Deutschen Bundestages*, 12. *Wahlperiode*, 44, *Sitzung am* 26.9.1991, p. 3687ff. *Vgl. Bundestags-Drucksache* no. 12/551, 16.5.1991, 14). They do not take into account that the situation has changed since 1975 and that experience gained by the implementation of abortion has demonstrated that the assumptions of the Constitutional Court were wrong. In spite of all the facts that speak well for a liberalization as pro- posed in the bill of the Social Democratic Party (SPD), the argument "this bill will be invalidated by the Constitutional Court" is not only "window-dressing" in parliamentary debates, but has substantial influence on policy-making.

The case of abortion shows how in the legislative decision-making process members of Parliament adjust their bills to accommodate former decisions of the court and anticipate possible future judicial review. Often the politicians ask jurists to give them detailed interpretations of the decisions of the Court, and sometimes the experts are asked for "Karlsruhe-astrology." Of course it is difficult to document the impact of these anticipated reactions. I would agree, however, with Malcolm Feeley's guess that even if one cannot verify such anticipated adjustments, they do constitute an important component of the power of Constitutional Courts over policy-making (Feeley 1978, 226).

THE IMPACT OF JUDICIAL POLICY-MAKING ON POLITICS AND SOCIAL CHANGE

The decisions of the Constitutional Court have always been respected by Parliament. The problem is not so much the absence, but rather the excess of deference by members of Parliament toward the court. Let us take the example of the financing of political parties. In this area the legislature has followed as closely as possible the standards set by judicial review. In its judgment of July 1966, the Second Senate of the Constitutional Court ruled that grants from public funds to support the general activities of parties were unconstitutional (BVerfGE 20, 56). The court interpreted political parties as freely competing organizations of society acting independently of the state. The judges considered it to be unconstitutional to give continuous financial support from public funds to such organizations. But as the activities of parties were necessary for the operation of Parliament, the court ruled that reimbursement of the costs of an appropriate election campaign would be admissible, provided that it was extended to smaller parties gaining votes considerably below the five percent of the second votes required for representation in Parliament.

Parliament reacted immediately. After politicians had failed for nearly twenty years to pass a parties law, this became possible after judicial review. Politicians discussed in Parliament how to adjust the law to survive judicial review. As Member of Parliament Arndt from the SPD warned his colleagues: "We should not kick against the pricks" (*Stenographische Berichte der Verhandlungen des Deutschen Bundestages*, 5. *Wahlperiode*, 116. *Sitzung am* 28.6.1967, 5801A).

The parties law was passed in 1967 by a great majority. But in spite of all the caution of the politicians, the law was invalidated by the Constitutional Court. The court ruled that only 0.5 percent of the second votes, not 2.5 percent as required by the law, would qualify a party for reimbursement of election campaign costs (BVerfGE, 24, 300). Parliament amended the law accordingly.

Members of Parliament sometimes also want the Constitutional Court to solve delicate political problems. Politicians wanted to allow higher tax deductions for donations to political parties. According to the law of 1967, the amount of tax-deductible donations was limited to 600DM per year. In 1979 the government of lower Saxony attempted via the abstract judicial review procedure to get instructions from the court as to whether this sum could be increased. The court, however, refused to play the desired role of problem solver, ruling instead that any regulation of donations to parties had to take into consideration the right of equal participation of every citizen in the political process.

In 1980 the amount of tax-deductible donations was increased, but the problem of the financing of parties was not solved. This became obvious in the "Flick scandal." As a result, a commission of experts was established to make proposals on the future regulation of the financing of parties. The report of the commission became the basis of a new bill. There was a public hearing of experts—all lawyers—in a committee of the Bundestag to clarify the question of just how the court would judge the bill in a potential future decision. The debate centered not so much on where the Basic Law draws the line for the financing of parties but on where the Constitutional Court would draw the line in a judgment. As Hans-Peter Schneider said in the hearing: "In my opinion there is no risk of unconstitutionality as long as one looks at the constitution . . . but there is a certain risk if one looks at judicial review" (*Stenographisches Protokoll über die 12. Sitzung des Innenausschusses des Deutschen Bundestages vom 9.11.83*, 79). The experts in the hearing had quite different opinions about the constitutionality of the bill. While Friauf and Schneider held the bill to be constitutional, Isensee had doubts about its constitutionality, and von Arnim and Seifert held the bill to be unconstitutional.

The amended parties law of 1984 declared political parties to be nonprofit associations, thereby allowing donations to parties to become tax deductible up to 5 percent of income or 20 percent of the taxes owed. This privilege granted for big donations and for political parties that are attractive to big donors was to be compensated for by a difficult system called "*Chancenausgleich*" that involved giving public money to parties that could not get as many donations and membership subscriptions as other parties. Irrespective of the inconsistencies of the compensation system itself, there is a qualitative difference between the big donation of a private person to a political party and public money. A citizen who is able to give a large amount of money to a party thereby gains political influence that should not be strengthened by a generous tax deduction. Such an unequal participation of citizens in the political process cannot be compensated for by public money. The Green party appealed to the Constitutional Court, claiming that the new law meant a privilege for people with high income.

The decision of the Second Senate in July 1986 was a surprising deviation from previous judicial review in this area. The Second Senate ruled by a 6-2 vote that it is unconstitutional to give tax-deductions for donations to parties corresponding to a certain percentage of income or taxes owed. But the court gave politicians specific information on what would be constitutional: each year individuals and firms would be permitted to give up to 100,000DM per year in donations to parties and thereby reduce their taxes. Such a limit in reality means a privilege for the well-to-do not much different from that in the percentage solution. As Judge Böckenförde wrote in his dissenting vote: "There continues to be the fact that the political opinions of some people are privileged compared to the opinion of others" (BVerfGE 73, 40 [110]). The majority of the Senate ignored the principle of equal participation of every citizen in politics.

Now the parties law had to be amended again. A bill passed in 1988 replaced the percentage solution with a provision that permits tax deductions for donations up to 60,000DM per year. Though this solution was not as unjust as it could have been under the Constitutional Court's ruling, one has to take into account the context of the law. One of the new provisions reduced the transparency of donation policy because only donations greater than 40,000DM have to be published. The combination of high tax-deductibility and low publicity gave a great privilege to big donors. The Green party once again filed an abstract review procedure at the Constitutional Court. The Second Senate decided on the constitutionality of the parties law of 1988 in April 1992. In this decision the court again changed its view and held tax, deductions for big donations to parties to be unconstitutional (EUGRZ 19 1992, 153-171).

Policy-making in the area of party financing demonstrates that the political decision-making process is overloaded with legal arguments. While members of Parliament are looking for solutions to political problems they have to consider the constitutional interpretations of the Court in Karlsruhe and to find their way through the labyrinth of headnotes and obiter dicta. Because politicians do not want to get into conflict with the Court, they often respect not only the main arguments of a judicial review decision, but nearly every sentence as well. The more often the court is appealed to, the more close-meshed constitutional interpretations will become. The abstract judicial review procedure can be misused by the opposition in Parliament to attain its political goals by legal means. Yet one has to realize that abstract judicial review is an important procedure for the protection of minorities. The contribution of members of Parliament to the judicialization of politics is strengthened when politicians expect a solution for a political or a social problem to come from the court. In addition to all this, members of Parliament anticipate judicial review and try to formulate policies to comply as nearly as possible not only with previous but also with predicted judicial review. What does this expansion of judicial power in politics mean for societal change?

"The fact is . . . that the policy views dominant on the [Supreme] court are never for long out of line with the policy views dominant among lawmaking majorities of the United States" (Dahl 1957, 285). Robert Dahl claimed with this thesis that policymakers and the U.S. Supreme Court were not very far apart and that the existence of the Supreme Court had altered policy-making and the conditions of liberty not more than by "a hair's breadth" (Dahl 1957, 292). A very similar thesis has been formulated for the German Constitutional Court by Ulrich Preuß. The Constitutional Court in his view is part of the power elite and tries to find judgments that please the political and social mainstreams. Consequently, the court, being itself part of or at least in a "near location" to politics, is not able to control the legislature and protect the rights of minorities. According to this thesis the court "makes politics in the spirit of consensus" and decides in harmony with the powerful forces of political life (Preuß 1987).

The reason for this harmony between court and lawmaking majorities is, according to Dahl and Preuß, the way judges are appointed or elected. For the United States it is claimed that presidents do not appoint justices that are hostile to their views on public policy nor to the dominant majority in the Senate. For Germany it is argued that the election by a committee of the Bundestag and by the Bundesrat has led to a certain pattern of selection of judges. Once a party is in possession of a seat on the court, it holds onto it. Judges elected on "party tickets" represent the political mainstream and this will show up in judicial review.

The thesis that Constitutional Courts will judge in conformity with the politically dominant interests of society is an inadequate simplification of the reality of judicial review. In the United States the president's nomination power is no guarantee of judicial review in the political interests of the president. The conservative Burger Court, for example, sometimes failed to please a conservative president and the conservatives in Congress. And in Germany party affiliation of the judges does not seem to play a decisive role in the decision-making process inside the court. The publication of dissenting opinions was first permitted in 1971 (Lamprecht 1992), the voting behavior of the judges since then can be analyzed. Such an analysis indicates that there have been decisions in which party affiliation did play a role. This was evident, for example, in the decision on abortion law when a majority of judges connected with the conservative Christian-Democratic Party invalidated the law over the protests of two dissenting members affiliated with the Socialist Party. But, all in all, party membership does not influence judicial review to any great extent.

Of course one might ask why politicians are eager to have "their" share of judges in the court and why there are such strict party quotas if party affiliation does not make a difference.[1] Party membership does indicate the general political views of a judge, and this is important when questions like abortion have to be decided. But there are many decisions for which party affiliation is of no importance.

Of course there have been decisions of the Constitutional Court like the 1986 judgment on the financing of parties (BVerfGE 73, 40) that legitimated the power politics of the established parties. But there are also decisions of the Constitutional Court, for example, those concerning the rights of prisoners (BVerfGE 70, 228) that are certainly more progressive than the attitude of the dominant forces toward this minority. If one analyzes the impact of judicial review on societal change and asks the cuibono question, one has to differentiate according to policies. The court has been effective in protecting the basic rights of individuals in such areas as the protection of privacy and data (*Persönalichkeitsrechte*) and has made new policies in this area. It has been less effective in protecting the political rights of equal participation of every citizen. The Constitutional Court has maintained the status quo and has been least effective when it comes to problems concerning the structure of the economy (von Brünneck 1988, 237).

Judicial review cannot thus be characterized as altogether in the interest of the political mainstream. Nor is it possible to divide the history of the Constitutional Court into clear "pro-" and "anti-" government periods. In the 1950s the Constitutional Court often decided in favor of the CDU/CSU-dominated governments, for example in the rejection of the petition of the SPD against rearmament (BVerfGE 1, 396) in 1952, or in the decision of the Saar statute in 1955 (BVerfGE 4, 157), which judged the cession of the Saar territory to be compatible with the Basic Law. On the other hand there was the television decision in 1961 (BVerfGE 12, 20, 1) that forbade Konrad Adenauer to establish a state-owned television channel called Deutschland Fernsehen GmbH. Furthermore, many decisions cannot be clearly characterized as favoring one political side.

Under the socialist-liberal governments from 1969 to 1982, many important reform laws failed to pass muster in Karlsruhe: the law on codetermination in the universities in 1972 (BVerfGE 33, 303), the law on abortion in 1975 (BVerfGE 39,1) and the law on conscientious objection in 1978 (BVerfGE 48, 127). Though the impact of the court on policy-making in the 1970s cannot be characterized as systematic resistance (Dopatka 1979, 45) to the Social Democratic-Free Democratic Party (FDP) government, it is obvious that the court did prevent important social reform projects.

The change in government to a CDU/CSU/FDP coalition in October 1982 has not been accompanied by a "turning point" in judicial review. The court has continued to control the government. In the Flick-case, brought to the court by the Greens and the SPD, the Second Senate of the Constitutional Court expressed the opinion that the government had no right to withhold documents from a parliamentary fact-finding committee for reasons of tax secrecy and that, in doing so, it had violated article 44 of the Basic Law. In the decision on the census law in 1983 (BVerfGE 65, 1) the First Senate invalidated parts of the law and voted in favor of more liberty for the individual. This decision, however, was not a real antigovernment decision, because all parties had voted unanimously for the law.

In two important decisions the court ruled in favor of the CDU/CSU/FDP-government. In its judgment that legitimized the stationing of Pershing-II and Cruise missiles (BVerfGE 68, 1) the court held that it was within the competence of the government to consent to the stationing of the missiles. And in a 1986 judgment the court ruled that it was constitutional for the government to deny the Greens a seat in a special committee controlling the economic plans of the security services (BVerfGE 70, 324). But when the first elections in the united Germany were being planned in 1990, it was the Constitutional Court that protected the rights of the smaller parties of the former DDR. In a decision of 29 September 1990 the court ruled that the election law was unconstitutional because it discriminated against the smaller DDR parties and their chances in the election.

This judgment documents that the Constitutional Court does not always decide in favor of the established parties.

CRITERIA FOR A BALANCE OF POWER
BETWEEN CONSTITUTIONAL COURT AND PARLIAMENT

As the Federal Constitutional Court has only a limited democratic legitimacy, it is detrimental to democracy when such a court frequently makes policy decisions and, with a dense network of constitutional interpretations, reduces the political alternatives of future generations. This is why we have to ask whether there are criteria by which we can judge where the appropriate boundaries between the Constitutional Court and Parliament should lie.[2]

Criteria for an appropriate division of labor between court and Parliament have to be consistent with the functions of both institutions. The boundaries between the institutions might change with their respective functions (Grimm 1988, 170). According to a most influential theory of judicial review, judges of constitutional courts have to ensure that the political process is "open to those of all viewpoints on something approaching an equal basis." As long as judges do not decide on competing values and political concepts and as long as they control "legitimate processes" instead of "legitimate outcomes," judicial review is compatible with democracy (Ely 1980, 74).

With regard to the problem of a proper balance of power between court and parliament in a representative democracy, the distinction between legitimate processes and legitimate outcomes is convincing. There are, however, cases in which a constitutional court has to make choices between competing values. If one defines justice not only by democratic procedures and legitimate processes but also by substantially just and legitimate outcomes, a constitutional court will not always be able to avoid a value-oriented judicial review. Therefore I do not share the assumption that it is illegitimate for a constitutional court to decide on legitimate outcomes as well.

I would suggest using John Ely's distinction to develop a more flexible interpretation of the balance between court and Parliament that would still be compatible with the principle of democracy. Concerning decisions on legitimate processes, for example, decisions of the rights of small parties in parliamentary decisions, the Constitutional Court has broad competencies and the boundaries between the two powers shift in favor of the court. Concerning decisions on legitimate outcomes, for example, a decision on abortion, the court has only restricted competencies, and the boundaries shift in favor of Parliament.

In cases where the Constitutional Court decides on legitimate outcomes, we must apply strict criteria to judge whether the specific value-oriented judgment was necessary and adequate or a transgression of competence. Such criteria could be:

1. The commitment of a decision to the text of the Constitution. Though many provisions of the Constitution are open to different interpretations, one has to keep in mind that there are also many clear-cut articles. Following a thesis developed for the historical method—a document cannot tell us what we have to say but rather prevents us from making statements that cannot be made—the Constitution can at least tell what policymakers are not allowed to do (Koselleck 1977, 45).

2. The rationality of the argument. Quite often, irrational argumentation and methodological shortcomings can be an indication that it was unnecessary for the court to make a value-oriented decision and that it nevertheless did so because of judicial power politics. The court's legal procedures are not just a "play on the stage," and the persuasiveness of the arguments is not "suggested" (Preuß 1987, 6) in order to veil the fact that judicial review is after all oriented to correspond with the political power elite. There must always be, and so far there has been, the possibility for the judges to interpret the Constitution independent of the political mainstream in accordance with convincing arguments derived from the Constitution.

3. The constitutional system of separation of powers. A theory of constitutional interpretation (Böckenförde 1976) that contains standards for a balance of power between Constitutional Court and Parliament cannot be derived from a subjective viewpoint or from an existing social consensus, but must be construed from the text and the genesis of the Constitution.

Just as there can be "no such thing as a complete separation of judicial and political power" (Denninger 1985, 1024), there can be no separation of a Constitutional Court as "negative" and Parliament as "positive" legislature as Hans Kelsen (1929, 56) proposed. A Constitutional Court does take part in policy-making often more by way of telling Parliament how a certain law has to be interpreted than by telling it that a law is unconstitutional.[3] But when the Constitutional Court is a policymaker, we have to be aware of its restricted democratic legitimacy. It is the competence of Parliament to shape politics and policies. Parliament is also better qualified than the Constitutional Court to adapt law to social change and to initiate social change by a process of trial and error. Judges are not very much inclined to revise judicial review and to adapt it to a changing political and social situation.[4] Therefore, it is all the more important for the solution of political problems in modern societies that judges do not gain too much influence on policy-making (Grimm 1991, 436).

NOTES

1. Kommers (1976, 128-44) documents for the period 1951-1971 that Constitutional Court vacancies were almost invariably filled by judges with the same party identifications as the judges being replaced. My own research (Landfried 1992) confirms that this pattern has continued into the 1990s.

2. The following argument is drawn from my "Introduction" (Landfried 1988, 16-20).

3. This has been emphasized for the U.S. Supreme Court as well: "In order to bring theoretical concepts into line with empirical reality, emphasis should be placed upon the Court's 'yea-saying' power rather than upon its 'nay-saying' power. . . Students of judicial policymaking should be paying more attention to the Court's statutory, as distinct from its constitutional, interpretation. In the areas of selective service, welfare, and civil rights, to cite but a few recent examples, the Court has been making public policy of tremendous consequence" (Funston, 1976:809).

4. The unwillingness to revise previous decisions is seen in interviews with the judges themselves (see Christine Landfried 1984, 172).

REFERENCES

Benda, Ernst. 1979. *Grundrechtswidrige Gesetze. Ein Beitrag zu den Ursachen verfaßungsgerichtlicher Beanstandung*. Baden-Baden: Nomos.

Böckenförde, Ernst-Wolfgang. 1974. "Grundrechtstheorie und Grundrechtsinterpretation." *Neue Juristische Wochenschrift* 27:1536.

———. 1976. "Die Methoden der Verfaßungsinterpretation—Bestandsaufnahme und Kritik." *Neue Juristische Wochenschrift* 1976:2089-2099.

Cappelletti, Mauro. 1979. "The Modern System of Judicial Review." In *Comparative Constitutional Law*, ed. Mauro Cappelletti and William Cohen. New York: Bobbs-Merill.

Dahl, Robert. 1957. "Decision-Making in a Democracy: the Supreme Court as a National Policy-Maker." *Journal of Public Law* 6:285.

Denninger, Erhard. 1985. "Judicial Review Revisited: The German Experience." *Tulane Law Review*.

Dopatka, Friedrich-Wilhelm. 1979. "Zur Bedeutung des Bundesverfaßungsgerichts in der politischen und gesellschaftlichen Entwicklung der Bundesrepublik 1951 bis 1978." In *Verfaßungsgericht und Politik*, ed. Wolfgang Däubler and Gudrun Küsel. Reinbek: Rowohlt.

Ely, John Hart. 1980. *Democracy and Distrust: A Theory of Judicial Review*. 4th ed. Cambridge: Harvard University Press.

Favoreu, Louis. 1988. "The Constitutional Council and Parliament in France." In *Constitutional Review and Legislation: An International Comparison*, ed. Christine Landfried.

Federal Constitutional Court. 1991. *Gesamtstatistik per 31.12.1990*. Karlsruhe: Bundesverfaßungsgericht.

Feeley, Malcolm. 1978. "Power, Impact and the Supreme Court." In *The Impact of Supreme Court Decisions: Empirical Studies*, 2d ed., ed. Theodore Becker and Malcolm Feeley. New York: Oxford University Press.

Funston, Richard. 1976. "The Supreme Court and Critical Elections." The *American Political Science Review*. 69:795.

Grimm, Dieter. 1988. "Comment on Report on Germany." In *Constitutional Review and Legislation: An International Comparison*, ed. Christine Landfried.

———. 1991. *Die Zukunft der Verfaßung*. Frankfurt.

Kelsen, Hans. 1929. *Wesen und Entwicklung der Staatsgerichtsbarkeit.* *Veroffentlichungen der Vereinigung der Deutschen Staatsrechtslehrer.*

Kommers, Donald. 1976. *Judicial Politics in West Germany: A Study of the Federal Constitutional Court.* Beverly Hills: Sage.

Koselleck, Reinhart. 1977. "Standortbindung und Zeitlichkeit. Ein Beitrag zur historiographischen Erschließung der geschichtlichen Welt." In *Objektivität und Parteilichkeit. Theorie der Geschichte,* ed. Reinhart Koselleck, Wolfgang Mommsen, and Jörn Rüsen. Munich: dtv.

Lamprecht, Rolf. 1992. *Richter contra Richter: Die abweichene Meinung und ihre Bedueting für die Rechtkultur.* Baden-Baden: Nomos.

Landfried, Christine. 1984. *Bundesverfaßungsgericht und Gesetzgeber.* Baden-Baden: Nomos.

————, ed. 1988. *Constitutional Review and Legislation: An International Comparison.* Baden-Baden: Nomos.

————. 1992. The Judicialization of Politics in Germany. Paper presented to the Interim Meeting of the Research Committee on Comparative Judicial Studies, International Political Science Association, *Centro Studi e Richerche Sull'Ordinamento Giudiziario,* University of Bologna, Forlí, Italy, June 14–17, 1992.

Preuß, Ulrich. 1987. "Aus dem Geiste des Konsenes: Zur Rechtsprchung des Bundesverfaßungsgerichts." *Merkur* 1987:1-12.

von Brünneck, Alexander. 1988. "Constitutional Review and Legislation in Western Democracies." In *Constitutional Review and Legislation: An International Comparison,* ed. Christine Landfried.

18.

Reunification and Prospects for Judicialization in Germany

H. G. PETER WALLACH

Currently, the increasing unlikelihood of a German constitutional referendum further empowers the institutions of continuity originally established by the Federal Republic of the West. This empowerment
inferentially adds to the authority of the Constitutional Court and the
other established courts. But to call this as part of a global expansion of
judicial power would be an overanxious application of the concept.

As far as the history of German political development is concerned,
the years since 1990 have promoted the bureaucratically oriented
Rechtsstaat as it has been tempered by the democratic reforms of the
postwar era. For the moment the role of the courts, in the unification
process, is centered on property issues and the settlement of accusations
against former officials of the Democratic Republic of Germany (DDR).
The most important constitutional determinations are firmly in the hands
of political and administrative officials.

This chapter will hardly touch on the relationship of the *Rechtsstaat*
concept to Vallinder's observations on judicialization. But the description
and analysis that follows will indicate that in Germany the role of the
judiciary is merely part of a bureaucratic panorama—defined by elected
officials. Where the second part of Vallinder's definition applies, further
care must be taken to differentiate standard setting from mediation and
the settlement of particular problems.

This chapter focuses on the nonjudicial decision making that is reforming the German Constitution. In the following sections this focus will be trained on the potentialities for revision offered by unification, the pressures to develop a new constitution, the counterpressures that provided for a continuation of the formerly "temporary" West German Basic Law, the continued processing of potential constitutional conflicts, and the meaning this has for future judicialization. Progress through these sections is marked by decreasing emphasis on description and technical detail, and increasing analysis wrapped in professional conjecture.

THE BASIC LAW AND UNIFICATION

After two world wars, amid occupation by three powers, and facing a separate East Germany, the writers of the 1949 West German constitution were well aware of impermanence. So they allowed for future change by giving their document the temporary name of Basic Law, recognizing in the preamble the transitional nature of the document, and including two provisions for unification with East Germany and with other territories once under the German flag. When, after forty years, unification became a reality, the choices made under those two provisions define the new constitutional reality (see Wallach and Francisco 1992).

Under the terms of Article 146 unification would have required a national referendum, including a referendum on the resulting new constitution. In effect the article encompassed the creation of a new, more permanent, Germany.

Article 23, which became the actual article of unification, implied piecemeal absorption of eastern territory and thus did not necessarily require a new constitution or a national referendum. It provided for accession of individual eastern *Länder* (states) by the western German Federal Republic.

From the November 9, 1989, break in the Berlin Wall to the March 1990 federal elections in the German Democratic Republic, while unification was still very much in question, both articles were discussed publicly and in the halls of government. Article 146 was considered the expected path by those who thought unification would be a matter of serious negotiation between two relatively equal sovereign powers. Social Democrats in the West even dreamed that this would be the opportunity to transform status quo features of the Basic Law that they had long resented. But by July of 1990, when the first unification steps took place, Article 23 was perceived as the most desirable path toward progress. Then interior minister Wolfgang Schäuble, in his book, *Der Vertrag*, points out that as early as January 1990 he had promoted the benefits of rapid unification and simple adaptation inherent in Article 23. He was not only persuaded that neither East Germans nor West Germans, had the patience to await the writing of a new constitution: he was also convinced that the negotiation and politics of convening a constitutional convention and holding a referendum could destabilize the political, economic, and social conventions in both parts of Germany to the point where even unification might fail (Schäuble 1992b, 55).

Once the DDR elections gave a majority of parliamentary seats to the Christian Democratic associated parties, the question of Article 146 took a back seat. The implementation of Article 23 dominated all treaty negotiations until the October 6 unification took effect.

Pressures for a Referendum

It is not that Article 146 was forgotten. Even Schäuble occasionally raised the threat of that route in his negotiations. But it had become necessary to consider immediate needs and long term pressures separately. If the public was to have a plebiscitary voice, the argument went, this could still be achieved after unification under Article 23. But in light of the economic decline and public impatience in the East, unification, the governments agreed, should take place as soon as possible. Schäuble was able to underscore this argument to his cabinet colleagues with figures on the large numbers of East German citizens resettling in the West (1992b, 77-78).

So the progress toward an Article 23 unification was paralleled with continued discussions about a new constitution. Not only were the advantages of a popularly based constitution evident to politicians and citizens alike; discussions of reforms in the Basic Law were tactically useful in detracting active reformers and publicly useful in promoting discussion of the character of the established charter.

Revisionists in the West understood the opportunities. More conscious of democratic pressures than the public of 1949, and fully capable of effective organization, they encouraged media discussion of abortion law and property rights, claims to governmental support, and desires for more participatory decision making.

Abortion was an especially relevant topic. It was legal in the East, but largely prohibited in the West by a well-known 1975 decision of the Constitutional Court. The Court had applied the Article 2 right-to-life provision of the Basic Law to prevent the then Social-Liberal government from decriminalizing abortion in the first trimester under Section 218a of the Criminal Code (39 BVerfGE 1). This promoted feminist mobilization in the West through simple reference to "Article 218" (see Mushaben 1989) and it provided an inequality-of-women argument for those in the East who were opposed to unification

The equality of women and the social benefits they received in the East fostered other constitutional arguments. Should the equality provisions of Article 3 not have more force? Had the court given sufficient respect to the complaints of single mothers? Should the government be required to provide day-care facilities, job opportunities for mothers, and guaranteed social services?

As we will see in the analysis of the two unification treaties, a comprehensive social agenda was incorporated into the negotiations. Rights to jobs, education, living quarters, and use of public property were all part of the political and constitutional discussion.

The authority of the Constitutional Court was also questioned. For the opportunity to reconsider the implied conservatism of that Court was not lost on promoters of change. Ever since the first important decision of that Court, in the *Southwest State case* (1 BVerfGE 14), a doctrine of cohesive interrelationship joined with one of a hierarchy of articles seemed to have bound the court in a nonactivist position.[1] Discussion of how to counteract this situation has included a suggestion that the court receive specific directions to consider articles in isolation as well as more moderate suggestions on changing the means of Court appointment to give Social Democratic state governments a greater role. Since the concept of stultification through allegiance to doctrinal cohesiveness is not easily explainable to the public, this issue has reached voters through proposals for referenda that could overrule the court. As a result unification provided opportunities for the kinds of populist approaches that are well known to Americans.

Other constitutional issues raised at one point or another included codified recognition of social, economic, and environmental goals (Häberle 1990, 247-254), more direct forms of democratic participation, a presidential form of government, and greater autonomy for the states. The question of federalism ultimately became basic to the ongoing discussion of unification and continues to be important. It involves issues of autonomy, dependence, and the responsibility of well-to-do states to aid those less wealthy. Insofar as the upper parliamentary house, the Bundesrat, gained strength with the Unification Treaty the states gained power. In addition issues of state (*Land*) responsibility emerged when the choice between Berlin and Bonn as capital was resolved and when the Kohl government tried to pressure the Social Democratic government of Brandenburg.

Discussion of these particularities and others has often been separated from discussion of whether there should be a new constitution and a referendum. As the following sections indicate, resolutions to some of the constitutional problems have been established, but interest in a referendum declines. Not only did the rush to an Article 23 unification sidetrack the referendum issue, but the Unification Treaty procedures for dealing with constitutional issues, joined with reminders about negative Weimar referenda experiences, have justified lessened effort to rewrite the Basic Law (Stern 1992b, 27-30; Schiedermair 1992).

Pressures That Prevented a Referendum on Unification

Once the March 18, 1990, DDR election had demonstrated convincing support for unification and for Christian Union oriented guidance, the issue of method was both determined and placed in the arena of party competition. For the Christian Union parties of the West, facing a national election in December, an early unification, favoring their party, was deterministic. For the Social Democrats, as well as the successor to the eastern Communist parties, the Party for Democratic Socialism (PDS), a constitutional referendum was the best opportunity to reform a unification dominated by the status quo perspectives of the Federal Republic. In those late spring months of 1990 Green Party opposition to unification and Social Democratic efforts to slow it down were identified with Article 146 initiatives.

Meanwhile western tutelage of DDR prime minister de Maiziere and the organization of negotiations by Interior Minister Wolfgang Schäuble inexorably led to the Article 23 procedures. Schäuble writes that western satisfaction with the Basic Law, combined with eastern interest in a rapid unification, was so overwhelming that his attention quickly passed from the choice between Article 23 and Article 146 unification to the question of what exceptions to immediate imposition of western law, in the East, were necessary (Schäuble 1992a).

Thus the two treaties he negotiated implemented Article 23 and then abolished it. In a sense he was well aware that the successful acceptance of those treaties reduced any felt need for an Article 146 constitutional convention or referendum.

THE UNIFICATION TREATIES

The first of the unification treaties, the Treaty Establishing a Monetary, Economic and Social Union,[2] provided for Article 23 procedures to integrate the property law and economic instruments of the then two Germanys and for reform of the welfare institutions that would undergird these instruments. Abolishment of non "social market" conventions in the DDR constitution and law was introduced in the beginning of the Treaty, and each country agreed to change any legislation that interfered with the full implementation of western currency, property law, environmental law, and banking institutions in the DDR. An arbitral tribune, as well as the Court of Justice of the European Community, would settle major disputes, and where possible local courts would settle local difficulties. Ultimately the governments of the two Germanys were given joint responsibility to overcome obstacles.

The social and welfare provisions countenanced full future unification and recommended that although the East German government could continue current practices, it would strive to adapt these to western conventions.

On September 28 the second treaty, The Unification Treaty, was signed. It deals with most of the pertinent legal and constitutional issues or provides timelines for resolving them. In the process it significantly amends the Basic Law and effectively makes it a permanent constitution (Stern 1992b). Most notably the phrase regarding the transitional nature of the document, in the preamble, is replaced by references to the responsibility of the German people and the interest in serving "world peace" and "a united Europe," along with the statement "This Basic Law is thus valid for the entire German People" (Art. 4, Sec. 1 of the Unification Treaty).[3]   Article 51 of the Basic Law is rewritten to empower the new states and localities of the former DDR with constitutional authority and to reorganize the upper house of the Parliament to account for the new states. An Article 143 is added to the

Basic Law to allow treaty-defined exceptions to the constitution until December 1992 and in some cases December 31 of 1995.

For the purposes of this chapter the most important changes are in Articles 23 and 146. Once the first is recognized as the instrument of unification, it is abolished to meet the fears of Poland and other eastern neighbors that the constitution provides for a new "*anschluss*." Article 146 is rewritten to account for a completed, rather than a prospective, unification. It reads: "This Basic Law, which is valid for the entire German people following the achievement of the unity and freedom of Germany, shall cease to be in force on the day on which a constitution adopted by a free decision of the German people comes into force" (Art. 4, Sec. 6 of the Unification Treaty).

The question of whether a referendum will be necessary under Article 146 is left for future amending procedures. Other matters to be dealt with by future amendments include the restructuring of the relationship between Berlin and Brandenburg[4] and further development of the relations of the states to the federal government (art. 5).

These formalistic changes to the Constitution are only two pages of the treaty. Most of the document concerns law, property, and adjustment in social and governmental institutions. Where DDR courts had settled prior claims, the decisions are recognized by the Treaty. So are treaties and obligations of the DDR government. But where there is a contradiction between the current applicability of a DDR court decision and unified German law, appeal to the courts is possible. In most instances, however, the united legislature is instructed to evolve procedures and standards of adjustment. Only on some of the most important issues does the treaty provide precise guidelines or deadlines for bringing about integration of laws.

A potentially thorny problem that was temporarily resolved by the treaty, more permanently resolved two years later, and still divides the nation, is abortion. It is the topic of Section 4 of Article 31. The treaty requires that a solution for the problem of "the protection of human life" be found by December of 1992. It also provides for the establishment of "advice centers" to aid prospective mothers. But it allows each part of Germany to continue to treat abortion as has been done thus far, until the determination resolving the differences has been reached. For women in the former West Germany this continued the prevention of abortion, while the women of the former East Germany could continue to have them. What was not resolved was whether women of the West, who had abortions in the East, could be prosecuted.[5]

Where the legislature was not given a deadline to provide a solution the treaty establishes a point at which the support of day-care centers or rent controls disappear. For taxes it provides a series of transitional dates.

For the purposes of this chapter it is important to point out that there are practically no problem resolutions officially left to the courts. On a few property issues arbitrators have defined responsibilities. But even Chapter 5, which concerns the "Administration of Justice," leaves most responsibility to the *Länder* and their parliamentary and bureaucratic bodies, rather than the courts.

Appropriate as this is in a parliamentary nation with a codified legal system, where bureaucracies administer law that is democratically determined, it contradicts the idea of judicialization. Nevertheless an American observer might suggest that enough is left indefinite to provide for court decision making. Even where definiteness seems evident, areas such as the unequal support of financial institutions leave room for the expression of constitutional authority. Constitutional Court might have potential authority. In Germany legislators and state governments can bring constitutional cases that they feel contradict their understanding of the Basic Law. Every citizen has the right to bring "civil liberties" cases (Kommers 1989). But the introduction of the new Article 143 prevents most such litigation. Furthermore, the tradition of the court thus far has been to decide issues in terms of constitutional consistency, rather than to play a major mediating role (Wallach 1991). As this chapter will continue to demonstrate, the elected branches are not ready to give it other responsibilities.

In effect the treaty clearly places responsibilities in the *Land* or federal governments, or requires that laws and their administration be within the demands of the European Community. Within such requirements there is ample opportunity to bring individual difficulties to the courts. But in a system where cases are considered unique and thus there is little regard for precedents, even decisions on such cases have a limited impact on generalized decision making.

In Germany the states administer most of the laws, including the laws of the federal government. As a result consistency in bureaucratic administration is respected and the need for court determination of responsibilities is restrained. Attachment 1 of the treaty directly addresses this point. It provides for *Land* supervision of courts and carefully notes where federal courts can interject their authority in issues affecting the transition to full acceptance of federal law. In chapter 3 of the attachment detailed directions are given on manning courts, removing cases from or adding cases to their dockets, and introducing the authority of states' attorneys. Though it describes extensive procedures for upholding judgments by courts of the Democratic Republic, this Chapter of the Attachment gives the states' attorneys high responsibility for determining if reconsideration's should come before post unification courts. So far as those courts are concerned, the appropriate chapters of the law under which they can make determinations and even the reductions of penalties allowable to former DDR citizens without sufficient funds are prescribed.

The only point on which the treaty directly affects the Constitutional Court concerns the requirements for membership. The attachment amends the 1985 law on the requirement that members hold law degrees (963).

In the sensitive area of bureaucratic management, one that easily could have been left to the courts, the treaty provides a commission controlled by the president of the Bundestag to mediate differences (chap. 2, Problem Area A, sec. 3, 1150).

Only such relatively minor (but currently thorny) issues as the treatment of foreigners residing in DDR territory are specifically to be resolved by court direction (chap. 2 of supp. 2, Problem Area B, sec. 3, 1151).

In common-law nations property is one of the greatest areas of litigiousness. Where such litigiousness might arise in a unified Germany there are extensive guidelines for civil procedures to accommodate it. But every effort is made to prevent this by the establishment and codification of the responsibilities of the trustee for the state property of the former DDR. In an office established by the treaty for economic unification, the trustee is given primary responsibility for resolving disputes in the Unification Treaty. In the second supplement the office of the trustee is further given direction on property that cannot be properly disposed of. In effect the two treaties strive to make the bureaucratic determinations of the trustee as final as possible and thus serve to prevent judicial action (see Stein 1992a).

The logic of the two treaties determines many of the issues of integration, assigns particular problems to specific bureaucracies or newly established offices, and provides deadlines for resolving open issues. The decisional responsibility for these unresolved issues is clearly left with the legislature. Problems are not evaded in either treaty, and no more than the necessary room for political debate is left open. Wolfgang Schäuble seems to have furthered these results by persuading the conferees that only by establishing agreement on sensitive issues could they hope to gain the two-thirds majority in the two houses of parliament that was necessary to amend the constitution (1992b, 124-29). In preparation for this effort he had already consulted the relevant ministries (1992, 90-92). As the chief western negotiator he also notes, in an article on the implementation of unification, that he was concerned with bringing the differing interests into firm agreements and felt the legal order of society *(rechtsordnung)* had to be secured (Schäuble 1992a, 234-36).

Whatever the intent, the political universe rarely guarantees that issues and solutions can be finally tied down. Even though the justices of the Constitutional Court were consulted about the organization of the treaty agreement on the first all-German election, they forced a new solution in a series of September decisions. But in terms of this chapter the respected structure for unification has prevented a number of potential difficulties.

THE CONSTITUTIONAL DEBATE AFTER THE UNIFICATION NEGOTIATIONS

The ink was not dry when the first debate arose. The Greens, some smaller parties, and Gregor Gysi, the leader of the Party for Democratic Socialism challenged the agreement on the first all-German election. They were justifiably concerned that parties could only be represented in Parliament if they surpassed a 5 percent threshold for all of Germany. It was an issue on which Schäuble had consulted the judges in Karlsruhe (1992b, 92-97). Nevertheless, whatever his understanding two months earlier, the Court expressed dissatisfaction with this part of the treaty. Because of the equality-of-votes provisions in the Basic Law, it only allowed the five percent threshold to apply separately in each part of Germany, with the exception that parties that had established all-Germany election pacts could have the elected portions of their list seated for all parts of Germany if they received 5 percent in either part.[6] With this election decision the Court not only established a role in the unification process, but it also demonstrated approval of special consideration for the East.

Though Schäuble might have appreciated judicial restraint on this issue, it is one of the few cases where he needed to worry about judicial authority. Other efforts to involve the Court have regularly been referred to competent, usually nonjudicial decisional bodies.

The Abortion Issue

An issue that only involved the Court two years later, but is an excellent example of the way unification problems could be resolved, is that of abortion. Under a deadline of the end of 1992, with religious and feminist groups demonstrating direct interest, a resolution was seemingly reached six months before the Unification Treaty deadline. It respected the opposition Roman Catholic-oriented Christian Democratic leaders had long held against allowing a division on abortion within the new Germany for longer than necessary.[7] But it took place without majority support from Christian Union delegates. On an issue on which party whips were not applied, thirty members of the "Christian" parties joined with Social Democrats, Free Democrats, Alliance 90-Green delegates, and PDS members to provide just under the two-thirds necessary for a constitutional amendment. Under the law abortion on demand would be available if performed by doctors during the first trimester, providing the women underwent a three day waiting period, and obligatory counseling.

The agreement was immediately challenged before the Constitutional Court by the Christian Union delegates who had opposed it. They referred to the previous Article 2 decision of the Court, and the primacy of Article 2.[8] In September the Court postponed the implementation of the decision and failed to come to a decision until May of 1993. It then decided the life of the fetus required that abortion be illegal, but neither doctors nor aborting females could be prosecuted for partaking in it. Their recommendations to the Parliament effectively barred laws that would allow government funding, including medical plans, to support abortion. As a judicial resolution this maintained respect for Roman Catholic ideals while satisfying one, but certainly not all, of the demands of feminists. It may even have reduced pressures for a constitutional amendment.

Other Constitutional Revisions

A Constitutional Commission has been formed to consider other open issues, which means the question of revision under Article 146 is on the table. Though the usual amendment procedure continues, there is renewed discussion of a national referendum. Offhand this is opposed by those westerners who are satisfied with what has developed (see Heigert 1992, 5). More concretely, it allows focus on financial, émigré, and social problems that have expanded since unification. And for academics and lawyers interested in the constitutional issues, the overall question of a new constitution is once again in the air.

Many recent articles, including those by Stern (1992b) and Blumenwitz (1991) strongly oppose change, especially change by means of a referendum. In addition Hartmut Schiedermair argues that the change in the preamble of the Basic Law makes it a permanent constitution, which is sufficiently respected by all who agreed to unification (1992), and in the same issue of *Die Politische Meinung* Josef Isensee argues that thought of change is primarily the province of extremists (1992). He warns that introduction of a plebiscite will automatically weaken the current Constitution, and if then there is not an overwhelming support for a new document the country will be permanently weakened (1992, 13-14). As he analyzes the unification debate and the debate for constitutional reform, they have become the outlet for naysayers in the SPD (1992, 12). In the more judicially oriented *Neue Juristische Wochenschrift* Reinhold Zippelius offers an even stronger case against a referendum on the Constitution. He argues that the ultimate support for a democratically written constitution is in the years of support provided by the citizenry. Such a confirmed constitution ultimately has more force than one created by a referendum representing a political moment. Thus the Article 79 amendment procedures best process the changes the public desires; a referendum offers too great an opportunity for an unwanted break with the past. He also takes the position that Article 23 should not have been abolished in light of the procedure whereby other successful democratic bodies such as the European Community and the United Nations expand their positive influence by added associationship, rather than by writing new charters (Zippelius 1991, 23).

AN ALTERNATE TO A NEW NATIONAL CONSTITUTION

In light of such articulate opposition to a new constitution and a referendum, as well as the little expressed public support for such a process, new methods for constitutional revision have been sought. The most interesting is the writing of a new constitution for the state of Brandenburg, the one territory of the former Democratic Republic that elected a Social Democratic government in the October 1990 state elections.[9] Developed by a multiparty committee, this constitution was submitted to the public in a June 14, 1993 referendum. It includes the possibility of referenda for special economic and political purposes, a guarantee of rights for citizens and foreigners that is stronger than that of the Basic Law, an espoused state commitment to environmental quality, and implied redistribution of wealth. As might be expected the CDU has used many of these points to request a postponement of the date of the referendum. It is the Christian Democratic position that the guarantee of rights that goes beyond those established in the Basic Law is unconstitutional and that the articulation of political goals such as those on the environment and citizen equality removes the goal-setting purpose of political parties ("Erneut Position bezogen," 1992). Especially irritating to them is a statement that "Every citizen owes everyone else a recognition of his or her worth." ("Union legt 'Eckwerte' im Verfaßungsstreit vor" 1992).

For those who support the Brandenburg efforts the potential implications on the Basic Law are not forgotten. The head of the Brandenburg Commission for rewriting the constitution argued against the Christian Democrats that ultimately the two constitutions have to come to harmony, but that he expected the Brandenburg document would be a model for changes to the federal document. He seemed to place special emphasis on the elements of voting rights for foreigners and the respect for human worth, which he finds support the purposes of the European Community (Thiessen 1992, 1). However, playing into these proposals were the very sensitive economic issues of preventing continuation of returned property and retribution payments where the productive use of the property would thus hinder further investment and financial development of the state (Bräutigam 1992).

Ultimately, the Brandenburg effort may be isolated by national politics and provide a series of new tests for the Federal Constitutional Court. Only if they gain SPD support in other states is it possible they will become a focus for further constitutional change. But as means for a state to influence national affairs they serve a unique function.

CONCLUSION

The immediate effect of the unification process has not expanded judicialization in Germany. For the most part, unification through accession to Federal Republic conventions under Article 23 of the Basic Law has continued the relationships of the bureaucracy and legal institutions that existed prior to 1989. This does not mean judicialization will not follow. The immediate results were gained through

1. Identification and immediate resolution of issues identified by pertinent ministries.
2. The setting of appropriate deadlines for differences not resolved.
3. Clear placing of responsibility for resolving open issues on the first national Parliament to be elected by all Germans.
4. A constitutional amendment justifying differing legal standards in the two parts of Germany during a transitional period.
5. The rearticulation of support for the possibility of a new constitution and a public referendum.
6. The ability of the parliamentary parties to come to terms on open issues.
7. A parliamentary tradition imposed on a Codified legal system that demands comprehensive laws and clear responsibility among decision makers.
8. A bureaucracy that is expected to administer politically determined regulations impartially and faithfully.

As the deadlines for the resolution of open issues pass, however, differences may result in new efforts to resort to nonelected forums. At that time the courts could become increasingly important. In addition, the current upheaval in the Federal Republic, which is increasing the Social Democratic majority in the upper house of Parliament and could even result in a grand coalition, portends additional pressure for a national referendum. The efforts in Brandenburg further make it evident that as independent means to resolve political difficulties are reached, the Constitutional Court may be forced to play an increasing role in resolving differences between the states and the national government.

This is especially likely on questions of economic responsibility, inequalities in social services, and the redistribution to the poorer states of tax moneys collected in the richer states.

Since Christine Landfried has also authored a chapter related to judicialization in Germany, I will say little more about other internal pressures for or against judicialization. However, in light of the Brandenburg effort to link constitutional revision to European Community interests, it is worth noting that a prime potential for judicialization is evident from that organization. As a body in which bureaucratic decision making supplants much political decision making, the Community leaves open contests on responsibility that will require court resolution.

In Germany divisions of responsibility are relatively clear. The federal and state governments have separate spheres of decision making, but the states are given integrative responsibility for administering government programs and most laws. Even the cities, especially their lord mayors, have broad powers, if they wish to exercise them, which do not require state or national oversight. Where bureaucracies have been established a conscious effort is made either not to create potential friction with other bureaucracies or to establish consultative bodies that will overcome differences. In addition the parliamentary provision of strong, unified parties eliminates another level of potential friction. All of this was respected by the writers and implementors of the unification treaties.

Such practices will not overcome the continued incapacity of the courts to resolve conviction-centered issues such as abortion, an incapacity the German Constitutional Court shares with the Supreme Court of the United States. However, political processing of such issues is also difficult. Therefore an aspect of judicialization worth studying further is where the lines are appropriately drawn between judicialization and political decision making. In Germany political decision makers, even on such highly charged issues as immigration, usually provide guidance, even if belatedly. The courts usually have not been prone to overrule them, and for this reason the public does not depend on the courts. It is a panorama distinct from that of the United States.

The German example may provide insight on the cultural and institutional factors that lend themselves to effective bureaucratization of decisions made. All such questions, though, lead to more fundamental issues concerning the relationship between institutions and political problem solving. Majority political decisions are typically supported in court. But minorities that lose political battles in majoritarian institutions have found constitutional guarantees effective means for mounting judicial challenges to majorities. Thus a parliamentary majority originally gained court victory on abortion, and other minorities have gained voting rights and taxing benefits in the Constitutional Court. Unification has exposed a variety of emotions that can lead to greater use of the courts. It is another possible path toward judicialization.

NOTES

1. Dispute over this point is evident among scholars. Donald Kommers, author of the seminal *The Constitutional Jurisprudence of the Federal Republic of Germany* (1989), has taken the position that the German Constitutional Court is highly activist. I take a relatively opposite view in "The West German Courts" (Wallach 1991).

2. All quotes are from the official translation provided by the German Information Center in New York City.

3. Translations are those supplied by the German Press Office in Bonn. The full treaty, with supporting documentation and ancillary protocols, was published as *Vertrag zwischen der Bundesrepublik Deutschland und der Deutschen Demokratischen Republik* by the Press and Information Office in Bonn in 1990.

4. In effect leaving open, if Berlin were not to be the national capital, the integration of those two states.

5. The author was doing research in the library of the Constitutional Court in Karlsruhe on the day this article was agreed to. Though he did not discuss it with any of the judges, he found that every employee who was asked thought the court would wish to allow prosecution of western women who had abortions in the East and were then arrested in the West under Article 218 of the Criminal Code.

6. *Vertrag zwischen der Bundesrepublik Deutschland und der Deutschen Demokratischen Republik über die Herstellung der Einheit Deutschlands*, 921-58.

7. During the final unification negotiations the abortion issue nearly buried resolution on the whole treaty when the Free Democrats and Social Democrats demanded a lengthening of the transition time and that the availability be based on where the abortion happened, not on where the woman was resident. The Christian Democrats were just as absolute in their demands that only women resident in the East be able to have abortions and that the transition period be as short as possible. The compromise provided the two-year transition period and the determination that the place of the abortion, not the residency of the woman having the abortion, would determine availability (Schäuble, 1992b:229-250).

8. In the South West State case the Court declared an amendment unconstitutional in light of larger constitutional principles (1 BVerfGE 14).

9. For materials on this effort, and for information on the procedure, I thank Gottfried Dietzel, former research director for the Federal Republic's Ministry of Health and Family, who now holds a similar position with the European Community Commission, after serving as special assistant to the minister-president of Brandenburg.

REFERENCES

Blumenwitz, Otto. 1991. "Braucht Deutschland ein neues Grundgesetz?"

Bräutigam, Otto. 1992. Statement of Brandenburg Minister of Justice Otto Bräutigam on March 13, 1992. Released by Press office of the State of Brandenburg *Aktuaelles der Woche*, March 19.

"Erneut Position bezogen." 1992. *Brandenburgishe Neueste Nachrichten*, March 1.

Guggenberger, Bernd, ed. 1991. *Die Verfaßungsdiskussion im Jahr der deutschen Einheit*. Munich: Karl Hanser Verlag.

Häberle, Peter. 1990. "Verfaßungspolitik für die Freiheit und Einhet Deutschlands: Ein Wissenschaftlischer Diskussionbeitrag im Vormärz 1990." *Juristenzeitung* 45, no. 8:289-307.

Heigert, Hans. 1992. Article in *Süddeutsche Zeitung*, March 11, 1992. Translated and reprinted in *The German Tribune* no. 1508, March 20, 5.

Isensee, Josef. 1992. "Die Künstlich herbeigeredete Verfaßungsdebatte." *Die Politische Meinung*, no. 269 (April): 11-16.

Kommers, Donald. 1989. *The Constitutional Jurisprudence of the Federal Republic of Germany*. Durham, N.C.: Duke University Press.

Mushaben, Joyce M. 1989. "Feminism in Four Acts: The Changing Political Identity of Women in the Federal Republic of Germany." In *The Federal Republic of Germany at 40*, ed. Peter H. Merkl. New York:New York University Press, 76-109.

Schäuble, Wolfgang. 1992a. "Der Eirdgungsvertrag in seiner praktischen Bedwahrun." *Deutschland Archiv* 25 (March): 233-242.

———. 1992b. *Der Vertrag*. Stuttgart: Deutsche Verlags Anstalt.

Schiedermair, Hartmut. 1992. "Hände weg vom Grundgesetz!" *Die Politische Meinung*, no. 269 (April): 17-22.

"SPD, FDP, and Some Conservatives and Alliance '90 Members Reach Compromise on Abortion Issues." 1992. *The Week in Germany*, May 15, 1.

Stern, Klaus, ed. 1992a. *Deutsche Wiedervereinignung: Die Rechtseinheit.*

———. 1992b. "Eine neue Verfaßung?" *Die Politische Meinung*, no. 268, March, 27-30.

Thiessen, Uhich. 1992. "Brandenburger schreiben am Grundgesetz mit." *Märkishe Oderzeitung*, March 23, 1.

"Union legt 'Eckwerte' im Verfaßungsstreit vor." *Der Tagesspiegel*, March 23, 8.

Vertrag zwichen der Bundesrepublik Deutschland und der Deutschen Demokratischen Republik. 1990. Bonn: Press and Information Office.

Wallach, H. G. Peter. 1991. "The West German Courts." In *Judicial Activism in Comparative Context*, ed. Kenneth M. Holland. New York: St. Martin's.

———, and Ronald A. Francisco. 1992. *United Germany.* Westport, Conn.: Greenwood Press.

Zippelius, Reinhold. 1991. "Quo vadis Grundgesetz?" *Neue Juristische Wochenschrift* 44 (January 2): 23.

The Smaller Democracies

19.

Sweden

BARRY HOLMSTRÖM

Has judicial power really expanded in Sweden? Has politics in Sweden really become more judicialized? An affirmative answer to this query presupposes some preliminary clarification of what we are talking about when we say that politics is judicialized. As a matter of fact, I would argue that dejudicialization in one respect has prompted judicialization in another.

The term judicialization can denote at least three distinct phenomena. From a public-administration point of view it can refer to the manner of dealing with matters in the state apparatus. The juridical procedure—or legalistic, to give it a slightly negative touch—has strengthened its hold on activities. Administrative behavior is permeated by procedural forms and techniques drawn from legal processes. The prototype is the impartial, rule-applying judge passing "sentences" or deciding "cases" brought before him by "litigants." The scope for discretionary action is narrow. This model of a Weberian inclination is closely linked to a hierarchical organizational structure and a basic conception of citizens as subjects.

A second and closely related meaning of judicialization takes note of education and training. We can call it the sociological conception. What about the rise or fall of a distinct type of public official, raised in the faculties of law and trained in public or private legal work? What about the professional basis of the pressure group personnel? And to what extent is the body of elected representatives, the Riksdag in Sweden, populated by people educated in law?

A third aspect focuses on control of the executive and legislative branches of the state by the judiciary. Judicialization means that the rule of law is increasingly attributed to the activities of the genuinely political branches of the state. Political activity and political decisions are increasingly bound to comply with the legal and constitutional rules as interpreted by the ordinary courts or a special court. Even the representatives of the people, chosen by them in general elections and politically responsible to them in the next contest, are subject to judicial review. Their decisions, ordinances, decrees, and acts can be quashed by a court verdict.

From the point of view of democratic theory, this last conception is the most interesting. My argument in this chapter will be that judicialization in this third sense has taken place in Sweden. However, at least part of the explanation of this slow but significant judicialization process is dejudicialization of politics in the other two senses.

THE LEGALISTIC SWEDISH STATE

A distinctive feature or the Swedish state apparatus before the democratic—and social democratic—era was its juridical or legalistic appearance. It looked like a machine staffed by legally trained people dealing with public matters in a formal, rule-applying manner. The scope for discretionary decision making was small.

The cabinet with its ministries resided at the top of this apparatus. At the end of World War I the principle of parliamentary supremacy was finally established, followed by the extension of the right to vote to all adult citizens. But still, this democratic government spent much of its time with administrative matters, investigating and deciding on complaints about decisions made by boards and county agencies, or giving permissions of various sorts. To the extent that politics was part of this undertaking, it was wrapped in a legalistic robe.

Recruitment stipulations reflected this character of public affairs. For members of the government the old constitution stipulated that at least two ministers (of about fifteen at that time) should be qualified jurists (Constitution of 1809, sec. 6). Prior to 1964 law degrees were formally required for all employees in the ministries and for the higher posts in many departments and boards.[1] This requirement was slowly eroded by exemptions before its abolition. But, even in the 1970s more than 50 percent of the director-generals (*generaldirektör*) and about one-third of the principal assistant secretaries (*byråchef*) were graduates of the faculties of law (Christofferson 1983, 169). At the ministries 84 percent of the top civil servants and 63 percent of the total were law graduates in 1964. In 1981 the proportion of law graduates was still rather high for the top civil servants, 70 percent. But now only one-third of all the ministry employees were law graduates (Christofferson 1983, 175; see *Series of Public Reports, Government Committees* [hereafter SOU] 1953, 16, 116-127 for the proportion of law graduates in 1953).

In the old two-chamber Riksdag,[2] replaced in 1970 by a unicameral parliament, the Upper House was densely populated by state employees from the higher echelons. Prior to the electoral reforms around 40 percent of its members were state employees and about one-third were law graduates. Permanently about 10 percent of its deputies were judges; in Sweden judges are not forbidden to participate in electoral politics. In the Lower House—before the democratic reforms heavily dominated by farmers—civil servants constituted about 25 percent of the deputies. About 10-15 percent of its members were law graduates and 6-8 percent were judges (*Studier* 1936; Sköld and Halvarson 1966, 463, 465).

On the other hand, private lawyers have never formed a prominent part of the Riksdag; there have been only a few of them at a time (*Studier* 1936; Sköld and Halvarson 1966, 463, 465). This accurately illustrates the character of the predemocratic Swedish state. The judicial element of the state powers rather constituted more a *Beamtenherrschaft* of the German type than a bourgeois or liberal state of the revolutionary French or U.S. type.

What about the courts? The old constitution was framed in the separation-of-powers fashion, but its judicial power was definitely not meant to function as a check on the other branches. At most it was seen in the Montesquieuan vein, as an autonomous branch but with no political functions whatsoever. In fact the judicial branch was not even completely separated from the executive. The Supreme Court judged in the name of the king. For more than a century the king in person had a right to participate and cast two votes. For some decades even the first minister of the time (*justitiestatsministern*) was a member of the Supreme Court (Malmgren 1965, 25; Herlitz 1957, 217; Stjernquist 1989, 108). The administrative and the judicial branches of the state just slowly and casually emerged as two specialized and distinct parts, both originating from the same executive power, that of the King. No wonder that judicial review of administrative decisions did not stand out as an acute necessity.

However, to ensure system and coherence in the complex of laws the Instrument of Government provided that bills had to be reviewed by the Supreme Court before they were passed to the Riksdag. In 1909 this judicial preview, resembling that of the Conseil d'etat in France, was transferred to a new body, the Law Council.[3] The Council was staffed by justices from the Supreme Court and a new Supreme Administrative Court (*regeringsrätten*) (Constitution of 1809, sec. 21).

This preview function is still part of the Swedish legislative process, even though the Law Council no longer is an exclusive auxiliary to the government; today minorities in the Riksdag standing committees can refer bills to the Law Council for judicial preview.[4] The Council's dicta are not binding. Insofar far as they concern legal technicalities, they are regularly accepted, less so in evaluative matters bordering on expediency or balancing of interests (Constitution of 1974, chap. 9, sec. 18; Riksdag Act, chap. 4, sec. 10).[5]

If judicial review of administrative action was scanty, judicial review of legislation was nonexistent. Long before parliamentary supremacy was finally accepted, established practice held that the courts could not quash laws. Historical antecedents had it rather the other way round: if a court found inconsistencies between the law and a fundamental law, it was bound to ask the legislators to "declare the law."[6] This power of interpretation was later transferred to the Supreme Court, but it was not understood as a right to invalidate laws or set them aside in specific cases (Malmgren 1934, 179-82; Stjernquist 1990, 108).

Obviously, this did not settle the question. But as the fundamental laws mainly contained rules of procedure—no Bill of Rights was included—it was mostly a theoretical problem as long as the legislative powers, the Riksdag and the king (government), did not quarrel. The courts, then, could take a narrow view. Like their French and British counterparts they refused to engage in constitutional review of legislation, comforting themselves with reviewing the correctness of the never-ending ritual of countersignatures, seals, promulgations and publications. It is true that public law scholars showed some interest in judicial review. But at most they defended the view that courts were authorized to void legislation made in flagrant contradiction to explicit rules of competence or procedure in the Constitution (Westerstahl 1941, 114-125; Stjernquist 1990, 109-111).

THE DEMISE OF THE LEGALISTIC STATE

Today things look different. Public activities have changed and radically decreased the relative importance of administrative techniques styled in the judicial fashion. Of course, public activities are still authorized by law, statutory instruments, or decree, and public regulation penetrates more and more of society. But the manner of doing things and deciding matters is less influenced by judicial procedures than before. Welfare-state ambitions are often difficult to achieve by traditional rule-applying procedures. Steering by goals flourishes, giving authorities wide scope for discretionary action. The legal basis for action establishes frames and defines general principles rather than proving specified directives, automatically applicable to a case.

As a consequence the legal profession has gradually lost its hold on the state apparatus. This decline, relatively speaking, has occurred simultaneously with a transformation of the social structure of the Riksdag. Two general phenomena explain this "dejudicialization": the victory of democracy and the growth of public duties in the welfare state era.

Democracy widened and changed the recruitment base of the political elite. Still, legislators in Sweden are recruited mainly from the public sector. But these employees are no longer law graduates from the higher bureaucracy or the judicial branch. In the 1988-1991 Riksdag only twelve deputies (3.4 percent) were educated in law, and six of them were public officials (two judges, three prosecutors, and one local government administrator) (*Fakta om folkvalda* 1989). There is nothing left of the old civil-service deputies of the legal-bureaucratic sort. They have been supplanted by administrators of another bent, often from the lower strata, placed in regional or local administration. The administrators now dominant in the Riksdag also have different educational equipment, not necessarily academic.

This development clearly reflects the democratic breakthrough and the subsequent social democratic dominance in Swedish politics during the last six decades. One of the social democratic strongholds nowadays is the lower strata of the public sector employees (see Oskarsson 1990, 237).

At the same time this reflects the growth and change of the public sector. The jurists no longer monopolize higher posts in the civil service, and they are outflanked as the most numerous profession in the bureaucracy. They still dominate the very top posts in the ministries (see Christofferson 1983, 175), but this is next to inevitable. The small Swedish ministries are highly occupied with drafting legislation, trying appeals and granting permits. Activities like these virtually require people educated in law.

The slow but steady "dejudicialization" of the state in these respects—the recruitment of the legislative and the executive branches, the scope and character of public affairs—clearly occasioned a growing propensity to call for a more active role for the judicial branch proper. Judicialization in this respect, the possibility of court intervention and invalidation of administrative norms and decisions or legislative acts, in short, an active judicial power in a checks-and-balances system, will be the focus of the rest of this chapter.

THE RISE OF JUDICIALIZATION

To understand the process of judicialization it is important to have in mind the point of departure. No rules authorizing judicial review of legislation were laid down in the old constitution, in force 1809-1974. The courts, at least up to World War II, did not recognize such review and it was largely ignored in the political realm and challenged by legal scholars.[7]

Administrative review was permitted and eminently so since 1909 when the Supreme Administrative Court was installed. But judicial control of the executive was quite restricted. The main reason for creating the Administrative Court was the felt necessity to relieve the government from hearing and deciding on many complaints (Holmgren 1967, 209-210). Seen in this light it was only natural that government decisions could not be challenged in the new court. The court was a substitute for the government, not a check on it. The Administrative Court Act enumerated the appeals the court was authorized to hear. The rest remained a task for the government. The "catalogue" distributing cases between juridical and governmental deliberation has since been revised several times, mainly in order to relieve the government from dealing with cases of a primarily juridical character.

But the administrative and the judicial processes were intermingled in a rather confusing way. The Supreme Administrative Court was something of a head without a body. There was an old administrative court, the Fiscal Court of Appeal (Kammarrätten), which deal with taxes, fees, allowances, and the like. The possibility of appealing from this court to the Supreme Administrative Court was established. But in most cases the ancient right to petition the king had meant the right to appeal to higher authorities in the administrative hierarchy. Now a final appeal could become either a case for the government or for the Supreme Administrative Court, although, except in cases such as tax complaints, preliminary appeals were still to administrative bodies, not courts.

Not until the beginning of the 1970s was a complete administrative court system established. The old Fiscal Court of Appeal was transformed into a court of appeal covering the same ground as the Supreme Administrative Court and the latter became a genuine court of precedent. The number of courts of appeal is now four.

At the same time a number of administrative courts of first instance were created. Three different types of administrative courts were set up in each county, taking over tasks from the county administration and the county Tax Appeal Boards. In 1979 these courts were fused into one administrative court in each county. They were also completely separated from the county administration, as the head of the court was henceforth an independent judge and no longer a high county administrator (Wentz and Hermanson 1970; Stromberg 1990, 180-90).

Many items have since been transferred to the court system. But in spite of all these reforms the "mix" remains between administrative dealings with complaints and appeals and court dealings. For instance, an appeal can be dealt with first by the county administration and then, on appeal, by an Administrative Court of Appeal. However, once a case is placed in a court, it is not possible to appeal to an administrative board or to the government (Petersson and Soderlind 1992, 255).

Many countries distinguish between questions of law and questions of expediency, or appropriateness. The first are eminently for courts to decide, the second a job for the administration and the government. In the Swedish system of administrative appeals—the Swedish term is *besvär* (compare the German *Beschwerde*)—this distinction is of minor importance. The authorities deal with all aspects of the case, the ordinary courts with none.[8]

This mode is also followed when drawing the line between the Supreme Administrative Court and the government. All complaints concerning, say, driver's licenses or compulsory treatment are heard by the court, irrespective of the exact nature of the complaint. One can say that the court, and the government as well, deals with both juridical and political (expediency) matters. Of course, the goal when enumerating the appeals to be referred to the Supreme Administrative Court has been to make a divide along this line. Through the decades the separation has also been trimmed by the complementary method of stipulating in each specific act, or part of an act, where to proceed.

In any case, the plaintiff cannot choose to bring whatever he claims to be an illegal decision before an administrative court. The right forum for hearing appeals is strictly defined, and sometimes the final instance is not a court, regardless of the citizen's preference. The courts simply have no general competence to hear complaints or review administrative matters.

During the last decades, however, this absence of a general right to court proceedings has become a delicate problem. Sweden was one of the first states to ratify the European Convention for the Protection of Human Rights and Fundamental Freedoms. From the beginning individual applications under the convention were admitted, and since 1966 the jurisdiction of the European Court at Strasbourg has been recognized. Because the Convention has not yet been incorporated in Swedish law,[9] national judges are not authorized to use the convention's clauses as part of their *ratio decidendi*. Plaintiffs wanting to adduce the convention have to stick to the expensive and time-consuming European track. But now they have found their way to Strasbourg—sometimes with a little help from their friends, certain interest organizations.

At the end of 1990 Sweden had been found guilty of violations of the convention in fourteen cases. In nine of these the European Court found that Sweden did not protect the right to have a dispute concerning the determination of an individual's "civil rights and obligations" adjudicated by an independent and impartial tribunal (Article 6:1 of the convention). Three policy areas were particularly exposed: planning and building, restraint of industry and commerce, and social security.

For instance, Sweden was convicted in the *Sporrong-Lönnroth* case because the property holders could not get their dispute with the city administration of Stockholm tried in court. For more than a decade the city had been indecisive whether to use an expropriation permit or not, causing great damage to the property holders, who could not sell their property and were forbidden to build anything new (Judgment 1982-09-23, ser. A, no. 52. [see the similar cases 1989-10-25, ser. A, no. 163; 1990-06-28, Ser. A, no. 180A and no. 180B]). In another case the same clause was violated because a restaurant, having had its permission to serve liquor withdrawn, could not take court action against the authorities (Judgment 1989-07-07, Ser. A, no. 159).[10] In a third case the court invoked the clause when a mother, who had lost, in a lawsuit, the right to take care of her daughter was not permitted challenge in court the restrictions on her right to see the child set by the social authorities (Judgment 1989-06-22, Ser. A, no. 156).

These convictions, increasing in number, were embarrassing, and something had to be done. In 1988 the Riksdag approved of a new way to bring about a court trial. From then on private litigants were permitted to appeal to the Supreme Administrative Court if discontented with decisions hitherto finally made by the government or by an administrative board not headed by a judge.

However, this departure from the traditional way of differentiating between juridical and executive routes for appeals was counteracted by another rule that confined the review of the court to questions of law. The Supreme Administrative Court was authorized to judge only "if the decision violates a legal rule." In the *travaux préparatoires* (legislative history) the legislators explicitly stated as a fundamental presumption that the court would refrain from intervening in "political" questions of expediency, or "passing judgments of a markedly discretionary or political character" (Prop. 1987/88:69, 24, 26, 30).[11] Finally, the court could only quash the decision. If necessary, the case had to be remanded to the administration.

In sum, the development of the administrative system and the changed rules of procedure and competence have clearly extended the scope for judicial review of administrative and governmental action. Further, matters formerly decided by the executive branch have been transferred to the judiciary. Parts of these reforms are certainly most aptly characterized as a politicization of the judicial branch rather than the other way around. More "political" deliberation and judgment—discretionary action, questions of expediency, balancing of interests, deciding priorities—penetrate the business of the courts. Other parts, for instance the transfer of cases of a law-applying character, can even be said to dejudicialize the executive branch.

Nevertheless, it is also evident that the judiciary has strengthened its powers to check the activities of the executive. The legality of administrative and governmental decisions can now, with a few exceptions, be challenged in court. In this respect the expression "judicialization of politics" is convenient. The rule of law, that is, the legal bounds defining—and restricting—the activities of the state apparatus, has been emphasized and has been given teeth bite by this opening up for judicial review.

What about the politics behind these reforms? The government bills were accepted by the Riksdag without much controversy. It should be stressed, though, that the social democrats, in power most of the time, had the initiative. They were staunch defenders of democracy conceived as parliamentary or people's sovereignty, and they were deeply suspicious of judicial checks on the political branches. For them the main objective was to relieve the executive of routine business of minor political importance, in order to make it an effective machinery for political reform and government.

For bourgeois politicians, some of them law professors and very active, reforming the court system and checking the executive had a more ideological motivation.   They argued for a strengthening, or restoration, of the *Rechtsstaat*, which they thought was threatened by the social democrats.   The social democrats' zealous expansion of the welfare state, administered by a modern bureaucracy armed with wide discretionary powers, was a permanent thorn in the flesh to the political Right. These fundamental differences were more clearly demonstrated in the party dispute over judicial review of legislation or, more exactly, of legislative norms.

THE DEBATE OVER JUDICIAL REVIEW

The case for judicial review of legislation got a bad start. When put on the political agenda it was explicitly stated that it was necessary because of the democratic breakthrough. The intention was to stem the tide, to put a check on the Parliament and the government, now equally "infected" by the principle of popular sovereignty. In other words, judicial review was from the beginning, even by its proponent and initiator, presented as an antidemocratic reform.

The argument for judicial review of the American type was presented by a law professor and conservative politician, C. A. Reuterskiöld. "Democracy is the twin of autocracy," he wrote. "None of them can stand an independent and equal power, for both freedom is an abomination" (Reuterskiöld 1918, 70).[12] Naturally, he got no applause from the victorious parties that had struggled for decades, against the conservatives supported by the royal family, to obtain democracy.

The inclination of the dominant part of the victorious left, the social democrats, was rather the opposite of Reuterskiöld's. They were, for instance, deeply suspicious of the Law Council's preview of draft legislation, even though its opinions were not binding. The Law Council was depicted as a conservative bastion acting as a brake on social reforms. Several times members of the party proposed the abolishment of the Council or at least that its opinions should be strictly confined to legal matters. These projects were not realized, as the other part of the victorious left, the liberals, voted for the status quo (Algotsson 1992, chap. 2.2). At any rate, it was evident that Reuterskiöld's stand for the time being was completely out of date. For two decades judicial review of legislation remained in the dark.

Judicial review is intimately related to the existence of a justiciable bill of rights. If the constitution does not pronounce material rights for individuals against the state, judicial review is confined to procedural matters. Of course, these can be hotly disputed sometimes, but ordinarily the probability for intervention by the judiciary in highly political, or politicized, issues is rather low in these circumstances.

Characteristically for the political climate in Sweden the increasing interest in a bill of rights around World War II did not ignite a corresponding interest in judicial review of legislation. To the contrary, even in a proposal from the Conservative party, demanding an investigation into the possibility of incorporating a bill of rights in the Instrument of government, the party dissociated itself from combining such a reform with judicial review. The main argument was that one should protect the courts from getting involved in politics (Motion FK 1938, 12). The Standing committee on the Constitution agreed. It stated that judicial review of legislation neither existed—a clear rebuttal of certain law scholars' views that the courts in fact practiced judicial review of legislation[13]—nor should be admitted (*Standing Committee on the Constitution, Reports* [hereafter KU] 1938:16). The Riksdag did decide to demand an investigation, but in the resulting official report the investigators declined to take a stand on judicial review (SOU 1941:20, 16).[14]   Its return to the political agenda was incidental and a consequence of the work on a complete revision of the Constitution of 1809. During two decades governmental committees composed of representatives from the four big parties worked on the project that finally resulted in the Instrument of Government of 1974. Part of this work, admittedly perceived as a minor question, was devoted to the construction of a bill of rights and judicial review.

From now on it was evident that the stand on the issue of judicial review of legislative norms tended to follow the ordinary left-right dimension. The social democrats, in power for all but six years (1976-1982), were the skeptics, the liberals and the conservatives were favorable and the agrarians (Center Party), former coalition partners of the social democrats, were undecided. The development of constitutional politics and decisions can be described as a gradual erosion of the leftist position corresponding to the weakening of the parliamentary dominance of the social democrats.

In the official reports preceding the new constitution the social democrats acknowledged the courts' right to judicial review. This was a concession in order to get an unanimous report; initially they had demanded an explicit prohibition in the constitution (SOU 1972:15, 108). But the concession was very constrained. Judicial review was narrowly interpreted as a right to ignore rules in flagrant or obvious conflict with higher norms. Furthermore, it was only effective in the special case (*inter partes*).

The social democrats also stressed the point that no court had ever refused to apply an ordinary law[15] and that their acceptance of the convention rested on the belief that judicial review would remain a highly extraordinary court activity. Last but not least, as long as they controlled the Riksdag the social democrats blocked every attempt to add an article to the Instrument of Government transforming the recognized European Convention on Human Rights to written fundamental law.

In the bill proposing the new Instrument of Government the minister of justice argued that an article would give the wrong impression. The government did not want any change whatsoever in the practice of the courts, and the inclusion of certain rights and "fundamental aims of the activities of the community" were definitely not meant to be a weapon in the hands of an activated judiciary (Prop. 1973:90, 200-201).

In public speeches party representatives repeatedly stressed the point that these rights and aims, defining the very existence of a civilized democratic state, could survive and progress only if they were a vital part of political life proper, espoused by the political community. Judicial review tended to weaken this shared responsibility, making the protection of civil rights and democratic rule a business for the courts and implying that the elected representatives of the people were the presumptive crooks threatening these rights and freedoms. The social democrats revolted against such a "separation-of-powers state" and defended a representative and parliamentary democracy of the British type.[16]

The Instrument of Government was the result of a political compromise. The bourgeois parties accepted it in return for a promise that the committee inquiry would be pursued, aiming at the inclusion of an entrenched and encompassing bill of rights. Their common stand also signaled a growing convergence on the problem of judicial review. In a new official report presented in 1975 they had forced the social democrats to make new concessions. Unanimously the committee proposed an amendment to the Instrument of Government empowering—and obliging—the courts not to apply provisions contrary to higher norms, or provisions decided in violation of the procedure prescribed. But provisions stated in statutes or statutory instruments, viz. decided by the Riksdag or the government, could be set aside only if the violation was obvious (SOU 1975, 75, 47).

The concessions, however, did not survive the heavy criticism launched by the Confederation of Trade Unions and the social democratic press. The government abandoned its party fellows in the committee and returned to the old position (Algotsson 1987, 168-180). In the Riksdag debates Prime Minister Olof Palme defended the English, one might say the Rousseauan, version of democracy against an American and—as he thought—Montesquieuan conception modelled on the separation of powers theory (RD 1975/76:149, 136-41, 157-59, 162-63).

In the autumn of that year, 1976, after 44 years in power, the social democrats lost the elections and resigned. The new coalition government initiated constitutional reforms in line with the bourgeois parties' ambitions to strengthen the protection of fundamental rights and freedoms. To be sure, they had never formed a solid front on the matter of judicial review. But at least they could revive the unanimous position from the latest committee report. An amendment to the Instrument of Government was proposed, and now it showed that the social democrats, too, returned to the committee position. After the elections in 1979, when the coalition parties defended their majority position, the Riksdag finally approved the amendment (Algotsson 1987, chap. 5).

ESTABLISHING JUDICIAL REVIEW

The extended political process resulted in a constitutional recognition of the courts' right to exercise judicial review. As a matter of fact, this right holds for every public authority applying a legal rule, not only for the courts. What does this mean in the context of our query about the judicialization of politics in Sweden? First, one should note that in many countries, some of them with very active courts, judicial review is not recognized in the constitution at all. This power for the judicial branch has evolved by case law through decades or centuries to become established practice. The absence of a written clause is patently not the same as the absence of an extensive exercise of judicial review.

Second, a written clause establishing judicial review of legislation can be a restraint as well as a weapon. The Swedish case is a good illustration. The article reads as follows:

If a court, or any public organ, considers that a provision is in conflict with a provision of a fundamental law or with a provision of any other superior statute, or that the procedure prescribed has been set aside in any important respect when the provision was inaugurated, then such provision may not be applied. However, if the provision has been decided by the Riksdag or by the Government, the provision may be set aside only if the inaccuracy is obvious and apparent. (Instrument of Government, chap. 11, art. 14)

There are several restraints here keeping judicial review within narrow bounds. Due procedure must be violated "in any important respect" to justify court action. As to legislative norms decided by the Riksdag or the government the violation or inaccuracy must be "obvious and apparent" to justify court exception from the norm. Putting the government in the same privileged position as the Riksdag makes this a very strong restriction, indeed, seemingly peculiar to Swedish legislation. The court judgment, finally, is narrowly confined to the special case and does not invalidate the provision as such.

Furthermore, in Swedish jurisdictions intentions expressed and statements made in the *travaux préparatoires* are important sources for a court's reasoning and judgment. Here you find more restrictions, reminiscences of the old social democratic—and Center Party—position. The new majority coalition was obliged to accept these formulas to get an unanimous stand; unanimity between the four big parties is a cherished value when changing the constitution.

In the commission report, the bill and the report from the Standing committee on the Constitution, it is clearly stressed that codification must not be interpreted as a change in existing practice. To the contrary, the intention was precisely to codify this extremely cautious practice (SOU 1978:34, 109; prop. 1978/79, 195; KU 1978/79:39, 10-14). The Riksdag committee added an "important advantage": that codification would be an obstacle to the evolution and expansion of the activity of the courts (KU 1978/79:39, 13). A judge reading this would hardly take it as an invitation to intrusive scrutiny.

Nevertheless, in spite of these reservations and statements I will argue that political life in fact has been influenced by this constitutional development. There has been some sort of a mental shift, partly caused by the adjustments of the legal system just described, opening up for an accelerated judicialization of politics. Codification of the right to judicial review has probably played a minor role. But the present focus on individual rights and the rule of law in political discourse, combined with some other changes in the conditions of politics in Sweden, have definitely lifted legal reasoning, the courts, and the judiciary out of the political darkness. I will give some evidence, admittedly scanty, for this conjecture.

The first observation concerns the preview activity of the Law Council. The new Instrument of Government, with its extended chapter on fundamental rights and freedoms decided in 1979, has forced—I am not inclined to say invited—the Council to deliberate on the conformity between draft legislation and fundamental law. Karl-Göran Algotsson has made a thorough analysis of the opinions of the Council during the 1980s. He concludes that deliberation on the Constitution and rights reasoning has increased, even if there are few cases where the Council states that a draft is incompatible with higher law provisions. The increasing number of convictions and pending cases at Strasbourg have influenced the Council's deliberations in the same manner (Algotsson 1992, English summary).

The most well-known case is the Law Council's observations on a new planning and building act, in which it referred to the Instrument of Government as well as the European Convention on Human Rights. The opinion aroused a heated debate on property rights and delegated legislation, but also on the role of courts and the judiciary in democratic decision making (see Algotsson 1992, chap. 5.6). The government made some changes in the bill to disarm and circumvent the Council's remarks, but this did not satisfy the bourgeois parties, which made heavy use of the observations of the legal authority. The government, lacking a majority of its own, was forced to negotiate and to make further concessions in the Riksdag (Prop. 1985/86:1; BoU 1986/87:1). This shows that even an opinion from a seemingly innocent advisory body can have important political repercussions. Anticipation of the Law Council's views has become an important element of political deliberations in ministries and government when preparing new legislation. The convictions of Sweden by the Strasbourg court, as well as an increasing number of complaints and cases pending, have had the same effect. As to exposition in the mass media, some of the Strasbourg cases have been highlights. Scoring political points by way of court action is becoming an attractive political option.

My second observation pertains to a sensational court ruling. The constitutional constraints imposed on judicial review of Riksdag acts appear next to insurmountable, and the Swedish courts have shown no eagerness to strengthen their power of review. But the political climate, fueled by the regular and more comprehensive scrutiny of the Law Council, has apparently loosened some chains. For the first time a Swedish court last year ruled that an act of Parliament "obviously and apparently" contradicted a fundamental law provision—the right to compensation for expropriated property. The court consequently refused to apply the law (*Linkopings tingsratt, fastighetsdomstolen*, Dom. 1991-11-13, no. DF 33).

The disputed law, abolishing certain exclusive fishing rights of some land owners, was controversial, as most property rights legislation. The Law Council made some observations and suggestions that were ignored by the government. But the Council certainly did not argue that the proposals obviously and apparently contradicted the Constitution. The court of first instance took another stand, repudiating the Law Council justices from the supreme courts and, in practice if not by intention, sided with the political opposition. Such boldness—or lack of good judgment—would have been unthinkable a decade ago.

This court judgment is truly exceptional, and it was later reversed on appeal. But my third observation implies that it can become more common. Seen as a probing action directed against the monistic conception of democratic rule espoused by the social democrats, the prospects of success are better than ever. Since October 1991 the Riksdag has had a nonsocialist majority. Four bourgeois parties form a minority government with the conservatives as the dominant party, holding the premiership and the ministry of justice.

This government has made a rapid start. It appointed two committees to consider constitutional changes. One of these committees is directed to report on the possibility of giving certain rights, cherished by the bourgeois parties better protection. The committee is also authorized to consider an extended use of judicial review of legislative norms as well as of administrative decisions. The government explicitly stated that the obvious-and-apparent condition protecting Riksdag and government provisions was too strong. It ought to be abolished or, at least softened. Finally, the government ordered an analysis of the constitutional court alternative (Dir. 1991:119).

This shows that the time perhaps is ripe for further movement toward greater court latitude to intervene in matters formerly defined as political. The social democrats have protested, but their countermove does not seem well advised in the long run. They have presented a list of their own, containing favorite rights and policy aims (statement by the representatives of the party in the committee, R&D 1992, no. 7, 4). Of course, the social democrats strongly oppose every attempt to activate the courts. Their proposals are meant to stall the bourgeois parties' propensity to use this technique to sanctify matters highly political in nature. But their strategy does not hit the heart of the matter: intervention in matters political by an unelected and unaccountable profession, the judiciary.

The social democrats can certainly block the constitutional court alternative, which is not very attractive for some bourgeois parties either. The slow but steady drift toward an encompassing judicial review seems to continue, however. The Center party public representative, for instance, has recently stated that he can vote for the abolishment of the obvious-and-apparent clause (Bertil Fiskesjo, in *Forfattningsdomstol och lagprovning* 1991, 12). This party has traditionally sided with the social democrats as the skeptics of judicial review.

CONTINUING JUDICIALIZATION

I will conclude with some general reflections on why I think judicialization of politics will continue and perhaps accelerate. I will ignore the probably most crucial event, Sweden's application for membership in the European Community, and pursue a line of argument closely related to the domestic development outlined above.

In the 1960s the late Norwegian scholar Stein Rokkan described the political system of his country as twofold. On the one hand, it was similar to that in other pluralist democracies: power and goods were distributed through the regular system of party politics, elections, and parliamentary politics. Here numbers are crucial. On the other hand, politics in Norway was characterized by the high degree of interest organization. Each important interest had an organization of its own. Initially these organizations acted as pressure groups, trying to influence the actors making politics by means of "the numerical channel." Parallel to this, however, they gradually developed corporatist forms of interest promotion and realization: exclusive rights to negotiate on behalf of certain interests, representation in public bodies, and participation in the implementation of public politics (Rokkan 1966).

This picture of the political system holds good (perhaps it is even truer for Sweden). It was recently confirmed once again in a book called *The Corporate State* (Rothstein 1992).[17] But there are signs that old corporate arrangements and networks are moldering. An extensive research project on the power structure of Sweden, now completed, amply demonstrates the complexity and vagueness of the present patterns of influence.[18]

One of the new channels of influence, I will maintain, is the judicial one. Court litigation on violations of rights and freedoms is usually depicted in terms of individuals fighting for their rights against an insensitive and inflexible state. There are indeed cases of that kind. But there are indications that it is also organized interests, frustrated by the ineffectiveness of the traditional pressure and negotiation types of influencing public policies, that are probing a new political strategy.

In the most conspicuous case, the *Sporrong-Lönnroth* litigation at Strasbourg, the real plaintiffs behind the scenes were the organized Swedish building and housing interests. Their organization had in fact chosen the case, convinced the owners to proceed, selected the lawyers, and financed the process (see Brunfelter, head of the action, in Sundberg 1985). In the property rights case resulting in the first exception to an act of Parliament, the plaintiff apparently made use of legal counsel provided by the farmers' union. A recent tax case, finally, highlighted by the media, seems to have been directed by organized business interests.[19]

The same phenomenon can in fact be found in the social security sector. Here the social democrats themselves have encouraged the participation of interest groups by using the legal technique of codifying general aims and objectives, giving them the form of positive individual rights: the right to health care, the right to a decent dwelling, the right to education, and so forth. In hard economic times this turns out to be declaratory or symbolic politics, empty words. But the rights talk implies that you can get your fair share by complaining or, in the last resort, by court litigation. The organization of the mentally retarded, for instance, has traveled the court route, with good results, in order to promote the right, established in law, to an owned dwelling for this group of people. In case after case administrative courts have convicted local public authorities for their failure, in part due to the shortage of dwellings, to comply with the law.

In conclusion, then, it may be the case that "the corporate state" is moldering. But the organized interest groups are not. They have found new ways of doing politics and promoting their concerns. One of these is the court option, or the American way: if you cannot win by negotiation or pressure group politics, sue them!

NOTES

1. The Swedish ministries are, comparatively speaking, small bodies. A great part of the executive function is administered by rather independent departments and boards (*ämbetsverk*), not responsible to a ministry but to the cabinet as a whole. They can be guided only by way of general decrees, not by orders or advice in specific cases (See *Constitutional Documents of Sweden* 1981, 30).

2. The two houses had identical powers. In budgetary questions, where joint voting was used in case of differences, the Lower House had an advantage due to its greater numbers (230 to 150).

3. The Law Council is a more independent institution. Its dicta are public documents, not, as in the French case, something the cabinet or the minister can keep secret if they so prefer.

4. Committee majorities can block a referral, though, if a delay is held to cause "considerable harm."

5. For governmental reception of the Law Council's advice, see Algotsson (1992). The reports are regularly appended to the bills and commented on by the government.

6. See the famous French command of 1790: "the courts will address the legislature at all times when they believe it necessary, to interpret a law or to make a new one" (translation by the editors) (Troper 1980, 60).

7. The situation in Sweden was much like that in France during the Third Republic (see Duez 1929; Barthélemy and Duez 1933, 219-227; Beardsley 1975).

8. Of course, it was possible to sue public officials for fraud, taking bribes and other criminal offenses.

9. A proposal to this effect backed by all political parties was presented to the *Riksdag* in December 1993.

10. See judgment 1987-10-27, Ser. A, no. 125 concerning the prohibition on challenging the withdrawal of a permit to keep taxicabs.

11. As a further threat a time limit was set. After three years a new legislative decision was necessary to prolong the act.

12. Reuterskiöld represented the Agrarian Party in the Upper House from 1919 to 1938 and was chairman of the Standing Committee on the Constitution during the 1930s.

13. See for instance Sundberg (Fahlbeck, Jagerskiold, and Sundberg 1947, chap. 1, sec. 3; Petrén 1956; Petrén 1964).

14. The report, proposing the constitutionalization of some rights, did not result in legislation.

15. The proponents of the existence of judicial review of legislation had difficulties in finding cases establishing the practice. At last, in 1964, they got a Supreme Court judgment in which the court decided on the conformity of an ordinary law and the Instrument of Government. The court ruled, however, that the law was not contrary to the fundamental law (NJA 1964, 471; see Petrén 1966, 432).

16. See, e.g., RD 1973:110, 28; RD 1974:30, 117-119, 121 (Olof Palme, prime minister); RD 1973:110, 97; RD 1974:30, 67 (Hilding Johansson, public representative of the party). There are striking resemblances between the views of Swedish social democrats and those who defended the Third and Fourth Republics in France, or the dominating defense of the British system in the United Kingdom.

17. There is a great deal of research on this theme; in English see, e.g., Ruin 1974; Rothstein 1987, 1988; Heclo and Madsen 1987.

18. The project, headed by Olof Petersson, has produced a great number of books, articles, and papers. The concluding report is SOU 1990:44, where references to specific reports can be found.

19. The Alvgard case; see, e.g., articles in *GoteborgsPosten*.

REFERENCES

Algotsson, K-G. 1987. *Medborgarrätten och regeringsformen. Debatten om grundläggande frioch rättigheter i regeringsformenunder 1970-talet* (Citizen rights and the instrument of government. The debate on fundamental rights and freedoms in the instrument of government during the 1970s). Stockholm: Norstedts.

————. 1992. *Lagrådet, rättsstaten och demokratin* (The Law Council, democracy and the rule of law). Stockholm: Norstedts.

Barthélemy, Joseph, and P. Duez. 1933. *Traité de droit constitutionnel.* Paris: Dalloz.

Beardsley, J. 1975. "Constitutional Review in France." *Supreme Court Review*, 189-259.

Christofferson, U. 1983. "De statligt anställda i Sverige" (Public employees in Sweden). In *Byråkrater i Norden* (Bureaucrats in the Nordic Countries), ed. L. Lundquist and K. Ståhlberg. Åbo: Publications of the Research Institute of the Åbo Akademi Foundation.

Constitutional Documents of Sweden. 1981. Published by the Swedish Riksdag.

Dahl, R. A., ed. 1966. *Political Oppositions in Western Democracies.* New Haven: Yale University Press.

Duez, P. 1929. "Le côntrole juridictionnel de la constitutionnalité des lois en France: Comment il convient deposer la question." In *Mélanges Maurice Hauriou*, ed. Faculty of Law and Economic Sciences, University of Toulouse. Paris: Sirey.

Fahlbeck, E., S. Jägerskiöld, and H. G. F. Sundberg. 1947. *Medborgarrätt* (Citizen rights). Stockholm: Institutet för offentlig och internationell rätt.

Fakta om folkvalda: Riksdagen 1988-1991. (Facts about the representatives. The Riksdag 1988-1991). 1989. Stockholm: Riksdagen.

Författningsdomstol och lagprövning i nordisk och europeiskbelysning (Constitutional Court and judicial review of legislation in Nordic and European comparison). 1991. Stockholm: Rättsfonden.

Heclo, H., and H. Madsen. 1987. *Policy and Politics in Sweden: Principled Pragmatism.* Philadelphia: Temple University Press.

Herlitz, N. 1957. *Grunddragen av det svenska statsskickets historia* (Fundamentals of the constitutional history of Sweden). Stockholm: Norstedts.

Holmgren, K. 1967. "Förvaltningsdomstolsreformen" (The reform of the administrative courts), *Förvaltningsrättslig Tidskrift*.

Malmgren, R. 1934. "Riksdagen och lagstiftningen" (The Riksdag and the power of legislation). *Sveriges Riksdag*, Vol. 14. Stockholm: V. Pettersons Bokindustriaktiebolag.

———. 1965. *Sveriges grundlagar* (The fundamental laws of Sweden). 8th ed. Stockholm: Norstedts.

Oskarson, M. 1990. "Klassröstning på reträtt" (Class voting in retreat). In *Rött, blått, grönt. En bok om 1988 års riksdagsval* (Red, blue, green. A book about the Riksdag election in 1988), ed. M. Gilljam and S. Holmberg. Stockholm: Bonniers.

Petersson, O., and D. Söderlind. 1992. *Förvaltningspolitik* (Administrative politics). Stockholm: Publica.

Petrén, G. 1956. "Domstols lagprövningsrätt" (Judicial review of legislation), *Svensk juristtidning*, 500-509.

———. 1964. "Lagprövningsrätten än en gång" (Judicial review revisited), *Statsvetenskaplig tidskrift*, 403-7.

———. 1966. "Lagprövningsrätten" (Judicial review of legislation), *Svensk juristtidning*, 432.

Regeringsformen 1809-1959 (The instrument of government 1809-1959). 1959. Stockholm: Fritzes distr.

Reuterskiöld, C. A. 1918. "Vår rättsordnings omvandling" (The change of our machinery of justice"). *Statsvetenskapligtidskrift*, 69-97.

Rokkan, S. 1966. "Norway: Numerical Democracy and Corporate Pluralism." In *Political Oppositions in Western Democracies*, ed. R. A. Dahl.

Rothstein, B. 1987. "Corporatism and Reformism: The Social Democratic Institutionalization of Class Conflict." *Acta Sociologica* 30.

———. 1988. "State and Capital in Sweden: The Importance of Corporate Arrangements." *Scandinavian Political Studies* 11.

———. 1992. *Den korporativa staten* (The corporate state) Stockholm: Norstedts.

Ruin, O. 1974. "Towards a Corporate Society?" *Scandinavian Political Studies* 9.

Series of Public Reports, Government Committees (SOU). various years. Stockholm.

Sköld, L., and A. Halvarson. 1966. "Riksdagens sociala sammansättningunder hundra år" (The social structure of the Riksdag during a century). In *Samhälle och riksdag* (Society in the Riksdag), vol. 1, ed. Arthur Thomson. Stockholm: Almqvist and Wiksell.

Standing Committee on the Constitution, Reports (KU). various years. Stockholm.

Stjernquist, N. 1990. "Judicial Review and the Rule of Law: Comparing the United States and Sweden." *Policy Studies Journal* 19:106-115.

Strömberg, H. 1990. *Allmän förvaltningsrätt* (General administrative law). Stockholm: Liber.

Studier över den svenska riksdagens sociala sammansättning (Studies in the social structure of the Swedish Riksdag). 1936. Uppsala: Almqvist and Wiksell.

Sundberg, J., ed. 1985. *Sporrong-Lönnroth. En handbok* (The Sporrong-Lönnroth case. A handbook). Stockholm: Institutet föroffentlig och internationell rätt, 63.

Troper, M. 1980. *La séparation des pouvoirs et l'histoire constitutionnelle française*. Paris: Pichon and Durand-Auzias.

Wentz, N., and W. Hermanson. 1970. "Utbyggnad och reformering avförvaltningsrättskipningen" (Expansion and reform of administrative jurisdiction). *Förvaltningsrättslig tidskrift*, 251-66.

Westerståhl, J. 1941. "Frågan om domstolarnas judiciella lagprövningsrätt i Sverige" (The problem of judicial review of legislation in Sweden). *Statens offentliga utredningar*, 20.

ABBREVIATIONS

BoU	Standing Committee on Housing, Reports
Dir.	Government Directives to Investigatory Committees
FK	Upper Chamber, Debates
KU	Standing Committee on the Constitution, Reports
Mot.	Proposals from members of the Riksdag
NJA	Publication of Judgments from the Supreme Court
Prop.	Government bill
RD	Riksdag debates, unicameral period
R&D	Review, published by the Riksdag
SOU	Series of Public Reports, Government Committees

20.

The Netherlands: Toward a Form of Judicial Review

JAN TEN KATE AND PETER J. VAN KOPPEN

On 23 October 1985 the European Court of Human Rights made a decision in the *Benthem* case (ECHR 23 October 1985, AB 1986, no. 1) that caused much turmoil among Dutch judicial authorities and legal scholars. Albert Benthem owned a garage in the village of Noordwolde. In 1976 he applied for a license under the Nuisance Act of 1952 for operating an installation for the delivery of liquid gas to motor vehicles, involving use of a surface storage tank with a capacity of eight cubic meters. The Regional Health Inspector advised against granting the license, because of the excessive risks to the neighboring houses. The municipal council nevertheless granted the license. The health inspector lodged an appeal with the Crown as head of the executive (*in casu* the minister of public health and environmental protection).

When such an administrative appeal is brought before the Crown, the Crown will not make a decision until the Administrative Litigation Division of the Council of State (Afdeling Geschillen van Bestuur van de Raad van State) has looked into the matter and prepared an advisory decision. The Crown's decision (a Crown's Decree, Koninklijk Besluit) almost never departs from the Litigation Division's advise.

In 1979 the Crown decided that Benthem should be refused the license and quashed the decision of the municipal council. Subsequently Benthem was ordered by the municipal authorities to cease operating his installation.   He appealed against this decision, but the decision was confirmed by the Crown. Meanwhile Benthem filed an application with the Commission of Human Rights, claiming that his case had not been heard by an independent and impartial tribunal, contrary to the requirements of Article 6, paragraph 1 of the European Convention for the Protection of Human Rights and Fundamental Freedoms (The Treaty of Rome of 1950). In its decision the European Court ruled that Article 6, paragraph 1 indeed was applicable because in this case a civil right was at stake. Thus the court had to determine whether the proceedings in appeal to the Crown satisfied the requirements of Article 6. The Dutch government stated that the Crown followed the Litigation Division's advice in the vast majority of the cases. This did not provide, in the court's view, the determination by a tribunal of the matters in dispute, because the Crown still is entitled to depart from the advice. Thus the Crown—hierarchical superior to the regional health inspector and to the ministry's director general, who had submitted the technical report to the Litigation Division—could not be seen as an independent and impartial tribunal that guarantees a judicial procedure.

As a result of the judgment of the court, the Dutch legislature had to abandon the provision in many statutes of an appeal to the Crown. The Administrative Litigation Division of the Council of State was subsequently upgraded to an independent administrative court (*Tijdelijke Wet Kroongeschillen* 1987). This change of law caused by the court's judgment is an example of the judicialization of politics in the Netherlands; as a result of this decision some disputes can no longer be decided upon by the Crown, but instead have to be referred to a truly independent administrative judge.[1]

In the Netherlands politics has been increasingly judicialized: there has been, in Vallinder's words, a substantial "transfer of decision-making rights from the legislature, the cabinet or the civil service to the courts." Not only did the European Commission of Human Rights (ECHR) further the protection of civil rights against the Dutch executive, but decisions of the Dutch Supreme Court (Hoge Raad der Nederlanden) have also been of great importance.   This development in the Netherlands is not unique.   The Dutch government, legislature, and judiciary have been propelled by international developments and the perhaps not fully expected dynamics and consequences of international treaties, such as those on human rights. In the following pages we will give some examples of this tendency to shift decision-making competence from political to judicial bodies. We will end with some remarks on one of the major points in which the Dutch constitutional law differs from that of adjacent countries: the absence of constitutionally-sanctioned judicial review of Acts of Parliament.

THE ADVANCE OF ADMINISTRATIVE LAW

The roots of the Dutch Constitution (*Grondwet*) lie in the *Trias Politica*, the separation of the legislative, administrative, and judicial powers. The first Constitution of 1814 has been changed and enlarged many times, but even after the last important revision in 1983,[2] several concepts establishing the *Trias Politica* still remain (Kortmann 1990, 30). Constitutional development has brought changes in different fields, including the extension of the fundamental human rights, the superiority of self-executing provisions of treaties, and the maturation of administrative law. But not only have the contents changed; so have the interpretation and nature of some provisions. For example, originally human rights were considered to guarantee the right to defend oneself in the field of criminal law; nowadays these rights make it possible to demand the conditions for fulfillment of these rights from the government (Akkermans, Bax, and Verhey 1988, 30).

Constitutions that stem from the *Trias Politica* can have different forms, witness the French and American constitutions. The original Dutch Constitution incorporated the French version of the idea of separation of powers, in which the democratic element of political decision making was dominant. In essence, majority rule determined political questions and therefore the outcome of the legislative process. The question of constitutional incompatibility had to be decided by the Parliament itself, not by the judiciary; the judiciary merely was the *bouche de la loi*, which should strictly apply legislation without its own interpretation. Thus, contrary to the American version given by Hamilton (see Kramnick 1987), according to which the division of powers led to a system of checks and balances, the French and Dutch versions led to a *separation* of powers (Cliteur 1989). This may be one of the reasons why in the nineteenth century little emphasis was given to the possible mistakes of the executive or the legislature. One could not imagine that these bodies would make mistakes or make decisions that were unjust or disproportionately disadvantageous for individuals or groups of citizens. Dominant legal doctrine considered democratic decision making the best guarantee against these kinds of failure (Struycken 1910; Stroink 1990, 5).

More recently has come the realization that, for instance, withdrawing a subsidy could be unjust; that changes in zoning-regulations can be unduly disadvantageous to individual citizens; or that either granting or denying a license can involve abuse of power by the executive. Starting in 1887, some statutes provided for a right to appeal decisions of the executive. Usually, decisions had to be appealed to the next hierarchically superior authority or to a special administrative court. Gradually, several special administrative courts were introduced, each with a limited jurisdiction based on a specific statute. The Dutch legislature did not create administrative courts with general jurisdiction. Therefore, today the field of administrative law is considered rather chaotic and complicated and hard for the ordinary citizen to understand (Scheltema 1986, 39; Kortmann 1990, 253).

The increasing demand for civil protections against executive actions led to the AROB Act of 1976 (Administratieve Rechtspraak Overheidsbeschikkingen [Administrative Jurisdiction on Public Authorities' Decrees]). This statute granted individuals the right to appeal any decree of a public authority to the newly formed Judicial Division of the Council of State (Afdeling Rechtspraak van de Raad van State) if no other special administrative court was available for an appeal. Since then the Judicial Division has energetically built a strong position by elaborating on the general principles of proper administration (*beginselen van behoorlijk bestuur*) in its case law (Stroink 1990, 5). The AROB Act proved to be very important. Appealing to the Judicial Division became so popular that the workload of this court became unmanageable: in the near future lower administrative courts in each district will be created and incorporated into the ordinary courts of first instance. The final piece of this development may be that the coming reorganization of the judicial system will lead to the creation of a chamber of the Supreme Court dealing with cassation in administrative law cases (Remmelink 1992, 15). So not only has the number of decisions by which the public authorities can influence the position of individuals and groups grown in the last decades so also have the possibilities of appealing these decisions, and of having these appeals decided by an impartial judge.

THE ROLE OF THE SUPREME COURT

The Dutch Supreme Court has come far from the *bouche de la loi* ideology of the nineteenth century (Hirsch Ballin 1988; Schoordijk 1988). The Supreme Court always had some influence on the law, merely by the interpretations given to statutes in the court's decisions. These interpretations, of course, set precedents, both for the court itself and for lower courts. But the important task of looking after the uniformity of the law has gradually come to be equalled by the court's function of developing the law. Starting with the famous decision in *Lindenbaum v. Cohen* (HR 31 January 1919, *NJ* 161, *WvhR* 10365; see van Koppen 1990), the Supreme Court has taken up the role of deputy legislature. That very decision, in which the Supreme Court widened the definition of tort from a mere breach of written rights or duties to any kind of breach of duty of care, made a bill on the same subject superfluous.

In recent years the Supreme Court has given new interpretations to existing statutes or formulated new rules for unforeseen problems in many decisions, making legislation unnecessary, even on issues where a clear political majority in Parliament would have produced legislation relatively swiftly. More important, the court produced case law on issues, such as the right to strike, euthanasia, and abortion, on which Parliament was unable to pass legislation. Supreme Court decisions play such an important role in these matters because of some peculiarities of Dutch politics.

For a long time the Dutch government has been built on a coalition of more than two or three, sometimes even five political parties. No party has ever reached a majority in Parliament. When one of the coalition parties agrees with the opposition on a hot issue and could join with the opposition to create a majority vote on such an issue, that party still has to consider the opinion of the coalition partner(s) in order to avoid the risk of breaking up the coalition. So even if there is a majority for a political choice on a certain issue, it is not certain that that choice will be made. More often the decision on these issues is postponed and the Supreme Court has to fill the gap (see van Koppen 1990, 1991).[3]

The permanent coalition character of the Dutch government also introduces compromise into the content of legislation: conflicting coalition opinions have to be assimilated in the text of new laws. Clear-cut legislation on controversial issues would often endanger cooperation within the coalition. This means that the compromise imparts a diffuse and vague nature to statutes. Such legislation often needs extensive interpretation before it can be applied in practice, which opens up the opportunity for the judiciary to play an important role in many controversial matters (Schuyt 1988, 332).

In the last two decades coalition parties became even more bound to each other through the introduction of the *regeeraccoord* (government agreement), an extensive written document dealing with all major and many minor political issues. The agreement is binding not only on members of the cabinet, but also on members of the parliamentary majority. Voting against any government proposal covered by the agreement is considered a breach of political contract and endangers the coalition. The government agreement, made in covert negotiations, in fact ties members of Parliament to cabinet decisions and thus turns the traditional dualism between cabinet and Parliament into a monistic ruling by the cabinet, thus enabling the government to run bills through Parliament by sheer political force, sometimes producing acts of low quality. In such political circumstances the Supreme Court may receive a new function: guardian of the quality of the law (van Koppen 1990).

Considering the growth of the public policy-making function of the Supreme Court it is not surprising that politicians nowadays seem to pay more attention to appointments to the Supreme Court than they have for decades. According to the law, Parliament has an almost decisive influence on the appointments in the Supreme Court, because it is Parliament's[4] competence to put forward a list of three nominees, from which the Crown (that is, the cabinet) has to choose. In practice, however, co-optation takes place. When there is a vacancy in the Supreme Court, the court draws up a list of six candidates, who are recommended for the position. Thereupon Parliament, without any discussion or public attention, puts the first three candidates of that recommendation list on the list of nominees, from which the first always is appointed by the Crown (van Koppen and ten Kate 1987; van Koppen 1990).

All justices appointed after World War II have had very low political profiles, compared to the appointments in the nineteenth century. No specific strategy or political prevalence can be discerned, except that lawyers who have extreme points of view do not have a chance to be appointed. Nevertheless we cannot rule out the possibility that, in private, the sitting justices, when they draw up he list of candidates, take into account the recommended lawyers' political affinities and philosophies of life in order not to depart too much from the proportional composition of the Second Chamber of Parliament. This could explain why the Supreme Court has succeeded in maintaining this co-optation system.

Nevertheless, in the future appointments to the Supreme Court will not take place so automatically and unobtrusively as they have in the past. In the summer of 1991 a Christian-Democratic member of Parliament started to ask questions about the procedure for the appointments of justices of the Supreme Court because he had the impression that too many judges and justices were adherents of one of the opposition parties (D66, a mildly liberal party). For the first time this question was covered heavily by the press. The Supreme Court promised to give more biographical data on the candidates in the future, and we may expect more debate about forthcoming appointments in the Supreme Court.

FROM NATIONAL LAW TO INTERNATIONAL LAW

Since World War II Dutch law has become more and more interwoven with international law, international treaties, and the law and case law of supranational institutions. This development has restricted Dutch political autonomy largely because many important decisions are no longer made in The Hague, but in Brussels, as a result of the Dutch membership in the EC, and because the government and the legislature are committed to the case law of some international courts. The fact that the interpretation of many treaties is reserved to independent international courts has had a rather unexpected impact on Dutch politics, especially in the field of fundamental human rights.

A major step toward the internationalization of law was made in the 1953 change in the Constitution, which explicitly stated that national law shall not be applied if it is incompatible with a self-executing provision of a treaty.[5] So the Constitution made it possible to subject national law, including constitutional law, to certain provisions of treaties, with no distinction made between treaties that were entered into before and after the enactment of the national law. Throughout the following decades this prevalence of treaties was properly taught in the law faculties, but it was of no great practical importance. The Supreme Court tried to avoid any reference to international law by giving an interpretation, sometimes rather strained, of a comparable constitutional provision that corresponded to the international treaty. The year 1980 was a turning point. By then the Supreme Court had begun to review openly the compliance of national law with international law, especially with the European Convention of Human Rights (for examples, see Van Dijk 1988).

After 1980 many citizens started to use the right to appeal individually to the European Court of Human Rights for alleged violation of the convention. This resulted in judgments of the European Court in which Dutch national law was considered to be in conflict with specific provisions of that convention (van Dijk 1988). International and supranational law, as interpreted by the European Court or the EC Court, has a considerable influence on national law, for instance by prohibiting the legislature from making any rule that is in conflict with that interpretation.[6] Thus, one of the major components of the judicialization of politics can be found in the restrictions of government authority by the development of the international and supranational law, including the case-law of the international courts.

TOWARD CONSTITUTIONAL REVIEW?

As we noted, the Dutch Constitution stems from a tradition in which there is no supremacy of the judiciary over the legislature. Since 1848 the Dutch constitution has included the principle that the judiciary is not allowed to review the compliance of any Act of Parliament with the constitution.[7] Any Act of Parliament supersedes the provisions of the Constitution and the principles that are incorporated in the Constitution: the decision of the Parliament's majority makes an Act inviolable. This rule has been restricted to Acts of Parliament explicitly. All the ordinances of lower legislative bodies, the provinces, the local government and so on, have to be in accordance with higher ones, Acts of Parliament and the Constitution. In that sense there is judicial review by judges in different layers of the judiciary that very often finds ordinances of lower bodies incompatible with an Act of Parliament or the Constitution.

An important argument for the inviolability of Acts of Parliament was that Parliament itself, as the representative of the people, was best equipped to judge whether a certain Act of Parliament was incompatible with the Constitution. This opinion had many strong adherents in the first half of this century (Struycken 1910). Nevertheless, the discussion of the appropriateness of judicial review was revived from time to time. During the preparation of the 1983 revision of the Constitution, a draft to create a form of judicial review was even circulated. Eventually, no constitutional review was incorporated in the Constitution, but ever since the discussion has continued.

The discussion of judicial review was fed by the increasing influence of international law on the case law of the Supreme Court and the lower courts. Nowadays we find ourselves in a peculiar situation: an Act of Parliament can be declared incompatible with self-executing provisions of international treaties, but not with the Constitution. This holds even when in the treaty and in the Constitution essentially the same principle is included in about the same words.[8] This inconsistency is nearly impossible to explain to non-Dutch scholars (Kortmann 1990, 336).

Another argument in favor of the ban on judicial review, the argument that Parliament itself is able to maintain a certain degree of quality in its legislative function, has become less convincing in recent years. As we mentioned earlier, the decreasing dualism between government and Parliament and the speed and pressure under which some drafts have passed Parliament, have occasionally resulted in botched-up legislation.[9] A notorious example is the so-called Harmonization Act of 1988, in which the rights of students were curtailed in a retrospective way. Ultimately an appeal to the judiciary failed, because the principle that an Act of Parliament is inviolable was upheld by the Supreme Court. The Court, however, noted that some aspects of the Harmonization Act were in conflict with general, though unwritten, rules of law and announced that it would not exclude a kind of judicial review in the future (van Koppen 1992).

It is not our purpose to sum up all the pros and cons that arise in the discussion on the question of judicial or constitutional review.[10] What matters here is that there is an overall tendency toward advocating a form of judicial review or creating a constitutional court (Kortmann 1990, 336; Stroink 1990, 25; Cliteur 1989, 1375; Van Boven 1990, 149). At the annual meeting of the Dutch Lawyers Association in June 1992, a clear majority favored the abandoning of the prohibition on constitutional review. The fact that most West European countries have a constitutional court will inevitably play a role, especially now that these constitutional courts "are intervening in legislative processes at an increasing rate" (Stone 1990, 89).

EPILOGUE

The growing complexity of modern society and the development of international law, especially in areas such as fundamental human rights, have resulted in a judicialization of politics in some fields. We may assume that this tendency has not yet stopped, given the ongoing discussion about judicial review and the relatively unique position of the Netherlands at this point. This increase in the judiciary's power may also have some less favorable aspects. For example, until now the appointments to the judiciary in the Netherlands have had a relatively unpolitical character, but it is not certain that this will last for long. So perhaps the benefits of the judicialization of politics may partially be overridden by the politicization of the judiciary.

NOTES

1. We use the designation "judge" only when the decisive authority, as in this case, can be seen as impartial and independent.
2. The 1987 revision is not relevant here.
3. In about the same way the Court of the European Community had to decide in questions that presumably were within the competence of the Council of European Ministers because that Council had too often failed to reach a clear political decision (Kortmann, 1990: 159).
4. To be exact: the Second Chamber of the Parliament, comparable with the House of Commons in the UK or the Bundestag in Germany.
5. Now Article 94, Constitution.
6. The only way to evade this situation would be the denunciation of the treaty, which is not an easy way out.
7. Now Article 120, expressing the same principle in other words.
8. See, for instance, Article 1 of the Constitution and Article 26 of the International Treaty on Civil and Political Rights.
9. See, for example, Damen & Hoogenboom (1989) on the extremely hurried legislation on the internment of refugees, after the Supreme Court had held this practice to be unlawful detention.
10. For a recent survey of these arguments, see, for example, Cliteur (1989), Van Boven (1990), and Stroink (1990).

REFERENCES

BOOKS AND ARTICLES

Akkermans, P. W. C., C. J. Bax, and L. F. M. Verhey. 1988. *Grondrechten: Grondrechten end grondrechtbescherming in Nederland*. Groningen: Wolters-Noordhoof.

Cliteur, P. B. 1989. "Argumenten voor en tegen constitutionele toetsing." *Nederlands Juristenblad* 64:369-75.

Damen, L. J. A., and T. Hoogenboom. 1989. "Na 'confectierechtspraak' nu ook 'confectiewetgeving'?" *Nederlands Juristenblad* 64:145-153.

Hirsch Ballin, E. M. H. 1988. "Onafhankelijke rechtsvorming: Staatsrechtelijke aantekeningen over de plaats en functie van de Hoge Raad in de Nederlandse rechtorde." In *De Plaats van de Hoge Raad in het Huidige Staatsbestel: De Veranderingen in de Rol van de Hoge Raad als Rechtsvormer*. Zwolle, The Netherlands: Tjeenk Willink.

Kortmann, C. A. J. M. 1990. *Constitutioneel recht*. Deventer, The Netherlands: Kluwer.

Kramnick, I., ed. 1987. *Federalist Papers*. Harmondsworth, Middlesex: Penguin.

Remmelink, J. 1992. *Past, Present, and Future of the 'Hoge Raad der Nederlanden.'* Arnhem: Gouda Quint.

Scheltema, M. 1986. "Een nieuwe uitdaging voor de administratieve rechtspraak?" In *Kroonberoep en artikel 6 EVRM*, ed. N.S.J. Koeman et al. Deventer, the Netherlands: Kluwer.

Schoordijk, H. C. F. 1988. "Hoe vat(te) de burgerlijke kamer van de Hoge Raad zijn rechtsvormende taak op?" In *De Plaats van de Hoge Raad in het Huidige Staatsbestel: De Veranderingen in de Rol van de Hoge Raad als Rechtsvormer*. Zwolle, The Netherlands: Tjeenk Willink.

Schuyt, C. J. M. 1988. "De veranderende plaats van de Hoge Raad in de samenleving." In *De Plaats van de Hoge Raad in het Huidige Staatsbestel: De Veranderingen in de Rol van de Hoge Raad als Rechtsvormer*. Zwolle, The Netherlands: Tjeenk Willink.

Stone, A. 1990. "The Birth and Development of Abstract Review: Constitutional Courts and Policy-Making in Western Europe." *Policy Studies Journal* 19:81-95.

Stroink, F. A. M. 1990. *De plaats van de rechter in het staatsbestel: Enige beschouwingen over de positie van de rechter ten opzichte van wetgever en bestuur, topgespitst op het vraagstuk vand e constitutionele rechtspraak.* Zwolle: Tjeenk Willink.

Struycken, A. A. H. 1910. *Administratie of rechter: beschouwingen over de moderne rechstaatsgedache naar van de aanhangige ontwerpen tot regeling der administratieve rechtspraak.* Arnhem: Gouda Quint.

van Boven, W. 1990. "Naar een schendbare wet?" *Ars Aequi* 39:143-50.

van Dijk, P. 1988. "De houding van de Hoge Raad jegens de verdragen inzake de rechten van de mens." In *De Plaats van de Hoge Raad in het Huidige Staatsbestel: De Veranderingen in de Rol van de Hoge Raad als Rechtsvormer.* Zwolle, The Netherlands: Tjeenk Willink.

van Koppen, P. J. 1990. "The Dutch Supreme Court and Parliament: Political Decision-Making versus Nonpolitical Appointments." *Law and Society Review* 24:745-780.

———. 1992. "Judicial Policy-Making in The Netherlands: The Case by Case Method." *West European Politics* 15, 80-92.

van Koppen, P. J., and J. ten Kate 1987. *Tot raadsheer benoemd: Anderhalve eeuw benoemingen in de Hoge Raad der Nederlanden.* Arnhem: Gouda Quint.

CASES CITED

ECHR 23 October 1985, *AB* 1986, 1, with note Hirsch Ballin.

HR 31 January 1919, *NJ* 161, *WvhR* 10365, with note Molengraaff.

HR 15 January 1960, *NJ* 1960, 84, with note LEHR.

HR 14 April 1989, *NJ* 1989, 469 (*De Staat der Nederlanden v. De Landelijke Studenten Vak Bond (LSV)*), with note MS.

21.

The Judiciary and Politics in Malta

CARMEL A. AGIUS AND NANCY A. GROSSELFINGER

BACKGROUND

In this chapter we take the term judicialization of politics to mean the process whereby the fundamental rights and freedoms of the citizens are secured and upgraded at the expense of the rights and obligations of the legislative and executive branches of the state. Politics is interpreted as the science or art of government, or the administration and management of public or state affairs, which entail the elements of public authority and legitimacy. Given this wide definition, the judiciary and its decisions assume a political connotation and the administration of justice becomes a specialized subsystem of the political whole (see Galligan 1989, 1).

The Maltese courts function as an interdependent part of a larger and much more complex political culture and history. We shall first try to locate the courts and their functioning within the larger Maltese political system in order to identify the broader factors and interdependent relations that have usually fashioned the kinds of constitutional and political cases that have come before them.

The 1964 Independence Constitution established Malta as a liberal parliamentary democracy, protecting the fundamental human rights of citizens and guaranteeing a separation between the executive, the legislative,and the judicial branches, with regular elections based on universal suffrage. Malta's legal system retained its civil-law origin and basis, which were already deeply rooted when the British arrived, though various common-law principles have been introduced in Maltese public law. There is no counterpart of the French Conseil d'Etat or the Italian Consiglio di Stato; the Administration does not have any special courts of its own. The common-law doctrine of precedent, as followed in various other civil-law countries, does not apply to Malta. Courts of first instance normally follow the principles laid down by the Court of Appeal and the Constitutional Court, even though they are not strictly bound to do so. When they do not, they are expected to give reasons for their departure in their written judgments. The Court of Appeal and the Constitutional Court are not bound to follow their own previous decisions, though they customarily do. Judges are appointed by the president acting in accordance with the advice of the prime minister, from among advocates who have at least twelve years practice at the bar or have served as magistrates.

Like their British counterparts, Maltese judges do not hold office at the pleasure of the executive, and their salaries do not require annual sanction and cannot be altered to their disadvantage. The post of a judge cannot without his or her consent be abolished during his or her continuance in office. Judges retire on attaining the age of sixty-five. Only in the event of proven misbehavior or incapacity may a judge be removed from office by the president and then only under set stringent conditions, which include a two-thirds majority vote of the House of Representatives. However, since the introduction of the present British type of judiciary in 1815, no judge has ever been removed from office, nor have any proceedings been ever instituted by Parliament for such a removal.

Through the exercise of judicial review, the Maltese Superior Courts play an important role in Maltese politics that is both adjudicative and constitutional. In their adjudicative role, the Superior Courts are guarantors to the private citizen against abuse or misuse of executive discretion. In their constitutional role, the Superior Courts, particularly the Constitutional Court, authoritatively interpret the Constitution and decide on various questions of a political nature.

The Constitution contains a judicially enforceable bill of rights affording protection of specified human rights and fundamental freedoms, subject to certain limitations. Malta is also a state party to the European Convention on Human Rights and has recognized the right of individual petition and the compulsory jurisdiction of the European Court of Human

Rights established by that convention.   Since 1987 the substantive provisions of the convention have been integrated into domestic law, though in the case of inconsistency between the convention and the Constitution, it is the Constitution that prevails.

An application for redress may be brought before a competent court if it is alleged by someone that a human-rights provision has been, is being, or is *likely to be* contravened in relation to him or her. Concurrent examination of human-rights cases under the Constitution and the convention is now automatically assured. Judgments of the European Court are directly enforceable by the Constitutional Court of Malta. This has given the international protection of human rights a new dimension in that judgments of the European Court, in which Malta is a party, are now vested with executory, not merely obligatory, force, which by themselves they did not otherwise have (see Cremona, 1990).

Under the Constitution, the Constitutional Court deals with:

1. questions or laws regarding membership in, voting for, or election to the House of Representatives;
2. appeals of decisions of the Civil Court, First Hall, relating to the enforcement of the fundamental rights and freedoms of the individual;
3. appeals of decisions of any court of original jurisdiction as to the interpretation of the Constitution;
4. appeals of the decisions of any court of original jurisdiction on the question of the validity of laws;
5. appeals of any question decided by a court of original jurisdiction dealing with any of the above mentioned matters.

The Court of Appeal, apart from its normal role as a court of appeal for decisions of courts of first instance, including judgments on review of legislative acts and executive discretion, is also entrusted with the hearing of various appeals of decisions of the executive and of administrative tribunals.

In their constitutional role, the Superior Courts, particularly the Constitutional Court, stand above the political system and the political process.   But in their role as guardians and interpreters of the Constitution, these courts serve a primary political function.

GENERAL OBSERVATIONS AND REALITIES

At face value one might get the impression that Malta has found the magic formula for holding the Constitution in perpetual equilibrium. This would be an optimistic picture of the real situation. In reality, the Maltese courts have approached their right to review executive discretion in a haphazard manner. Certainly, the absence of specific legislation on the subject for a long time and the different attitudes taken by the various administrations that have governed the Maltese nation, in regard to their discretionary powers and the reviewing role of the courts, have contributed to the wilderness that emerges. But judicial review in the Maltese context has involved predominantly judge-made law: Maltese judges thus carry quite a measure of responsibility for this shortcoming. It is, however, to the credit of some judges that over the years, the administration, including that of the colonial era, has been restrained in the arbitrary exercise of its wide discretionary powers, in spite of the absence of specific legislation.

When faced with cases involving the exercise of administrative discretion, the validity of legislative acts, and other issues of a political nature, the Maltese judiciary has not historically been homogeneous in character and approach: periods of negative indifference have alternated with others of creativity and activism. Very few judges, however, have been creative or activist; the great majority seem to have been more concerned with limiting the availability of judicial review and avoiding a direct confrontation with the other two branches of the state.

To a lesser extent, this applies also in the field of human rights. Since 1961, the courts have dealt with 370 human rights cases and in many instances, especially in the last decade, have decided against the executive. Yet, even in this field, the Maltese courts' contribution to human-rights development has been plagued by the excessively formalistic view taken of human rights and redress and the reluctance in some instances to embark on an imaginative and liberal development of the human-rights provisions.

Nevertheless, any analysis that places the judiciary in Malta in a subservient position to the executive misreads history and mistakes the source and nature of the Maltese legal system. That Malta enables its citizens to live in freedom is to a large extent a consequence of the Maltese judicial system and the Maltese judges. In spite of the criticism that the courts over the years have worked in an inevitable tandem with the executive, always proving it right, it is undeniable that it is they that have on several occasions ensured the enforcement of the rule of law and the respect of the fundamental human rights and freedoms of the Maltese.

THE MALTESE COURTS IN THEIR ADJUDICATIVE ROLE

In Malta the concept of judicial review owes its origin to the courts' invention in 1894 of a doctrine of governmental liability that needs some explanation, as it put the executive well-nigh beyond the control of the courts when acting to regulate social and economic interests.

In *Busuttil v. La Primaudaye* (*Collection of Decided Cases* [this title omitted hereafter], vol. 14, 94), an action for damages against the state, the First Hall of the Civil Court introduced the notion of the dual personality of the state. As guardian of the common good the state has two personalities: in the first one it administers its own public property and patrimony; in the second it acts politically through laws to preserve law and order and to regulate the nation's life. In the first capacity, it acts *iure gestionis* and administers its property as everybody else does with no special privileges. In the second capacity, the state employs political sovereign authority as the supreme arbiter of the common good: it acts *iure imperii*, and the courts are limited to inquiring into the form the proceedings have taken.

This two-headed Leviathan was imported by the presiding judge from the Continent, where the distinction had already lost its resplendence. This, nevertheless, was the accepted doctrine of the Maltese courts until the applecart was upset by the Court of Appeal in 1935 (in *Cassar Desain v. Forbes*, vol. 29.1.43), which explained that the doctrine of the dual personality of the state was a wrongful proposition law with no foundation in the Maltese legal system. This judgment was followed in the same year in only one case—decided by the same set of judges (*Galea v. Caruana Galizia*, vol. 34.1.345).   Immediately after the composition of the Court of Appeal changed, the same court went back to the old doctrine without the least hesitation (*Buttigieg v. Cross*, vol. 31.1.398; *Cilia v. Cuschieri*, vol. 33.1.356).

By 1958 this doctrine had been extended to include as acts *iure imperii* laws providing for administrative discretion, with the corollary that the courts may not substitute their own discretion for that of the administration in such matters (*Aquilina v. Ellul Mercer noe*, vol.

42.1.165; *Attard Montalto v. Cuschieri noe*, vol. 38.1.749), even though the courts hinted that they would review the dishonest exercise of such executive discretion (*Pace v. Anastasi Pace*, vol. 32.2.217).

Throughout this period the courts accepted a wide variety of formal restrictions on their ability to exercise judicial review of administrative discretion.[1] However, at the same time these limitations were being self-imposed by the courts, they did on occasion come up with surprisingly far-reaching and avant-garde judgments. For instance, in 1954 when the executive tried by all means to stop the release of a number of Soviet films for public viewing, the courts firmly ruled against political control and in favor of freedom of expression. Despite the Cold War political environment, the opposition of the Catholic Church, and, apparently, the personal views of the judges who dealt with the cases, the courts refused to stop the release of the films (*Baldacchino v. Caruana Demajo*, vol. 38.1.61).

Judicial Review in the 1960s

In the 1960s there was a sharp decline in the number of cases in which the reviewing jurisdiction of the courts was sought. This was certainly due in part to the less frequent use of requisitioning powers by the Housing Department. However, the approach that the courts had adopted in the past discouraged attempts to challenge the exercise of administrative discretionary powers in court. There was a general awareness within the legal community of the limitations that the courts had imposed upon themselves in matters of judicial review. In addition, the theory of the dual personality of the state was not in any way tampered with by the Independence Constitution and was even reaffirmed in postindependence judgments (*Mintoff v. Borg Olivier noe*, Civil Court, First Hall, 09.17.70).

During this period the Maltese courts also continued to establish or reaffirm principles further limiting their right of review.[2] There were only two exceptions:

1. In *Masini v. Podestá* (Court of Appeal, 04.26.61) the court ruled that discretion exercised by the competent authority, and in the correct form, may yet be attacked if it is not fairly and honestly exercised. Even in this case, however, the court reiterated that it did not have the authority to substitute its own discretion for that of the competent authority.

2. In *Pellegrini v. Arrigo noe* (Vol 42.2.869) the court decided that the discretion exercised by the executive had to be reasonable, in good faith, and not the fruit of corruption.

Judicial Review under Labour Government, 1971-1987

Things began to change in 1971, when the Malta Labour Party won the general election after nine years in opposition. With the new Administration, the style of government changed too. In particular, the administration conferred upon itself more and more discretionary powers and tried to keep these outside the jurisdiction of the courts. The period 1971-1987 when the Labour Party remained in power was marked by several instances of confrontation between the two main political parties in which the courts became involved, and by direct conflicts between the executive and the judiciary. It became common at this time for the executive to accuse the judiciary of encroachment into the powers and discretion of the administration for political motives. This resulted in an attempt to reverse the process of judicialization of politics that the courts had just embarked upon, by introducing laws and measures that at best could be considered an attempt to politicize the judiciary and at worst a threat against the independence of the judiciary. This period was also marked by a wide and indiscriminate use of the Housing Act of 1949 that gave the Housing secretary wide powers to requisition houses. This became, in due course, a much disputed issue.

The first case of abuse of executive discretion that came up for judicial review soon after the Labour Party's election resulted in a revolutionary judgment (*Lowell v. Caruana*, Civil Court, First Hall, 08.14.72) in which a court questioned, for the first time, the executive's claim to an unrestricted right to withdraw permits and licenses. But more important, it gave what could then appear to be the "coup de grace" to the lingering *jus imperii* doctrine.[3]

This judgment provided the same court (presided over by a different judge) with the proper framework for a thorough examination of the motives and reasons behind the issuing of a housing requisition order in *Sciberras v. Housing Secretary noe* (Civil Court, First Hall, 07.21.73). The court held that exercise of administrative discretion can be controlled:

1. when an exercise of discretion has not complied with the conditions provided by statute for the exercise of that power,
2. when power has been used for any purpose extraneous to the legislation that conferred the power,
3. when there is a violation of the principles of natural justice (if the authority is vested with quasi-judicial powers);
4. when the authority has acted according to the directions or instructions of its departmental superior, rather than exercised the independent discretion with which it had been vested.

The court also held that, in general, the courts retain the power to prevent discretionary power from being transformed into arbitrary power.

The stage was set for further development, but within five months the same court, differently constituted, ignored the principles of the *Sciberras* case and harked back to the old trite and convenient formula (in *Muscat v. Housing Secretary*, and *Debono v. Bugeja noe et*, Civil Court, First Hall, 12.05.73 and 08.14.74) even though ten years earlier the Court of Appeal had expressed doubts as to the validity of the *jus imperii* doctrine (*Butler v. Camilleri*, Court of Appeal, 01.08.65).

At this point, the executive rushed through Parliament a new Interpretation Act (1975) that thwarted what had been decided in the Sciberras case, subjecting those senior public officers who previously exercised their discretion independently to the control, supervision, and direction of the minister.[4]

The great breakthrough came in 1980 in the Blue Sisters case (*Prime Minister v. Sister Luigi Dunkin*, First Hall, Civil Court, 06/26/80). The case established the following principles:

1. the power to impose conditions on a license "as the minister may deem fit" did not mean that the minister had absolute power to subject the license to conditions that are arbitrary or irrelevant to the purposes of the enabling law;
2. although the minister had the power to issue a license, subject to those conditions that he or she may deem fit, these must be reasonable conditions related to the purposes of the law under which the license was issued.

This judgment seemed to have developed the position that the Maltese courts could review administrative discretion in the following cases: (a) if there was plain *ultra vires*; (b) if jurisdictional facts were nonexistent; (c) if there were procedural defects; (d) if the decision was bad on the face; (e) if there was abuse of discretion, whether by taking into account improper purposes or by the consideration of extraneous considerations, or if the decision was one that no reasonable person would have reached; (f) if there was a violation of any of the principles of natural justice.

All this was seen by the administration of the day as an encroachment by a politically motivated and hostile judiciary into the powers of Parliament and ministerial discretion or as a threat to its permanency in power. In Parliament as well as in public meetings, the prime minister, ministers and Labour Party members of Parliament proclaimed that the judges were a reactionary lot and that together they formed a club of the party in opposition. Also, in the previous seven years the executive had failed to constitute the Constitutional Court for a good three years,[5] with the declared aim of forcing the opposition to accept changes in the Constitution that required a two-thirds majority in Parliament. It had played musical chairs with some judges in politically sensitive cases, transferring them to different jurisdictions, and had on another occasion suspended the function of all the courts (except the Constitutional Court before which it had to appeal) for five weeks.[6]

Immediately after the Blue Sisters Case, Act 8 of 1981 was rushed through Parliament, restricting judicial review to three cases only, namely, (a) when the act is ultra vires, (b) when it is in violation of an explicit provision of a written law, and (c) when the due form and procedure has not been followed in a material respect and substantial prejudice has ensued as a result. Essentially this enactment was intended to eliminate the power of the courts to test the reasonableness of the executive's exercise of discretionary powers. It amounted to a radical departure from British principles, which had begun to be applied by the courts.[7]

Act 8 of 1981 may be said to have restricted, conceptually at least, the courts' right of review of executive discretion, but it left their review rights under the Constitution untouched. In the next section we shall deal with the Maltese courts' performance in this field of review.

The Constitutional Role of the Maltese Courts

The Beginning

The following discussion will be limited to cases that established principles of importance in the field of judicial review, which declared legislative acts of Parliament unconstitutional, or that had a direct bearing on the executive's policy and the political well-being of the nation, and that eventually brought the courts and the executive into direct confrontation.

In spite of the several constitutions that Malta had during colonial rule, the only constitution that contained a chapter on fundamental human rights was the 1961 Constitution, that immediately preceded the present one.   The very first case in which the Maltese court denounced a violation of a human right by the administration was in 1963.   In the 1960s there was a dispute between the Catholic Church and the Labour Party that resulted in that party's newspapers being condemned by the Church.   The then Nationalist minister of health forbade the party papers from entering state hospitals.   On an application by the Labour Party, the first court and later the Court of Appeal and the Privy Council (*Buttigieg v. Borg Olivier noe*, Civil Court, First Hall, 03.11.63; Court of Appeal, 01.10.64; Privy Council, 04.19.66) declared the minister's order to be violating the right of freedom of expression.   In turning down the defendant's appeal, the Court of Appeal laid down two important principles: (a) the executive could not pretend immunity from court proceedings when exercising an extralegal administrative act; and (b) in deciding what was permissible or justifiable in a democratic society, one could not ignore the ethical and social values of the judge himself and the consideration that the point at issue was one of balance between the power of the administration and the freedom of the individual.

This was indeed a promising start by the Maltese courts.   In subsequent years, however, though more was to come, a number of decisions departed from this course.   Periodically, the Maltese courts in their constitutional role have been asked to decide on the constitutionality of laws, what is reasonably justifiable in a democratic society, what amounts to an "emergency," what constitutes discrimination on political grounds, what are their duties when the executive seeks to stifle the right of access to the courts, what are Parliament's rights in matters of contempt and breach of privilege, and generally to delineate the frontiers of human rights in the jungle world of administrative discretion. What follows depicts the stand taken by the Maltese courts in some of these diverse spheres of review.

The Legitimacy of Executive Acts

One of the very first principles in this area was established by the Constitutional Court when it rejected the contention of the executive that to impugn an act done under a law as a violation of human rights the law itself must be impugned (*Police v. G. Camilleri*, Constitutional Court, 04.23.65). The same contention was turned down again in two subsequent cases, but when in 1982 it was once again brought forward, the same court, differently constituted, reversed the judgment of the first court, holding that no administrative act done in virtue of a law or regulation could ever be considered to be in violation of the human rights provisions unless the law or the regulation itself were in violation (*Galea v. Commissioner of Police et*, Constitutional Court, 10.20.82). Fortunately, in 1988 the same court, differently presided and once more differently constituted, reverted to the original position, asserting that every act of a public authority can be challenged by the individual on the ground of an alleged violation of human rights provisions without the need also to challenge the law by virtue of which the act is alleged to have been done (*Galea v. Commissioner of Police*, Constitutional Court, 11.25.88).

Constitutional Review of Legislative Acts

Through constitutional review of Legislative Acts, Maltese courts have established that:

1. The Maltese Parliament is supreme only within the limits of the Constitution[8] and in terms of the same Constitution, the courts have the right to review the legality and constitutionality of legislative acts (*Mintoff v. Borg Olivier*, Constitutional Court, 11.05.70).
2. When a law is passed by Parliament, the courts will accord to it the presumption of constitutionality until the contrary is proved by plaintiff (*Vassallo v. Prime Minister*, Constitutional Court, 02.27.78; *Debono v. Prime Minister*, Constitutional Court, 08.28.84).

3. When Parliament applies a "social purpose" label to an enactment, the courts ought to respect and not to question it (*Debono v. Prime Minister*). In 1987, however, the Constitutional Court, once more differently constituted, went back on this statement, holding that it was not bound to decide in compliance with the administration's social policy (*Debono Grech v. Mizzi noe*, 12.24.87).

4. The courts will enquire whether a law infringes human rights even though Parliament declares the object of that law to be "in the national interest."[9]

An illustration of constitutional review of legislative acts arose in 1986 with regard to the powers and privileges of the House of Representatives. The editor of a satirical weekly was summoned before the House to face charges of contempt. The editor challenged in court Parliament's right to try anybody for contempt or breach of privilege, submitting that such proceedings made mockery of the fundamental right of access to a court and for a fair hearing. The first court decided in his favor, but on appeal the Constitutional Court reversed the judgment, holding that proceedings for contempt of Parliament constituted an exception to the constitutional rights of personal freedom and freedom of expression and that this restriction applied also to the right to a fair trial (*Demicoli v. Speaker of the House of Representatives*, Civil Court, First Hall, 05.16.86; Constitutional Court, 10.13.86). Subsequently, this case was heard before the European Court of Human Rights, which decided that proceedings for contempt of Parliament violated the basic right to a fair trial and access to an impartial and independent tribunal (ECHR, Case of *Demicoli v. Malta*, 33/1990/224-288, 08.27.91). Steps have been taken to revise the whole parliamentary procedure on contempt and breach of privilege, transferring Parliament's right to prosecute, try, and punish offenders to the ordinary courts.

A further decision of the Constitutional Court of particular interest involved a 1977 act that prohibited lawyers who were also members of Parliament from appearing in any civil proceedings against the executive and from defending persons charged with certain specified crimes. In the same year the editor of one of the opposition's weekly papers was charged with sedition and engaged as his defense counsel the deputy leader of his party who was also a member of Parliament. The question whether the accused could be defended by him arose and was referred for decision by the Civil Court, which found the Act to be in harmony with the Constitution. On appeal, the Constitutional Court reversed this judgment declaring that in limiting the choice of a defense counsel in criminal proceedings, the act violated the right of an accused to be assisted by a lawyer of his or her own choice (*Police v. Falzon*, Civil Court, First Hall, 07.29.83; Constitutional Court, 09.26.88). In a subsequent judgment the same court further extended this unconstitutionality to the other part of the act, which made the same prohibition applicable to constitutional cases (*Police v. Ellul Sullivan*, Constitutional Court, 04.05.89).[10]

In September 1982, Parliament passed the so-called Foreign Interference Act, allegedly necessary to avoid big-power interference in the domestic affairs of a small country. This law, which attracted widespread international censure, prohibited the holding of any activity by foreigners in Malta except with the permission of the minister of foreign affairs. The executive interpreted the act as requiring permission even for lectures by foreigners to groups of businessmen and trade unions. In February 1985, an Italian citizen, Massimo Gorla, president of the European Union of Young Christian Democrats, was charged under the act after addressing a Nationalist Party rally. He was released on bail and allowed to leave Malta, but his case progressed before the court, which declared that parts of the act violated the fundamental freedom of expression and communication and were, hence, unconstitutional (*Police v. M.Gorla*, Civil Court, First Hall, 07.16.86).

Constitutional Review of Executive Discretion

A decision of major importance that cut a further inroad in the field of constitutional judicial review of administrative discretion relates to the decisions of the Public Service Commission. This commission is created by the Constitution for the purpose of advising the prime minister in making appointments to public offices and taking disciplinary measures against them. The Constitution provides that the question of whether the commission has validly performed any of its vested functions shall not be inquired into in any court. The Constitutional Court, however, has asserted the principle that the commission in its deliberations had to observe the constitutional provisions on human rights and that any violation of those provisions would be reviewed by the courts (*Galea v. Chairman, PSC*, Constitutional Court, 11.25.85).

The courts have been less enterprising when they came to deciding what constitutes an emergency. The Maltese Constitution suspends certain human rights in the event of an emergency. For example, two types of emergency—a state of public emergency formally proclaimed by the president of the republic or by Parliament, and "any other emergency or calamity that threatens the life or well being of the community"—can suspend the fundamental protection against forced labor (Constitution, Sec. 35 (2)(d)). There is no definition or example of this second type of emergency in the Constitution though there are sufficient pointers to distinguish it from other situations of crisis, public discomfort or uneasiness.

In 1977 the majority of breadmakers who manufacture the traditional Maltese loaf staged a strike, ignoring a ministerial order forcing them to return to work under threat of penal sanction. One of the bakers who had contravened the order challenged the ministerial order. During the hearing of the case, the ministry of Trade announced that the bread supply had remained constant and normal. Nevertheless, the court decided that the bakers' strike constituted "an emergency or calamity, threatening the life and well being of the community" and did not overturn the ministerial order (*Mula v. Minister of Trade*, Civil Court, First Hall, 03.21.77).

Also in 1977, after a partial strike by state-employed physicians, Parliament quickly passed a law providing that striking doctors who did not sign a declaration withdrawing from all industrial action could no longer exercise their profession in private hospitals, which had had nothing to do with the dispute. The doctors' union attacked this law as a violation of their constitutional rights. The executive, meanwhile, locked out the doctors from all government hospitals, recruited other local and foreign doctors, and repeatedly claimed that the situation in the hospital sector was not only well under control but had also considerably improved. A later law summarily dismissed all the doctors who had taken part in the strike. The court of first instance recognized the existence of an emergency *ex officio* and rejected all the doctors' complaints on that basis (*Cuschieri v. Prime Minister*, Civil Court, First Hall, 08.29.77; confirmed on appeal by the Constitutional Court, 11.30.77).

These two cases attracted widespread criticism, especially since the presiding judges had taken upon themselves the task of declaring a state of emergency when the executive branch itself had categorically excluded it. This criticism and general feeling of discontent and disillusion with what was considered as the courts' passive attitude to the executive's strong hand grew as more and more cases came before the courts and were repeatedly decided in favor of the administration. In 1980 one of the judges of the Constitutional Court resigned, and in 1981 the chief justice and president of the same court followed suit. The Constitutional Court was reconstituted, but until 1983 no significant progress was registered. When the courts then began to overturn the executive, the inevitable happened—the judges and the administration came into direct confrontation, and by 1987 the situation had precipitated near-collapse of the whole system. Three cases are of major significance in this development.

Confrontation Between the Executive and the Judiciary

In 1983, the Parliament passed a law vesting in the state "certain rights over immovable property acquired by any Church or other Pious or Religious Institution." This law in effect transferred to state ownership over 80 percent of the Catholic Church's property. In September 1984, the court of first instance declared the law unconstitutional because it violated the freedom of conscience, confiscated church property without adequate compensation, and discriminated against the Catholic Church.[11] Four days later there was a mob assault on the law courts in which parts of the court building were gutted by fire.

In April 1984 a law was passed that gave the state direct control over all private schools in Malta. The constitutionality of this law was challenged by the Catholic Church as well as by associations representing teachers of private schools and parents of children attending those schools. What followed has been described as the "Calvary of the School Cases (*Sunday Times of Malta*, October 6, 1985, 13)." At one stage, the judge of first instance was challenged by counsel to the prime minister,[12] but the judge refused to step down. The prime minister appealed from a preliminary decree of the same judge to the Constitutional Court. Following various spontaneous abstentions and challenges, only three judges were left to constitute that court to hear and determine the appeal. The prime minister challenged them as well. The three judges, however, refused to step down, issuing a judgment in which they declared (*The Archbishop v. The Prime Minister et noe*, Constitutional Court, 10.22.1984) that (a) the Constitution requires that there must be, at all times, a Constitutional Court, even if the executive fails in its duty to constitute it; and (b) even though only three judges remained to decide the case, because all the others had been disqualified, the doctrine of necessity imposed on them the duty to remain, in spite of attempts to challenge them because the fundamental right of access to a court would be meaningless without the existence of a court.

The case went back to the first judge, who was again challenged by the prime minister and again refused to abstain. On November 7, 1984, following an incident that had arisen two days earlier during a sitting, the prime minister once more requested the judge's abstention. At the same time a motion was tabled in Parliament threatening the judge with suspension from his duties should he continue to refuse to abstain.[13] In spite of the protests of the bench and a threat by all the judges to resign en bloc, Parliament proceeded to pass the resolution, and the judge in question did what he had thrice declared he was not prepared or entitled to do—he disqualified himself from hearing and deciding the case. The executive did not appoint another judge to hear the cases, which were thus left desperately in search of a judge for the following years.[14]

The final confrontation came toward the end of 1986 in what has since come to be known as the Zejtun Case. The opposition party applied to hold a mass meeting at the village of Zejtun, well known as a Labour Party stronghold. A permit was originally issued, but, following protests by a number of Zejtun Labourites, allegedly on the insistence of the commissioner of police that he was not in a position to guarantee order, the prime minister withdrew the permit. The matter ended up before the courts. The defendants, the prime minister and the commissioner of police, contended that they were solely responsible for public order and that they, not the courts, had the final say in such a matter. Both the court of first instance and the Constitutional Court declared that the ban imposed by the commissioner of police and the prime minister violated the fundamental rights of freedom of association and freedom of speech (*Fenech Adami v. Commissioner of Police*, Civil Court, First Hall, 11.28.86; Constitutional Court, 11.29.86). Both courts held that the burden of proving a clear and present danger, sufficient to justify the restraint of fundamental freedoms, fell on the authorities, and that in this case the executive had failed to provide sufficient evidence to prove the existence of this danger. The Constitutional Court also expressed its faith that Maltese society was sufficiently organized to ensure the existence of fundamental human rights by preventing abuses by those who allegedly would stifle such rights, and it proceeded to annul the ban.

After the judgment, according to newspaper reports (*The Times of Malta*, November 30, December 1, 1986; *Sunday Times of Malta*, December 7, 21, 1986), the executive, instead of deploying the police to ensure observance of the court's order, allowed a large number of thugs to disrupt the meeting.   The end result was tear gas, shots, arson, seventy persons wounded, and a full-scale public attack by the prime minister on the judges who had decided the case, holding them responsible for what had happened, accusing them of ignorance and irresponsibility, and affirming that in future he was prepared to go to prison and disobey the order of the court.[15]

All this happened during the heat of the election campaign, which ended six months later with the Labour Party being defeated.   Under the new administration the confrontation between the judiciary and the executive came to an end, but a taste of what could have been in store had this change not taken place was given soon after the 1987 elections: on June 19, while some Labourites were being arraigned in court on charges of corrupt practices, a second mob assault resulted in the looting and gutting of the law courts.

CONCLUSION

We have traced out the wandering route pursued by the Maltese judiciary in the field of the judicialization of politics and mapped the basis for a future scientific investigation.   For much of the period covered, Malta was a British colony, and the matter of judicial review was not in any way regulated by statute.   During this period the Maltese judges did assert a limited right of review of legislative acts and executive discretion, but in general they showed more restraint than activism in the judicial review.   In some areas, they seemed more willing to limit the exercise of discretionary powers, and in others less willing, sometimes even reluctant.   The question of the legitimacy of judicial review was never really contested at the political level by the other two branches of government; it was clarified by the judges themselves, who decided to impose limitations on their right of review of legislative acts and executive discretion.   The judges themselves created a measure of control that the rest of the political system tolerated.   In this way the legitimacy of the courts' right of review never became a controversial issue, and judicial decisions were considered authoritative and binding by the political community at large.

With the promulgation of the Independence Constitution, the judiciary was assigned the difficult task of restraining the other two branches of the state from working their momentary will. The Constitution also entrusted the judiciary with the role of interpreting this basic instrument of government and of reviewing the legality and constitutionality of legislative enactments. In this context the judiciary is placed by the Constitution above the other branches of government.

At the same time the courts, being an integral part of the machinery of government, have to contend with the actions and reactions of those who control the various levels of the other two branches and whose decisions are politically motivated. While the roles of the legislature and the executive necessarily entail giving voice to contemporary political sentiment, the judiciary was not conceived or designed as the third barometer of current public opinion. The political environment in which the courts operate, nevertheless, necessarily has a bearing on the extent and effectiveness of judicial review.

It is against this background that the Maltese courts' real political power, as distinct from their formal legal power, can be determined. The postindependence era has been a trying experience both for the judiciary and for democracy in Malta. As the judiciary emerged from a century-old dormancy to assume its new role as watchdog of the Constitution and guardian of human rights, it clashed with the other two branches of government mainly on the question of legitimacy of the extent of review they had undertaken, both in their normal adjudicative role and in their constitutional role.

The limitations that the judges themselves had imposed on their right of review in the past, the slow takeoff in their new role, the lack of uniformity and homogeneity among some judges in their approach to the question of review left room for the other two branches of government to try limiting these powers of review as soon as some judges became more activist than others. The administration of the day also tried to nip judicial activism in the bud by resorting to high-handed tactics and measures. But as these increased and as executive discretion became more arbitrary, judicial activism increased, and so did the homogeneity of the approach to judicial review by the bench in general.

During the last five years of the Labour administration, the Constitutional Court declared one violation of human rights provisions after another, and a final clash would have been inevitable had the 1987 election reconfirmed the Labour Party in power. Since 1987 the more arbitrary, judicial activism increased, and so did the homogeneity of the approach to judicial review by the bench in general.

During the last five years of the Labour administration, the Constitutional Court declared one violation of human rights provisions after another, and a final clash would have been inevitable had the 1987 election reconfirmed the Labour Party in power. Since 1987 the introduction of the right of individual petition, the recognition of the compulsory jurisdiction of the European Court of Human Rights, and the incorporation of the convention into domestic law have somewhat changed the outlook for the future. These factors put the judiciary in a stronger position, provide it with a sounder foundation, and pave the way for a more vital and more meaningful expansion of judicial power.

NOTES

1. These included:

a. Matters of policy were not the proper concern of the law courts (*Zammit v. Ellul Mercer*, vol. 40.2.920).

b. The ultra vires doctrine was accepted as possible ground for review. Due, however, to the absolute *jus imperii* notion, the courts were bound to interpret the doctrine restrictively, limiting it to matters of necessary formalities and competence.

c. The administration cannot by an act *jure gestionis* fetter the exercise of a discretion *iure imperii* (*Buttigieg v. Cross*, vol. 31.1.398; *Ciantar v. Camilleri*, vol. 35.1.83) and an act *iure imperii* can be subsequently revoked by the same authority (*Ciantar v. Camilleri*; *Zammit v. Ellul Mercer*). Alternatively, a competent authority may by a subsequent act *iure imperii* limit the operation of a previous action (*Aquilina v. Ellul Mercer noe*, vol. 42.1.165).

2. The more important of these additional restrictions are the following:

a. The principle that the courts may not discuss the policy of a government department is the corollary of their basic function to ensure due observance of the law (*Micallef v. Podestá*, Civil Court, First Hall, 01.10.61).

b. It was doubtful whether the administration could fetter away its discretion by previous commitments or declaration of its policies (*Grech v. Farrugia noe*, Civil Court, First Hall, 11.18.64).

c. The court can review a discretionary exercise only to see whether the act was performed by the competent authorities and according to the formalities prescribed by law (*Vincenti v. Farrugia noe*, Court of Appeal, 06.26.67).

d. If the executive could by a departmental letter limit the scope of its future action, a fortiori the legislature could impose restrictions on the exercise of powers it had originally granted (*Camilleri v. Reginiano*, Court of Appeal, 05.04.73).

3. It did so by laying down three important principles to oust the *jus imperii* doctrine as a test of control in the exercise of executive discretion:

a. The executive and its servants are always liable before a court of law unless excluded by express provision of the law.

b. In the absence of special administrative tribunals as in other continental countries have, the Maltese system adopted the Anglo-American principle, that the ordinary courts should ensure due observance of the law even by the organs of the State within the limits of judicial review.

c. Maltese public law derives from English public law, a principle recognized by various Maltese judgments and by no means abrogated or modified by the granting of independence.

The court went on to assert the principle that a discretion should be exercised according to law and that a court of law may examine the motives of the administrative action to see whether discretion has been properly exercised or whether extraneous considerations were taken into account.

4. Act 35 of 1990 amended the Interpretation Act (1975) to restore to these public officers the exercise of their discretion, but reserving for the minister the power to give directions in writing relative to the exercise of that power, including a direction ordering the reversal of a decision.

5. This occurred because of some loopholes in the Constitution that have since then been remedied. Prior to the amendments which were made to the Constitution in 1974 the president had as one of his functions assigning judges to the Constitutional Court when the need arose. But the Constitution did not impose a time limit on the president and did not provide for the automatic composition of the court in case the president failed to nominate the judges. By Act 58 of 1974 these shortcomings were taken care of.

6. This has been possible as a result of a legacy of colonial times during which the governor as head of the executive had the right to assign to each judge his duties. This prerogative was retained after independence. Throughout this century, in practice, however, saving this exception, the distribution of work has always been decided by the judges themselves and then rubber-stamped by the head of the executive branch. Talks are under way with the ministry of justice to transfer this power to the projected Supreme Council of the Judicature.

7. In 1990, the then minister of justice, speaking at an international conference, stated that the 1981 law was to be reviewed. This has yet not taken place.

8. With the coming into force of 14 XIV of 1987, the supremacy of the Maltese Parliament is also limited by the European Convention on Human Rights.

9. This important principle was established by the First Hall of the Civil Court in the Church Property case (*The Archbishop v. The Prime Minister*),

decided on 09.24.84. That court had then proceeded to annul the Devolution of Certain Church Property Act of 1983.

10. As a result of this judgment and international pressure, the act was subsequently amended to conform to the Constitution and the European Convention.

11. The state appealed from this judgment to the Constitutional Court, where the case dragged on until 1987, when it was withdrawn by the Nationalist administration which was elected in that year.

12. The presiding judge was challenged on the ground that during the first sitting he had declared that as a child he had attended a private school. The prime minister had initially lodged no objection to this statement.

13. The text of the motion read as follows:

> This House resolves that should Mr Justice Carmelo Scicluna decide to continue hearing the case himself, the Minister of Justice shall take all necessary steps according to law in order that the said judge would be prevented from doing so. Furthermore, this House urges the Minister of Justice, in cases of similar abuses in the future, to consider first whether it would be less harmful to the people that a judge should continue to receive his salary whilst being relieved of his duties than to be allowed to decide cases according to his passions; and then to table a resolution in this House in order that such judge would be removed from his duties as judge although he would continue to receive his salary.

For censures of this resolution, see the *Bulletin of the Center for the Independence of Judges and Lawyers* (1985), the *Report of the International Helsinki Federation for Human Rights on Human Rights in Malta* (1985), and *The Review* of the International Commission of Jurists (1984).

14. The Church Schools dispute eventually was taken up between the state and the Vatican authorities, and an agreement was reached in 1991. The resolution was never applied and lapsed with the dissolution of Parliament in 1987.

15. See the *Unofficial Debates of the House of Representatives* (sitting of December 10, 1986) wherein the prime minister is reported as saying

> I regret to say that I made a mistake not to stick to my decision to ban the meeting a second time after that the court had decided, and I accepted the advice of others, after what had already happened in Zejtun. No judge can take away from me the responsibility. No judge has any rights, according to law, to do this. When those responsible for public order, the Commissioner of Police and the Prime Minister feel in conscience that public order will be broken, the courts must bow their heads. This they must do according to the law. If there will be another case, and in my

conscience, I feel the same as I felt about the Zejtun meeting, I am prepared to go to prison and disobey the order of the court.

This followed a statement that the prime minister had made some days earlier and in which he is reported to have said "Whether we acted according to law can be said by the courts, but if it was a good decision or not, will be said by the people. I am amazed how so many men of wisdom in the courts fail to see this. Even the courts will one day learn to perform their duties properly." (*Sunday Times of Malta*, December 21, 1986, 13).

REFERENCES

Bulletin of the Center for the Independence of Judges and Lawyers. 1985. no. 17.

Cremona, J. J. 1990. "The European Convention on Human Rights as part of Maltese Law." In *Selected Papers, 1946-1989*, ed J. J. Cremona. Malta: PEG Ltd.

Galligan, Brian. 1989. *Politics of the High Court: A Study of the Judicial Branch of Government in Australia.* Brisbane: University of Queensland Press.

Harding, H. W. 1968. *Maltese Legal History Under British Rule (1801-1836).* London: Progress Press.

International Commission of Jurists. 1984. *The Review*, No.33 (December): 12.

Mercieca, A. 1969. *The Making and Unmaking of a Maltese Chief Justice.* Malta: Muscat Press.

Report of the International Helsinki Federation for Human Rights on Human Rights in Malta. 1985.

Sunday Times of Malta. October 6, 1985-December 21, 1986.

The Times of Malta. November 30-December 1, 1986.

Unofficial Debates of the House of Representatives. 1986. Malta.

22.

Israel

MARTIN EDELMAN

The judicialization of politics has probably proceeded further in Israel than in any other democratic country. In the strong sense of the definition propounded by Torbjörn Vallinder, the civil judiciary in Israel, particularly the Supreme Court justices sitting as members of the High Court of Justice, are exercising power at the expense of politicians and administrators. The justices now claim the authority even to review the internal workings of the theoretically sovereign Knesset (parliament).

The expansive nature of judicial power within the current governmental system of Israel is a marked change from the situation just forty-four years ago when the state came into existence. Then, power and authority was concentrated in the elected agencies—the Knesset and, particularly, the government. Rampant partisanship, arbitrary and self-interested policies, and, worst of all, an inability to deal with crucial problems besetting Israeli society, corroded that authority and, ulti- mately, the power of the elected leadership. The default of Israel's democratically elected leadership has led to the judicialization of politics.

Rampant partisanship has been a feature of the state since before its inception in 1948. Most of today's political parties had their origins in the Zionist movement, which created Israel. They were voluntary associations formed to build the homeland in Palestine, each with its own vision of what the future Jewish state should be like. Each party sought to influence the course of events not only by direct political action in

Mandate Palestine and within the World Zionist Organization, but also by establishing institutions that reflected its own ideology. Throughout the prestate period (1920-1948), the Jewish political parties tended to be more like "totalistic" movement type parties than the specialized electoral mechanisms found in the United States. (Duverger 1954; Medding 1990)

In the early years of the state the same pattern continued and was actually reinforced by government policies. The mass immigrations, first from the displaced-persons camps in Europe and then from the Arab countries was handled largely by the Jewish Agency. Agency officials followed the established pattern of allocating "resources" on a proportional basis to the various Zionist parties. The new immigrants were apportioned among the political parties on the basis of a party key, and each party was responsible for integrating its quota of immigrants into society. As with the earlier, prestate immigrants, the new arrivals were supplied housing, education, employment, and so forth, by party-affiliated institutions.

Gradually, state institutions replaced party ones. In 1953 a state school system replaced those run by the political blocs.[1] In 1959 state labor exchanges replaced those operated by the political parties. A state Ministry of Immigration and Absorption was created, though the division of functions between it and the Jewish Agency remain less than fully articulated. Moreover, the initial disposition of the new immigrants had no legitimacy in the law or the fundamental ideology of the new state; it had simply been the product of expediency. Hence when the economy began to expand in the mid-1950s, the new immigrants felt free to move outside the party orbits to which they had been assigned, and they were given practical encouragement to do so by the increased demand for manpower in the urban centers.

Thus, over time, the extragovernmental role of the Israeli political parties has been reduced. It has not been eliminated; the parties still provide their members with a variety of ancillary services—youth movements, athletic activities, health services, and so forth. Furthermore, the creation of government agencies did not invariably displace the parties. Except for the Israel Defense Forces and the civil judiciary, Israeli government bureaucracies show an excessive tenderness toward partisan considerations. Through appointments, patronage, contracts, and administrative rulings, government ministries have been turned into party institutions under other names. In Israel, the emergence of a state bureaucracy has not resulted in the implementation of Max Weber's rationalistic, legal norms or in the withering away of the political parties. By all accounts, partisan influence still matters a great deal in Israel.

It should also be noted that until May 1977 Israeli politics was dominated by Mapai and its successor, the Labor Party. For the first twenty-nine years of statehood, and indeed throughout most of the thirty years of the British Mandate, which preceded independence, the Jewish community in Palestine was led by socialists. Although the Mapai-Labor leadership group was more pragmatic than doctrinaire, and although they were never able to enact their complete program, they were ideologically disposed to a state-run society. By design, the "House of Labor" permeated all aspects of Israeli society (Perlmutter 1970; Medding 1972). The governments elected in 1977 and 1992 were dominated by Likud, a party that is more ideologically inclined toward a market economy. But the temptations to utilize the "spoils of office" for partisan advantage outweighed Likud's ideological commitment to privatization. Israel remains a society dominated by government institutions directed by highly partisan political parties.

Thus the key political institutions of Israel are not the formal governmental agencies but the political parties. This is particularly true of the parties that form the cabinet coalition and thereby control the ministries. Israel is a highly politicized nation. From the early days of the British Mandate, political parties have been omnipresent and powerful institutions within the Jewish community. This role has diminished somewhat under the growing impact of state institutions, yet political parties in Israel still "occupy a more prominent place and exercise a more pervasive influence than in any other state, with the exception of some one-party states" (Akzin 1955, 509).

As might be expected in this environment, overt partisan considerations are inescapable elements in the workings of the Knesset and the government (cabinet). Parliamentary parties act to further, in that arena, the ideological goals of the Zionist groups that spawned them. Party discipline is exceptionally strong; the member of Knesset is expected faithfully to carry out the party's program. Despite the multiparty system, and despite the failure of any single election list ever to obtain a parliamentary majority, decisions reached by the government are rarely overturned by the Knesset; the centralized hierarchical nature of Israeli political parties all but insures a parliamentary majority for any government proposal. As a result, Israelis expect that public policies emanating from these institutions will reflect the partisan concerns of the parties in the governing coalition.

Since Israeli democracy has always been based upon a wide-open, robust competition among a multitude of political parties, Israelis have been keenly aware that their security from arbitrary governmental coercion is based upon a rather strict adherence to the ideal of the rule of law. The clash of partisan and ideological values has even prevented Israel from adopting a written constitution (Edelman 1980; Edelman 1992b). Without a written constitution, Israelis perceive that the rule of law is the only way to limit some of the more egregious consequences of their highly partisan politics. And like the rest of the Western world, Israelis see the courts as the guardians of that value.

The rule of law "means that government in all its actions is bound by rules fixed and announced beforehand—rules that make it possible to foresee with a fair certainty how the authority will use its coercive powers in given circumstances and to plan one's individual affairs on the basis of this knowledge" (Hayek 1944, 72). The idea that all governmental action must be authorized by law is the residue of the long, historical struggle against tyrannical rule. And the horrors perpetrated by so many regimes during the twentieth century have powerfully reinforced the importance of the rule of law as a hedge against arbitrary, ad hoc governmental action, that can be potentially brutal to the point of genocide.

From this perspective, law is seen as something quite distinct from politics. In politics, values and principles are perceived as instrumental tools for achieving certain results. Law, on the other hand, is perceived as flowing from an impartial, objective analysis of rules and principles. Law and politics are seen as distinct methods of conflict resolution (Wechsler 1959).

To protect the rule of law, the Israeli political elite, consciously and with considerable effort, decided to insulate the judiciary from the political environment. To maintain the civil judiciary's independence from the partisan political arena, the judges, particularly the Supreme Court justices, are selected on professional criteria rather than on the basis of economic, social, or political characteristics. And the separation between the civil courts and partisan politics is systematically reinforced by an array of operating practices and norms (Edelman 1992a).

Because the civil courts, particularly the Supreme Court, are seen as "the traditional repository of independent, objective, and impartial decision" (Elman 1971, 405), they have come to play an increasingly important role within Israeli society. In the thirty-two-year period from 1956 to 1987, the number of cases entered on the Supreme Court docket increased a staggering 632 percent while the population increased by 230 percent. In the exercise of its broad equity jurisdiction, the Supreme Court sitting as the High Court of Justice received 1,466 petitions in 1987, more than seven times as many as thirty-two years earlier (Central Bureau of Statistics 1956, 328; 1958, 8). Israelis are asking the civil courts—especially the High Court—to render judgment on an increasingly large number of matters.

Moreover, the Israeli public plainly trusts the judgment of the civil courts. Recent Israeli surveys indicate that the civil courts are second only to the Israel Defense Forces—the quintessential guardian of the national interest—in public support. And as table 22.1 indicates, that trust greatly exceeds the public's confidence in the overtly partisan policy institutions—the Knesset, the government, and especially, the political parties themselves.

It is also important to note that the deep support for the civil courts is held throughout society. Trust in the civil courts does not vary from group to group, between the politically liberal and the politically conservative (Yuchtman-Ya'ar 1989, 10-11). That would indicate that support for the civil courts is indeed based upon the public's respect and concern for the rule of law.

It is also possible that the data reflect the Israeli public's almost total disdain for the immobilism that has beset Israeli political institutions for at least the last decade. Israeli surveys do not, like their American counterparts, probe *why* people view the judiciary as they do. But as table 22.1 indicates, the political parties are consistently the least trusted Israeli institutions. And in recent years the Knesset, and particularly the government, have suffered a precipitous decline in public esteem. The reason is clear to all: the partisan political agencies of the Israeli government are unable to deal with important, clearly recognized problems.

Israeli governments are preoccupied with maintaining their parliamentary coalitions rather than with formulating and implementing public policies. The precarious nature of government stability is undoubtedly linked to the multiplicity of parties within the single chamber Knesset. Because no single party list has ever won a majority

of the 120 seats since the establishment of the state, all governments
have, of necessity, been based upon parliamentary coalitions.

Table 22.1: Trust in Israeli Institutions (rank indicated after slash)

	1987	1989	1990	Total
IDF	90.3 /1	91.5 /1	88.5 /1	90.1 /1
Courts	82.5 /2	79.3 /2	77.8 /2	79.9 /2
Universities	75.5 /3	68.8 /4	68.0 /4	70.7 /3
Police	62.0 /4	69.8 /3	72.5 /3	68.1 /4
Knesset	59.8 /5	52.3 /5.5	48.0 /7	53.4 /6
Government	59.5 /6	52.3 /5.5	46.8 /9	52.9 /7
Local Govt.	58.5 /7	50.8 /7	53.0 /5	54.1 /5
Histadrut	45.3 /8	34.5 /11	40.3 /10	40.0 /10
Rabbinate	43.5 /9	50.5 /8	50.5 /6	48.2 /8
Big Business	43.3 /10	38.5 /9	47.5 /8	43.1 /9
Press	40.3 /11	38.0 /10	38.8 /11	39.0 /11
Pol. Parties	34.8 /12	30.3 /12	32.0 /12	32.4 /12
Average	57.9	54.7	55.3	55.5

Source: Yuchtman-Ya'ar and Peres (1991, 24).

For most of Israel's short history, its multiparty system has not
precluded strong government. From 1948 to 1977, the Labor Party (or
its predecessor, Mapai) was the dominant party. Any and all public
policy successes and failures could fairly be attributed to its leadership.
After the 1977 elections, a Labor-led government, that had begun to drift
aimlessly, was replaced by a Likud-led coalition. And in the first two
Likud-led governments (1977-1984) that party was clearly directing the
ship of state.

Since 1984, however, neither of the two large parties has had a
dominating plurality in the Knesset. There has been a continual, fierce
jockeying for power. At times a National Unity government based upon
both large parties imposed a temporary cease-fire in the political wars.
But the significant ideological differences between Labor and Likud
—especially over the future control of the areas Israel has administered

since the 1967 Six Day War—has precluded strong, sustained government policy-making; the ministers were more concerned with possible future coalitions with some of the smaller parties. At other times, Likud formed a government with several smaller parties. But their policy demands, particularly those of the Orthodox (Jewish) religious parties, also resulted in policy stalemate. As a result, the political system, dominated by the party structures, seems incapable of utilizing governmental agencies to deal with social problems.

Therefore, public cynicism born of governmental immobilism may also account for the expansion of judicial power in Israel. Within the existing structures, the civil judiciary appears to provide the only rational, objective policymakers.[2] In contrast to the politicians, the judges appear willing to decide matters (rather than to postpone) regardless of the political fallout and to decide on the basis of standards and principles rather than on electoral considerations. The courts, therefore, are continuously being asked to rule on an ever-wider range of matters.

The partisanship and immobilism besetting Israel's elected institutions explains the judiciary's increasingly important role. In 1948 the Supreme Court functioned very much like the House of Lords in the British system; its impact on governmental policies was on the margins. Now the Israeli Supreme Court is exercising power akin to that of its American counterpart; it is an important player in the public policy process.

This change was facilitated by the dual nature of the Supreme Court's jurisdiction. One part is quite unexceptional. Within Israel (including all of Jerusalem),[3] the civil courts—the Magistrates Courts, the District Courts, and the Supreme Court—have basic jurisdiction in criminal and civil matters. The Israeli Supreme Court, as the final authoritative interpreter of the law of the state, has full appellate jurisdiction over the procedure and substance of criminal, civil, and administrative cases decided by the District Courts. It also hears appeals from such other tribunals as the labor courts, worker's compensation boards, and rent tribunals. (Basic Law: The Judiciary 1984; Courts Law 1984)

Another part of the Israeli Supreme Court's jurisdiction is quite distinctive. It exercises an equity jurisdiction both as a court of first instance and on appeal. In this capacity, sitting as the High Court of Justice, it deals with matters in which it may be necessary to grant relief in "the interest of justice." Palestinians in the occupied areas were granted access to the Israeli High Court by a decision of the government not to oppose such applications.[4] Thus the High Court of Justice deals with claims by Palestinians that the Israeli occupying authorities—the Civil administration—have exceeded or misapplied their powers in the same way that it hears petitions by Israeli citizens against their government.

The High Court is also authorized to review the actions of the military court. But it will interfere with the judgment of a military court only if that court plainly exceeded its authority or if a clear injustice has been done to the petitioner. In the High Court's review of decisions from the various religious courts,[5] only questions of whether a case is properly within the jurisdiction of a religious court will be entertained.

This jurisdictional arrangement has permitted the civil courts, particularly the Supreme Court functioning as the High Court of Justice, to change their focus to match the changed environment in which they have functioned. In the early years of the state, the Supreme Court was necessarily concerned with establishing its authority by generating respect for its decisions. The justices were aware that in the turbulent domestic and international situation of their new state, appeals to practical necessity could be used to evade or ignore court orders. Therefore, the early Supreme Court opinions were characterized by highly formalistic legal style, narrow interpretations of statutes and precedents, adherence to stare decisis, and deference to the decisions of the Knesset, the government, and the Israel Defense Forces. Throughout, the civil courts emphasized the importance of the rule of law and their own adherence to those rules (*Zeev v. Gubernick* 1948; *Bezerano v. Minister of Police* 1949; *Al-Couri v. Chief of Staff* 1950).

Gradually the civil courts, particularly the Supreme Court, expanded its conception of the rule of law. In a number of important cases, the Supreme Court asserted the right to interpret legislation in light of the principles of natural justice. Rights to a hearing and to cross-examination were required in statutory proceedings that did not provide such safeguards. Administrative discretion to deny licenses, to determine election lists, to register companies, and to censor newspapers was substantially curtailed (Albert 1969; Goldstein 1982). By 1974 it was clear that the Israeli courts' concern for the rule of law was being extended to protect human rights (Shapira 1974).

Israeli citizens and even the Palestinians in the occupied areas responded by turning to the courts, particularly the High Court, with the increasing frequency noted above. The judges came to understand this new situation as the result of an increasing concern for the rule of law—the very ideal that they had helped establish. They recognized that the civil courts were perceived as the guardians of that value. In the absence of a written constitution, the judges now believe that the civil courts must be active policymakers: in the Israeli system, the courts provide recourse from arbitrary governmental decisions driven by partisan considerations; there is no other mechanism for protecting the individual rights and political liberties essential for maintaining Israeli democracy. "When the Court does not become involved," declared the justices, "the principle of the rule of law becomes flawed. A government that knows in advance that it is not subject to judicial review, is a government likely not to give dominion to the law, and likely to bring about its breach" (*Segal v. Minister of Interior* 1980). Justice Aharon Barak (1989) maintains, for example, that unlike their American counterparts, Israeli judges need not be constrained by exercising an undemocratic authority since in the absence of a written constitution their decisions can always be overridden by a legislative majority.

Israeli judges have responded to the ever-increasing appeals for judicial intervention by handing down decisions on an increasingly wider range of issues. The High Court has held that it has jurisdiction to examine the *internal* decisions of the Knesset itself, including a decision on whether a proposed bill can be tabled (*Sarid v. Speaker of the Knesset* 1982; *Kahane v. Speaker of the Knesset* 1985; *Kahane v. Speaker of the Knesset* 1986), and whether to remove the immunity of a Knesset member (*Mi'ari v. Speaker of the Knesset* 1987). Similarly, a government's highest policy objectives, like the Likud-led coalition's settlement policy in the West Bank, has been successfully challenged in the High Court (*Dweikat v. Government of Israel* 1980; *Samara v. Commander of Judea and Samaria* 1980; *Kfar Vradim and Others v. Minister of Finance, Eliyahu v. Minister of Defence and Others* 1989). As David Kretzmer (1990) says, "The net of judicial review extends over all arms of government, and over almost all types of activities." Only an explicit legislative act of the Knesset that does not conflict with an entrenched provision of a Basic Law is immune from judicial control (Edelman 1992b).

In Israel, a fascinating pattern has emerged from the sharp dichotomy that is seen between the operating norms of the political and legal realms. It is a phenomenon with significant consequence. Israeli politics is marked by intense ideological partisanship, a partisanship that is more extreme than in any other Western-oriented democracy. Policies emerging from the institutions rooted in the electoral system are therefore perceived as essentially partisan. The Israeli legal world is seen as operating on the basis of formal criteria. Decisions emerging from the civil courts are perceived as being rooted in the type of rule of law first enunciated by Max Weber ([1925] 1954). Precisely because the judges, particularly the Justices of the Supreme Court, are seen as the guardians of the fundamental values embedded in the rule of law, precisely because they are not seen as using their positions to advance special causes, they possess considerable authority.

Israel, like other Western societies, has inherited the ideal that the public realm ought to be based on the common good, that public policy ought to be made in the spirit of disinterestedness. In the actual political system of Israel, only the civil courts approximate that ideal. Therefore, in the highly politicized democracy that is Israel, authority—and considerable political power—has flowed toward its premier nonpartisan institution, the civil judiciary.

The judicialization of politics in Israel has been further accelerated by the functional immobilism of its elected agencies. At least since the 1982 Lebanon War, the government has been unable to formulate and implement systematic policies to address the most obvious problems confronting the nation: economic stagnation; absorption of the massive influx of Jewish immigrants from the countries of the former Soviet Union and from Ethiopia; and stable peace and/or security arrangements with the Palestinians and the rest of the Arab world. The coalition politics emerging from the multiparty Knesset have produced government policies that, at best, can only be characterized as temporizing, ad hoc efforts to muddle through. In that context, court decisions have a strikingly different character: they appear to be decisive policies based on fixed standards. The default of Israel's democratically elected leadership has produced a vacuum, and the people have turned to the courts to resolve an ever-increasing range of problems.

The civil judiciary in Israel is exercising power at the expense of politicians and administrators. At this writing, the judicialization of politics is an inexorable feature of Israeli society.

NOTES

1. The 1953 Act did not impose a single uniform system of education. There are four types of educational systems in Israel today: a state secular (Jewish) system; a state religious (Orthodox Jewish) system; a state Arab system; and a set of independent, largely ultra-Orthodox Jewish, religious schools, which are heavily subsidized by the government.

2. This frustration with the existing system accounts for the upsurge of institutional reform.   Currently Israel elects its Knesset via a proportional (closed list) system. In the closing days of the twelfth Knesset (March 1992), the percentage of votes needed to guarantee at least one seat in the Knesset was increased from one percent to 1.5 percent. More importantly, in 1996, the Israelis will elect their prime minister directly instead of having the premier emerge from the bargaining among the parliamentary parties.

3. Israel annexed East Jerusalem after the 1967 Six Day War and codified that annexation in Basic Law: Jerusalem (1980).

4. That action, allowing residents of an occupied area to have access to the civil courts of the occupying power, is unprecedented in international law and was not authorized by Israeli statutes. With the passage of time, it has become accepted practice in Israel.

5. There are fourteen state-recognized religious communities in Israel, each with its own court system: the Rabbinical Courts (Jewish); the Shari'a Courts (Muslim); the Druze Religious Courts; the Bahai Courts; and the courts of ten Christian communities—Eastern (Greek Orthodox); Latin (Catholic); Gregorian Armenian; Armenian (Catholic); Syrian (Catholic); Greek Catholic (Melkite); Maronite; Syrian Orthodox; Chaldean (Uniate); and Evangelical Episcopal. The religious courts have exclusive jurisdiction over members of their communities on matters relating to marriage and divorce; many of these courts also resolve other private law matters within their communities.

REFERENCES

BOOKS AND ARTICLES

Akzin, B. 1955.   "The Role of Parties in Israeli Democracy." *Journal of Politics* 17:507-545.

Albert, J. 1969. "Constitutional Adjudication without a Constitution: The Case of Israel." *Harvard Law Review* 82:1245-1265.

Barak, A. 1989. *Judicial Discretion*. New Haven: Yale University Press.

Central Bureau of Statistics. 1956. *Government Yearbook*. Jerusalem: Government Printing Office.

———. 1988. *Judicial Statistics*. Jerusalem: Government Printing Office.

Duverger, M. 1954. *Political Parties*. trans. B. North and R. North. New York: Wiley.

Edelman, M. 1980. "Politics and the Constitution in Israel." *Statsvetenskaplig Tidskrift* (Swedish Journal of Political Science) 3:171-181.

———. 1992a. "The Judicial Elite of Israel." *International Political Science Review* 13, 235-248.

———. 1992b. "Israel's Struggle for a Written Constitution." In *Comparative Judicial Review and Public Policy*, ed. D. W. Jackson and C. N. Tate. Westport, Conn.: Greenwood.

Elman, P. 1971. "The Commissions of Inquiry Law, 1968." *Israel Law Review* 6:398-409.

Goldstein, S. 1982. "The Influences of Constitutional Principles on Civil Procedure in Israel." *Israel Law Review* 17:467-510.

Hayek, F. A. 1944. *The Road to Serfdom*. Chicago: University of Chicago Press.

Kretzmer, D. 1990. "Forty Years of Public Law." *Israel Law Review* 24:341-355.

Medding, P. 1972. *Mapai in Israel*. Cambridge: Cambridge University Press.

———. 1990. *The Founding of Israeli Democracy, 1946-1967*. Oxford: Oxford University Press.

Perlmutter, A. 1970. *Anatomy of Political Institutionalization: The Case of Israel and Some Comparative Analyses*. Occasional Papers no. 25. Cambridge: Harvard University Center for International Affairs.

Shapira, A. 1974. "The Status of Fundamental Individual Rights in the Absence of a Written Constitution." *Israel Law Review* 9:457-511.

Weber, M. [1925] 1954. *Max Weber on Law in Economy and Society*. Trans. M. Rheinstein and E. Shils. Cambridge University Press.

Wechsler, H. 1959. "Towards Neutral Principles in Constitutional Law." *Harvard Law Review* 73:1-35.

Yuchtman-Ya'ar, E. 1989.   "The Israeli Public and Institutions: Who
Do You Trust?" *Israeli Democracy* (Fall): 7-11.
Yuchtman-Ya'ar, E. and Y. Peres.   1991.   "Public Opinion and
Democracy   after Three Years of Intafada."   *Israeli Democracy*
(Spring): 21-29.

STATUTES

Basic Law: Jerusalem. 1980.
Basic Law: The Judiciary. 1984.
Courts Law. 1984.

CASES

Al-Couri v. Chief of Staff. 1950. 4 P.D. 34.
Bezerano v. Minister of Police. 1949. 2 P.D. 80.
Dweikat v. Government of Israel. 1980. 34(i) P.D. 1.
*Kfar Vradim of Others v. Minister of Finance; Eliyahu v. Minister of
Defense and Others.* 1989. 43 (ii) P.D. 503.
Kahane v. Speaker of the Knesset. 1985. 39 (iv) P.D. 85.
Kahane v. Speaker of the Knesset. 1986. 40 (iv) P.D. 393.
Mi'ari v. Speaker of the Knesset. 1987. 36 (ii) P.D. 169.
Samara v. Commander of Judea and Pamaria. 1980. 34 (iv) P.D. 1.
Sarid v. Speaker of the Knesset. 1982. 32 (iv) P.D. 197.
Segal v. Minister of Interior. 1980. 34 (iv) P.D. 249.
Zeev v. Gubernick. 1948. 1 P.D. 85.

PART IV

RAPIDLY CHANGING NATIONS

Post-Communist States

23.

The Attempt to Institute Judicial Review in the Former USSR

CHERYL A. THOMAS

One of the major developments in the Soviet political system during the Gorbachev era was the elevation of both the Constitution and the judiciary in the political life of the state. In the late 1980s, judicialization of politics clearly occurred in the former Soviet Union in Vallinder's first sense of the term—the expansion of the province of the courts and the judges at the expense of the politicians or administrators. This development is notable, not only in a historical context, but for its potential effect on the long-term political complexion of post-Soviet Russia.

With the establishment of first the Soviet Committee of Constitutional Supervision in 1989 and then the Russian Constitutional Court in 1991, substantive judicial decision making developed in the former Soviet Union and today in Russia includes the basic conditions outlined by Vallinder: a special staff or judges with legal training, who resolve conflicts between two parties according to preordained rules, with prospective effects on similar cases in the future. Although remarkable for the swiftness with that this development occurred, it was not the first time that any form of judicialization of politics could be said to have occurred in the former Soviet Union. During at least two earlier periods of Soviet legal history, attempts were made to extend the influence of the courts and judges at the expense of politicians or bureaucrats. However, these brief forays into judicialization clearly did not result in either the promotion of an independent judiciary or substantive, long-term extensions of individual rights.

By examining the development of judicial review in both the Soviet Union and the Russian Federation from 1989 to 1992, and by assessing the extent of judicialization achieved by these judicial review bodies, this chapter addresses two questions: Why was judicialization of politics in the Soviet Union under Mikhail Gorbachev and in the Russian Federation under Boris Yeltsin fundamentally different from earlier attempts to increase judicial decision making?   To what extent can these recent moves toward judicialization be considered positive developments?

JUDICIAL REVIEW AND THE SOVIET LEGAL SYSTEM

Historically, the Soviet legal system demonstrated a great reluctance to give courts the power to review either the constitutionality or the legality of acts of officials and state agencies (Butler 1988, 161). In part this can be seen as a necessary means of ensuring the Communist Party's control over the state apparatus; virtually all communist societies rejected judicial review as incompatible with parliamentary (and thus, party) supremacy (Ludwikowski 1983; Held 1983, 229).   Yet it may also be indicative of a more fundamental aspect of Russian political culture, in which the Russian tendency toward the acceptance of autocracy fostered a historical and deep-seated resistance to a strong independent judiciary (Berman 1963, 196-222; see also White 1984).   For either or both reasons, from the earliest days of the revolution, the Communist regime viewed constitutional review not as a judicial power but as a joint legislative and executive power, exercised under the guise of parliamentary supremacy.

The 1918 RSFSR Constitution vested all constitutional review power in the legislature (All-Russian Congress of Soviets) and the executive (All-Russian Central Executive Committee), and with the adoption in 1924 of the first USSR Constitution, the principle of legislative and executive supervision over their own actions was continued, with supreme constitutional control over the Soviet system delegated to the USSR Congress of Soviets. When the Congress was not sitting (most of the time), the USSR Central Executive Committee, and specifically the Presidium of the Central Executive, exercised supreme constitutional control over legislation it promulgated itself. The Presidium's mode of operation in reviewing constitutional questions did not follow a judicial-style procedure, and decision-makers were not judges or specially trained legal staff. Findings of unconstitutionality usually did not result in repeal of legislation or suspension of actions; instead, proposals were made by the Presidium to the political body responsible (potentially the Presidium itself) to bring the law or action into conformity with the Constitution. Such "decisions" also had no prospective effect.

However, in this early period of Soviet legal history, a brief experiment in what could be termed judicialization of politics did occur. From 1923 to 1933 a very limited extension of constitutional review power was made to the USSR Supreme Court, in which the Court was granted the power to make advisory opinions on the constitutionality of actions of republics and to resolve jurisdictional disputes between republics (Kazimurchuk 1991). The Supreme Court also had the power to refer questions of invalid action by ministries, departments and administrative agencies to the Central Executive Committee Presidium, and reportedly two-thirds of all cases considered between 1924 to 1928 by the USSR Supreme Court concerned the constitutionality of decrees and regulations issued by state agencies (Butler 1988, 162). Thus at some point prior to the 1980s, some constitutional review power was given to an actual court in the Soviet Union. This brief period does point to the existence of limited judicialization of politics during the Communist period, and knowledge of it, especially among legal scholars, may have had some influence on the moves toward the expansion of judicial power in the 1980s (Fogelklou 1992).

The early experiment in judicialization was short-lived, however, and the rise of Stalinization and the cult of personality in the mid-1930s resulted in the elimination of any constitutional control by the judiciary—a feat achieved with the enactment of the 1930 Constitution of the USSR. The new Constitution signaled the ultimate triumph of the Presidium over the judiciary, stripping the Supreme Court of its limited constitutional review powers and openly declaring the supremacy of the Supreme Soviet in all matters of constitutionality, with the Presidium acting on its behalf (see the 1936 *Constitution of the USSR*).

De-Stalinization in the 1950s and 1960s brought about no change on the issue of constitutional review, but it is worth noting that other moves toward some form of judicialization of politics did occur, especially during Khrushchev's reforms of the late 1950s. Here, the rise of the concept of "socialist legality" included the view that there was a need to protect the procedural and substantive rights of citizens in relation to the state. Gordon Smith suggests that "Unlike either the utopian or dictatorial concepts of law, socialist legality began to resemble the Western concept of 'rule of law'" (Smith 1988, 141). It was far from being a state under the rule of law, but the main development in this direction was that Soviet jurists began to urge the ratification of a new constitution that would extend the notion of citizens' rights. Specifically, they argued that cases involving citizen's personal and property rights should be examined by the courts, not by administrative agencies, and that state officials should be held responsible for rights violations.   In 1962 a drafting commission for a new constitution was created, with the aim of injecting judicially ensured citizen rights into the constitution.

Yet, once again, this period of judicialization proved fleeting and was eclipsed by a resurgence of legal utopianism and the dictatorial trend in the law in the early 1960s.[1]   The 1962 drafting committee's attempts at constitutionally guaranteeing individual rights were not finally approved until the 1977 Brezhnev Constitution and not brought into force through legal codes until 1988.[2]   Even then, however, the spirit of the 1960s reforms was denied, as constitutional rights were restricted by the extent to which citizens fulfilled their obligations to the state (Smith 1988, 151).

Most importantly, this second period of judicialization in the Soviet Union did not extend to the issue of judicial review of the Constitution. The 1977 Constitution sanctioned and reinforced the old process of internal review, with permanent legislative commissions carrying out internal reviews of legislation for compliance with the Constitution. Along with the dominance of the USSR Presidium at the national level, constitutional control of republic laws was exercised by republic presidia. There were still no clear procedures for the exercise of constitutional control by the Presidium, and its "decisions" on constitutionality were usually characterized by a lack of legal argument—openly giving the political reasons for its rulings.[3]   Furthermore, the Soviet Constitution was not a binding legal document from which articles were cited in court decisions.[4]   Constitutional provisions in the Soviet Union had legal force only when they were implemented in one of the codes of law of the various republics, with the consequence that numerous constitutional provisions remained unrealized (Butler 1988).

THE EXPANSION OF JUDICIAL POWER IN THE 1980s

With the rise to power of Mikhail Gorbachev and his promotion of perestroika and glasnost, much was made (as in the Khrushchev era) of the need to develop the concept of the rule of law in the Soviet Union. One of the main tenets of this new thinking was the need to change the position of the judiciary in Soviet society, particularly through the institutionalization of some form of judicial independence. A number of factors prompted this move toward judicial reform in the late 1980s, including extensive interest in the glasnost media in reporting such phenomenon as "telephone law," in which a party of soviet officials would telephone a judge and "advise" him what the outcome of a particular case should be (Hosking 1990, 144). Such exposés led to widespread discussion in the Soviet Union in the latter part of the 1980s on how to begin to create a "law-governed state," in particular how best to establish the conditions for an independent judiciary (Fogelklou 1992; see also Kerimov and Ekimov 1990).

Gorbachev, a lawyer himself, seemed especially influenced by the types of reforms that initially had found favor under Khrushchev.[5] Harking back to the attempts in the 1950s to institute "peoples' courts," he argued, "It is especially important to enhance the role of courts as an elective body very close to the population, to guarantee the independence of judges, and to observe most strictly democratic principles in legal proceedings, objectiveness, contested election, and openness" (Gorbachev 1987, 107). Many Soviet legal scholars, jurists, and political reformers were eager, however, to push judicialization much further than this, and the issue of judicial review emerged early on as a core component of achieving the rule of law and an independent judiciary in Soviet society.[6] During 1987-88, proposals were made to extend constitutional review power to some type of judicial or quasi-judicial body. Some reformers wanted to grant the USSR Supreme Court the right to declare invalid the decisions of ministries and departments as well as legislative acts that violate the Constitution—a return to the practice of the 1920s and 1930s. Others favored the creation of a constitutional council attached to the USSR Supreme Soviet or its Presidium, while a third group argued for the formation of a separate constitutional court of the USSR.[7] In July 1988, the 19th Conference of the Communist Party of the Soviet Union (CPSU) issued a resolution "On Forming the Socialist Legal State," in which, among other things, it recommended that "to make law and government decisions conform strictly to the requirements of the Constitution of the USSR, it would be useful to set up a Committee for Constitutional Supervision" (CPSU 1988).

THE SOVIET COMMITTEE OF CONSTITUTIONAL SUPERVISION

Later that year, as part of its reform of the 1977 Brezhnev Constitution, the USSR Supreme Soviet created a new constitutional article establishing the Committee of Constitutional Supervision (revised *Constitution of the USSR* 1988, 103-5). This was only the first stage in establishing what many legal scholars hoped would be a truly independent constitutional review body, but which the CPSU apparently saw as another vehicle for endorsing party policies, this time in the guise of judicial review. Debates in the Congress of Peoples' Deputies in June 1989 over the election of the new committee highlighted the deep divisions within the Congress over the nature of the committee in particular and constitutional reform in general. Gorbachev's list of nominees drew immediate fire from the Congress because it did not include a single nonparty member, and his nominee for Chairman, Vladimir Kudrisvtsev, was widely criticized as a "party compromiser" (*Current Digest of the Soviet Press* [hereafter CDSP] 1989, 22). This all reflected a general sense in the Congress that the creation and appointment of the committee was being rushed through the Congress in the interests of the party.

But the most vociferous opposition to the establishment of the Committee of Constitutional Supervision came from a number of Baltic deputies (CDSP 1989, 24), who argued that the most pressing need was for the Union Constitution to be revised, not for a new form of supervision for an outdated one. Their other more fundamental objection was that the committee would infringe upon the sovereign rights of the republics through its authority to review republic constitutions and laws. During the subsequent vote to elect committee members, most of the Lithuanian delegation stunned the Congress by walking out in protest over the proposed law, forcing Gorbachev to ask the Congress to form a commission to consider these objections and prepare a new draft law (*Izvestia* June 10, 1989, 9). Six months later the commission submitted a draft law to the Congress, although four commission members openly opposed the provisions to review republic laws without their consent.[8] Final approval was reached on December 23, 1989, and the Committee of Constitutional Supervision came into force on January 1, 1990 (see *Izvestia* December 26, 1989, 1, 3).

Officially a legislative committee, not a court, on the surface the Committee of Constitutional Supervision seemed to be yet another example of internal constitutional review. The committee was made up of specially trained legal experts who resolved disputes between two parties, but no clear procedures were proscribed in the law, and no indication of the binding nature of the committee's decision in future cases was made. However, these points should not obscure the fact that the committee, in its powers and actions, was a significant move toward empowering an independent judicial body with the authority to review constitutionality in the Soviet state. Specifically, there were important elements of separation of powers explicit in its creation. First was the open declaration that the committee was to be independent—subordinate only to the Constitution—and the prohibition against any committee member belonging to any group or institution subject to committee review, which, most importantly, included the Communist Party. Other provisions promoting judicial independence related to the protection of the twenty-five-member committee from removal from office and prosecution, and to their right to silence over pending cases. This move toward the principle of separation of judicial power from legislative and executive power was the fundamental break with the past that the committee represented; it clearly signalled a far mare profound shift toward the expansion of judicial power in Soviet politics than had occurred during the previous seven decades of Communist rule.

In spite of not being a full-fledged court, the committee clearly did possess the power of judicial review and was set up to operate, in large part, as a judicial body. It had the power of constitutional review over national legislative and executive actions (including executive agencies) and some limited review of decisions of other judicial bodies.[9] The committee was also empowered to review division-of-powers disputes between the center and the republics and between republics. Additionally, even though no strict procedures were laid down in the enabling legislation for committee procedure, the committee, especially through its Chair, Sergei Alexeseyev, followed judicial-style procedures in hearings, and decisions of the committee were written as legal decisions, focusing exclusively on the constitutional legality of laws and acts.

The committee possessed three basic constitutional review powers: advice, temporary suspension for three months and total immediate suspension. To placate republican opponents, the committee's authority to review republic constitutions was suspended until a new federal structure could be agreed upon. However, republic laws affecting fundamental human rights still fell within the immediate scope of the committee. If an act was ultimately deemed unconstitutional, the committee would communicate its finding to the organ issuing the law, the body initiating the review, and the Presidium. A finding of unconstitutionality then suspended the application of the act until the nonconformity was eliminated, with a maximum period of three months to do so. However, if the act in question was found to violate fundamental human rights and freedoms secured in the Union Constitution or in international acts to which the Soviet Union was party, then the act was deemed immediately invalid. The Congress of Peoples' Deputies had the power to override a finding of unconstitutionality of an act of the Congress or of a republic constitution by a two-thirds vote. Technically, this meant that the extent of judicialization of politics achieved by the creation of the committee was moderated by legislative override. However, the actual decisions of the committee in its brief history are perhaps more indicative of the extent of judicialization achieved by this body.

In one of its first decisions, the committee clearly signalled its intention to distance itself from the political leadership, especially the CPSU, and to pursue a course of judicial independence. It ruled unconstitutional President Gorbachev's decree transferring control of all demonstrations and public events in Moscow from the Moscow City Soviet to the USSR Council of Ministers, a move designed by the party to prevent demonstrations at the 1990 May Day parade in Red Square. Although this decision had little effect on the actual May Day parade, it was a bold move in which a newly created quasi-judicial institution with little entrenched political power pitted its authority against both the most powerful political figure in the state and the CPSU.

None of the committee's subsequent decisions had such a high political profile, but over the next year and a half the committee set about revoking numerous old all-Union laws, many of which represented some of the worst deprivations of individual rights perpetrated by the Soviet state. In these decisions, the committee focussed primarily on questions of violations of fundamental human rights, thereby giving itself the greatest scope for the exercise of judicial review. The committee ruled unconstitutional the long-despised law giving officials the right both to determine whether laws and information should be classified as secret and the application of such unpublished acts (as published in *Sovetskaya Yustitsiya* [hereafter SY] 1991a); it also nullified the Soviet law requiring the registration of citizens (SY 1991d, 22-23). A number of other decisions revoked all-Union laws detrimental to the labor rights of workers (SY 1991c, 23) and abolished labor provisions preferential to state and party workers (SY 1991c, 23). The committee also addressed the often-compromising relationship between the military and the public in a number of decisions and showed particular interest in protecting individual rights in the legal process (SY 1991c, 22). The committee confined its constitutional review almost exclusively to the suspension of all-Union laws. Only a few committee decisions dealt with the division of powers in the Soviet federal system, and most of these came in the final months of the committee's existence and seemed particularly futile as the Soviet state disintegrated.

Ultimately, the Committee of Constitutional Supervision was only as viable as the state that created it. In the rapidly changing constitutional order (or, more precisely, disorder) that followed the August 1991 putsch, Union institutions like the committee became increasingly obsolete.[10] With the establishment of the Commonwealth of Independent States in December 1991, the Committee of Constitutional Supervision, like other Soviet governmental institutions, ceased to function. Yet, while the end of the Soviet state in December 1991 spelled the end of the committee, it did not result in the end of judicial review (and thus judicialization) within the old Soviet Union.

THE RUSSIAN CONSTITUTIONAL COURT

Two months before the coup attempt, the RSFSR Congress of Peoples' Deputies passed legislation creating a Russian Constitutional Court (see SY 1991e, 37-53),[11] and in October 1991 appointments were finally made to this republic-level body.[12] Like the Soviet Committee of Constitutional Supervision, the Russian Court represents a fundamental break with the previous adherence to internal constitutional review. But unlike the Soviet committee, the formation of this fifteen-member body constitutes a far greater shift toward the separation of judicial from legislative and executive power. The Russian Constitutional Court is an actual judicial body that more accurately conforms to Kelsen's model of a special constitutional court with the power of judicial review operating outside the normal judicial system, It is empowered to rule on the constitutionality of proposed and enacted legislation, as well as on actions of government officials (Constitution, sec. I, art. 1) and has the power to initiate proceedings to remove the Russian president from office for violating his constitutional responsibilities. In addition, the Court is subject only to the Russian Constitution, has the power of immediate nullification for all findings of unconstitutionality, and operates under specific judicial procedures. Its decisions have prospective effect, and no legislative override exists (see SY 1991e).

Like the Soviet committee, the Russian Court wasted no time in giving a clear and early signal of its intent to follow a strict path of judicial independence from the political leadership. In January 1992 the Court acted on a request from the Russian Congress of Peoples' Deputies to review the legitimacy of President Yeltsin's decree merging the RSFSR Security ministry and Interior ministry into a single super security agency. In a unanimous decision without the right of appeal, the Court threw down the constitutional gauntlet to the most powerful politician in the nation, ruling that the Russian president had exceeded his constitutional powers and immediately nullifying the decree (*Izvestia* January 15 1991, 1). Following this, the Court agreed to hear the even-more-contentious case on the legality of Yeltsin's 1991 ban on the Communist Party and then agreed to rule on whether the Russian parliament's attempt to take control of *Izvestia* newspaper was an unconstitutional violation of press freedom.

THE COMMITTEE OF CONSTITUTIONAL SUPERVISION AND RUSSIAN CONSTITUTIONAL COURT AS JUDICIALIZATION

According to Vallinder: "The judicialization of politics may roughly be said to signify the upgrading of fundamental rights of citizens at the expense of the rights and obligations of the (legislative) majority." The Soviet Committee of Constitutional Supervision was able, in a remarkably short time, to establish a reputation for judicial independence and protection of human rights within a state that had little or no experience of operating under the rule of law. Hosking suggested that in order for the Soviet legal and political system to move toward becoming a state under the rule of law in the 1980s, it was necessary to remove vaguely worded laws used to restrict individual rights, to ensure judicial observance of proper procedures, and to institute judicial independence (Hosking 1990, 144). The committee's early rejection of the Gorbachev decree was a clear departure from past judicial subservience to the party line, and its rejection of numerous old, discredited laws fulfilled an important psychological function within the Soviet Union, authoritatively purging the state of old laws, long despised and discredited but still on the statute books. These developments may seem somewhat insignificant now because of the dissolution of the committee along with the entire Soviet Union. But judicialization has been perpetuated in the post-Communist Soviet Union through the Russian Federation's adoption of judicially enforced constitutional review.

The committee and the Russian Constitutional Court were both conceived of as means of protecting individual rights against government abuse. But they were also meant to be judicial mediation bodies that could resolve jurisdictional disputes between regions and the center—a function widely recognized as necessary within a fully functioning federal system (Duchacek 1961). Yet both bodies were particularly weak on judicial review of the federal system, perhaps not surprisingly, considering the fragile state of both the former Soviet federation and the current Russian Federation. The Committee of Constitutional Supervision concerned itself primarily with individual-rights guarantees, encouraged perhaps by the provision granting it total and immediate suspension power over laws found to violate fundamental human rights. This provision in itself is an indication of a movement toward Tate's judicialization factor, a "Politics of Rights," in Soviet society, which movement encouraged those interested in challenging existing legislation and official action to frame constitutional issues in rights terms, as this was the course most likely to bring about nullification. Such a politics of rights has continued in the Russian Federation, but because the Russian Court has the power of immediate nullification over all unconstitutional acts, not only human-rights violations, the scope of constitutional questions being presented to the Court is broader and usually includes a mixture of individual-rights and separation-of-powers issues.

If the elevation of individual rights through judicial protection is seen as the essence of Vallinder's conception of judicialization of politics, then judicialization clearly came to the former Soviet Union before its dissolution and now survives within the former state most prominently in the Russian Federation. However, Tate argues that "it is the choices judges make to be more or less active in imposing their own policy solutions that determine just how far judicialization will go under favorable sets of facilitating conditions." In the Soviet Union the debates among jurists and legal scholars over judicial review in the mid-1980s strongly indicated a judicial desire to expand its role (see Fogelklou 1992). In 1988 Smith could point to an increasing role for jurists in the policy-making process, as their opinions were respected and sought by policymakers, especially in drafting new legislation (Smith 1988, 143). Legal experts and jurists have been aided in this by a high degree of group awareness and interaction, fostered throughout the 1980s through conferences, symposia, and writings in legal journals.

In their earliest decisions, the Committee of Constitutional Supervision and the Russian Constitutional Court made a point of sending obvious signals to the political leadership that they intended to actively exercise this new power of constitutional review. The Soviet committee decision on Gorbachev's demonstration ban and the Russian Court decision on Yeltsin's security agency merger were high-risk decisions, guaranteed to throw the new constitutional review bodies into conflict with the political leadership. Today, this activist stance has continued to be embraced by the Russian Court, especially with its decision to review President Yeltsin's ban on the Communist Party. This case was perhaps the most highly politicized issue the court or any political body could address in post-Soviet Russia, and the highly volatile nature of the issue has been reflected in the verbal and physical attacks and threats made against some court judges and their families. Such threatening behavior might have been expected to encourage a less activist stance by the court, but instead it has only seemed to strengthen the court's commitment to take on highly politicized cases. Its willingness to become involved in such cases has in turn encouraged opposing political forces within the Russian state to work the most fundamental and deeply divisive policy questions into constitutional issues to present to the court for resolution.

Vallinder sees judicial review of executive and legislative actions as one major form of judicialization of politics, and it is the adoption of this practice that most clearly demonstrates the extent of judicialization that developed first in the former Soviet Union and later in the Russian Federation during the years since early 1990. Although Soviet legal and constitutional history indicates that it is possible for some limited forms of judicialization to occur even in authoritarian regimes, the power of judicial review over the constitution seems to be an exception. The creation of a specialized court (or even a quasi-judicial body) with independent powers to review and invalidate actions of the national executive and legislature appeared to be the dividing line between technical and substantive judicialization of politics in the former Soviet Union.

One of the distinguishing features of Communist states is the subordination of law to politics, a situation in which the legal system is firmly under the control of the party leadership (Held 1983, 228). With the establishment of judicial review in the former Soviet Union, it became possible, perhaps for the first time, to create some distance between the party and the judiciary. The enabling legislation for both the Soviet committee and the Russian Court openly declare that the Constitution (not the party or the legislature) represents the supreme law of the land. This is a formal but important rejection of the long-standing Soviet (and Russian) adherence to the principle of parliamentary supremacy that was simply a euphemism for party supremacy. Both bodies wasted no time in exercising their independent powers of constitutional review, including challenges to party control over the political and legal system.

The creation of the Committee of Constitutional Supervision and the Russian Constitutional Court was fundamentally different from earlier periods of judicialization under socialist legality in the former Soviet Union. Their powers of constitutional review were removed from the control of the party, and their creation elevated the position of the judiciary within the political system for perhaps the first time in more than seventy years of Communist rule. This raises the question, What separates judicialization of politics in authoritarian regimes from judicialization in democratizing or democratic states? Although this is far too large a question to be addressed here, it may be suggested that, while judicial review is not a necessary prerequisite for any form of judicialization of politics to occur (for example, developments in the 1920s and in the Khrushchev period), in transitional authoritarian states it may be one element that distinguishes true extensions of judicial decision-making power from procedural or technical changes that do nothing to loosen the regime's total control over the political decision-making process.

THE PROBLEM OF LEGITIMACY AND JUDICIAL REVIEW
IN THE FORMER SOVIET UNION

Like the soul-searching Vallinder discusses that went on in much of postwar Western Europe over how to protect the rights of citizens in the future, and in parallel with developments in postwar Germany and Italy, in the late 1980s the Soviet Union and the Russian Federation also moved to address this issue by creating (1) a new Constitution, (2) a bill of rights, (3) a Constitutional Court, and (4) judicial review. Yet the expansion of judicial power through the institution of judicial review in the former Soviet Union and the Russian Federation in the last three years has been different from the process followed in postwar Western Europe in one fundamental respect. In the former Soviet Union, the adoption of judicial review has proceeded in the face of a lack of consensus over the constitutional order of the state, with both the Soviets and the Russians finding it immensely difficult to achieve the first element of this four-part formula.

Without a new constitution reflecting the ideological and structural change, at first in the Soviet Union and now in the Russian Federation, the two judicial bodies would inevitably face serious problems of legitimacy, or what is often termed "diffuse support" (Easton 1965). Among the conditions for judicial legitimation identified by Murphy and Tanenhaus is the perception that the judicial institution should interpret and apply the fundamental principles of the polity to legal disputes (Murphy and Tanenhaus 1969). Yet here lies the crucial problem faced by judicialization in the both the USSR and Russia. Both the Soviet committee and the Russian Court have had to exercise judicial review under defunct constitutions.

As Vallinder points out, judicial review can be defended against claims of usurping the power of the elected executive and legislature only because it is based on a popularly enacted constitution of the state. But the process of enactment and the content of the constitutions under which the committee and the court exercised judicial review were discredited even before these judicial bodies began to interpret them. In both the former Soviet Union and in the Russian Federation, it was far easier for the legislature to achieve consensus on the need for a constitutional review body than it was to achieve a new constitution for the state. Such a move inevitably places the judicial review body in a highly problematic situation.

The case of the Committee of Constitutional Supervision was resolved most dramatically by the disintegration of the Soviet state.   In some respects the Russian Federation seems to be dangerously close to replaying the constitutional
mistakes of the former USSR, especially in its development of a constitutional review body.   Like its Soviet predecessor, the Russian Parliament has created a constitutional review body before it has resolved the larger and more difficult issue of constitutional reform.   This places the Russian Constitutional Court in the unenviable position of having to interpret what is widely viewed as a lame duck constitution, one that owes far more to the discredited Communist past than to postcoup Russian politics.   The lack of a new constitution also places the future of the Court in question, creating uncertainty over whether it will be radically altered in the new constitution[13] or whether the Russian Federation will also disintegrate, once again taking a constitutional court with it into the footnotes of history.

The longer constitutional reform remains unresolved and the Russian Constitutional Court continues to exercise judicial review in highly contentious cases, the greater the likelihood that pressures to limit "government by the judiciary" will increase.   The constitution is the source of legitimacy for the Constitutional Court, and with the court now facing strong challenges to its authority, especially with its highly visible role in deciding the future of the Communist Party, the current constitutional limbo in Russia can only threaten the establishment of a strong independent judiciary.   The difficulties the Russian court faces with compliance were highlighted in the KGB/Interior Ministry case, with the ministries' refusal to submit documents to the court during its deliberations and President Yeltsin's resistance to abiding by the decision once it was announced.[14]   These problems are not likely to abate in the immediate future, as the Russian Constitutional Court continues to be used as an umpire for resolving disputes within the Russian legislature and between the legislature and the executive.

CONCLUSION

In most respects the judicialization of politics in both the Soviet Union and Russia through the adoption of judicial review can be viewed as positive developments.   The creation and actions of these constitutional review bodies helped to break the Communist Party control over the political process, encouraged judicial independence, authoritatively purged the statute books of laws that flagrantly violated human rights and in doing so promoted a politics of rights—all of which may be viewed as developments toward the rule of law in a state with little practical experience of such a concept. As such, Gorbachev's Soviet Union and now post-Communist Russia can be seen as a continuation of the trend toward the international judicialization of politics in the postwar era. The creation of the Soviet committee and the Russian Constitutional Court are clear signals of intent to move toward judicially supervised government, and this experience strongly supports Vallinder's belief that judicialization is not likely to be either stopped or reversed in the near future. Perhaps the surprising aspect of judicial activism in the former Soviet Union and Russia has been the speed and determination with which the judicial review bodies embraced their new responsibilities. In this respect, the actions of both the committee and the Russian court also support Cappelletti's belief in the inevitability of judicial activism in countries where constitutional adjudication by the judiciary is sanctioned (Cappelletti 1989, 30).

The one worrying aspect in this shift toward judicialization in the former Soviet Union is the apparent desire to elevate the role of the judiciary without providing it with a sound source of legitimacy. For this reason, the creation of both judicial review bodies can be seen to some extent as exercises in expediency. In both cases, the primary interest in the political arena was in achieving the *appearance* of an independent judiciary, with little political will to provide the necessary constitutional support to protect the fledgling judicial bodies from challenges to their authority. The disintegration of the Soviet state has eliminated this problem for the Committee of Constitutional Supervision. Yet in Russia, the Constitutional Court and the problem remain. The major stumbling block to continued judicialization of politics in Russia is the lingering uncertainty over the future of the Russian Constitution. If judicial review is seen as the benchmark for achieving substantive judicialization, especially in transitional authoritarian states like the Russian Federation, then the lack of consensus over the Russian Constitution leaves the Russian Constitutional Court vulnerable and the future of judicialization of politics within the heart of the former Soviet state in question.

NOTES

The author would like to thank the Kennan Institute for Advanced Russian Studies of the Smithsonian Institution, Washington, DC for its generous financial support of the research for this chapter.

1.   For example, public participation in the administration of justice, expansion of police powers, and the reintroduction of capital punishment for a wide variety of offenses.

2.   The provisions of Article 58, paragraph 2, of the 1977 USSR Constitution guaranteeing that the "actions of officials committed in violation of law, in excess of their powers, and impinging upon the rights of citizens may be appealed to a court" were not procedurally effected until 10 years later. On June 30, 1987, the USSR Supreme Soviet adopted the law titled Procedure for Appealing to a Court the Unlawful Actions of Officials which impinge upon the Rights of Citizens, effective January 1, 1988. The law itself experienced a stormy passage in the Supreme Soviet and had to be amended on October 20, 1987 to further strengthen its provisions (see Butler 1988).

3.   See, for example, "Edit of Presidium of USSR Supreme Soviet on Nonconformity of Estonian Legislation to USSR Constitution and Law," in Butler (1991, 149).

4.   "Judicial decisions and judgements are legal actions since they bear legal consequences, but they do not create and do not formulate legal norms" (Mokicheva, 1970, 1).

5.   He conceded that "courts, procurators' offices, and other bodies called upon to protect public order and combat abuses were often ruled by circumstances, and found themselves in a dependent position and forfeited their principled stand in the struggle against law violators" (Gorbachev, 1987, 107).

6.   Even after the Committee of Constitutional Supervision was created, some legal scholars continued to press for greater reforms in the legal/constitutional system. See Chetverin's "A Socialist State Committed to Law: A Democratic State" (1990) (see also Fogelklou 1992).

7.   These proposals had been in circulation within legal and academic circles for many years (see Russinova and Rianzhin, 1975; see also Toporin 1989).

8.   Not surprisingly, these commission members were from Estonia, Latvia, Lithuania, and Gruzia (*Izvestia*, December 22, 1989, 10).

9.   This last power was extremely limited as it excluded judicial decisions in civil, criminal, administrative, and *arbitrazh* cases.

10.   For a discussion of the Committee's role in the coup see *Izvestia*, August 19, 20, September 2, 1991; for a discussion of the legal issues involved in the abortive coup attempt, see Thorson (1991).

11. This paper was originally written in the summer of 1992, and the following discussion of the Russian Constitutional Court covers its decisions and activities up to that point. At press time, the Court has been suspended, and its future remains in doubt. In the immediate aftermath of the October 1993 confrontation between President Yeltsin and the hardline parliamentarians, the chairman of the Constitutional Court, Valery Zorkin, was forced to resign, and the president suspended the Constitutional Court.

12. Almost immediately, questions were raised about the competency of the judges, with *Moscow News* suggesting that only two or three of the 13 judges appointed in October were known to be "experienced lawyers of unquestionable authority." But many fears were allayed with the appointment of Valery Zorkin as Chairman of the Court. Professor at the Higher Law School of the USSR Interior Ministry and head of a working group on the Russian Constitutional Commission, Zorkin's credentials were greatly enhanced in the public's view by his signing of a declaration on August 19 condemning the Emergency Committee as unconstitutional (See *Moscow News* 1991).

13. When this chapter was originally drafted in summer, 1992, virtually all proposals for a new Russian Constitution included provisions for the continued exercise of judicial review of the constitution. At press time, the draft Russian Constitution developed by President Yeltsin envisaged the continuation of the Russian Constitutional Court, but with far more restricted powers.

14. It reportedly took the chairman of the Constitutional Court, Valery Zorkin, almost an hour to explain to Yeltsin that the Court, as interpreter of the Constitution, served as a higher authority than the President, and that Yeltsin would have to comply with the Court ruling. In a subsequent interview, the seeds of future conflict were sown when Zorkin expressed the view that Yeltsin had to realize that "Russia's President has his mandate, not an indulgence." *Moscow News* (1992).

REFERENCES

Berman, Harold J.   1963.   *Justice in the USSR: An Introduction.*   Cambridge: Harvard University Press.

Butler, W. E.   1988.   *Soviet Law.*   2nd ed.   London: Butterworths.

———.   1991.   *Basic Documents on the Soviet Legal System.*   2nd ed.   London: Oceana.

Cappelletti, Mauro.   1989.   *The Judicial Process in Comparative Perspective.*   Oxford: Clarendon.

Chetverin, Vladimir. 1990. "A Socialist State Committed to Law: A Democratic State." trans. Natalia Belskava. In *Authoritarianism and Democracy*. Moscow: Progress Publishers.

Communist Party of the Soviet Union [CPSU]. 1988. "On Forming the Socialist Legal State." English translation in *Moscow News*, supplement to no. 29 (July 17): 6.

Constitution of the USSR (revised). 1988. *Review of Socialist Law* 1989, no. 1, 7:103-05.

Current Digest of the Soviet Press (CDSP). 1989. Vol. 61, no. 31.

Duchacek, Ivo. 1961. *Comparative Federalism: The Territorial Dimension of Politics*. New York: Holt.

Easton, David. 1965. *A Systems Analysis of Political Life*. New York: Wiley.

Fogelklou, Anders. 1992. "New Legal Thinking in the Soviet Union." In *The Emancipation of Soviet Law*, ed. F. J. M. Feldbrugge. Deventer, The Netherlands: Kluwer.

Gorbachev, Mikhail. 1987. *Perestroika: New Thinking for Our Country and the World*. London: Collins.

Hazard, John N., William E. Butler, and Peter B. Maggs, eds. 1977. *The Soviet Legal System*. Dobbs Ferry, N.Y.: Oceana.

Held, David. 1983. *States and Societies*. Oxford: Blackwell.

Hosking, Geoffrey. 1990. *The Awakening of the Soviet Union*. London: Heinemann.

Izvestia. June 10, 1989-September 2, 1991.

Kazimurchuk, V. E. 1991. "On Constitutional Supervision in the USSR." In *Perestroika and the Rule of Law*, ed. W. E. Butler. London: Tauris.

Kerimov, D. A. and A. J. Ekimov. 1990. "Constitutsionni nadzor i SSSR." *Sovetskor Gosudarstvo i Pravo* 9:3-13.

Ludwikowski, R. R. 1983. "Judicial Review in the Socialist Legal System: Current Developments." *International and Comparative Law Quarterly* 89.

Mokicheva, K. A. 1970. *Teoriia Gosudarstva i Prava*. 2d ed. Moscow.

Moscow News. 1991. "Man from the Top." No. 46:4.

———. 1992. "Russia's President has his mandate, not an indulgence." no. 5:16.

Murphy, Walter F. and Joseph Tanenhaus. 1969. "Public Opinion and the Supreme Court: A Preliminary Mapping of Some Prerequisites for Court Legitimation of Regime Changes." In *Frontiers of Judicial Research*, ed. Joel B. Grossman and Joseph Tanenhaus. New York: Wiley.

Russinova, S. I. and V. A. Rianzhin, eds. 1975. *Soverskoe Konstitutsionnoe Pravo*. Leningrad. Reprinted in *The Soviet Legal System*, ed. John N. Hazard, William E. Butler, and Peter B. Maggs.

Smith, Gordon B. 1988. *Soviet Politics: Continuity and Contradiction*. London: Macmillan.

Sovetskaya Yustitsiya (SY). 1991a. 11 (February).

———. 1991b. 11 (April): 23.

———. 1991c. 11 (June): 23.

———. 1991d. 11 (October): 22-23.

———. 1991e. 11 (November): 37-53.

Thorson, Carla. 1991. "Constitutional Issues Surrounding the Coup." *Report on the USSR* 3, no. 36:19-22.

Toporin, B. N. 1989. "Konstitutsiia v sotsialistichekom pravovom gosudavstve." In *Sotsialisticheskoe Pravovoe Gosudavstvo*, ed. B. N. Toporin.

White, Steven. 1984. "Soviet Political Culture Reassessed." In *Political Culture in Communist Studies*, ed. Archie Brown. London: Macmillan.

24.

Legal Reform and the Expansion of Judicial Power in Russia

WILLIAM KITCHIN

[Author's Note: This chapter was originally written in mid-1992.
Since 1992, events have led to the abolition of the Russian
Constitutional Court, the fall of Valery Zorkin, the adoption of a new
constitution for Russia, the adoption of a revised regime of judicial
review, the attempted mainstreaming of the criminal jury, and the
further progression of legal reform in Russia. History has overtaken
some of the cast of characters and institutions referred to in this
chapter. Nevertheless, the basic conceptual observations have been
confirmed by events in Russia that have occurred since the chapter
was written—not only is *politics* being judicialized in Russia, but on
a more fundamental level *law* itself is being judicialized as Russia
confronts the profoundly politicized law and legal system inherited
from the Communist era.]

Not only politics, but law itself is being "judicialized" in Russia.
Domains of policy off-limits to courts from 1917 until 1989 are now
subject to judicial review by the Russian Constitutional Court. Thus, the
most political type of judicial decision-making has become a part of the
Russian judicial landscape. This, of course, did not occur in a vacuum;
the Soviet committee on Constitutional Oversight from 1989 until late

1991 exercised an advisory power of judicial review (Kitchin 1991a, 98) of these two judicial institutions, novel in the Soviet/Russian context, is that arenas of what used to be political decision-making are becoming judicialized.

But something even more preliminary is also occurring in Russian judicial progression—law itself is being judicialized. For the entire Soviet period until 1989, law was understood as a tactical extension of the political system and was a control mechanism at the service of the elite (the Communist Party). Law did not exist apart from politics except in the most routine of cases. However, beginning in 1988, the centerpiece of *juris perestroika* was the "law-governed state." A prerequisite to the development of this notion was the depoliticization of law itself. Law was to be thought of as something separate from politics with an independent potency of its own. Thus, the process of judicializing law is now under way. The judicialization of law is evident in every sphere of Russian law.

This chapter examines these two parallel developments now going on in Russia—the judicialization of politics and the judicialization of law. The first is most clearly and controversially illustrated by the mandatory power of judicial review of the Russian Constitutional Court. The second is well demonstrated by current reform of Russian criminal procedure.

JUDICIAL REVIEW

Judicial review is the power of a court to declare a law or other normative document (such as a presidential order) null and void. *Soviet* practice from late 1989 until December 1991 allowed laws to be struck down on any of three bases: (1) they violated the 1977 Constitution; (2) they violated basic rights and liberties contained in international agreements to which the Soviet Union was a signatory; (3) they violated the rights of ethnic groups (Kitchin 1991a, 97-100).

Russian practice, commencing in late 1991, allows laws and normative acts to be struck down if (1) they violate the 1977 Constitution or (2) they violate the principle of separation of powers (Malysheva 1992, 1).

Thus, judicial review was created for the Soviet Union in 1989 and continued until the Soviet Union ceased to exist. It was exercised by the Committee on Constitutional Oversight. A strengthened variant of judicial review was created by Russia in late 1991 and is today the focal power of the Russian Constitutional Court.

Judicial review is arguably a necessary condition for an advanced stage of judicialization. By definition, judicial review represents a legal or judicial constraint on the making of otherwise political decisions. Without judicial review, judicialization may take place but can hardly be secure. In a sense, judicialization without judicial review will be judicialization by grace, under the constant possibility of cancellation by political forces.

Judicial Review in the Soviet Union from 1989 to 1991

The Soviet Committee on Constitutional Oversight was established in December, 1989. The committee had the power to declare as invalid laws, presidential decrees, and almost any other law-like, normative instrument issued by the Center. A committee decision could be overturned by a two-thirds vote of the Congress of People's Deputies, but in fact no decision of the committee was ever overturned (Kitchin 1991a, 97-100).

In the two years of its existence, the committee on Constitutional Oversight struck down, among others, the following laws and decrees:

1. President Gorbachev's decree banning public demonstrations inside the Moscow Ring Road.
2. All-Union laws providing for the compulsory treatment of alcoholics by the Ministry of Internal Affairs.
3. President Gorbachev's January 1991 decree that the Soviet Army be used to enforce the law and safeguard public order.
4. Army regulations requiring garrison commanders to follow orders of local Communist Party of the Soviet Union (CPSU) officials.
5. Soviet laws requiring residency permits.
6. Provisions in the Labor Code that denied to certain occupations the right to judicial review of job dismissal.
7. The Soviet practice of enforcing unpublished or secret laws and substatutes.
8. The Soviet practice of depriving one of citizenship by unreviewable administrative decree.

9. The Soviet consumer protection law whereby the buyer had no recourse against the seller in case of undiscovered defects in a product if the product had been accepted by the buyer.

10. Republics' refusal to spend allocated money for Soviet servicemen's housing.

11. A Lithuanian law creating vicarious criminal liability of an individual for actions of sociopolitical organizations to which the individual belonged.

12. Armenia's annexation of Nagorno-Karabakh.

13. Azerbaijan's liquidation of Nagorno-Karabakh's autonomy.

The major criticism from within Russia of the committee's performance during its two-year life was that its decisions were at the periphery of the turmoil sweeping the country and that the committee did little to abate that turmoil (Maylsheva 1991). Such criticisms misunderstand the committee's statutory functions as well as its judicial and jurisprudential missions. The primary statutory functions of the committee were (1) to establish supremacy of the Constitution over all-Union laws and decrees and (2) to protect the rights and liberties of the individual. These were the functions of the committee as specified in the statute that created it. Moreover, the enabling statute explicitly precluded the committee's ruling on most conflicts between laws of the various republics and laws of the Center. Thus, the nationalities issue, probably the most divisive issue in the Soviet Union during 1990 and the first half of 1991, was off-limits to the committee. Nevertheless, a perusal of the topics addressed by the committee (above) confirms that it was hardly at the periphery of the political and social turmoil in 1990 and 1991.

The judicial mission of the committee was to increase the processes and pace of judicialization. The Soviet legal system in 1989 was extraordinarily politicized. Judicial review did not exist at all. A law-governed state was a remote abstraction. After decades of Communist rule, law had become thoroughly discredited as just another tool of the cynical Communist elite. From 1917 until 1988, judicial matters had been thoroughly politicized. In 1988 and 1989, a few half measures were enacted to hint at the possibility of judicialization. Finally, in December 1989, the establishment of judicial review reversed the seventy-two-year policy of politicization, and judicialization began in the Soviet Union.

The decisions of the Committee on Constitutional Oversight, however, were often enforced belatedly or not at all. Though certain decisions were implemented quickly, the political institutions and political culture lagged behind the ideals of judicialization and the liberal concepts that underlay the committee's human-rights decisions.   In spite of enforcement problems, the committee accomplished the mission bestowed on it by history—that is, the starting of the engines of judicialization.

In retrospect we can see a historic jurisprudential mission of the committee. It energetically and institutionally established a Soviet theory of the separation of law from politics and the supremacy of law over politics. Until the committee's experience, Soviet law was thoroughly politicized. The committee represented the judicialization of law and the rejection of Communist and nihilistic conceptions of law, which had dominated Soviet legal theory since 1917.   What had previously been heresy—judicial review and the supremacy of legal principles—the committee transformed into accepted jurisprudence.   As such, the committee, though it was besieged by criticism and enforcement problems, opened a jurisprudential door that had heretofore been locked closed. At this point the Russian Constitutional Court enters.

Judicial Review in Russia from 1991 to the Present

After the August 1991 coup, Russia, then the Republic of Russia, established its own Constitutional Court. By the time the Soviet Committee on Constitutional Oversight disbanded in December 1991, the Russian Constitutional Court was staffed and operating Maylsheva 1991). Its mandatory power of judicial review is stronger than the Soviet concept had been, in that the Russian Court's decisions about the constitutionality of laws and decrees are not subject to legislative override. Moreover, the Russian Constitutional Court can levy fines against officials who refuse to comply with its decisions and even impeach the president if he refuses to comply with a ruling of the Constitutional Court.

The court has the following specific powers (Feofanov 1992, 2): (1) to strike down as null and void laws and other normative instruments; (2) to abrogate Russia's treaty obligations if they contravene the 1977 Constitution; (3) to resolve disputes between geographic entities within Russia; (4) to strike down as unconstitutional rules of procedure and judicial instructions promulgated by courts, including plenary instructions issued by the Russian Supreme Court; (5) to impeach the president if his actions are unconstitutional.

Valery Zorkin, chairman of the Russian Constitutional Court and for years an ardent proponent of a law-governed state, has made clear that the court's dual missions are to create a rule of law and to prevent a relapse into totalitarianism.   The following passages, taken from an interview published in *Komsomolskaya Pravda* in January 1992, show Zorkin's strong belief in the rule of law (Malysheva 1992, 1):

Zorkin: In any totalitarian system, the law *(pravo) is* reduced to the level of a means.   And that is dangerous, when what you mean by the law is whatever comes from "above."

Q: Who is the creator of the law, if not the authorities?

Zorkin: The law is supreme justice.   It exists in nature, it is just as much an immutable law of nature as, for instance, the law of gravity.

Q: Is it possible to disregard the law "temporarily," to substitute revolutionary expediency for the duration of some particularly difficult period?

Zorkin: History shows that you cannot do that, even for a short time. There are only two paths, the path of law, or the path to dictatorship.

Q: It is highly likely that in the public consciousness such strict adherence to the letter of the law will be perceived as a hindrance to future prosperity.

Zorkin: Prosperity has never preceded the triumph of the law.   And conversely, countries that gravitate intuitively toward a rule-of-law civilization have prospered.

Q: But is it possible to build a rule-of-law state at a stroke?   Maybe you have to get there by stages, building up the legal potential, so to speak?

Zorkin: By stages, but resolutely and rapidly.   A man standing on the brink of a precipice cannot allow himself the luxury of drawing back from the brink millimeter by millimeter.

Q: So you are trying to stop the people from falling over the precipice?

Zorkin: That is the main task of the Constitutional Court.   The very existence of this body is a guarantee of public security.   We should and must protect the borders of the legal ground beyond which lie the abyss, the precipice, perdition.

This passage is a clear expression of the process of judicialization now under way in Russia. Judicial review, thus, is the major manifestation of the rule of law and in contemporary Russia has been institutionalized in the Constitutional Court.

The 1977 Constitution as an Obstacle to Judicialization

The Russian Constitutional Court, like the Soviet committee on Constitutional Oversight before it, measures the constitutionality of laws and decrees according to their consistency with the 1977 Soviet Constitution (often referred to as the Brezhnev Constitution). Thus, built into Russian judicial review is an inherent incongruence: the 1977 Constitution is an expression of politicization of law whereas Russian judicial review of 1992 represents the judicialization of law and is an extension of judicialization into politics.

The 1977 Constitution embraces a number of concepts that have been abandoned by contemporary Russian legal practice, yet the 1977 Constitution remains in force. For example, that Constitution does the following: (1) prevents private ownership of the means of production and distribution; (2) prevents private possession of unearned income; (3) prevents the hiring of one individual by another; (4) establishes "socialist legality" in criminal law; and (5) relegates individual rights to secondary importance behind the "interests of society and the state" (Art. 37, 1977 Constitution, RSFSR [Russian Soviet Federated Socialist Republic]).

Russian law is now contrary to each of these fundamental concepts. Thus, when the Constitutional Court rules on "constitutionality," it is engaged in a fictional undertaking. It is called upon to make rulings of constitutionality, yet the Constitution itself has for all practical purposes not existed since the repeal of Article 6 in 1989 (Kitchin 1991b, 2-4). D. A. Kerimov, chairman of the Supreme Soviet committee that drafted the Soviet Law on Constitutional Oversight, recognized the deceptive endeavor of constitutional review in a system in which the Constitution had been repudiated. He said the Constitution was "a fiction, performing the hypocritical role of a democratic facade designed to conceal from the onlooker the lawlessness and tyranny of the era of the personality cult, voluntarism, and stagnation" (Kerimov 1989, 2).

Valery Zorkin is similarly aware of the problem of being saddled with the obsolete Constitution, but Zorkin is willing to participate in the fiction of constitutional review, probably because the Constitutional Court must *appear* to be *judicial* as opposed to just *political*. Zorkin described the court's dilemma as follows (Malysheva 1992, 1):

Q: You have taken on the mission of protecting the Constitution. Yet it is being said increasingly insistently that we have no Constitution. What precisely are you protecting?

Zorkin: We have a Constitution. True, it is not complete, not all-embracing, it is contradictory. It takes a strange form—one sleeve is cut from a medieval caftan, the other from a modern business suit. But even this must be observed, until a new one is adopted.

The Constitutional Court's first ruling was to strike down President Yeltsin's decree that had established a consolidated security institution composed of the old KGB and the MVD (Interior Ministry) (Rudnev 1992a, 1). The court's ruling said squarely that Yeltsin's order was unconstitutional but cited no specific provisions of the Constitution that the order violated—probably because the order was consistent with the 1977 Constitution. The court's ruling instead was based on the emerging Constitution—a partially articulated set of democratic and capitalistic principles, with a separation-of-powers governing structure characterized by a clear demarcation of powers. The court's declaration that Yeltsin's order was unconstitutional thus transferred from the political system into the judicial realm a policy decision that before 1989 would have been untouchable by a court. This is a concrete example of the judicialization of politics in Russia.

However, the court's transparent appeal to a Constitution makes for a very high-risk version of judicialization because upon even the most cursory analysis, the court's ruling was not based on the 1977 Constitution but was a political decision based on the emerging Constitution. (Indeed, the irony of judicial review is that as a value-allocation decision, it is the most political of a court's functions, yet what the Constitutional Court needs is an image of being apart from the very type of policy-making that judicial review requires.) The text of the court's decision is as follows (Rudnev 1992a, 1):

> After examining in open session the case relating to verifying the constitutionality of the Russian President's Decree "On the Formation of the RSFSR Ministry of Security and Internal Affairs [MSIA]," the court resolved: to adjudge this Decree inconsistent with the RSFSR Constitution from the point of view of the division of legislative, executive, and judicial powers within the republic, as well as the demarcation of competence among the higher organs of state power and management as enshrined in the Constitution. The said Resolution is final: It is not subject to appeal, and will come into force immediately after its proclamation. In legal terms, this means that the Russian President's Decree on the formation of the MSIA and all other normative acts and their individual clauses based on or derived from it lose judicial force and are considered invalid. All juridical relations based on the said Decree revert to the status they possessed before the adoption of the unconstitutional Decree.

Likewise, the court's second ruling was an extension of the judiciary into matters heretofore the exclusive province of the executive and legislative branches of government. The court ruled that the attempt of Tatarstan to hold a referendum on Tatar sovereignty was a violation of the Russian Constitution (Rudnev 1992b, 63). The court's ruling was simply a political necessity. Without it, the door to disintegration of Russia itself would have been opened.

The most recent issue confronting the Constitutional Court is President Yeltsin's decree that banned Communist Party activities and confiscated party property. The basic argument advanced by the petitioners in the May 26, 1992, hearing before the court was that the Constitution simply does not give the Russian president the power to ban a party or to confiscate property. In a cross-petition, a group of deputies argued before the court that the party never had a legal existence in the first place and that the ban and confiscation, therefore, are not at legal issue. The court has consolidated the two petitions and will reconvene to hear the consolidated case in July, 1992.

The Constitutional Court, thus, represents judicialization of phenomena previously beyond the reach of courts. However, the absence of a viable constitution on which to base its rulings places the credibility of the Constitutional Court in some jeopardy. Although it claims a constitutional standard, because that standard is implicit, it is elusive. Thus, constitutional review by the Russian Constitutional Court could quite likely be perceived as just another aspect of politicized decision-making. Judicialization implies something different, but the absence of an explicit constitutional standard arguably is resulting in the loss of some of the credibility of the expansion of judicial power in Russia.

Judicialization by judicial review is dependent on the image that the court is different from the other political institutions. If the court's rulings compromise that difference in appearance by seeming to be politically inspired rather than constitutionally required, the by-product of that compromise may well be the weakening of the processes and trends of judicialization.

Procedure on the Russian Constitutional Court

Before 1989, Soviet judicial procedure was socialist-inquisitorial, that is, a mixture of continental-European and Russian customary procedure with an ideological layer of socialism superimposed upon the mixture. In 1989 with the creation of the Soviet Committee on Constitutional Oversight, "judicial" procedure took a decidedly noncontinental turn to a more academic-legislative approach. This was perhaps to be expected of a committee, as opposed to a court, which was an adjunct to the legislative system rather than an integrated component in the judicial system.

In contrast to the past, the procedure of the Russian Constitutional Court is markedly but not rigidly adversarial.[1] Only juridical and governmental institutions can petition the court; individual citizens cannot carry cases to this court. Thus, this is abstract judicial review in the sense that there is not an actual case or controversy before the court.

The court procedure is a variant of public, appellate-type procedure known to Western appellate courts. First, a member of the court lays out the issue and the major arguments on each side of the issue. Thus, litigants can gain immediate insight into how the court understands the case and thus can emphasize and deemphasize certain parts of their arguments.

Second, the litigant who petitioned the court to hear the case gives an oral analysis of the issue and explains and supports a recommendation that the law or decree at issue be struck down. This analysis in the first six months of the court's life has often resembled a speech or a lecture more than a dialogue, since interruptions and questions from the judges have not been frequent.

Third, the response is given by a representative of the governmental institution that issued the law or decree. Thus, in the case involving the consolidation of the MVD and the KGB, the analysis from the presidential branch was given by Sergei Shakhray, vice premier of Russia. Again, the response has so far been more in the nature of a speech than an appellate dialogue such as is found in oral argument before an American appellate court. Interruptions and queries from the court do occur, but not yet in great abundance, though they are becoming more frequent.

During both of these speeches as well as for all portions of the court's public procedure, the relevance rule applies. Thus, all statements must be relevant to the issue at hand. No remarks about the court's alleged biases or political motives are allowed.

Fourth, the court hears from "experts." including legal, academic, and political speakers, as well as representatives of nongovernmental organizations. Members of the court have shown greater willingness to quiz the experts than the litigants.

Fifth, the court can exercise a *sua sponte* power of subpoena before or even during the oral argument. Thus, for example, during the oral argument of the MVD-KGB consolidation case, reference was made by an expert to certain documents that the court until that time had known nothing about. The court ordered the documents produced and recessed for two hours until they were produced.

The sixth and seventh steps of the public procedure are the closing statements by the two litigants. So far, these have been brief and summary in nature.

Next the court immediately considers the issue in private. Little is known about the procedures followed in the private conference. So far, secrecy has been complete; leaks have been nonexistent. *Sobratia* has not yet been published for this court.

Finally, the court publicly announces its decision through a press release.

The rules of procedure governing the whole process have not been finalized, but the court has shown a willingness to hear evidence, "witnesses," and experts and also to require the production of specified information. Forms of address ("Esteemed Judges," "Esteemed Court") are rigorously enforced. Unlike its predecessor, the Committee on Constitutional Oversight, the Constitutional Court is a court, operates as a court, projects a judicial image, and is perceived as an adjunct component of the judicial system.

Thus, it is fair to conclude that the procedure of the Constitutional Court is representative of a definitive process of judicialization. The court's procedure exemplifies the aspects discussed by Vallinder (see chap. 2 of this volume) and adds its own flexible variations to those procedures to enhance its ability to discern "the truth."

JUDICIALIZATION OF RUSSIAN CRIMINAL PROCEDURE

Whereas judicial review is largely concerned with the judicialization of *politics,* when we turn to Russian criminal procedure we encounter judicialization of *law.* In the past, routine criminal cases were handled in a manner relatively free of political intrusion, but the political elite exercised the power at will to control the decisions in specific criminal cases; moreover, the elite shaped criminal procedure to facilitate that control. Today we are seeing a major depoliticization of Russian criminal procedure.

Vallinder (chap. 2) notes that the judicial decision-making model has different characteristics and methodology from those of a legislative model. I shall discuss the changes in Russian law using the organizational scheme Vallinder proposes.

Actors

Since 1988 Soviet, and now Russian, law has entered a period of legal reformation. In this new reform period, the actors in criminal cases remain the same as before (a three-judge court; defendant and advocate; and prosecution), but now Russia has haltingly added a fourth actor—the jury.

In 1864 Russian law began its experience of jury trials, but the Bolsheviks abolished the jury in 1917. Today, Russia is once again experimenting with the criminal jury, but to date actual impaneling of juries has been exceptional and has seldom happened outside of Moscow (Interviews). The Russian jury, thus, is completely outside of the legislative model and represents an infusion of democratic sentiment into judicial decision-making. Indeed, the Russian rationale for the jury is very similar to Justice White's in *Duncan v. Louisiana*, (392 US 947 [1968]). The jury is seen as a check on unfair prosecution or a biased judge. The jury is also a general restraint on arbitrary law enforcement. The ultimate power of the criminal jury in America is its power to nullify laws. To date there has been no discussion of that power in the Russian legal literature.

The prosecution in Russian criminal law in the prereformation period was the procuracy. The procuracy also was supposed to serve an ombudsman (protector-of-rights) function for the defendant (Oda 1987). These two roles of the procurator—prosecutor of the defendant and ombudsman for the defendant—are perceived as incompatible by many Russian observers. Consequently, the Russian Supreme Soviet is today considering reducing the procuracy to only a prosecutor (Interviews). The ombudsman role as defender of rights will be taken by defense counsel.

The role of defense counsel has also undergone major change since the beginning of the Russian legal reformation. The most far-reaching change is that since 1991, defense counsel can enter the criminal process on behalf of the defendant within twenty-four hours of the filing of charges (Interviews). This permits defense counsel to protect the interests and rights of the defendant during the preliminary investigation. Before 1991, defense counsel could not enter the case until the conclusion of the preliminary investigation. This could easily be up to six or even eight months after the crime. Usually by this time the defendant would have made incriminating statements, evidence would be stale or no longer available, and witnesses would have become corrupted or would no longer be alive (Osakwe 1983, 460).

In the past, the files of defense counsel were accessible to the ministry of justice. Thus, communications between a defendant and counsel were hardly privileged. The concept of work product was unknown. Today, there is an embryonic advocate-defendant privilege developing in Russian criminal practice (Interviews). Card files are no longer accessible to anyone, and the concept of work product is developing.

The actors are the same today as they were in the Soviet period in name only. There have been major changes, however, in the direction of judicializing the roles and functions of the actors so as to protect individual rights. As Vallinder implies, protection of individual rights is the fundamental principle of the judicial model of decision-making (Vallinder, chap. 2).

Working Methods

The judicial methodology is usually open hearings with arguments offered by two opposing parties. This contrasts with the legislative methodology of negotiation, bargaining, and compromise.

In the prereformation period, Soviet criminal procedure was a hybrid judicial-administrative model in which information was theoretically processed according to two basic operating rules: (1) A defendant was formally charged only if the procurator, after an autonomous preliminary investigation, had an "inner conviction" that the defendant committed the crime charged (Osakwe 1983). (2) The court's legal and procedural presumption was that a properly charged defendant was guilty.

Thus, the methodology of charging and conviction was not an open hearing, but instead was a closed administrative process. The open hearing that the court eventually held was a ratification hearing—to confirm the accuracy of the procurator's charge—and a sentencing hearing. The sentencing function itself did often feature an open hearing and the weighing of aggravating and mitigating factors.

Today, changes are afoot, but it would still be an overstatement to conclude that the two operating rules have changed. Both still apply. The "inner conviction" standard is theoretically so demanding at the pretrial stage, so the argument goes, that presumption of guilt is fully justified at trial. However, as defense counsel becomes more prominent in the pretrial phases, the presumption of guilt at trial will be more frequently and successfully challenged (Interviews). Likewise, the "inner conviction" standard itself, arguably a more rigorous protector of the innocent defendant than the American "beyond a reasonable doubt" standard, could in the hands of a thoroughly professionalized procuracy protect individual rights.

A reasonable expectation, therefore, is for routine criminal cases to continue to be processed under the same operational methodology as in the past, albeit with greater protection of individual rights. Nonroutine cases—more sensational crimes and those carrying heavier penalties as well as those with energetic and resourceful defense counsel—will feature a weakening of the application of the two operational rules. The result for those cases will be more meaningful trials, in which the court ceases merely to ratify a charge and becomes a more active participant in a weighing-of-information process. Thus, for these cases, at best, the methodology is becoming more judicialized, but for the great majority of criminal cases the methodology continues to be primarily administrative.

The Basic Decision-making Rule

The basic decision-making rule in the judicial model is that an impartial judge decides cases. The legislative model, in contrast, is based on the majority-rule approach.

In the prereform era, the majority rule approach was not used in Soviet courts, nor is it today, but Soviet judges could hardly be described as "impartial!" Impartiality is a function of judicial independence, and the typical Soviet judge was notoriously dependent on the Communist Party for his (most were males) appointment to the post of judge and for his continuing to be a judge. Judges who strayed from party dogma in general or deviated from party wishes in particular cases would be judges no longer.

Today, judicial independence is a major goal of legal reform. Four mechanisms are enhancing the chances of achieving that goal. First, the appointment process when it involves elections uses a large electoral basis so that judges do not become dependent on a small geographic area for reelection. Thus, town judges are elected by a large region. In addition, terms of office are being lengthened—in some case to ten years as opposed to five years as it was during the Soviet era. Members of the Constitutional Court are appointed for life by the Supreme Soviet. Moreover, Yeltsin has called for life terms for all judges (Osakwe 1991, 2).

Second, conflict-of-interest rules are being strengthened so that it is considered ethically improper for judges to receive ex parte advice from anyone. This is an attempt to eradicate the old practice of judges' receiving and following party orders in cases in which the party desired certain results. To date, the conflict-of-interest rules have probably not had a major impact because many of today's judges are the same individuals who were judges in the prereform period. Though they may not seek or formally receive party guidance, many still sympathize with and, therefore, automatically follow the party's approach and do accept ex parte communications from their colleagues of a Communist persuasion.

Third, contempt rules are being strengthened. This trend began in 1990 and is continuing today. The All-Russian Congress of Judges in its October 1991 meeting called for heightened penalties for contempt and significantly called for the redefinition of contempt as a criminal offense (Kornilov 1991, 3). This would in effect put contempt cases on the criminal docket instead of treating contempt administratively as is currently done.

A fourth mechanism to strengthen the independence of judges was Yeltsin's decree that as of January 1, 1992, substantially increased judges' salaries (Osakwe 1991, 2). Though the uncertainty of the Soviet economy and the impending convertability of the ruble reduce the financial significance of this increase, the symbolism is nevertheless important. It is a step in the direction of an independent judiciary.

Thus, the concerted efforts to increase judicial impartiality and independence are indications of the process of judicialization currently under way in Russia. In the past, politics was frequently and prominently injected into the decision-making mode of courts. Eliminating that practice is still a major problem in the Russian judicial system, but at least now there is deliberate movement toward depoliticizing judicial decision-making.

Output

Russian judicial practice follows Vallinder's model in that Russian criminal courts settle individual cases and generally do not issue general rules. The output and decisions of Russian cases are not precedent and do not form general rules to guide subsequent policy-making. This is a typical characteristic of the civil-law tradition and continues to be the Russian practice.

There are two exceptions to this general practice. First, the Russian Supreme Court can issue "plenary instructions," which are interpretations of law and procedure that bind the lower courts (Osakwe 1983, 494). Second, the Russian Constitutional Court has the power of judicial review, and this includes the power to overrule plenary instructions issued by the Supreme Court.

Implications

The model of judicial decision-making assumes that judicial application of law to the facts of a case results in "the only correct solution" to the problem at hand (Vallinder, chap. 2).

The two dominant Soviet schools of jurisprudence (legal nihilism and Communism) rejected the idea of there being only one correct solution. Legal nihilism disavows the conflict-resolution function of law and instead maintains that all that matters is the appearance of legality, that conflicts are resolved and policy is made by the political elite. The Communist variant of legal nihilism simply maintains that the law is an instrument by which the party achieves its objectives. Neither legal nihilism nor Communism assumes that there is only one correct solution to a legal problem. (Thus, scientific socialism, which would philosophically endorse the "one correct solution" hypothesis, was never compatible with basic Soviet theories of judicial decision-making and in practice was considered relevant only to the preliminary investigation in criminal cases.)

A newer, developing school of Russian jurisprudence is the current reform approach, that might be called "democratic legalism." The twin tenets of this approach are that (1) law should not serve the elite but should serve the people equally and (2) judges must be guided by legal and democratic principles rather than by the needs of policy. The law-governed state is, thus, based ultimately on these two principles. Democratic legalism does not seem to accept the "one correct solution" hypothesis for individual cases, but neither have its proponents clearly rejected that idea. Both the use of the jury in criminal cases and the use of arbitration courts in civil cases would seem to reject the idea that there is only one correct solution to a legal controversy.

Does this mean that as far as implications are concerned, Russian legal reform is less judicialized? Not at all. Judicialization concerns the ultimate content of the decisions made and whether that content is based on known principles or on situational practicalities. A legislative model of decision-making produces output, which circumstances and votes make possible. Political output results from possibilities, practicalities, and power relationships among the relevant actors.

Judicialization emphasizes the principles that guide decisions. Judicial output results from doctrines, rules, and only secondarily from power relationships among the actors. Seen in this fashion, Russian judicial decision-making is undergoing pronounced judicialization. As recently as 1988, the principles that allegedly guided judicial decisions were still under the day-to-day control of the political elite. Today that control has been substantially weakened.

NOTES

1. This section of this chapter is based on Rudnev (1992a) and on interviews—cited herein as "Interviews"—which I conducted with lawyers and journalists in Moscow in the summer of 1992.

REFERENCES

Feofanov, Yuri. 1992. "Structure of Law. . ." *Izvestia*, March 19, 2.

Kerimov, D. A. 1989. "Fiction." *Pravda*, December 22, 1.

Kitchin, William. 1991a. "The Implications for Judicial Review of the Current Legal Reforms in the Soviet Union." *Policy Studies Journal* 19:96-105.

―――. 1991b. "A Preliminary Assessment of the Soviet Committee on Constitutional Oversight." Paper presented at the 1991 Meeting of the Law and Society Association, Amsterdam, June 26-29.

Kornilov, Sergei. 1991. "Judiciary: Starting from Scratch." *Rossiyskaya Gazeta* , October 22, 3.

Maylsheva, A. 1991. "Candidate on Functions of Constitutional Court." Foreign Broadcast Information Service Daily Report. Soviet Union October 30, 1.

―――. 1992. "The Constitutional Court Itself Will Henceforth Assess Parliament's Laws and the President's Decrees." *Komsomolskaya Pravda*, January 15, 1.

Oda, Hiroshi. 1987. "The Procuracy and the Regular Courts as Enforcers of the Constitutional Rule of Law." *Tulane Law Review* 57:439-601.

Osakwe, C. 1983. "Modern Soviet Criminal Procedure." *Tulane Law Review* 57:439-601.

―――. 1991. "Dismantling the Obsequious Judiciary." *Rossiyskaya Gazeta* (Oct. 19): 2.

Rudnev, Valery. 1992a. "Constitutional Court Abolishes B. Yeltsin's Decree . . ." *Izvestia*, January 16, 1.

———.   1992b.   "Constitutional Court Chairman on Tatarstan."
Foreign Broadcast Information Service Daily Report. Soviet Union,
March 13, 63-64.

Troubled Democracies

25.

The Philippines and Southeast Asia

C. NEAL TATE

The expansion of judicial power is a phenomenon that is highly relevant
to the politics of the nations in several of the world's regions: North and
South America, Western and Eastern Europe, including the Eurasian
giant, Russia, and the Indian subcontinent. Articles contained in this
work and in other sources (see the studies by Russell, Stone, Kitchin,
Volcansek, Sunkin, and Edelman in Jackson and Tate 1992; Di Federico
and Guarnieri 1988; Waltman 1988; and the studies collected in Holland
1991) document aspects of this phenomenon.

The picture is different in most of Africa and Asia, however. In
Africa, incipient democratization efforts may bring increased
judicialization of politics as they bring increased demands for the rule of
law. But so far it appears that the judicialization of politics is potentially
imminent only in the changing South Africa and in some of the nations
surrounding it (see chapter 26; Gouws 1992). Aside from India, it may
be that the Philippines is the only nation in Afro-Asia where the
expansion of judicial power can be said to be a significant, current
political development.

To document the importance of the judicialization of politics in the
Philippines, it may be useful to survey the role of the judiciary in the
other nations of Southeast Asia. Although this survey will be distinctly
cursory, there is little danger of drawing wrong conclusions about the
importance of the judiciary or the likelihood of the judicialization of
politics in the region's political systems (Burma [Myanmar], Thailand,

Laos, Cambodia [Kampuchea], Vietnam, Malaysia, Singapore, Indonesia, Brunei, Papua-New Guinea, and the Philippines).

A majority of the Southeast Asian countries are unlikely candidates for the judicialization of politics because they are ruled by regimes that, by any standard of judgment, are distinctively, if not ruthlessly, undemocratic and nonconstitutional. As evidence, one might cite the political and civil-rights ratings given Burma, Laos, Cambodia, Vietnam, Indonesia, and Brunei in recent surveys of *Freedom in the World* (for example, see McColm 1990).[1] These nations are among the world's "not free." Since it appears that the judicialization of politics is likely to occur mostly, if not only, in regimes that have adopted the institutions and norms of liberal democracy and accepted the principle of judicial independence (see chap. 3), there is little present basis for the judicialization of politics in these countries.[2]

The situation is quite different in Thailand, Malaysia, Singapore, Papua-New Guinea, and the Philippines. These nations are all, in form at least, liberal democracies with independent judiciaries. But in practice, Thailand's persistent problem of military intervention against civilian (or civilianized) regimes, Malaysia's rule by strong prime ministers representing an ethnically based and defensive political party organization, and Singapore's long domination by strong-man ruler Lee-Kuan Yu and his designated successors have meant that in these nations, too, there has been little room for the judicialization of politics.[3]

Thus, at present, only Papua-New Guinea and the Philippines represent nations in which one could expect the liberal democratic preconditions for the judicialization of politics to be present. To the best of my knowledge, the relatively recent independence of Papua-New Guinea (1975), its continued dependence on Australia, and its conservative British judicial tradition have prevented significant judicialization of politics in that country. The Philippines is another matter, however. Several factors—liberal democracy, separation of powers, a politics of rights, interest group and opposition use of the courts, and frequently ineffective majoritarian institutions with limited public respect (see chap. 3)—appear to make substantial judicialization of contemporary Philippine politics possible, if not likely. The remainder of this chapter, therefore, focuses on the Philippine case, concentrating on the role of the Supreme Court in the judicialization of that nation's politics.

THE JUDICIARY IN THE PHILIPPINES: BACKGROUND

For seven decades, through the periods of American colonialism, prewar Commonwealth, and postwar independence, the Supreme Court was a respected, independent, and powerful legal force in Philippine politics and government. Indeed according to most informed observers, its reputation for competence and rectitude generally exceeded that of other government institutions.[4] But in 1972 incumbent President Ferdinand Marcos established his military-backed one-man rule, declaring martial law, disbanding the Congress and political parties, and restricting freedom of the press and other democratic liberties that Filipinos were used to exercising. The president did not abolish the Supreme Court or change its membership or structure. To the contrary, Marcos defended himself against the charge that he was a dictator by noting that his actions were still subject to challenge in the Supreme Court.

This defense may have sounded a little hollow to those who noted that the president's martial-law decrees also pronounced that his edicts could not be challenged in court and established jurisdiction for military courts over offenses that previously would have been the province of the civilian judiciary. Martial law thus clearly posed a threat to the power, independence, and ultimately, popular respect the Supreme Court had always enjoyed.

Despite Marcos's martial-law rule, the power, independence, and respect of the Supreme Court did not immediately disappear. Critics of the president's rule took seriously his remark that his actions were subject to challenge in the Supreme Court. They brought suits asking the Supreme Court to overturn, on constitutional grounds, the president's martial-law declaration and his effectively unilateral ratification of a new constitution that gave him absolute authority until he should choose to give it up. Though they found some support among the Supreme Court's justices, actually getting a majority to declare that the new constitution had not been validly adopted, Marcos's opponents were unable to persuade a majority to rule against the effectivity of his rule (*Javellana v. Executive Secretary*, 50 *Supreme Court Reports Annotated* [SCRA] 30 [1973]). The result was an opinion stating that there was "no further barrier" to the effectivity of the new constitution with its grant of unlimited power to Marcos. Though hardly a ringing endorsement, this language served as a precedent justifying Marcos's authoritarian rule against subsequent direct challenges.

The consolidation of Ferdinand Marcos's one-man rule effectively removed the liberal democratic environment and most other factors facilitating the judicialization of politics and sharply reduced the ability of the Philippine Supreme Court to judicialize politics by ruling on matters the president would have preferred to keep under his own jurisdiction.   That ability was further reduced as the president increasingly appointed to the Court justices who, though nominally legally well qualified, were widely regarded as "cronies" of the president. The consequence was that, well before the end of Marcos's rule, the public respect formerly accorded the Supreme Court, as well as its reputation for independence and its political power, had dissipated.

Marcos was finally brought down in February 1986 as a result of a combination popular revolt/military mutiny (the People Power Revolution) that followed his attempt to remain in power after a rigged election that he allegedly lost to Corazon ("Cory") Aquino.   Cory Aquino was the widow of Benigno Aquino, a political opponent of Marcos's who had been imprisoned and tried under military auspices in the early years of martial law, allowed to go into exile in the United States for medical reasons, and assassinated while under military escort upon his return to the Philippines in 1983.   Aquino and his supporters had on several occasions been rebuffed by the Supreme Court in their efforts to win him freedom from imprisonment or to transfer his case from a military tribunal to the civil courts.

When the People Power Revolution installed Cory Aquino as the new president of the Philippines, it seemed possible—because of the experience of the Aquino family and their political allies with the Supreme Court under Marcos—that whatever new government was established to replace the Marcos regime would hardly be favorably inclined toward the judiciary, especially the Supreme Court.[5]   Indeed, Aquino appeared to reinforce that possibility when, in her inaugural address, she called for the resignation of all incumbent government officials, "beginning," as she noted pointedly, "with the justices of the Supreme Court."

However likely it appeared at the beginning of the Aquino regime that the judiciary would be weakened, it was not to be.   Instead, Aquino almost immediately reestablished a Supreme Court, staffed with several new justices, which quickly ascended to a position of respect that nearly matched that of its premartial-law predecessor.   Furthermore, the new president manifested a "hands-off" attitude toward disputes that ended up in the judiciary, an attitude that gave the new Supreme Court latitude to rebuild its reputation for independence and, perhaps, its political power. Finally, and most importantly, the new constitution that was drafted in 1986 and ratified in early 1987 reestablished a liberal democratic regime with an independent judiciary headed by a powerful Supreme Court and expanded the power of the judiciary through several constitutional provisions intended to make it a stronger bulwark against the possibility of new abuses by a would-be authoritarian ruler. These provisions have established the foundation on which an expansion of judicial power can be built in the new Philippine Republic.

CONSTITUTIONAL FOUNDATIONS FOR THE JUDICIALIZATION OF POLITICS

The current (1987) Constitution of the Republic of the Philippines certainly provides the structural foundations for the judicialization of politics. It sets up a liberal democratic regime with an impressive separation of the executive, legislative, and judicial branches of the government. It assigns the judiciary, headed and managed by the Supreme Court, new and expanded powers and responsibilities that give it great potential to judicialize a wide variety of policy processes that would otherwise be the responsibility of the executive and the legislature, that is, the majoritarian institutions. It also contains an elaborate Bill of Rights capable of sustaining a vigorous politics of rights that would promote the judicialization of politics.

Constitutional Provisions Regarding the Judiciary

All the effective constitutions of the Philippines have established a structurally separate and independent judiciary with full formal powers of judicial review. The current constitution goes farthest in this direction, however. It provides such usual protections for judicial independence as security of tenure during good behavior (until a mandatory retirement age of seventy) and security of compensation. In addition,

1. *It grants to the judiciary broad powers over judicial selection.* All judges, including those of the Supreme Court, are selected by the president from a list of at least three nominees prepared by a constitutionally mandated Judicial and Bar Council. The members of this

council are nominated by the president and approved by the Congress-based Commission on Appointments. But the Council is chaired by the chief justice of the Supreme Court, and includes only one representative of the legislative and executive branches of government. Its other four members represent the Integrated Bar (which is regulated by the Supreme Court), professors of law, retired members of the Supreme Court, and "the private sector." The council's membership thus is clearly biased toward the point of view of the judiciary.

2. *It grants the judiciary fiscal autonomy.* Congress may not reduce the Court's budget, and that budget must be immediately made available to the courts.

3. *It grants the judiciary self-government and provides additional formal protections for judicial independence.* The Supreme Court (a) appoints all officers and employees of and exercises full administrative control of the judiciary; (b) exercises disciplinary control over all judges and all officers and employees of the judiciary; (c) has exclusive power to promulgate rules governing "protection and enforcement of constitutional rights, pleading, practice, and procedure in all courts, the admission to the practice of law, the Integrated Bar, and legal assistance to the underprivileged" (Constitution, 1987: art. 7, sec. 5(5); see also De Leon 1987, 337), such "Rules of Court" having the force of law; (d) exercises exclusive control over the transfer of judges,[6] while guaranteeing judges against permanent or lengthy temporary transfers to other stations without their consent.

4. *It grants the Supreme Court broad powers and jurisdiction that may not be altered by Congress, protects the Court from expansions of its jurisdiction without its consent, and prohibits judges from serving on nonjudicial bodies.*

Though limited to ruling in disputes involving actual controversies, the judiciary is assigned the *duty* to rule in "controversies involving rights which are legally demandable and enforceable, and to determine whether or not there has been a grave abuse of discretion amounting to lack or excess of jurisdiction on the part of any branch or instrumentality of the Government" (Constitution, 1987, art. 7, sec. 1). This authority and duty is so broad that Philippine constitutional-law authorities contend that it sharply restricts the ability of the courts to use the "political question" doctrine to avoid ruling on the challenged actions of even the highest government officials (see Cruz 1987, 81-83; De Leon 1987, 317; Nolledo 1987, 77).

The Bill of Rights and Potential Judicialization

The current Constitution of the Republic of the Philippines has a very extensive Bill of Rights, that should be regarded as both cause and effect of a Philippine politics of rights that has intensified in the post-Marcos era. The current Bill of Rights has its origins in the 1935 Constitution, drafted under American supervision to serve as the governing framework for the Commonwealth of the Philippines, inaugurated in 1935. This Bill of Rights provided for the following rights:

1. Due process of law
2. Equal protection of the laws
3. Just compensation for private property in eminent domain
4. Security against search and seizure except on proper order of a judge after proper hearing
5. Freedom of travel: freedom of abode and of changing abode
6. Privacy of communication
7. Freedom of association
8. Separation of church and state
9. Freedom of worship
10. Freedom of speech, press, and assembly
11. Prohibition of nobility
12. Prohibition of emoluments from foreign states
13. Security of contracts
14. No ex post facto laws or bills of attainder
15. No imprisonment for nonpayment of debt
16. No involuntary servitude
17. No suspension of the writ of habeas corpus except in cases of invasion, etc
18. Due process of law in criminal cases
19. Right to reasonable bail
20. Presumption of innocence
21. Right to counsel
22. Right to be informed of charges against one
23. Right to speedy public trial
24. Right to confront witnesses against one

25. Protection against self-incrimination
26. Prohibition of excessive fines and cruel and unusual punishment
27. Protection against double jeopardy
28. Right to access to courts even if poor

Extensive as it was, the 1935 Bill of Rights was expanded in the constitution of 1973, drafted just before and adopted just after the beginning of Marcos's establishment of martial-law authoritarianism. Nominally, the 1973 constitution added the following to the 1935 Bill of Rights:

29. Prohibition of means of obtaining confession that vitiate free will
30. Inadmissibility of improperly-seized evidence whether from an unconstitutional search, a violation of the constitutionally guaranteed privacy of communication, or obtained by coercion (as in 29 above)
31. Freedom of information on matters of public concern
32. Right to speedy proceedings before all judicial, quasi-judicial, or administrative bodies
33. Production of evidence in the behalf of an accused
34. Right to be informed of one's right to remain silent and to have counsel while under detention
35. Right to an "impartial" as well as a "speedy" and "public" trial[7]

Unfortunately, the expansions in words of the 1935 Bill of Rights meant little in practice. The ineffectiveness of the Bill of Rights of the 1973 Constitution was obviously due to the president's one-man rule made "legitimate" by the Transitory Provisions of and later amendments to the 1973 Constitution.[8]

Although many of the rights guaranteed under the 1973 Constitution were not respected under Marcos's authoritarianism, approval of the rights provisions of the 1973 constitution by Marcos's successors is evident. The 1973 Bill of Rights is subsumed under the even broader Bill of Rights of the 1987 Constitution. Where the drafters of the 1987 constitution felt the phrasing of specific provisions of the previous bills of rights was inadequate to prevent abuses by the Marcos regime, they added new language in an attempt to make the new Bill of Rights as dictator-proof as possible.

Specifically, the 1987 Bill of Rights

1. Adds that any warrant issued in a judicial hearing in a search-and-seizure case must result from probable cause to be determined "personally" by the judge.

2. Adds "as prescribed by law" to regulate government violations of privacy of communication when public safety or order require it.

3. Rewrites and strengthens the right to travel and adds "as may be prescribed by law" to the clause allowing limitation of the right under constitutionally prescribed conditions.

4. Adds "research data" to that subject to the freedom of information.

5. Adds to freedom of association a specific right to form unions.

6. Reorders the list of rights to list property rights after personal rights.

7. Adds a guarantee of "adequate legal assistance" to the right of free access to court for the indigent.

8. Rewrites the right to counsel and to remain silent to include the right "to be informed of" the right to remain silent and to have "competent and independent counsel preferably of his own choice," to be provided with counsel if one cannot afford one, and requires that any waiver of these rights must be "in writing and in presence of counsel."

9. Specifically adds "torture" to the list of prohibited activities in investigations.

10. Adds "admissions" to the list of evidence inadmissible if improperly obtained.

11. Provides for "penal and civil sanctions" for violations of the rights of persons under investigation and the right to "compensation and rehabilitation" for victims of "torture or similar practices."

12. Guarantees the right to bail except for life sentences when evidence is strong, even during suspension of habeas corpus.

13. Specifically prohibits detention for political beliefs.

14. Abolishes the death penalty, unless reinstated by Congress for "heinous crimes"

The rights protections contained in these telling changes in the Bill of Rights are augmented by other provisions. For example, the 1987 Constitution (a) contains a prohibition on physical, psychological, or degrading punishment on prisoners and requires adequate prison conditions, and (b) establishes a Human Rights Commission to investigate claims of rights violations.

Even more significantly, the Constitution contains other modifications of the provisions of the 1973 (and 1935) documents that represent clear reactions to Marcos's one-man rule.   In contrast to the earlier constitutions, the 1987 charter contains restrictions on the president's authority to suspend the privilege of the writ of habeas corpus that make the declaration of such a suspension almost a futile gesture.   To declare the suspension of the privilege of the writ or to declare martial law now requires an actual invasion or rebellion, not just an imminent threat thereof, and that public safety mandates it.   In addition, a declaration of martial law does not automatically suspend the privilege of the writ of habeas corpus.   The suspension of the privilege, if justified, is allowable only for those who have been judicially charged, and a judicial charge is required within three days if release of detainees is to be avoided.   The right to bail is not impaired even if the privilege of the writ is suspended, and any suspension may not exceed sixty days.

The president, if she or he suspends the writ or declares martial law, must report to Congress on the declaration within forty-eight hours. Congress must convene itself within twenty-four hours to hear the report, if it is not in session.   Congress may revoke the president's proclamation, if it sees fit, and the president cannot reinstate it.   In addition, the Supreme Court may review the factual basis of such proclamations and must its promulgate decision on the matter within thirty days.

Any declaration of martial law does not suspend the operation of the Constitution;   the civilian authorities remain in charge.   If it feels the proclamation is justified, Congress may extend the proclamation beyond 60 days, at the president's initiative.

Potential Judicialization in the 1987 Constitution

The legal effect of the martial law/habeas corpus provisions of the new constitution is as clear as its origin: it seeks to prevent the use of authorized presidential powers to abuse rights.   A similar, if less obvious, effort is evident in the already-discussed provisions of the 1987 Constitution that greatly strengthen the formal independence and power of the judiciary.   The net result is to provide a very broad basis for the judicialization of politics in the Philippines: liberal democracy, separation of powers, the legal basis for a vigorous politics of rights, and a jurisdiction tailor made for interest group and opposition use of the courts.

NATIONAL INSTITUTIONS, JUDICIAL ATTITUDES AND THE FULFILLMENT OF THE POTENTIAL FOR JUDICIALIZATION

The fulfillment of the potential for the judicialization of politics in the Philippines does not depend entirely on constitutional or legal provisions. The extent to which the potential is fulfilled is also affected by the actual and perceived characteristics of the national majoritarian institutions and by the constellation of attitudes characterizing the judiciary. Actual judicialization becomes more likely if majoritarian institutions are ineffective in handling important policy disputes, are negatively perceived by the public, at least as compared to the judiciary, or actually delegate difficult policy problems to the judiciary. However, even under these circumstances judicialization may not occur unless there is an appropriate conjunction of conditions favorable to judicialization and activist judicial attitudes.[9]

To what extent has there been such a conjunction in the Philippines? Certainly the majoritarian institutions established under the 1987 Philippine Constitution must be judged to be more effective and to have higher prestige than their nominal equivalents during the last years of the Marcos dictatorship. Nevertheless, during her six-year Presidency Cory Aquino was plagued by attempted military coups and frequently criticized as weak and ineffective.[10] In addition, the Congress elected under the new constitution was distinguished more by its maneuvering for partisan and personal political advantage than by the vigor of its attack on the nation's crucial problems. As a result, public support of both the president and the Congress declined over the first five years of the life of the new constitution,[11] and influential commentators regularly remarked on the ineffectiveness of the new institutions of democracy.[12] In contrast, the Supreme Court retained substantial respect and support, even in the midst of a nasty conflict with an important Aquino administration official (see Tate 1992, 122), and, five years after its reconstitution under the Aquino regime, it continued to be editorially judged the branch of the national government "that the public seems to hold in highest esteem" (*Manila Bulletin*, June 11, 1991).

It would appear that both the constitutional and legal environment and the character of the majoritarian institutions favor the judicialization of politics in the Philippines. Whether or not the judiciary takes advantage of such favorable facilitative conditions to promote judicialization depends upon the attitudes of the judges, particularly the Supreme Court justices. Have the judges displayed activist attitudes? To the extent that they have, how much judicialization has occurred?

Interviews I conducted with incumbent justices of the Philippine Supreme Court in 1987-1988 indicated that, at the beginning of the new constitutional regime, an activist orientation was common among them.[13]   Almost all the justices indicated their awareness of the unprecedented strengthening of the formal powers of the Supreme Court under the new constitution and their approval of the larger role for the Court that these powers implied. A few spoke scornfully of the timid behavior of the Court under Marcos and enthusiastically embraced a broad policy role for their court. The first annual report issued by the Court's chief justice, Claudio Teehankee, also spoke forcefully about the breadth and importance of the Court's policy-making at the beginning of the Aquino regime (Teehankee 1987). Although there were several justices whose orientation seemed clearly restraintist, the bulk of the interview evidence suggests the presence of a substantial amount of activism in the attitudes of the Supreme Court justices initially appointed by Cory Aquino.

Have these activist attitudes, combined with the favorable facilitating conditions present in the Philippine legal and political environments, actually led to Supreme Court decisions that can be cited as evidence for a judicialization of post-Marcos Philippine politics? In the absence of firm empirical guidelines for judging just how much judicialization has occurred in a political system, the answer must of necessity be a matter of professional opinion and judgment. To support my tentative judgment that judicialization had occurred in the Philippines, I have examined reports of Supreme Court decision making appearing in a major Philippine newspapers during 1990 and 1991,[14] the fourth and fifth years of Philippine government under the 1987 constitution.

The assumption of this examination is that newspaper coverage of the Supreme Court's decision making will concentrate on the most newsworthy (sensational?) among the numerous decisions handed down by the Court at any given time, and that decisions marking the judicialization of politics will generally be represented among these newsworthy decisions. By examining 1990 and 1991 news reports, I hope to tap the Court's "regular" decision making after the initial rounds of decisions reflecting reactions to, or readjustments made necessary by, the period of authoritarianism.[15]

The most controversial decisions handed down by the Supreme Court during 1990-1991 do indeed appear to provide evidence for increasing judicialization in Philippine politics. In one of them, the Court thwarted the executive's plan to try Senate Minority Leader Juan Ponce Enrile for "rebellion complexed with murder" for his alleged part in the December, 1989 coup that came very close to unseating Aquino. This crime would have entailed much more serious punishment than the simple crime of "rebellion," punishable under the Spanish-influenced civil code by a relatively modest prison sentence.

Enrile was co-instigator—along with current President Fidel Ramos, of the 1986 military mutiny that touched off the People Power Revolution, a former minister of defense under both Marcos and Aquino, and a bitter rival of Aquino and Ramos. The leaders of the 1989 coup and several prior ones, for that matter, had been closely affiliated with Enrile. The suspicions and evidence linking Enrile to the coup seemed entirely reasonable. Nevertheless, the Court, following a 1950s ruling directed against President Ramon Magsaysay's efforts to thwart the Hukbalahap rebellion (see Tate and Sittiwong 1986), ruled that there was no such crime as rebellion complexed with murder and that, if Enrile were to be tried, he would have to be tried for simple rebellion (*Manila Bulletin*, September 14, 1990). Eventually, the Court freed Enrile altogether.

The Supreme Court's treatment of Enrile might be regarded as an instance of a judicial body merely requiring a majoritarian executive to obey the rule of law. Regardless, there is little question that the Court's actions restricted the ability of the president and her administration to respond effectively to the latest and most serious violent threat to her constitutionally sanctioned rule. From this perspective, the Supreme Court judicialized Philippine politics at least by "legalizing" a dispute that might have been better handled by the majoritarian institutions.

In other 1990-1991 decisions, the Supreme Court can be argued to have judicialized the political process when:

1. It erected legal barriers slowing or thwarting the efforts of the Philippine Commission on Good Government (PCGG) to recover for the nation billions of pesos in "ill-gotten assets" acquired by the Marcoses and their cronies during the long period of Ferdinand's rule. In particular, the Court consistently restricted the PCGG's efforts to recover assets from Marcos's cronies Roberto Benedicto and Eduardo "Danding"

Cojuangco, President Aquino's estranged businessman cousin (*Manila Bulletin* April 3, November 30, 1990). There can be little doubt that these and similar restrictions on the activities of the PCGG significantly reduced the ability of this agency of the majoritarian institutions to enrich the government's coffers by regaining substantial portions of the illegally obtained wealth of the Marcos cronies.

2. It declared unconstitutional the president's attempt to appoint an acting chair of the Commission on Elections, ruling that the commission should elect its own acting chair until a permanent chair could be confirmed by the Commission on Appointments (*Manila Bulletin*, December 19, 1990).[16] Critics of this decision might have argued that the Court should have left the operation of the commission to the majoritarian bodies who are supposed to select it, and to whom it reports.

3. In one of its most important constitutional decisions, it ruled that Aquino administration officials could not hold more than one government position for which compensation was paid (*Manila Bulletin*, March 5, 1991). Aquino had appointed numerous officials to two or more offices as a way of enhancing the otherwise "inadequate" incomes received by government officials and of enticing competent persons from better-paying private-sector occupations. Certainly it is possible to argue that this issue could have been left to the majoritarian institutions responsible for making and confirming such appointments.

4. In response to a suit by the political opposition, it prevented the government from selling a valuable piece of property in Tokyo to raise funds to be applied to reducing its foreign debt and land-reform spending (*Manila Bulletin*, February 21, 23, July 27, 1990), ruling that the sale required Congressional approval. This action allegedly caused the government to miss the opportunity for a lucrative sale that would have been of substantial benefit.

5. It prevented the Metropolitan Manila Commission from having police officers confiscate the license plates of some illegally parked vehicles or the operator's licenses of drivers in certain traffic violations (*Manila Bulletin*, July 23, 1990, February 24, 1991). Although sympathizing with drivers who might have been subject to such confiscations, anyone who has experienced Manila traffic might also regret any restriction that hampered the ability of the city to expedite traffic flow and wonder why such an administrative issue should have been decided by the Supreme Court.

6. On the petition of a Senator and a consumers' group, it disallowed prices increases planned by the National Power Corporation (NAPOCOR) (*Manila Bulletin*, March 13, May 30, June 1, 1991). NAPOCOR argued that it needed the price increases to finance additional power-generating capacity for metropolitan Manila and that disallowing the increases would only lead to increased power difficulties and "brownouts" for the metropolis. NAPOCOR appears to have been right: brownouts in Manila were subsequently a considerably bigger problem than they had been in previous years (personal communication from a Manila informant).

7. It engaged in a direct confrontation with the House of Representatives over the latter's power to remove one of its appointees to the House of Representatives Electoral Tribunal, on which three of its justices also serve (*Manila Bulletin*, April 18, 19, 25, 26, 1991). The Supreme Court justices on the tribunal and the Court itself sought to prevent what appeared to be partisan manipulation of the tribunal by the House majority to prevent an unfavorable outcome in an election dispute. But the position of the House of Representatives was that the Court had no right or jurisdiction to tell it how to appoint or remove its constitutionally guaranteed members on the Tribunal.

8. It restrained the government from enforcing a law that would have "desynchronized" local and national elections mandated for 1992 (*Manila Bulletin*, June 28, 1991). The president and the Congress had agreed that desynchronizing the 1992 elections would have made it easier to administer peaceful, fair, and honest elections. The Court's restraining order seemed to tell majoritarian institutions that, even when in agreement, they could not specify procedures for their own elections without challenge from the judiciary.

9. It required the University of the Philippines College of Medicine to admit four students who had been denied admission under a new and more stringent admissions formula devised by the college faculty (*Manila Bulletin*, February 28, 1991). Skeptics might be forgiven for wondering whether the Supreme Court should have been substituting its judgment for that of those qualified to judge the ability of students to become competent physicians.

10. It stopped Quezon City from raising real-estate taxes, even though the increases had been approved by the Ministry of Interior and Local Government (*Manila Bulletin*, March 23, 1991). Again, one might ask why the Supreme Court should substitute its judgment of the

reasonableness of a local tax increase for that of elected city officials and national administrators who report to the majoritarian president?

In arguing that these decisions represent celebrated instances in which the Supreme Court judicialized Philippine politics, I mean neither to praise nor denounce the Court's actions. The constitutional grant of authority given the Supreme Court certainly provides a foundation for it to substitute its judgment for that of any government official who has, in the Court's view, engaged in a "grave abuse of discretion amounting to lack or excess of jurisdiction." Furthermore, it would certainly be possible to cite examples of cases in which the Court refused the opportunity to judicialize Philippine politics. But it would also be possible to cite a number of additional examples that represent instances in which the Supreme Court judicialized politics during 1990-1991. Thus I believe the cited examples do constitute substantial evidence for the judicialization of Philippine politics by the Supreme Court under the 1987 Constitution.

The years since the establishment of the new Philippine Republic hardly constitute sufficient time for the potential for judicialization to manifest itself in a concrete continuing trend, even if highly activist judges were in place at the top of the judicial hierarchy. Furthermore, it may be that the regime of President Fidel Ramos, elected in 1992, will rejuvenate the majoritarian institutions and reduce the likelihood of continuing judicialization. Ironically, what might also contribute to reducing the likelihood of continuing judicialization is the domination of the Supreme Court appointment process by the Judicial and Bar Council, a body that strongly represents the judiciary and the legal community. There is some evidence, in the careers of the initial Supreme Court appointees, that the council nominations will predominantly represent career judges and court administrators with little direct experience of the political process.[17] Although such a career does not necessarily produce a justice with restraintist attitudes, the Philippine experience suggests that such appointees are more likely to be restraintist than justices with different, more partisan, careers. Thus it is likely that the Philippines will remain an interesting case in which to observe the process of judicialization.

NOTES

The research reported in this chapter was supported in part by grant no. SES-8710051 funded jointly by the Law and Social Science and Political Science Programs of the U.S. National Science Foundation (NSF) and by a Fulbright-Hays senior research fellowship to the Philippines received by the author in 1987-1988. The opinions expressed here are those of the author and do not necessarily reflect those of NSF or the Fulbright program.

1. This is not the place to engage in a discussion of the potential biases and reliability of the political and civil freedoms ratings awarded annually by Freedom House. Suffice it to say that recent, careful work by Steven Poe and the author (Poe and Tate, 1994) documents, on the basis of a cross-national and longitudinal empirical analysis of 153 nations, that the Freedom House Political Rights indicator is a reasonable and reliable indicator of the extent of democracy within nations.

2. Burma and Indonesia have experienced agitations for increased democracy that may bear fruit in the near future. But the probability and likely date of any future adoption of democratic government in these nations still appear to be low and distant.

3. I do not imply that there are not important political differences in the degree of democracy and political freedom between Thailand, Malaysia, and Singapore (as a group) and, especially, Burma, Laos, Cambodia, and Vietnam (as another group). The differences are rather substantial: whereas Freedom House rates the latter among the world's least free nations, with political-freedom and civil-rights scores at the most repressive end of the seven-point Freedom House scale, the former are usually included in the "partly free" category and given scores in the middle of the scale (see McColm, 1990, for example). In addition, there is some evidence that judges may be increasingly being called upon to resolve important and politically sensitive issues in Thailand, Malaysia, and Singapore.

4. The only exception was the years of the Japanese occupation of the Philippines during World War II. A Supreme Court substantially altered in membership maintained a very low profile in the occupation government. For discussions and documentation of the Court's importance and role, see Tate (1992, 1971) and the sources cited therein.

5. For speculation to that effect, see Tate and Sittiwong (1986, 18).

6. Previous constitutions had given this authority to the secretary of justice, with the approval of the Supreme Court.

7. The 1973 Constitution also added certain words and provisions that, given the circumstances of its adoption and ratification, appeared rather ominous. Aside from a provision allowing trial *in absentia* for a properly arraigned and notified defendant who unjustifiably fails to appear (retained in the 1987 Constitution), the 1973 Constitution (a) added the phrase "other responsible officer as may be determined by law" to the "competent judge" in specifying those authorized to issue search or arrest warrants, and (b) provided that freedom of abode "and travel" could be impaired not just on the "lawful order of the court" in constitutionally recognized circumstances, but "when necessary".

Despite these phrases, it is clear that, on balance, the human rights of Filipinos were more strongly guaranteed in the *words* of the 1973 Constitution than they had been in those of the 1935 document.

8. The Transitory Provisions provided essentially that the President could rule by decree for as long as he wished without seeking the approval of anyone. They did so by providing that (a) the "incumbent President of the Philippines" would continue to exercise the powers of the President under the superseded 1935 Constitution as well as those of Prime Minister and Cabinet under the new Constitution, (b) that all his laws, orders, and decrees were binding until altered either by him, or by the regular National Assembly, (c) that the regular National Assembly would assemble only after it was elected under rules established by an Interim National Assembly, and (d) that the Interim National Assembly, though it existed "immediately" upon the ratification of the 1973 Constitution, could be convened
only by the President.

The President never convened the Interim National Assembly and it was rendered obsolete by a 1976 amendment replacing it with an "interim Batasang Pambansa" (IBP).   Although the IBP did convene, and, indeed, was later replaced by a regular Batasang Pambansa, and although martial law was officially lifted in 1981, the President's ability to rule unimpeded was not removed. The constitutional amendments and other presidential proclamations making these changes carefully retained the incumbent president's power to rule by decree whenever he felt it necessary to do, without challenge from other government bodies.   His one man rule thus continued the elimination, suppression, or severe limitation of the rights guaranteed in the 1973 Constitution.

9. This paragraph follows the argument of Tate (1992).

10. With some justification, Aquino openly wondered how a woman who had survived six increasingly serious military coup attempts could be characterized as weak. Nevertheless, perhaps because of her political inexperience or her personal vision of how policy should be made in a democracy, Aquino did seem reluctant to use her (initially great) personal popularity and political support to lead important policy initiatives.

11. See the opinion polls conducted by the "Social Weather Station" and by the Ateneo de Manila University.

12. For example, the respected editor of the *Manila Chronicle*, Amando Doronila, filed in August 1990 a series of editorials entitled "Democracy in mortal danger" and "Prescriptions to a petrified Presidency" (Doronila 1990a, 1, 1990b, 1).

13. The interviews were conducted with 13 of the 15 incumbent Supreme Court justices. They did not seek systematically to measure activist role orientations on the Philippine Supreme Court; they were conducted for other purposes. The conclusions that follow represent my inferences as to the degree of activism that seemed to individual justices to be justified. These inferences are based on their comments about the constitutional position of the Court, its actual and desired behavior before, during, and after Marcos's authoritarianism, and their projections of its future.

14. The newspaper was the daily *Manila Bulletin*. The *Bulletin* is usually first or second in total circulation among Manila's numerous English newspapers and appears to try to be Manila's newspaper of record. At the time of my newspaper research, it was also the only Manila newspaper continuously available in the U.S. Library of Congress. I have been able to examine its contents through June, 1991.

For a different perspective, I also examined the annual reviews of Supreme Court constitutional lawmaking that have appeared in the *Philippine Law Journal* since the effective date of the new constitution. The *Philippine Law Journal*, published by the Law Center of the University of the Philippines, is the nation's leading legal journal. Unfortunately, for a number of reasons having mostly to do with the scarcity of resources available for scholarly publishing in the Philippines, the *Philippine Law Journal* was several years behind in its publication schedule. This led to the curious phenomenon of articles analyzing events that occurred in 1988-1989 appearing in journal issues dated 1987. But it also meant that it had not yet published annual reviews of constitutional law for 1990-1991.

15. For some discussion of these, see Tate (1992).

16. These first three cases were cited by the *Manila Bulletin*'s senior editorial writer as striking evidence that the High Court was reasserting its independence:

> Lately, the High Tribunal has been reasserting, through a series of landmark decisions, its independence. Bar and bench and the public all agree that in so doing it has bolstered people's confidence in it as the court of last resort for grievances. The Fernan Supreme Court may yet go down in history as a model for future Supreme Courts of this country. (Bigornia, 1990)

[Marcelo Fernan was the Court's chief justice at this time.]

17. This would not be at all inconsistent with the appointment pattern in the pre-martial-law period. Prior to 1969, the modal Supreme Court appointee was a career judge promoted most often from the most senior position on the Court of Appeals, even though the appointment process was controlled by the President and the Congress-based Commission on Appointments (see Tate, 1971).

REFERENCES

Bigornia, Jesus. 1990. "High Court Reasserts its Independence." *Manila Bulletin*, December 20, 6ff.

Cruz, Isagani A. 1987. *Philippine Political Law.* Quezon City: Central Lawbook Publishing Co.

De Leon, Hector S. 1987. *Textbook on the New Philippine Constitution.* Manila: Rex Book Store.

Di Federico, Giuseppe, and Carlo Guarnieri. 1988. "The Courts in Italy." In *The Political Role of Law Courts in Modern Democracies*, ed. Waltman and Holland, 153-80.

Doronila, Amando. 1990a. "Democracy in Mortal Danger." *Manila Chronicle*, August 28, 1ff.

———. 1990b. "Prescriptions to a Petrified Presidency." *Manila Chronicle*, August 30, 1ff.

Edelman, Martin. 1992. "Judicial Review and Israel's Struggle for a Written Constitution." In *Comparative Judicial Review and Public Policy*, ed. Jackson and Tate, 157-76.

Gouws, Amanda. 1992. "The Judicialization of Women's Issues: Implications for South African Women in the Post-Apartheid Society." Paper presented to the Interim Meeting of the Research Committee on Comparative Judicial Studies, Forlí, Italy, August.

Holland, Kenneth M., ed. 1991. *Judicial Activism in Comparative Perspective.* New York: St. Martin's.

Jackson, Donald W. and C. Neal Tate, eds. 1992. *Comparative Judicial Review and Public Policy.* Westport, Conn.: Greenwood Press.

Kitchin, William. 1992. "Establishing and Exercising Judicial Review in the Soviet Union: The Beginnings." In *Comparative Judicial Review and Public Policy*, ed. Jackson and Tate, 59-74.

McColm, Bruce. 1990. *Freedom in the World, 1989-90: Political Rights and Civil Liberties.* New York: Freedom House.

Nolledo, Jose N. 1987. *The Constitution of the Republic of the Philippines with Annotations.* Manila: Rex Book Store.

Poe, Steven C. and C. Neal Tate. 1994. "Repression of Human Rights to Personal Integrity in the 1980s: A Global Analysis." *American Political Science Review* 88:853-72.

Russell, Peter H. 1992. "The Growth of Canadian Judicial Review and the Commonwealth and American Experiences." In *Comparative Judicial Review and Public Policy*, ed. Jackson and Tate, 29-40.

Stone, Alec. 1992. "Abstract Constitutional Review and Policy-making in Western Europe." In *Comparative Judicial Review and Public Policy*, ed. Jackson and Tate, 41-58.

Sunkin, Maurice. 1992. "The Incidence and Effect of Judicial Review Procedures Against Central Government in the United Kingdom." In *Comparative Judicial Review and Public Policy*, ed. Jackson and Tate, 143-56.

Tate, C. Neal. 1971. "The Social Background, Political Recruitment and Decision-making of the Philippine Supreme Court Justices, 1901-1968." Ph.D. diss. Tulane University, New Orleans.

———. 1992. "Temerity and Timidity in the Exercise of Judicial Review in the Philippine Supreme Court." In *Comparative Judicial Review and Public Policy*, ed. Jackson and Tate, 107-28.

———, and Panu Sittiwong. 1986. "The Supreme Court and Justice in the Marcos Era." *Pilipinas: A Journal of Philippine Studies* 6:1-19.

Teehankee, Claudio. 1987. *A Year of Restoration, a Time of Renewal: 1986 Annual Report of the Supreme Court*. Manila: Supreme Court of the Philippines.

Volcansek, Mary. 1992. "Judicial Review and Public Policy in Italy: American Roots and the Italian Hybrid." In *Comparative Judicial Review and Public Policy*, ed. Jackson and Tate, 89-106.

Waltman, Jerold L. 1988. "The Courts and Political Change in Post-Industrial Society." In *The Political Role of Law Courts in Modern Democracies*, ed. Waltman and Holland 1988:216-34.

Waltman, Jerold L., and Kenneth M. Holland, eds. 1988. *The Political Role of Law Courts in Modern Democracies*. New York: Macmillan.

26.

The Judicialization of Namibian Politics

NICO STEYTLER

In introducing the global expansion of judicial power, Torbjörn Vallinder describes two variants of the phenomenon that is the focus of this book. The first variant, "judicialization from without," refers to the expansion of the courts' power at the expense of the other two branches of government. The prime example of this process is the judicial review of legislation and executive acts. This form of the expansion of judicial power entails the imposition of judicial decisions on the legislature and the administration. The second form of judicialization, termed "judicialization from within," involves the introduction or increased use of judicial staff or judicial decision-making methods in making policy decisions in the state administration.

The Namibian Constitution of 1990 is a good example of how provision is made for the judicialization of politics from without and from within. Through judicial review and the method of appointment of judges, the power of the judiciary and the legal profession has been increased at the expense of the legislature and the executive. Moreover, the ombudsman, overseeing the administration, may introduce judicial decision-making methods to the civil service.

I argue here that the judicialization of Namibian politics was one of the key devices for protecting minority interests, thereby facilitating Namibian independence under majority rule. Central to this device stands the justiciable bill of rights and the judges who will interpret it. It will be further argued that the unprecedented levels to which minority parties sought to judicialize politics may in the end undermine the potency of this device. The absolute entrenchment of judicial review and the built-in institutional distance between the courts on one hand and the legislature and the executive on the other hand, may lead to the breakdown of the constitutional order on which minority protection depends.

The judicialization of politics was among the political compromises that were made in order to effect independence, majority rule, and national reconciliation.[1] In this process the international community played a crucial role through the adoption in 1982 by the United Nations Security Council of the *Principles concerning the Constituent Assembly and the Constitution*.

1982 CONSTITUTIONAL PRINCIPLES

In 1978 the Security Council adopted Resolution 435, brokered by the five Western nations then in the Security Council (the United Kingdom, the United States, France, Canada, and West Germany—collectively known as the Contact Group). The resolution entailed a detailed plan for the achievement of independence and was accepted by South Africa. It included the holding of free elections under United Nations supervision for a constituent assembly that would draft a constitution. The resolution was not implemented initially because South Africa, backed by the United States, insisted on linking Namibian independence with the withdrawal of Cuban troops from Angola. This issue was to delay the implementation of resolution 435 for the next ten years.

In order to encourage implementation of resolution 435, the Contact Group sought to allay the fears of the internal parties (Wiechers 1991, 5). An all-party conference for preimplementation talks was organized in 1981 under the auspices of the United Nations, where the internal parties could meet SWAPO. The conference failed to produce any results because it became apparent that the South African government and the internal parties would seek independence not through the United Nations, but unilaterally.

The Contact Group sought to give assurances to the internal parties about the future because the latter sensed that the implementation of resolution 435 would reduce them to "minority" parties. Within the context of the Cold War there were also deep-seated fears about the Southwest Africa People's Organization (SWAPO), which was backed by the Soviet Union and its surrogate, Cuba. The perception was that "there [were] few in the upper echelons of SWAPO with a taste for liberal, multi-party democracy and acceptance of externally defined normative restraint on freedom of executive action" (Cleary 1988, 343).

The first attempt was the proposal by the United States to draft a complete constitution before the first election. This plan was rejected out of hand by SWAPO. The next attempt was to formulate a set of principles that would guide both the procedure of drafting a constitution and its contents. This was achieved by the *Principles concerning the Constituent Assembly and the Constitution* of 1982, contained in a letter from the Contact Group to the Security Council, and which was eventually circulated as a document of the Security Council (Wiechers 1991, 8). The *Principles* was accepted by both the South Africa government and SWAPO.

The *Principles* provided that a constituent assembly should be elected by means of free and fair elections in terms of proportional representation. Such an assembly then had to adopt a constitution by a two-thirds majority. The constitution, in turn, had to comply with a number of principles, including the following:

1. . . .

2. The Constitution will be the supreme law of the state. It may be amended only by a designated process involving the legislature and/or votes cast in a popular referendum.

3. The Constitution will determine the organization and powers of all levels of government. It will provide for a system of government with three branches: an elected executive branch which will be responsible to the legislative branch; a legislative branch to be elected by universal and equal suffrage which will be responsible for the passage of all laws; and an independent judicial branch which will be responsible for the interpretation of the Constitution and for ensuring its supremacy and the authority of the law.

4. . . .

5. There will be a declaration of fundamental rights. . . . Aggrieved individuals will be entitled to have the courts adjudicate and enforce these rights.

6. . . .

7. Provision will be made for the balanced structuring of the public service, the police service and the defence services and for equal access by all to recruitment to these services. The fair administration of personnel policy in relation to these services will be assured by appropriate independent bodies (*Principles* 1982).

The objective of the *Principles* was to place limits on majoritarian rule; the legislature and the executive would be subject to judicial review. Thus, the increase in powers of the courts at the expense of the legislature and the executive became "part and parcel of the overall peace plan" (Wiechers 1991, 8). For this very reason the *Principles* has been criticized. Richardson comments that the *Principles* was "more a balancing of outside interests than an expression of the constitutive expectations of the people in the territory" (Richardson 1984, 108).

The *Principles* received the support of SWAPO not only because of international pressure, but because its provisions were not inimical to SWAPO's stated policies and views on minorities. Already in 1975 the position was adopted in a discussion paper that a Namibian constitution should include "a detailed and effective Bill of Rights." The enforcement of a bill of rights by a constitutional court was justified, inter alia, as "the single most effective line of defence for any minority" (Cleary 1988, 294). This position was reiterated by the United Nations Institute for Namibia (UNIN), then under the direction of Hage Geingob, who became Namibia's first prime minister in the SWAPO government. In a publication on constitutional options, it was noted that the inclusion of a bill of rights was necessary, inter alia, "to safeguard the interests and aspirations of minority groups"(UNIN 1979, 50).

In the meantime the internal political parties were also embracing the idea of judicial review. A multi-party conference issued in 1984 the Windhoek Declaration of Basic Principles and the Bill of Fundamental Rights and Objectives. The internal parties formed in 1985 a Transitional Government of National Unity and by proclamation the

South African government instituted a bill of rights of limited justiciability for the territory.

Eventually in 1988, through trilateral agreements among South Africa, Angola, and Cuba, the withdrawal of Cuban troops from Angola and South African troops from Namibia was brokered, paving the way for the holding of an election for a constituent assembly in November 1989. In that election SWAPO gained 58 percent of the popular vote, while the second-largest party, the Democratic Turnhalle Alliance (DTA), received 28 percent. The Constituent Assembly convened in late November 1989. At its first meeting the assembly adopted unanimously the *Principles concerning the Constituent Assembly and the Constitution* as the basis for a new constitution. Eighty days later, in February 1990, the Constitution was accepted, also unanimously. Finally, on March 21, 1990 Namibia celebrated its independence with Sam Numjoma, the SWAPO leader, as its first executive president.

Most commentators have noted how remarkable it was that the Constituent Assembly could have agreed upon a lengthy constitution within the short period of eighty days that included the festive days of Christmas, Boxing Day and New Year's Day. It was the result, one commentator concluded, of "a remarkable readiness to negotiate and to compromise on the part of the parties who had been at daggers drawn for many years" (Carpenter 1991, 64). The key issues on which negotiations and compromise took place were, reportedly, that SWAPO got an executive president in return for two major concessions: a second house in the legislature composed of regional representatives, and elections by proportional representation (*Argus*, January 26, 1990). What was not mentioned in the media but is apparent from the reading of the Constitution, is that the judicialization of politics played an equally important role in the negotiations. This was, however, inevitable because in the 1982 *Principles* the judicialization of politics was made integral to the implementation of resolution 435 and Namibian independence.

1990 CONSTITUTION

The results of the 1989 elections to the Constituent Assembly confirmed the minority status of the internal parties. They commanded enough support, nevertheless, to veto SWAPO proposals and seek guarantees about the future. In terms of ideology the two sides were diametrically opposed.   SWAPO had a socialist orientation geared toward the redistribution of wealth to an impoverished black peasantry and working class.   The minority parties represented, on the other hand, a number of interest groups, from the propertied white elite to a range of black political and ethnic groupings, many of whom were the functionaries and beneficiaries of the old regime.

The minority parties had little faith in the politics of majoritarian rule. Their objective was to seek guarantees for the protection of their vital interests in the economy, multiparty politics, and the civil service.   The political system could not provide them with guarantees.   A share in the power through a minority veto in the legislature was not a viable option, as it would have contradicted the very basis of representative politics. Moreover, it would have smacked of ethnic and race politics.   The only other option was to seek judicial protection of their interests, provided, of course, that the judiciary shared their basic concerns and interests.

This was the solution the *Principles* of 1982 had offered.   At the Constituent Assembly all the minority parties aligned themselves closely to the *Principles* and pleaded that they should form the basis for negotiations.   SWAPO had little difficulty with this proposal, as it had been a party to the *Principles* when it was first formulated (*Argus*, November 22, 1989).   Negotiations could thus commence when the SWAPO secretary of foreign affairs proposed on the first day of the assembly that it should adopt the provisions of the *Principles* as guidelines (*Die Burger*, November 22, 1989).   The *Principles* thus presented to the assembly a useful common framework within which minority concerns could be addressed and the process of national reconciliation could take place.

The *Principles* contained only the rudimentary elements of limited government.   When flesh was added to the bones, a very limited government was the result; the Constitution empowered the judiciary at the expense of the legislature and the executive to unprecedented levels. If one compares the SWAPO draft constitution,[2] which was used by the Constituent Assembly as a working draft, to the adopted Constitution, a dramatic shift of power becomes apparent.   Three features stand out: first, judicial review in terms of a justiciable bill of rights was absolutely entrenched; second, judicial appointments were insulated from legislative and executive influence and control; and third, quasi-judicial supervision of the civil service was instituted through the establishment of the office of the ombudsman.

Judicial Review

Judicial review in terms of a justiciable bill of rights is a regular if not an essential feature of constitutions in new democracies. In view of the *Principles concerning the Constituent Assembly and the Constitution* of 1982 and the previous pronouncements of the parties, such a bill of rights was bound to be included in the Constitution. Where this Bill of Rights differs from comparable bills of rights is in the extent to which it was entrenched. The Namibian Bill of Rights includes the classical political and civil rights of a liberal democracy. In this respect there is a great deal of correspondence between the rights protected in the Bill of Rights and the SWAPO draft. Both incorporated the right to property (SWAPO draft, art. 45; Namibian Bill, art. 16). Socioeconomic rights, which would have given the state a definite social democratic orientation (le Roux 1991, 120), were limited in the Bill of Rights to the bare minimum. The SWAPO draft included the right to "equitable and satisfactory" working conditions (art. 23), social welfare rights "including, but not limited to housing, in accordance with the law" (art. 24) and the right to primary education (art. 25). The Namibian Bill of Rights included only the right to primary education (art. 20[2]), while the other socioeconomic rights were relegated to the nonenforceable principles of state policy contained in Chapter 11 of the Constitution. Significantly, rights relating to working conditions, which were listed first in the SWAPO draft and which would have affected the white-controlled private sector the most, were omitted.

Although no enforceable duties were placed on the state, administrative decision making was brought firmly under judicial supervision. The Bill of Rights provides that administrative bodies "shall act fairly and reasonably" (art. 18). The requirement of reasonableness, not mentioned in the SWAPO draft (art. 44), implies that a court may investigate the merits of the decision, not merely whether the administrative body has complied with all the procedural requirements, as is presently the position in South African law (Baxter 1991, 295).

The language and form in which the rights in the Bill of Rights are expressed are also much more precise and detailed than in the SWAPO draft. It seems as though the drafters sought to limit the uncertainty attendant on any bill of rights couched in broad strokes. They sought to achieve legal certainty by making the text less open-ended. Innovative (and also unpredictable) judicial interpretation was thus given a short leash.

The most striking feature of the Bill of Rights, when compared to the SWAPO proposal and other comparable bills of rights, is the level to which the minority parties succeeded in safeguarding it from legislative and executive encroachments. The SWAPO draft provided that for amendments to the Constitution, including the fundamental rights, a two-thirds majority in the National Assembly should be required (art. 133[1]). In contrast the Namibian Bill of Rights is entrenched absolutely. While the Constitution may be changed by a two-thirds majority, the chapter containing the fundamental rights and freedoms can never be changed (art. 131). The provisions relating to the required majority for amending the Constitution are likewise immune from amendment (art. 132[4]).

The legislature's power of placing limitations on rights (and thereby hollowing out rights) is also carefully circumscribed. First, there is no general limitation clause, and any limitation of a right should specifically be contained in that provision. For example, Article 21, which lists a wide range of the fundamental freedoms in subsection 1, permits in subsection 2 reasonable restrictions "which are necessary in a democratic society and are required in the interests of the sovereignty and integrity of Namibia, national security, public order, decency or morality, or in relation to contempt of court, defamation or incitement to an offence." The provisions that are not subject to limitations include the right to dignity, the right to equality and freedom from discrimination, certain procedural rights such as the prohibition against the creation of offenses with retrospective effect, and rights pertaining to administrative justice.

Second, the constitutional language curtails the impact of permissible limitations on rights. Article 22 requires that any law providing for a limitation "shall (a) be of general application, shall not negate the essential content thereof, and shall not be aimed at a particular individual; [and] (b) specify the ascertainable extent of such limitation and identify the Article or Articles hereof on which authority to enact such limitation is claimed to rest." A court is thus empowered to strike down legislation on the substantive test contained in paragraph a, as well as on the formal grounds of paragraph b where legislation does not explicitly refer to the enabling article in the constitution.

The binding force of the Bill of Rights on the executive is nearly complete. Even when a "a state of national defence or emergency" is declared by the president (the continuation of which can be vetoed by a third of the members of the National Assembly (art. 26[2]), the majority of the rights enshrined in the Bill of Rights cannot be derogated from. The only rights from which there may be derogation are: liberty, privacy, property, political activity, education, assembly, strike, and movement (art. 24[3]). The rights to equality, life, dignity, fair trial, family life, children's rights, administrative justice, culture, speech, thought, religion, and association remain absolutely protected. Moreover, the right of access to a lawyer and the courts, to protect these rights, may not be infringed (art. 24[3]; Erasmus 1990, 299).

Even where the executive acts in terms of a state of national defense or emergency, the judiciary may still hold sway. Any steps that the president may take in terms of the state of emergency are judicially reviewable (art. 26[5]; Erasmus 1990, 300). Detention without trial is carefully regulated in the Bill of Rights itself. Every detention must be reviewed within a month of arrest by a special Advisory Board (dominated by members of the judiciary), which has the power to order the release of the detainee (Erasmus 1990, 300). Thus, the supremacy of the Bill of Rights and, consequently, the judiciary, is secured even in times of political instability.

Judicial review of legislation places courts squarely within the legislative process and hence the political arena. Alec Stone has thus conceptualized constitutional courts as "specialized third legislative chambers" (Stone 1990). They are "legislative" in the sense that they, like legislatures, determine policy issues generally and prospectively. They are "specialized" because their legislative powers are restricted to the scope of a bill of rights. They are the "third" chambers after the lower and upper houses of legislative bodies. The "legislative powers" of such a court are the most unambiguous when the question of the constitutionality of legislation can be raised by way of abstract review. The effects of concrete review of legislation are, however, not necessarily less legislative (Stone 1990).

The "legislative powers" of constitutional courts, Stone argues (in chapter 12 of this volume), enable opposition parties to judicialize policy issues "in order to win what they would otherwise lose in 'normal' political processes." Tate (in chapter 3) describes this process as follows: "If the opposition can redefine a 'legislative' dispute as one that involves a 'right,' it can shift from a forum in which the majority's right to rule is accepted, into one in which minorities are acknowledged to have rights that can be asserted against majorities by nonmajoritarian institutions like courts." Opposition politicians can resort to this process most readily where the constitutionality of legislation can be tested by way of abstract review. Concrete review may achieve the same result, but the process may be more cumbersome.

Can the Namibian superior courts' power of judicial review can it be described as a "specialized third legislative chamber," after the National Assembly and the National Council? Can it be used to win legislative battles that minority parties have lost in the other two chambers? The Constitution makes provision for abstract review only at the initiative of the attorney-general[3] and the president (art. 64[2], 87[c]). Nevertheless, opposition parties may translate political battles in the legislature into courtroom dramas. Gerhard Erasmus, a lawyer who participated in the drafting of the Constitution, maintains that the *locus standi* requirement in Article 25(2) is flexible enough to allow parliamentarians as individuals to approach the court on constitutional matters (Erasmus 1990, 308).

Through an extensive, predictable, and immutable Bill of Rights, judicial review has been deeply entrenched and has created the legal framework for a powerful judiciary. However, critical to any faith minority parties may have in the Bill of Rights would be the trust that the judiciary as the "specialized third legislative chamber" shared their values and concerns. The minority parties thus sought to insulate as far as possible the judiciary from the influence of the majority-dominated executive and legislature.

Judicial Independence

Judicial independence is strenuously asserted in the Constitution (Erasmus 1990, 307). Article 78 states, first, that "The courts shall be independent and subject only to this Constitution and the law" (art. 78[2]). Second, "No member of the Cabinet or the Legislature or any other person shall interfere with Judges . . . in the exercise of their judicial functions" (art. 78[3]). Third, "all organs of the State shall accord such assistance as the courts may require to protect their independence, dignity and effectiveness" (art. 78[3]).

The significance of Article 78 lies more in the rhetoric than in its legal enforceability. The first provision, Gretchen Carpenter (1991, 54) argues, is no more than a manifesto, as independence is a quality attributed to a court rather than something that can be achieved by legal fiat. The second provision is already contained in the common-law offence of contempt of court, but is now elevated to a constitutional principle. Although Judge Brian O'Linn opined in *S v. Heita* (1992 [3] SA 785 [NmHC]) that the third provision places "a positive legal duty on all organs of State" to assist the courts (790B), it is difficult to imagine what possible remedies there may be for a breach of this "duty" other than the present contempt-of-court sanction, which is, in any event, dependent on executive assistance. The value of these provisions thus lies in the symbolic bolstering of the faith of the minority parties in the power of the courts vis-a-vis the legislature and the executive.

Of far greater importance than the ringing phrases about judicial independence is the institutional insulation of the judiciary from the executive and the legislature. The aim of the minority parties was to ensure that the judges would not be the handmaidens of the government, but the guardian angels of their interests. Of vital importance, thus, was the appointment and dismissal procedures for judges.

SWAPO had no difficulty with the concept of judicial independence, but already in 1979 caution was expressed that independence should "neither be construed as isolation from society nor license to behave anyhow" (UNIN 1979, 44). It was therefore thought inappropriate that the chief justice be appointed by anyone other than the head of state—certainly not by a judicial service commission. Such a commission would play a modest role; the head of state could consult with or seek its advice on the appointment of Supreme Court judges (UNIN 1979, 44).

The SWAPO draft reiterated this position and proposed that the chief justice and the judges of the Supreme Court should be appointed by the president (SWAPO proposal, article 85[d][ii]). This also happened to be the law and practice in South West Africa/Namibia. The draft also provided for a Judicial Service Commission (JSC), but with limited powers. It would advise the president on the appointment of judicial officers in the lower courts (art. 123), but with the removal of judges it would have the sole power to make a binding recommendation to the president (art. 124). The composition of the JSC, however, would be firmly under the control of the executive. The JSC would consist of the chief justice, the attorney-general and the chairperson of the Public Service Commission (art. 125), all of whom the president would appoint to their respective positions (art. 85[d]). SWAPO thus envisaged a limited role for the JSC, whose composition would be controlled by the executive.

The Namibian Constitution reflects a different perception of judicial independence. The appointment and dismissal of the judiciary is almost completely taken out of the hands of the legislature and the executive and entrusted to the Judicial Service Commission (JSC). The commission, unlike the one proposed in the SWAPO draft, falls not under the control of the executive, but under the various branches of the legal profession. The president appoints the chief justice, the judges of the Supreme Court and of the High Court, and the judge-president of the High Court on the recommendation of the JSC (art. 32[4][a][aa]). Likewise, a judge may be removed from office only by the president on the recommendation of the JSC (art. 84). The recommendation of the JSC to the president implies that the latter's decision to appoint or dismiss is a mere formality (Carpenter 1991, 46), a procedure that is unprecedented in the constitutions of English-speaking Africa (Corder 1992). The composition of the JSC is therefore of vital importance. Here again the legislature plays no role and the executive only a limited one.

The JSC consists of the chief justice, a judge appointed by the president, the attorney-general and two persons nominated by the professional organizations of the legal profession (art. 85[1]). The only person who is directly appointed by the president is thus the attorney-general (art. 32[3][i][cc]). Even the judge whom the president may appoint comes from the pool of judges appointed by the JSC itself. The effect of the composition of the JSC is that the power of appointing the judiciary is firmly in the hands of the judiciary and the organized legal profession. The entrenchment of this power within the old legal elite was facilitated by the transitional arrangements contained in the Constitution. All judges serving under the old regime before independence retained their positions (art. 141[1]). On independence, the JSC was to consist of four persons: two judges appointed by the president selected from the judges in office (one judge would serve until a chief justice was appointed), the attorney-general, and two members of the legal profession nominated by the Bar Council of Namibia and the Council of the Law Society of South West Africa, respectively (art. 139[1]). The first task of the commission so constituted was to recommend the appointment of a chief justice (art. 139[1]). This meant that from the five judges, all white (Berker, the judge-president under the old regime, Strydom, Levy, Hendler and O'Linn), President Numjoma had to select two judges. With the vast majority of legal practitioners being white, it was inevitable that two Whites were nominated by the Bar Council and the Law Society, the latter still operating under the "South West African" banner. The commission consisted then of Judges Berker and Strydom, advocate Frank of the Bar Council, Dicks of the Law Society, and Ruppel, the attorney-general (Du Pisani 1991). The JSC then recommended that Berker become chief justice and Strydom, the second most senior judge, the judge-president of the High Court.

The Constitution thus firmly ensconced the legal profession in a powerful position to exercise considerable control over the higher courts. The result is that a small, unrepresentative elite, dominated by Whites who have traditionally had little sympathy with SWAPO, will be able to wield a considerable amount of power. Moreover, their professional interests link them further to this propertied elite; the legal profession—its form, objectives and sources of income—is predicated on the continuance of the status quo. In the "specialized third legislative chamber" the minority parties have thus achieved a limited but effective veto over the legislature and the executive through an "independent" judiciary interpreting a rigidly entrenched bill of rights.

The Ombudsman

The establishment of the office of ombudsman is arguably an example of the second form of judicialization of politics—judicialization from within. The appointment of a lawyer as an ombudsman may introduce judicial decision-making methods into matters falling within the domain of the administration or executive. For the outgoing elite and the new minority in Namibia it may have been another way of seeking assurances about the maintenance of a fair and efficient civil service.

The SWAPO draft made provision for the office of an ombudsman (art. 78). Its functions would be to investigate instances of violation of laws or of human rights, discrimination, or unfair, harsh, or rude treatment of a citizen by an official; to advise the attorney-general on the constitutionality of preindependence legislation, and to investigate corruption among officials (art. 80). The president would appoint the ombudsman (art. 79 read with art. 85[d][ii]), and no requirement was set that the incumbent should have a legal background.

The ombudsman of the Constitution (see Hatchard 1991) differs in significant respects from the SWAPO draft. As in the SWAPO draft, the ombudsman may investigate complaints pertaining to the violations of fundamental rights and freedoms by any official or to any act of maladministration. The powers of the ombudsman go much further, however, and he or she is expected to deal with three very contentious policy areas, which, from a comparative perspective, are unprecedented (see generally Frank 1975; Rudolph 1983; Hatchard 1986; van Zyl 1989).

First, the ombudsman has the power to investigate complaints about the functioning of the Public Service Commission, the defense force, the police force, and the prison service "in so far as such complaints relate to the failure to achieve a balanced structuring of such services or equal access by all to the recruitment of such services or fair administration in relation to such services" (art. 93[b]).

The restructuring of the armed services was a high priority after years of war, and their "balanced structuring . . . and equal access by all to recruitment" were thus included in the *Principles* of 1982 (para. 7). The *Principles* contained, however, the important rider that "the fair administration of personnel policy" would be assured by "appropriate independent bodies" (para. 7). Striking a balance in the application of an affirmative action policy implies weighing the interests of two competing groups: the loss of jobs for members of the old regime and promoting the black majority, who were excluded from educational and work opportunities by that regime.

Second, the ombudsman may investigate "the over-utilization of living natural resources, the irrational exploitation of nonrenewable resources, the degradation and destruction of ecosystems and failure to protect the beauty and character of Namibia" (art. 93[c]). All these issues involve policy questions and value judgments. When are natural resources "over-utilized?" When is the exploitation of nonrenewable resources "irrational," and so forth? Many of these issues will be raised in respect of private sector mining, industry, and commerce, which form the core of the propertied elite's interests.

Finally, the ombudsman may investigate practices and actions by persons, enterprises, and other private institutions accused of violating the fundamental rights and freedoms (art. 93[d]). This power is unique because without exception the office of the ombudsman has traditionally been concerned with maladministration by *state* officials. Private-sector mining, industry, commerce, farming, and social clubs will certainly constitute the bulk of the "enterprises" and "private institutions." Again, the propertied elite would be a likely target of investigation.

The wide scope of the ombudsman's powers in both the public and the private domain, from the armed forces to ecology, makes the office a powerful one indeed. Again, as with the appointment of judges, neither the executive nor the legislature has the dominant say in this matter. The lawyers, through their mouthpiece the JSC, makes a binding recommendation to the president of who should be appointed to this important post (art. 90[1]). Moreover, their choice is limited to one of their own ilk, for the incumbent has to be a judge or a lawyer (art. 89[4]).

The comments expressed above on the "independence" of the JSC in the appointment of judges are also applicable to the appointment of the ombudsman. The JSC may be swayed by class interests in appointing a person who may not pitch the "balanced structure" of employment in the civil service and the armed services, contrary to the perceived interests of their socioeconomic class. The incumbent's decisions, dealing with difficult and controversial policy issues, may likewise not be inimical to minority interests.

JUDICIALIZING POLITICS

The adoption of a constitution that allocates considerable power to the judiciary at the expense of the legislature and the executive does not by itself constitute the judicialization of politics. Tate observes that this phenomenon implies "a *process* that substitutes the policy judgment of usually unelected representatives of the socioeconomic and political elite for that of majoritarian political institutions." Judicialization develops, he argues, "only because judges decide that they *should* (1) participate in policy-making that could be left to the wise or foolish discretion of other institutions, and at least on occasion, (2) substitute policy solutions they derive for those derived by other institutions."

This is, however, only half of the story. A further step is required—the other two branches of government must accept the substitution of the courts' policies for theirs and the consequent diminution of their power. Brunello and Lehrman (1991, 268) thus observe that the degree of influence courts may have on policy is dependent on the reaction of those actors in the political process entrusted with the execution of court decisions. They conclude that effect will be given to decisions "so long as there is sufficiently broad consensus on political norms" and the judicial review deals with relatively minor issues (at 295).

The question, then, is whether the *process* of the judicialization of Namibian politics will take place, as was intended by the minority parties. It is suggested that the unbridled use by the judiciary of its far-reaching powers of judicial review may lead to a confrontation with the government in which the Constitution may be the main casualty. The elaborate and watertight structure to secure the expansion of judicial power may paradoxically, then, be a contributing factor in subverting the process from taking root.

SWAPO's history is rooted in the ideology of the right to self-determination and being "the sole and authentic voice of the people." It came to the Constituent Assembly as the victor of an election with 58 percent of the popular vote and the ringing claim in its draft constitution: "All power in Namibia belongs to the people who shall control the activities of State organs" (art. 1[2]). Moreover, "the National Assembly shall be the supreme organ of State power" (art. 58). SWAPO left the Constituent Assembly as the new government, but with the powers of the legislature and the executive dramatically circumscribed. On the other hand, "White inhabitants of the country," Erasmus notes, "can be greatly satisfied with these provisions of the constitution regarding matters such as the protection of human rights, culture and private property" (1990, 309—[translation by the author]). Considerable power was placed in the hands of a small, unaccountable, and unrepresentative legal elite that historically, economically, and socially is more aligned to the minority groups, and over which the other two branches of government have little control. This was the price SWAPO was willing to pay for the expeditious achievement of independence, national reconciliation, and power.

Compromising on majoritarian rule in order to establish a political settlement is not a new phenomenon; the politics of political pacts are evidence of this (Anderson 1991; Hagopian 1990). Such pacts by design subvert notions of majority rule (Hagopian 1990, 151.). For the sake of stability which a pact produces, greater democratization is abandoned (Karl 1986). The *Principles concerning the Constituent Assembly and the Constitution* of 1982 was the first pact between elites in the international arena and local politicians. That pact, in turn, determined the process by which the Namibian Constitution was drafted and the compromises that consequently were made. The Constitution was the second pact; it provided "a degree of stability and predictability that is reassuring to the threatened traditional elites" (Karl 1990, 38). Unlike pacts that are aimed at a transitional period (but may gain permanency) (Karl 1990, 161), the Namibian Constitution was designed to bind the future. The pact may, however, carry the seeds of its own destruction, should the courts be seen to be "a specialized third legislative chamber" in which minority interests routinely veto majoritarian rule. This prospect is facilitated by the legal framework of judicial review; a rigid Bill of Rights enforced by a judiciary insulated from the legislature and the executive.

The rigidity of the Constitution pertaining to fundamental rights constitutes, ironically, the weakest link of their protection. It is a truism that an inflexible constitution breaks the most easily. A Supreme Court decision invalidating a statute closes the book on the issue, as no amendment of fundamental rights is permissible. There are numerous examples in Africa where a rigid constitution, instead of securing compliance, prompted its revolutionary overthrow (Carpenter 1991, 59; Reyntjens 1992, 41). In Namibia, where one of the purposes of judicial review is minority protection, the conflict is unlikely to be over minor issues (see Brunello and Lehrman), but will involve challenges to majority rule. It is then a question of how able and willing the executive or the legislature will be to finesse an adverse judicial decision by nonrevolutionary means.

The method of appointment of the Namibian judiciary may further exacerbate the conflict between it and the executive/legislature. A judicial decision is more likely to be accepted and executed if the executive and legislature have trust in the judiciary. This trust is engendered where the legislature and/or the executive have a say in who shall exercise the power of judicial review (Simba 1987, 10; Steytler 1992). Should the legal profession (in the JSC) pursue through their appointments the narrow interests of the propertied elite to whom it is closely aligned, and a judiciary so appointed returns decisions inimical to the majority, then the prospect of the revolutionary demise of judicial review is indeed great.

In Namibia an open and direct conflict between the judiciary and the executive or legislature has not yet occurred, but in September 1991 strains on their relationship surfaced for the first time. The events surrounding the Kleynhans treason trial, although not dealing with judicial review, illustrate dramatically some key issues pertaining to the judicialization of politics in a new democracy.

"CONTEMPT OF COURT EN MASSE"

Brian O'Linn was appointed to the South West African bench shortly before independence with a reputation as an implacable opponent of apartheid. There were even calls for his dismissal on the ground of his alleged sympathy with SWAPO (see *S v. Heita* 1992 (3) SA 785 (NmHC) 786G). In 1991 he presided over the trial of nine white right-wingers accused of treason. The prosecution was conducted by prosecutor-general Heyman, a prosecutor from the old regime who had remained in office after independence. The trial ran for several months and received intense publicity in the press because of a number of controversial decisions (Ruppel 1992). Five ringleaders skipped the country when bail was granted on what was thought to be too-lenient terms. The bail of the remaining accused was not withdrawn at the close of the state case, and another accused absconded. The remaining three accused, who were not the ringleaders of the conspiracy to overthrow the Namibian government, were found guilty of participating in or failing to report the theft of a large quantity of arms and ammunition from a police depot and planning the shooting and abduction of cabinet ministers. Very lenient sentences were passed down. The first accused received an effective four-years' prison sentence, the second a prison sentence of two years, and the third a wholly suspended prison sentence and a fine of R500 on the theft charge (*Windhoek Advertiser*, September 21, 1991).

The first reaction came from Windhoek's Central Prison when prisoners, on hearing the news over the radio, rioted and commenced a week-long demonstration because they claimed that they had received heavier sentences for lesser crimes (*Namibian*, September 23, 1991). Newspaper reports followed that criticized the judgment bitterly and demanded the sacking of Judge O'Linn (*Windhoek Advertiser*, September 25, 1991). Epithets such as "apartheid judge," "racist judge," and "colonial judge" were bandied about. There were calls for his dismissal, resignation, and even arrest (*Windhoek Advertiser*, October 23, 1991). The deputy minister of education and culture, Buddy Wentworth, probably expressed popular sentiment accurately when he said the decision confirmed many Blacks' perception "of the white dispenser of justice [acting] in favor of a white perpetrator of violence upon a black man and therefore . . . an attempt to retain the old status quo" (*Windhoek Advertiser*, November 11, 1991).

The seriousness of the matter was immediately sensed by the legal profession and those whose fate was dependent on the survival of the judiciary. An anonymous jurist reflected their fears as follows, "If the political assault against the judicial pillar of the Constitution is allowed to go unanswered Namibia's Constitution as a whole 'might as well be torn up'" (*Windhoek Advertiser*, September 30, 1991). Chief Justice Berker threatened contempt charges (*Namibian*, September 25, 1991). Judge-President Strydom thought that the root of the problem lay in a misunderstanding caused by poor newspaper reporting. He sought ways to make information more accessible to the newspapers. Not only will fully typed judgments be made available to the press, but if deemed necessary in a particular case, the trial judge will provide an explanatory note to the media (*Windhoek Advertiser*, September 28, 1991). Judge O'Linn issued such a detailed "explanatory note" in the form of a postsentence memorandum giving reasons for the sentences he had imposed (*Namibian*, September 25, 1991).

The Law Society condemned the "inflammatory statements" by influential people and organizations (*Namibian*, September 30, 1991). The Society of Advocates asked that the attorney-general and the prosecutor-general take action against those who were clearly in contempt of court (*Windhoek Advertiser*, September 25, 1991). In the National Assembly the opposition parties rallied to the defense of the judge and the independence of the judiciary (*Windhoek Advertiser*, October 12, 1991). The Prosecutor-General also came out in defense of the sentences (see his full statement in *S v. Heita* 1992 (3) SA 785 (NmHC) 786G, 794).

The SWAPO government's response to the crisis was ambivalent. On the one hand, the minister of justice, Dr. Tjiriange, issued a statement affirming the government's commitment to the Constitution and the independence of the judiciary (*S v. Heita* 1992, 793D-784A). On the other hand there was a well-orchestrated campaign by SWAPO officials against the judiciary. Moses Garoëb, SWAPO's chief coordinator, held a news conference after Dr. Tjiriange's statement where, in the opinion of Judge O'Linn, he was again "insulted and scandalized" (*S v. Heita* 1992, 794B). Garoëb said that "in the past the Namibian judiciary system was an exclusive mutual admiration and private club of the white minority." The office of the prosecutor-general also come under attack:

it "was the dispenser of selective justice using its legal authority to the detriment of the majority of black Namibians." Moreover, he asked rhetorically, "How many black Namibian patriots found their way to the gallows in the Namibian High Court of colonial times, represented at that time by the Prosecutor-General for just being in possession of a revolver?" (*Namibian*, October 18, 1991, as quoted in *S v. Heita* 1992, 795G-I; see also *Windhoek Advertiser*, October 23, 1991). Garoëb proceeded to organize a protest march, and three thousand SWAPO supporters demonstrated in Windhoek and committed what was described as "contempt of court en masse" (*Windhoek Advertiser*, September 30, 1991). In the crowd were printed banners demanding "Judge O'Linn and Prosecutor-General must go." Another slogan proclaimed "White Supremacist Tendencies," while the crowd chanted "Down with O'Linn, Down with Heyman." They handed a petition signed by 7,000 persons to Prime Minister Geingob, calling for O'Linn's dismissal and arrest and a retrial of the three accused as well as the sacking of all the other judges who were "biased and disloyal" (*S v. Heita* 1992, 794C). A similar march took place in Swakopmund, and pamphlets were distributed in Keetmanshoop (*Windhoek Advertiser*, September 30, 1991).

The deputy minister of education and culture summed up SWAPO's ambivalent attitude as follows: "We shall jealously protect the independence of the judiciary but equally jealously insist upon our newly-gained rights [of free speech]" (*Windhoek Advertiser*, November 11, 1991). The defense of the right of free speech was an obviously convenient cover for their sympathy for the public's sentiments. Judge O'Linn described this attitude "as an open invitation to the disgruntled and uninformed members of the public to do their damnedest, without fear of interference or action from the organs of government" (*S v. Heita* 1992, 790D-E). Indeed, this was the attitude of attorney-general Ruppel. In the National Assembly he defended the public's freedom of speech: "As long as the proceedings in court are not interfered with or threatened and as long as the judgments are respected by the organs of State, criticism, even outspoken and sometimes possibly misplaced and based on wrong perceptions, should not be criminalized lightly" (Ruppel 1992, 60). The "robust and accommodating approach to criticism" which Ruppel called for (1992, 60), has meant that no prosecution for contempt of court against any person has been instituted.

The SWAPO government's ambivalent attitude toward the judiciary made it painfully clear to the judges that they were indeed the weakest branch of government. Judge O'Linn expressed this reality as follows: "The judiciary has no own defence force or police force. They are not politicians. They cannot descend into the arena to defend themselves" (*S v. Heita* 1992, 791C).

Although they may initiate contempt-of-court proceedings, or even institute defamation actions, he concluded that on the whole they are dependent on the support of the other organs of government for "the protection of their independence, dignity and effectiveness and for the maintenance of the independence of the judiciary as a pillar of the Namibian Constitution, without which itself cannot survive" (791E). This required, Judge O'Linn opined, that "article 78 the Constitution is not merely regarded as part of a paper Constitution used as a public relations document at special occasions, but is enshrined in the hearts and minds of the Namibian people and respected and enforced by all concerned" (787C).

If their vulnerability became so apparent on a matter of sentencing, which shook the public's confidence in their impartiality, then judicial review of legislation and executive acts promoting majoritarian interests will set the judiciary on a collision course with the new government. For judicial review and the judiciary to survive, they will have to become "politicians," despite O'Linn's protestations to the contrary; the process of judicializing politics inevitably entails the politicization of the judiciary.

POLITICIZING THE JUDICIARY

When Canada adopted the Charter of Rights and Freedoms in 1982, Peter Russell wrote that the main effect of it would be "a tendency to judicialize politics and politicize the judiciary" (Russell 1983, 51-52). Ten years later he notes in this book (chapter 9) that the Canadian judiciary has constrained its growth of power. He argues that most members of the Canadian Supreme Court have exercised constraint for political reasons, namely, they did not desire "to push their power of judicial review so far as to antagonize leaders in other branches of government or the mainstream of public opinion." The judiciary, aware of its position as the weakest branch of government, is compelled to indulge in politics—the art of the possible. The judges are conscious of the political character of constitutional interpretation (Goldford 1990,

255), the power they may wield through judicial review, and their reliance on the executive for the execution of their decisions.

In Namibia the judiciary was earmarked to play a political role in protecting, inter alia, minority interests through judicial review. However, the judicialization of Namibian politics may require a more nuanced political role. The judiciary, in protecting minority interests, cannot antagonize majoritarian interests unduly without undermining their own position; the judicialization of politics requires political accommodation, no matter what the letter or spirit of the Constitution may be. This is the dilemma that the Judicial Service Commission and the Namibian judges face.

Immediately after independence the JSC sought to reduce the lily-white complexion of the bench. The first appointment was Ismael Mohammed, the renowned civil rights lawyer from South Africa, as acting judge. By the end of 1990 Mohammed and Enoch Dumbetshena, the retired chief justice of Zimbabwe with strong liberal views, were appointed to the Supreme Court. By September 1992 the first black Namibian, Pio Teek (previously the ombudsman), was appointed as judge of the High Court.

At the same time the judges of the Supreme Court have not hesitated to enter the political arena and defend their constitutional position of power. A month after the Kleynhans treason trial Judge O'Linn presided in *S v. Heita* over a trial of two ex-SWAPO guerrillas charged with murdering a white police sergeant. Without being requested to do so, he considered recusing himself because the political turmoil surrounding the Kleynhans trial created the following dilemma for him:

> Should I acquit the accused, or give them a so-called 'light' sentence, a section of the population will believe that I have been intimidated. Should I convict and impose stiff sentences, the onslaught on myself and the judiciary may be repeated, which will be fatal to the prospects of maintaining the rule of law, as enshrined in the constitution, with disastrous consequences to our fledgling constitutional democracy and to the country as a whole. (*S v. Heita* 1992, 786J-787B)

By raising the issue of recusal *mero motu*, he was able to set out the whole saga of the Kleynhans trial, the aftermath, and his response thereto. As Joel Mervis correctly observes, the judge "seems to have acted purposefully in entering the political arena." The recusal device was used effectively by him to launch from the bench "an all out political attack on political partisans" (*Sunday Times*, December 20, 1992).

In the first case in which the constitutionality of legislation of the new Namibian legislature was at issue, the High Court boldly asserted its powers of judicial review. The State Repudiation (Cultura 2000) Act sought to repudiate a donation of R8 million and the sale of a farm by the previous regime to an association called Cultura 2000, which the government alleged was a white racist organization. A year before independence the Representative Authority for Whites donated R4 million to Cultura 2000 to promote the cultures of "the Afrikaner, German, English and Portuguese or other communities of European descent." A loan of R4 million was also made, but two weeks before independence, it was converted into a donation. By relying on the provisions of the Constitution pertaining to the repudiation of acts by the previous regime (art. 140), the government seems to have sought to circumvent the right to property and the expropriation requirement of "just compensation" (art. 16[2]).

The High Court (*Cultura 2000* 1992) held that the Constitution allowed the repudiation of acts of the previous regime only if such acts would have saddled the new government with duties or obligations. The court argued that if the Constitution was "not interpreted to apply only to obligations, the Namibian government could by statute (such as the Repudiation Act), "repudiate sales, donations, legal settlements and any other obligation already performed by the previous government without paying any compensation despite the fact that it was performed very many years prior to independence" (34). A different interpretation would have rendered the property clause ineffective. In this case the court had little difficulty in finding that the donation and sale were completed before independence, although under very suspect circumstances, and that there remained no duties or obligations for the government to discharge. The Repudiation Act was thus *ultra vires* the Constitution and invalid.

In the *Cultura 2000* decision the court established an important precedent that would secure property relations as they existed at independence. Although the decision is of vital importance for protecting vested interests and preserving the old status quo, it did not involve the rejection of a major policy of the new government. To what lengths the courts will be willing and able to go in thwarting the legislative and executive will on major policy issues before sparking off a constitutional crisis remains as yet unknown. It will depend largely on the political wisdom of both the courts and the government.

CONCLUSION

The expansion of judicial power was one of the key ingredient in the pacts that facilitated Namibian independence under majoritarian rule. The judicialization of politics entails, however, more than a constitutional structure; it is a dynamic process. The Constitution provides only the legal structure; it does not constitute the process. The process will occur when the courts exercise their power of judicial review and the other two branches accept the lessening of their power. Such acceptance will be facilitated where there is trust and mutual support among the various branches of government. In Namibia such trust is not facilitated by a rigid Bill of Rights and a constitution that isolates the judiciary from the other branches of government. A lack of trust may in the end lead to the breaking of the constitutional order. It will then be ironic that the expansion of judicial power which facilitated the establishment of a constitutional order, might undermine the continuance of that order.

NOTES

1. For a historical background to Namibian independence, see Erasmus (1990), Cooper (1991), Landis (1987), Saxena (1991), and Soggot (1986).
2. *SWAPO's Proposed Constitution for Namibia—1989*, referred to as the SWAPO draft constitution.
3. See Articles 54(2), 64(2), 79(2), 87(c). See for example *ex parte Attorney-General: in re Corporal Punishment* 1991 (3) SA 76 (NmSC), where the attorney-general acted in terms of article 87(c).

REFERENCES

Anderson, L. 1991. "Political Pacts, Liberalism and Democracy: The Tunisian National Pact of 1988." *Government and Opposition* 26:244.
Baxter, L. 1984. *Administrative Law*. Cape Town: Juta.
Brunello, A. R. and Lehrman K. F. 1991. "Comparative Judicial Politics: Case Studies of the Federal Republic of Germany and the Republic of India." *Comparative Political Studies* 24:267-98.

Carpenter, G. 1991. "The Namibian Constitution—ex Africa Aliquid Novi after all?" In *Namibia: Constitutional and International Law Issues*, ed. D. van Wyk, M. Wiechers and R. Hill. Pretoria: Verloren van Themaat Center for Public Law Studies.

Cleary, S. M. 1988. "A Bill of Rights as a Normative Instrument: Southwest Africa/Namibia 1975-1988." *Comparative and International Law Journal of Southern Africa* 21:291.

Cooper, A. D. 1991. *The Occupation of Namibia: Afrikanerdom's Attack on the British Empire*. Lanham, MD.: University Press of America.

Corder, H. 1992. "The Appointment of Judges: Some Comparative Ideas." University of Cape Town. Unpublished paper.

Cultura 2000 and another v. The Government of the Republic of Namibia and others. 1992. Unpublished judgment of the High Court per Levy, AJP, June 10.

Du Pisani, A. 1991. *Rumours of Rain: Namibia's Post-Independence Experience*. Johannesburg: The South African Institute of International Affairs.

Erasmus, G. 1990. "Die Grondwet van Namibië: Internasionale Proses en innoud." *Stellenbosch Law Review* 1:277.

Frank, B. 1975. "The Ombudsman and Human Rights Revisited." *Israeli Yearbook of International Law*, 122.

Goldford, D. J. 1990. "The Political Character of Constitutional Interpretation." *Polity* 23:255.

Hagopian, F. 1990. "Democracy by Undemocratic Means? Elites, Political Pacts and Regime Transition in Brazil." *Comparative Political Studies* 23:147.

Hatchard, J. 1986. "The Institution of the Ombudsman in Africa with Special Reference to Zimbabwe." *International and Comparative Law Quarterly* 35:255.

———. 1991. "The Ombudsman in Africa Revisited." *International and Comparative Law Quarterly* 40:937.

Karl, T. L. 1986. "Petroleum and Political Pacts: The Transition to Democracy in Venezuela." In *Transitions from Authoritarian Rule in Latin America*, eds Guillermo O'Donnell, Philippe Schmitter and Lawrence Whitehead. Baltimore: John Hopkins University Press.

———. 1990. "Dilemmas of Democratization in Latin America." *Comparative Politics* 23:1.

Landis, E. S. 1987. "Namibia: A Transatlantic View." *South African Journal on Human Rights* 3:347.

le Roux, Pieter. 1991. "The Social Democratic Nature of the Charterist Economic Vision." In *The Freedom Charter and Beyond: Founding Principles of a Democratic South African Legal Order*, ed. Nico Steytler.

Marcus, G. and Davis, D. 1991. "Judicial Review under an ANC Government." *South African Journal on Human Rights* 7:93.

Mervis, Joel. 1992. "The judge judges the judge." *Sunday Times*, December 20.

Reyntjens, F. 1992. "Protecting Human Rights in Sub-Saharan Africa: Specific Problems and Challenges." *South African Public Law* 7:40.

Richardson, H. J. 1984. "Constitutive Questions in the Negotiations for Namibian Independence." *American Journal of International Law* 78:76.

Rudolph, H. 1983. "The Ombudsman and South Africa." *South African Law Journal* 100:92.

Ruppel, H. F. E. 1992. "A Bill of Rights: Practical Implications for Legal Practice—A Namibian Perspective." *South African Public Law* 7:51.

Russell, Peter H. 1983. "Political Purposes of the Canadian Charter of Rights and Freedoms." *Canadian Bar Review* 61:30.

Saxena, S. C. 1991. *Namibia and the World: The Story of the Birth of Nation*. Delhi: Kalinga.

Simba, L. 1987. "The Status and Rights of Judges in Commonwealth Africa: Problems and Prospects." *Lesotho Law Journal* 3:1.

Soggot, D. 1986. *Namibia: The Violent Heritage*. London: Resi-Collings.

Steytler, Nico C. 1992. "Democracy and the Administration of Justice." In *The Freedom Charter and Beyond: Founding Principles for a Democratic South African Legal Order*, ed. Nico C. Steytler. Cape Town: Wyvern.

Stone, Alec. 1990. "The Birth and Development of Abstract Review: Constitutional Courts and Policy-making in Western Europe." In Symposium on Judicial Review and Public Policy in Comparative Perspective, ed. Donald W. Jackson and C. Neal Tate. *Policy Studies Journal* 19:81-95.

SWAPO. 1989. *SWAPO's Proposed Constitution for Namibia—1989*.

United Nations Institute for Namibia (UNIN). 1979. *Constitutional Options for Namibia: A Historical Perspective.* Lusaka, Zambia:UNIN.

van Zyl, L. S. 1989. "Die Klassieke Ombudsman: 'n Herbeskouing." *De Rebus*, 299.

Wiechers, M. 1991. "Namibia: The 1982 Constitutional Principles and their Legal Significance." In *Namibia: Constitutional and International Law Issues*, ed. D. van Wyk, M. Wiechers and R. Hill. Pretoria: Verloren van Themaat Center for Public Law Studies.

CONCLUSION

27.

Judicialization and the Future of Politics and Policy

C. NEAL TATE AND TORBJÖRN VALLINDER

When one asks scholars to participate in a conference on The Judicialization of Politics and then asks them to prepare chapters appropriate for publication in a book entitled *The Global Expansion of Judicial Power*, perhaps one should not be astounded when they find that there is indeed a considerable amount of expansion of judicial power, or judicialization, around the world. Even so, the essays in this volume constitute persuasive evidence that the phenomenon is a good bit more than the self-fulfilling prophecy of the editors. No one mandated that the contributors to this book actually find that politics was being or had been judicialized in the settings they chose to analyze. Furthermore, their essays portray a variety of experiences with the global expansion of judicial power too great and too significant to be the product of editorial influence, even assuming the strong-minded contributors to this book to be subject to such influence. For better or worse, the expansion of judicial power does appear to be a phenomenon that is real and that is shaping and will shape global politics and policy for the foreseeable future.

Although it would be desirable to do so, we are not in a position to provide reliable and valid measures of the extent to which the two varieties of judicialization have developed within the nations treated in this book, much less for other nations. Nevertheless, it will be useful in this summing up to provide a qualitative assessment of the progress and likely future of judicialization in various nations, using as data these chapters and a variety of other research not included between these covers.

WESTERN COMMON-LAW DEMOCRACIES

We begin with the United States, the home of the expansion of judicial power, and the politico-legal systems most similar to that in the U.S., the Western common-law democracies. No one, least of all Martin Shapiro, denies that there has been in the United States over the last century a prodigious amount of what we shall call, for brevity, "Judicialization I," the expansion of judicial policy-making into realms that were previously or that, in the opinion of many, ought to be dominated by the majoritarian institutions, executives, and legislators. Similarly, no one disputes that there has also been in the U.S. a very substantial growth of "Judicialization II," the extension of courtlike procedures into negotiating and decision-making arenas not previously characterized by such procedures, and many are very critical of this development. Shapiro argues that the progress of Judicialization II, or "legalization," continues unabated in the U.S., but after an extensive survey, concludes that the growth of Judicialization I has leveled off or possibly even abated somewhat in recent years. Although it is not clear that everyone would agree with Shapiro's assessment, his conclusion is generally consistent with the prediction one would make on the basis of Tate's analysis of the conditions promoting the judicialization of politics. At the national level, a Supreme Court dominated by justices with rightist policy values has operated within a framework in which executive and (recognizing the normally effective coalition of Republican and conservative Democrats) legislative institutions have, almost all the time, been dominated by policymakers with rightist policy values. Under these conditions even activist justices would not find it necessary to judicialize politics further.

There is one caveat one must enter with regard to Shapiro's analysis, however: it is focused on the national level and takes no real account of what may be happening within the political systems of the American states. We have not surveyed the evidence necessary to document the point, but it seems highly likely that, regardless of what has happened at the national level, the expansion of judicial power—in both its facets—has proceeded apace within the subnational units. Given this as fact, the future seems to hold for the United States still more expansion of judicial power.

The adoption of the Charter of Rights in 1982 brought the issue of the expansion of judicial power to the center of debate over the future of the Canadian confederation and its governmental institutions and policies. Judicialization there has been—no one denies that. But the debates over whether there should be/should have been more or less judicialization, whether the phenomenon is/can be expected to be a positive or negative development in Canadian politics, have been vigorous, to say the least. Generally, the positions of the debaters have been very closely connected to their ideological views and to their expectations as to whether judges are more or less likely to produce policy consequences they favor, should judicialization continue. Bogart gives us an excellent summary of these debates, while also putting forward his own position. Though not unaffected by or without a position on the issues in the debates, Russell seeks in his analysis of the Canadian case to make another point: that the justices of the Supreme Court, after some experience with the possible consequences of the expansion of their own power and with a concern for their long-run effectiveness and legitimacy, appear to be adopting a self-limiting strategy that should slow the pace of judicialization. If Russell is right, the pace of expansion of judicial power in Canada may slow. But with the Charter of Rights still in place, with provincial and national officials still searching for an elusive unifying formula, and considering the drastic reorganization of national political power resulting from Canada's 1993 parliamentary elections, one should hardly expect to see judicialization stagnate.

The judicialization that has taken place in Australia does not appear to have resulted from as clear a stimulus as that in Canada. Nevertheless, the influences that Galligan and Slater and Power cite as promoting both Judicialization I and Judicialization II there have pushed the process far enough to challenge some of the traditional policy-making and administration assumptions of a system based firmly on the principles of parliamentary sovereignty and the British model. Galligan and Slater's account of the progressive intrusion of the judiciary into the prerogatives of the cabinet that occurred prior to the strategic withdrawal by the High Court would have seemed simply incredible to Bagehot, Mackintosh, Bryce, and the other classical expounders of the nature and procedures of cabinet government. Power's discussion shows how immigration policies and procedures have been so judicialized as to completely reshape a policy area that is of especial significance in Australia. If judicialization in Australia so far falls somewhat short of the levels it has achieved in the United States and Canada, the accounts of Galligan and Slater and of Power do not suggest that it has leveled off there or that it will not continue to grow in the future.

Maurice Sunkin's discussion of the case of the United Kingdom concludes that Judicialization II appears to be growing steadily, and according to his account suggests it is likely to continue to grow. Behind the pressure for instilling courtlike procedures into the decision making of administrative agencies on grievances and other client claims is the need to provide citizens a way to demand greater accountability from those who so significantly affect their lives in modern welfare states. Other contributors (Zannotti, for example) also suggest that life in such states encourages judicialization. Sunkin's conclusion suggests that these hopes for greater accountability are sometimes in vain: British judges often review the work of agency officials only to sustain it after little serious inquiry into its procedural quality or justice.

Sunkin does not see Judicialization I as having made much progress in the United Kingdom, and the situations he describes do not suggest that it is on the verge of doing so, at least in any dramatic way. Nevertheless, the specter of the supranational jurisdiction of the Court of the European Community looms today over British judicial decision making, and it is possible that that specter will yet cause the expansion of judicial power into parliamentary policy prerogatives.

Romano-Germanic Democracies

If one were to select the politico-legal culture most likely to spawn an expansion of judicial power, surely one would pick that of the Western common-law democracies. After all, it has long been recognized that the common-law judge creates or, traditionally, "finds" law where none existed before. When one combines the common-law method with the written constitutions that are present in most of those democracies and whose meanings are the prerogative of the judges to declare, certainly the structural elements for a substantial expansion of judicial power are present, at least under appropriate conditions.

In sharp contrast stand the Romano-Germanic democracies with their monolithic   codes   and   norms   of   deference   to   legislative interpretation—that are supposed to extinguish judicial creativity—and their traditional denial to judges of any power of judicial review. Yet it may be in these nations that one finds today the most significance contemporary instances of the global expansion of judicial power.

Judicialization in the larger Romano-Germanic democracies has been in part a result of political crisis. In the aftermath of World War II, Germany and Italy produced, under the watchful eye of the victorious common-law democracies, written constitutions that incorporated judicial review, established designated constitutional courts, and provided measures to protect the independence of judges. In France, the political chaos that caused the breakup of the Fourth Republic led to a new constitution that apportioned considerable power to an elected president, in preference to the traditionally sovereign French National Assembly, and also established a body with the power to advise government on the constitutionality of proposed policy enactments. As time has passed and the facilitating conditions for judicialization have developed, these institutional arrangements have served well as foundations for the expansion of judicial power in France, Germany, and Italy.

It is important not to stretch the argument too far. Stone finds considerable evidence for judicialization in France and Germany through "complex coordinate construction" involving the constitutional courts. But Lafon's careful account of the recognition of the development of judge-made law in French civil jurisprudence, countered in part by a formalization of what the French have always recognized as judge-made administrative law, does not suggest a rampant judicialization of French politics and administration. A balanced picture would show a considerable expansion of judicial power in France, especially as compared to earlier eras, but not the kinds of expansion experienced by Germany and Italy.

Stone and Landfried certainly agree that there has been an ample occurrence of Judicialization I in Germany. The role and influence of the Constitutional Court have expanded steadily since its creation, and it now regularly and authoritatively determines policies that might have been the prerogative of the majoritarian institutions. Landfried, for one, finds these developments disturbing. Like other critics (see those surveyed by Bogart for Canada), she is concerned that the Constitutional Court's expanding role weakens and distorts German democracy. Landfried is especially critical of the court's dogged determination to have the final critical word on abortion policy. Here she feels the court has unwisely prevented majoritarian institutions from making constructive or even rational policy.   On the other hand, she ends up being less critical of the court's efforts to regulate party finance policy.   Here, she thinks, the court has protected mass access to politics and government more effectively than the powerful parties would have done.   Landfried thus recognizes that there may be conditions under which the judicialization of a policy issue is warranted and others under which it is not.   She concludes her work by offering a set of principles that, in her view, can guide courts as to when they should and when they should not seek to expand their policy-making power.

Wallach wraps up our consideration of Germany by reviewing the process that led to its reunification.   His account suggests that judicialization is certainly not inevitable.   The difficult issues to be resolved in creating one Germany out of two might well have been the catalyst to a major increase in judicial policy influence in the unified nation.   That this did not occur—at least in the short run—is due to the careful work of the architects of reunification.

When we turn our attention from Germany to Italy, we encounter what may well be the most striking and significant example of the expansion of judicial power in a Romano-Germanic democracy.   The consequences of Italian judicialization are still being played out, even as this book goes to press, in the corruption scandals, the revelations, and the trials that have racked Italy for an extended period.   But it appears at this point that the "peculiar" judicialization described and explained by the contributors who focus on the Italian case may well be responsible for a revolution that could mark the most significant transformation of Italian politics since the turn to fascism.   The leading characters in this revolution have been magistrates, members of the unified Italian corps of prosecutor/judges.   Having been educated by Di Federico, Guarnieri, Mestitz and Pederzoli, and Zannotti, we are no longer the naive foreign observers described by Di Federico.   We recognize that the "judges" who are behind this revolution are actually "prosecutors," at least as Americans would understand that term.   But we also now understand that the Italian system does combine judges and prosecutors into a common corps of magistrates, all called "judge," and that the Italian public and media do not make careful distinctions as to who is and who is not, properly, a "true" judge.   In this sense, if in no other (and there are others), Italian politics has been massively judicialized.

The importance of the Italian case led us to include several contributions seeking to describe and explain it.   Mestitz and Pederzoli's chapter suggests that the origins of the expansion of judicial power in Italy may well lie in the training of Italian legal personnel, especially as compared to Germany and France. Guarnieri's analysis of the extraordinary steps taken to protect the independence of Italian magistrates shows how that independence has led to the development of a highly factionalized but effectively irresponsible judicial corps that may in fact barter that independence in factional politics. Zannotti's description of the efforts of Italian and American judges to protect and enhance their salaries by establishing judicial control of salary policy paints an unflattering picture of a self-centered and ultimately almost uncontrollable judicial hierarchy. Her characterization of the American courts as showing disciplined restraint may sound strange to observers of judicialization in the United States. Finally, running throughout all these contributions, but especially those of Di Federico and Guarnieri, is a concern that the expansion of the power of almost completely independent and irresponsible judges is causing serious harm to the liberties of Italians.

The last contribution to deal with the Italian case, that of Michael Mandel, begins from a more hopeful perspective on Italian judicialization. Mandel has been a strong critic of the expansion of judicial power in Canada because he sees it as both antidemocratic and antiprogressive. He turned his attention to Italy in the hope that in a political environment that, among other things, has persistently featured a strong political left one might find progressive judicialization. After recounting the constitutional and doctrinal bases that suggest a greater concern with progressive policies in Italy, Mandel examines the performance of the courts and legal system in several policy areas. His ultimate conclusion is negative. Judicialization in Italy appears no more likely to produce progressive policy than in Canada. Regardless, it appears likely to continue into the foreseeable future.

The section on the Romano-Germanic democracies concludes with case studies of four smaller democracies, Sweden, the Netherlands, Israel, and Malta. None of these nations appears to be a good candidate for the expansion of judicial power. Sweden and the Netherlands share the Romano-Germanic traditions that do their best to downplay any possibility of judicial creativity, and each has been dominated by parliamentary governments not afraid to exercise their policy-making powers in innovative ways. Neither has experienced the kind of political crisis that led to the instauration of constitutional courts in France,

Germany, and Italy. Yet Holmström and ten Kate and van Koppen find considerable evidence for some current and probably more future judicialization in the two countries.

Readers will recall that Holmström's account of the Swedish case portrays that country as having moved from a politics and an administration that were historically quite legalized, that is, that were characterized by Judicialization II, to one that is less legalized, but somewhat more dominated by Judicialization I, the emergence of judicial power in policy areas previously dominated by majoritarian institutions. Among the multiple reasons for this are a broadening acceptance of the appropriateness of judicial review and the discovery that once it has been practiced, it is not so easy to limit judicial review to what anyone other than the judges would regard as particularly egregious cases of constitutionality. Also among these reasons is the discovery of the courts by interest groups, a phenomenon familiar to students of American judicialization. These factors plus the influence of the European Community predict a bright future for judicialization in Sweden.

The Netherlands, too, is experiencing an intrusion of the courts into policy areas where administrators and legislators previously were rarely challenged. Dutch citizens, both individual and corporate, have increasingly turned to the courts to defend their interests against officials acting from a conception of the broader public interest. This judicialization has occurred partly through the development of Dutch administrative law, since Dutch judges, in contrast to some or all of their French, German, Italian, and Swedish counterparts, still lack any constitutionally sanctioned power of judicial review. But it has also occurred as the Dutch Supreme Court, under favorable political conditions, has steadily expanded its interpretative role. Finally, the incorporation of international-law norms into Dutch law has expanded the role of the judges. The result is the development of a form of judicial review that may be leading the Netherlands to a constitutional review and a continually increasing judicialization of politics.

The last Romano-Germanic democracies discussed, Israel and Malta, are different in important ways from the continental European systems considered. The Israeli political system embraces parliamentary sovereignty, has usually had coalition governments, and does not grant the power of judicial review to its judges, in part because it lacks a written constitution. Structurally, therefore, it looks like a cross between the systems of the Netherlands and the United Kingdom. Politically, however, Israel is a relatively new state with a multicultural society and a history of military tension and outright conflict with its neighbors that provide quite a different environment for its judges. In this environment, the judges—especially the Supreme Court—have played a controversial and extremely important role. Edelman's analysis shows that court to be very highly regarded by the public and increasingly able to determine important policy questions in spite of the lack of a written constitution or the power of judicial review, in large part due to the immobilism and partisanship of majoritarian politics and the great relevance of rights issues in Israeli society. His conclusion is as straightforward as it can be: "the judicialization of politics is an inexorable feature of Israel society." It is also a feature whose future appears secure.

Some of the differences between Malta and the other Romano-Germanic-heritage states we have discussed are obvious. Malta is a European polity that, as an independent state, is even newer than Israel. Within the lifetime of many of its adult citizens, it was a colony of Great Britain, attaining its formal independence only in 1964. It is also very small: it occupies only 122 sq. miles and has a population of around 350,000. There are fewer than thirty judges in the entire Maltese judiciary. These facts, however, have not prevented Malta from being an interesting case study of the expansion (and contraction) of judicial power. Agius and Grosselfinger's account of the alternate timidity and temerity of Maltese judges in protecting individual and group rights, variously interpreted, reveals clearly the interaction among (1) group assertion of legal claims, (2) the composition of the judicial decisionmaker or decision-making group, and (3) the composition and orientations of the government. In Malta, as suspected in numerous other settings, the conflict between the judiciary and the government resulting from the assertion of judicial authority occurred most prominently when a leftist party controlled the government. Unlike other cases, the response from supporters of the party to the judiciary's effort to assert its power was rather dramatic, as mobs stormed the Courts of Justice on two occasions. With a change of parties, the position of Malta's judiciary seemed more secure, and the prospects for continued judicialization of Maltese politics seemed to be enhanced.

RAPIDLY CHANGING NATIONS

Our final section presented analyses of rapidly changing nations, nations in which political activists were trying to establish viable democratic institutions after decades of totalitarianism, years of authoritarianism, or a history of racist colonial control. When one begins to analyze the occurrence of and prospects for judicialization in rapidly changing nations, one should not be too surprised when political change outstrips analysis. Of course we have directly in mind the Russian case, in which the ongoing expansion of judicial power involved in the effort to establish review in Russia and in the activities of the Constitutional Court under the leadership of Valery Zorkin was cut short by the events of 1993. Had the patterns described by Cheryl Thomas and William Kitchin continued, Russia would have been well on the way to joining the ranks of those nations whose politics have been significantly judicialized. The abolition of Russia's Constitutional Court by Boris Yeltsin in the wake of his violent 1993 conflict with the recalcitrant oppositionist parliament yields a dramatic example of the possible consequences for judges when the expansion of their power meets the objectives of a powerful opponent not constrained by the conventional rules of democratic politics. Of course one should remember that in the Soviet Union, the members of the Constitutional Court might have been given exciting new duties in a frontier region as well as having their court suspended. Furthermore, one should remember the Maltese case just described: when the courts offended the regime there, regime-supporting mobs sacked the courts, even though no one had changed the conventional rules of democratic politics.

Neal Tate's discussion of the prospects for the expansion of judicial power in the Philippines shows how, in the effort to reestablish democracy after years of personalistic dictatorship, constitution makers placed great hopes in a formally empowered judiciary. The initial years of experience under that constitution did show some evidence of an expansion of judicial power in a political system where majoritarian institutions were persistently troubled by political instability, in the form of several attempted military coups and a leadership that was certainly deferential to the courts if not as its critics frequently suggested, weak and aimless. A change of presidential and Supreme Court leadership in 1992 (the chief justice resigned to run, unsuccessfully, for vice president) were important developments that occurred after the period of Tate's research and left the Philippine situation somewhat uncertain. By the time of this writing, there was some evidence that majoritarian institutions were gaining strength, but the power of the judiciary had not yet begun to wane.

The last case study in the Rapidly Changing Nations section is Nico Steytler's examination of constitution making and politics in Namibia, a nation that after years of colonial control by the racist oligarchy of South Africa, a vigorous liberation struggle, and long delays caused by Cold War struggles in southern Africa, quite quickly and peacefully adopted a new constitution and established a majoritarian government. This was possible in no small part because of the willingness of the leadership of SWAPO to entrench the bases for an expansion of judicial power in the Constitution. Had they not been willing to do so, Steytler's account tells us, the minority of Namibian whites and former functionaries of the colonial regime would not have agreed to the document, with the likely result that Namibian independence and democracy would have been further delayed, and possibly that extensive political violence would have occurred. The problem that Namibia faced after the establishment of a democratic government under the new constitution was that assertions of judicial power by independent judges regarded as agents of the old ruling powers caused significant political turmoil accompanied by thinly veiled efforts to intimidate the judiciary. Significant judicialization in Namibia thus may pose a serious threat to the continuation of the democracy that was possible only because of that very judicialization.

The Namibian case described by Steytler seems very directly relevant to the process of democratization that, at this writing, is under way in South Africa. The constitution agreed to by the government and the African National Congress (ANC) is, in its inclusion of an entrenched judiciary and minority rights, remarkably similar to that of Namibia. Furthermore, government efforts to win white support for that constitution sound very similar to those made in the Namibian case. Though its prospects look good, it is too early to say whether the proposed South African Constitution will actually succeed in laying the foundation for a stable majority government. It may yet be derailed by opposition from powerful white opposition groups or by the evident disagreement between the ANC and its political opponents within the black community. But if it does succeed, it seems likely that the scenario that has played out so far in Namibia will be directly relevant to South Africa

SOME QUESTIONS ABOUT THE EXPANSION OF JUDICIAL POWER

We have tried to extract timid predictions about the future of judicialization from our discussion of the case studies included in this book. But let us begin to conclude by directly facing the question: Is the global expansion of judicial power a phenomenon with a future? A famous saying of the Danish cartoonist Storm P. runs like this: "It is difficult to make predictions, especially about the future." Generally speaking, that may be true. However, in discussing the expansion of judicial power around the world, it should be fairly safe to predict further advance in many countries. If our analyses are on target, this is because the conditions that appear to favor the development of that expansion continue to be on the rise. Perhaps the most important of these conditions is the presence of liberal democracy. The world has not yet been made safe for democracy, but it seems to be moving in that direction. However, democratization is not the only condition that is relevant. The others we have identified—separation of powers, a politics of rights, interest- and opposition-group use of the courts, ineffective majoritarian institutions, positive perceptions of the courts, willful delegation of troublesome issues by the majoritarian institutions—also are on the rise. With these facilitating conditions present, activist judges are likely to turn up with significant frequency to insure that the courts will continue to go marching in.

Let us now cease concluding by considering one last pair of questions:

- Is the global expansion of judicial power a good thing?
- If it is not a good thing, what can one do about it? What are the viable alternatives to the judicialization of politics?

It is not difficult to find defenders of judicial power when that power is expected to be exercised to protect interests one approves of from greedy, insensitive, or possibly even "tyrannical" majorities. If the American Supreme Court advances the rights and political power of disadvantaged minorities or protects a woman's right to have an abortion, many will applaud (though others will not), even if they recognize that what the court has done might have preempted any useful policy role for majoritarian institutions. Yet if the South African or Namibian judiciary were to become the frontline defender of the entrenched rights of another minority, the whites who constructed and for so long ably defended apartheid against the effective action of majority-controlled institutions, many of these defenders of judicialization would be less than pleased.

The contributors to this book are, by and large, more sophisticated than the anonymous defenders of judicialization just described. Their assessments of the wisdom of further expansion of judicial power are affected not (only) by their assessment of the appropriateness of the policies the courts make or would make. They are much more concerned about the implications of the expansion of judicial power for the viability of democracy and the robustness of majority rule. They are, in general, skeptical about the wisdom of judicialization. They see the expansion of judicial power as most likely to weaken majoritarian democratic institutions and sustain the rule of privileged and unrepresentative elites, shutting out those who should be represented in a democratic state from effective access to policy-making processes or to effective, responsive administration.

If it is the majority view of our expert contributors that the global expansion of judicial power is not a good thing, and we would argue that it clearly is, what, if anything, can one do about it? Some rulers have not found this to be a difficult problem. In Uganda, Idi Amin simply had the chief justice assassinated when the Supreme Court displeased him. In Nigeria and Pakistan, military regimes found that simple reprimands or transfers of judicial personnel would make clear to judges what they would stand for by way of judicial interference in their affairs (see Ojo 1977; Tate 1993). In not-yet-fully-democratized Russia, Boris Yeltsin suspended an offending Constitutional Court.

In democracies, answers are not so easy to come by. Judicialization does not result from an organized conspiracy—indeed, it does not result from any single factor that is easily controlled. Can one say to nations that have ineffective or ill-regarded majoritarian institutions "Straighten out your legislature and executive—make them more effective and more worthy of respect!"? Can one, in a democratic state with a modicum of political and civil liberties, take action to prevent interest groups or the political opposition from pursuing their interests through the courts when it appears advantageous to do so? Is it really wise to abolish separation of powers? Is it wise to try to reduce public confidence in the courts so that they will be less likely to find an atmosphere of acceptance when they judicialize? Of course one can try to train and select judges so that there will be less chance that they will become activists once on the bench. But what is one to do when some of them turn out to be activists, anyway? Destroy their independence? It might do some good to urge majoritarian policymakers to stop shifting troublesome issues to the judges and to stop turning policy disputes into matters of rights. But this may be unwelcome counsel to an elected official who sees his or her career as likely to be destroyed if he or she does take a position—any position—on a troublesome issue, or if he or she gains the reputation of being willing to bargain away the "rights" of a powerful group.

Doing something concrete and useful to prevent or reduce the expansion of judicial power thus turns out to be difficult. Martin Shapiro suggests that Americans seem to be comfortable with the substantial judicialization of their politics because the judiciary provides a significant redundancy mechanism in their policy process. Perhaps that is a position that most of the world's democracies will have to accept. Short of that, preventing or reducing the global expansion of judicial power will likely be a slow process, a process through which democratic rule will have to become not just more widespread, but also more effective.

REFERENCES

Ojo, Abiola. 1977. "Public Law, The Military Government and the Supreme Court." In *The Supreme Court of Nigeria*, ed. A. B. Kasunmu. Ibadan: Heinemann Educational Books (Nigeria), 90-106.

Tate, C. Neal. 1993. "Courts and Crisis Regimes: A Theory Sketch with Asian Case Studies." *Political Research Quarterly* 46:311-38.

Contributors

Justice CARMEL A. AGIUS is currently one of the three judges who make up the Constitutional Court and the Court of Appeal of the Island of Malta. He is also an examiner in the Faculty of Law of the University of Malta and has regularly been contracted to give lectures to law students. He has published a number of presented papers resulting from his participation in various international conferences. He is also the convenor of the Maltese section of the International Association of Judges.

W. A. BOGART is Professor of Law at the University of Windsor, Ontario, Canada. He is the author of articles dealing with civil procedure, the impact of litigation, and empirical research on legal policy. He is a coauthor of *Civil Litigation* (1991), a text used in many Canadian law schools, and *Courts and Country: The Limits of Litigation and the Social and Political Life of Canada* (1994); he is at work on a book about the impact of law on social and political issues. He is a frequent adviser and consultant to governments in developing legal policy.

GIUSEPPE DI FEDERICO is professor of political science at the University of Bologna, director of the Center for Judicial Studies, and director of the National Research Council Institute on Judicial Systems (IRSIG-CNR). For almost thirty years he has been engaged in research on the working of justice systems in Italy and other European countries. Recently, as a member of the board of directors of the Budapest Institute of Constitutional and Legislative Policy, he has been actively engaged in consulting activities for the reform of the judicial systems of various countries in Eastern Europe. His many essays, articles, and books deal with topics such as recruitment and training of judges and prosecutors, judicial independence, public prosecution, criminal proceedings, court organization, and court technologies.

MARTIN EDELMAN is chair of the Department of Political Science, Rockefeller College of Public Affairs and Policy of the University at Albany, New York. He is the author of *Democratic Theories and the Constitution* (1984); of *Courts, Politics, and Culture in Israel* (1994), and of articles dealing with American constitutional law and Israeli court systems.

BRIAN GALLIGAN is professor of political science and director of the Federalism Research Center in the Research School of Social Sciences at the Australian National University. He is currently engaged in research on the Australian constitutional system, citizenship, and rights. His major publications include *Politics of the High Court* (1987), with Ann Capling, *Beyond the Protective State* (1992), and *A Federal Republic: Australia's Constitutional System of Government* (forthcoming).

NANCY A. GROSSELFINGER has served as a senior Fulbright Scholar teaching criminology and consulting on the creation of an Institute of Criminology at the University of Malta. She has previously taught criminology at Gallaudet University in Washington, D.C. and at Niagara University in New York. She was an individual consulting expert at the 1985 and 1990 United Nations Congresses on the Prevention of Crime and the Treatment of Offenders.

CARLO GUARNIERI is professor of political science at the University of Bologna and an associate of the Centro Studi Sull'Ordinamento Giudiziario of Bologna. His principal research interests are in comparative politics, especially comparative judicial and administrative systems. He is the author of *L'indipendenza della magistratura* (1981), *Pubblico ministero e systema politico* (1984), *Magistratura e politica in Italia* (1992), and of many articles and chapters in Italian and English analyzing the performance of the Italian and other judiciaries.

BARRY HOLMSTRÖM is associate professor of political science in the Department of Government, Uppsala University. He has written books and articles on Swedish foreign policy and on land and planning policy.

JAN TEN KATE is senior lecturer in the Faculty of Law at Erasmus University, Rotterdam.   He studied law and psychology at Groningen University and 1984 received a doctorate of law from the Erasmus University, based on his research on judicial decision making conducted with Peter J. van Koppen.   He has also conducted research on the appointments of the justices of the Dutch Supreme Court and on negotiations between attorneys.

WILLIAM KITCHIN is on the political science faculty of Loyola College in Baltimore, Maryland.   His primary research interests and publications concern Russian legal reform and the development of the rule of law in Russia.

PETER J. VAN KOPPEN is senior researcher at the Netherlands Institute for the Study of Criminality and Law Enforcement (NISCALE) in Leiden.   He studied psychology at Groningen University and at the University of Amsterdam.   Formerly, he was senior lecturer in sociology and law at Erasmus University, Rotterdam, which awarded him a doctorate of law in 1984.   His varied research has appeared, in both English and Dutch, in major law and social science journals and scholarly books.   His most recent book is *Dubieuze Zaken: De Psychologie van Strafrechtelijke Bewijs* (1992), with Hans Crombag and Willem Albert Wagenaar.

JACQUELINE LUCIENNE LAFON teaches history of law in the Law Faculty-Jean Monnet of the University of Paris-South, where she was Associate Dean from 1980-1987.   She also teaches at the Institute of Judicial Studies (IEJ).   In English, she is coauthor with Mary L. Volcansek of *Judicial Selection: The Crossevolution of French and American Practices* (1987) and of "The Judicial Career in France: Theory and Practice under the Fifth Republic" (*Judicature* 1991).

CHRISTINE LANDFRIED is professor of political science at the University of Hamburg.   She is the author of *Bundesverfaßungsgericht und Gesetsgeber* (1984) and of other works analyzing the behavior and policy making of the German Constitutional Court.

MICHAEL MANDEL is professor of law at Osgoode Hall Law School of York University in Toronto.   He has frequently lectured on constitutional law and at the Italian Universities of Bologna, Padua, Calabria, and Trento, and at the European Universities Institute in Fiesole, where he was a Jean Monnet Fellow in 1990-91. The second edition of his book *The Charter of Rights and the Legalization of Politics in Canada* was published in 1994.

ANNA MESTITZ is research director of the Italian National Research Council Institute on Judicial Systems (IRSIG-CNR) in Bologna. She has conducted comparative research on topics related to judicial administration and on psychology and law. Her writings deal with the recruitment and socialization of legal professions in Europe, Italian juvenile courts, and the use of video technologies in Italian courts. At present she is head of the Judicial Psychology Division of the Italian Psychological Society. She is the author of *Selezione e formazione professionale dei magistrati e degli avocati in Francia* (1990) and has served as an expert on several national committees for the reform of the Italian judicial system.

PATRIZIA PEDERZOLI is a researcher in the Department of Political Science of the University of Bologna. Her principal research interest concerns cross-national analysis of judicial systems. She is the author of *Selezione e reclutamento delle professioni legali in Germania* (1992).

JOHN POWER is director of the Australian National Internships Program in the Australian National University and is Professor Emeritus of political science at the University of Melbourne. His principal research interest is the comparative study of mechanisms of executive responsibility. He is a coauthor with John Halligan of *Political Management in the 1990s* (1992).

PETER H. RUSSELL is professor of political science at the University of Toronto. He is a past president of the Canadian Political Science Association and of the Canadian Law and Society Association. His research interests are in the fields of constitutional and judicial politics—Canadian and comparative. His most recent books are *The Judiciary in Canada: The Third Branch of Government* (1988) and *Constitutional Odyssey: Can Canadians Become a Sovereign People?* (1993).

MARTIN SHAPIRO is professor of law at the University of California, Berkeley. He is the author of numerous books and articles on American and comparative law and politics, including *Law and Politics in the Supreme Court* (1964), *Freedom of Speech: The Supreme Court and Judicial Review* (1966), *The Supreme Court and Administrative Agencies* (1968), and *Courts: A Comparative and Political Analysis* (1981).

DAVID R. SLATER is a graduate in economics and law from Monash University. He worked as a research assistant in the Federalism Research Center at the Australian National University, and is now a practicing lawyer in Melbourne.

NICO STEYTLER is a professor of law in the Department of Public and Procedural Law at the University of the Western Cape, South Africa. He was previously professor of law at the University of Natal. Recently, with the process of democratization in South Africa under way, he has focused his research on public policy and constitutional law. He is author of *The Undefended Accused on Trial* (1987) and a coauthor of *A Charter for Social Justice* (1992). He is a coeditor of *Criminal Justice in South Africa* (1983), *The Freedom Charter and Beyond* (1991), and *Free and Fair: Election Law and Practice for South Africa* (1993).

ALEC STONE is assistant professor of political science at the University of California, Irvine. He is the author of *The Birth of Judicial Politics in France* (1992) and coeditor with Martin Shapiro of *The New Constitutional Politics of Europe*, a special issue of *Comparative Political Studies* (January 1994) devoted to the political impact of constitutional courts.

MAURICE SUNKIN is a senior lecturer in law at the University of Essex and a barrister. His principal areas of interest are public law and environmental law. During the past decade, he has conducted empirical research on the use and impact of judicial review in the United Kingdom. His articles have appeared in many of the leading British legal journals. He is a coauthor of *Judicial Review in Perspective: An Investigation in the Use and Operation of the Judicial Review Procedure in England and Wales* (1993).

C. NEAL TATE is Regents Professor of Political Science at the University of North Texas. His articles on comparative politics, especially judicial politics and behavior, have appeared in major political science and law and society journals. He is coeditor with Donald W. Jackson of *Comparative Judicial Review and Public Policy* (1992) and is a former Convenor of the Research Committee on Comparative Judicial Studies of the International Political Science Association.

CHERYL A. THOMAS is assistant professor of public law in the Department of Political Science at the University of Vermont and formerly was visiting fellow at the Center for Socio-Legal Studies at Oxford University. Her principal areas of research are in comparative judicial institutions and federalism.

TORBJÖRN VALLINDER has been associate professor of political science at the University of Lund, Sweden, and editor of the *Statsvetenskaplig Tidskrift (The Swedish Journal of Political Science)*. One of his publications in English is "The Swedish Jury System in Press Cases: Offspring of the English Trial Jury," (*Journal of Legal History* 1987).

H. G. PETER WALLACH is professor of political science at Central Connecticut State University and director of the Connecticut Institute for European and American Studies. He is a coauthor with Ron DeFrancisco of *United Germany* (1992) and coeditor with George Romoser of *West German Politics in the Mid-Eighties* (1985). His works on German politics, political leadership, and judicial affairs have appeared in U.S. and German political science journals and books.

FRANCESCA ZANNOTTI is professor of political science at the University of Bologna. She is a member of the Committee on Law and Politics of the Italian National Research Council (CNR) and a member of the executive committee of the Italian Political Science Association. Her principal research interests are in judicial organization and behavior and public law. She is the author of *Le attivitá extragiudiziarie dei magistrati ordinari* (1981), *La magistratura, un gruppo di pressione istituzionale* (1989), and of numerous other studies of the Italian and European judiciaries.

Index